Talking with the President

To Ivan

A big man
and a big
friend

Talking with the President

THE PRAGMATICS OF PRESIDENTIAL LANGUAGE

John Wilson

OXFORD
UNIVERSITY PRESS

OXFORD
UNIVERSITY PRESS

Oxford University Press is a department of the University of Oxford.
It furthers the University's objective of excellence in research, scholarship,
and education by publishing worldwide.

Oxford New York
Auckland Cape Town Dar es Salaam Hong Kong Karachi
Kuala Lumpur Madrid Melbourne Mexico City Nairobi
New Delhi Shanghai Taipei Toronto

With offices in
Argentina Austria Brazil Chile Czech Republic France Greece
Guatemala Hungary Italy Japan Poland Portugal Singapore
South Korea Switzerland Thailand Turkey Ukraine Vietnam

Oxford is a registered trade mark of Oxford University Press
in the UK and certain other countries.

Published in the United States of America by
Oxford University Press
198 Madison Avenue, New York, NY 10016

Library of Congress Cataloging-in-Publication Data
Wilson, John, 1954 December 12–
  Talking with the President : the pragmatics of Presidential language / John Wilson.
    p. cm.
  Includes bibliographical references and index.
  ISBN 978–0–19–985879–8 — ISBN 978–0–19–985880–4 1. Rhetoric—Political aspects—
United States. 2. Communication in politics—United States. 3. Presidents—United
States—Language. 4. Pragmatics—Political aspects. 5. Discourse analysis—Political
aspects. I. Title.
  P301.5.P67W55 2015
  973.9201'41—dc23
                              2014032367

9 8 7 6 5 4 3 2 1

Printed in the United States of America on acid-free paper

For Linda, my soul mate

CONTENTS

ACKNOWLEDGMENTS

There are several individuals I would like to thank for their encouragement and support in the process of producing this book: Dr. Karyn Stapleton, for her helpful discussions on the proposal; Dr. Diane Hazlett, Professor Paul Carmichael, and Dr. Cathy Gormely-Heenan for their support in helping me secure a leave of absence to complete the work. Thanks to Professor Deborah Tannen, Professor Heidi Hamilton, and staff and graduate students at the Department of Linguistics, Georgetown University, Washington, D.C., where I got to try out an early version of Chapter 2. Also a big thank you to the School of Communication, University of Washington, Seattle, and the Department of Linguistics, University of Florida Gainesville, for hosting me as a Visiting Professor while I worked on the final chapters of the book. In particular I need to thank here Professor Gerry Philipsen of the University of Washington, and Professor Diana Boxer of the University of Florida, who both initiated the invitations and looked after me while I was at the respective institutions. Finally, thank you to Hallie Stebbins of Oxford University Press for her patience, support, and encouragement.

Talking with the President

1

Hail to the Chief

PRAGMATICS AND THE PRESIDENT

Introduction

Consider the following brief exchange:

a. Should we trust John?
b. John is a Republican but he is honest.

The answer carries an implication that "Republicans are dishonest" and a statement that "John is a Republican"; hence John would be dishonest (see Lakoff, 1971: 67). This is denied, however, through the clause introduced by "but." Most readers will understand all of this intuitively, but where in (b) does it say "John is dishonest?" It doesn't, yet an expectation about Republicans in general, and therefore John in particular, has been set up; otherwise, what is it that the "but" clause denies? How does "but" do that? There is nothing in the conceptual nature of "but" that says it must mean a "denial of expectations." Indeed, it can be used in other ways. For example, one can use "but" for contrast, "John is fat but Fred is thin," or one can use it for correction, "John is not married but he has a partner." Given that "but" may be used in several different ways, it is sometimes called "procedural" (Blakemore, 2002). This simply means that we must look at how it is used in context, taking account of interactional expectations along with local and shared knowledge, and when we do this we are doing pragmatics. In (b) it only makes sense to say "but John is honest" if there is an implication from the first clause that Republicans are not normally honest. Pragmatics helps us understand how all this works, that is, it helps us understand the way(s) in which meanings are worked out in context; and this is not just a theoretical issue.

On April 17, 2013, President Barack Obama delivered a speech from the White House Rose Garden. This followed the Senate's rejection of an extension of gun control checks brought forward following a growing number of fatal shootings in various parts of the United States, and in particular the Newtown School massacre

1

Talking with the President. John Wilson. © Oxford University Press 2015.
Published 2015 by Oxford University Press

in Connecticut, when 20 children and several adults were killed. Reacting to the Newtown tragedy, Obama said he had a personal responsibility to help stop such events from occurring again; hence he brought forward plans for changes in gun control. Many considered the proposed changes relatively minor, so the Senate's rejection of even these minor changes made Obama visibly angry during his speech.

This is also displayed in the way he makes use of "but" to set up contexts where there is a "denial of expectations:"

> By now it is well known that 90 percent of the American people support universal background checks that make it harder for a dangerous person to buy a gun. . . . Ninety percent of Americans support the idea. Most Americans think it's the law. And a few minutes ago 90 percent of Democrats just voted for the idea. BUT it's not going to happen, because 90 percent of the Republicans in the Senate just voted against it.

We can see how Obama constructs a numerical context in which the overwhelming evidence suggests that universal background checks should proceed, but they won't, and the reason for this "denial of expectation" is given in the final statement, when we find it is the Republicans who are responsible. Variations of this use of "but" occur throughout the speech:

> That's why 90% of the American people supported it. BUT instead of supporting this program the gun lobby and its allies willfully lied about the Bill. They claimed that it would create some kind of "big brother" gun registry even though the bill did the opposite . . . plain and simple there in the text. BUT that didn't matter.
>
> A lot of Republicans had that fear BUT Democrats had that fear too.

In these brief examples we see how "but" is not only encoded pragmatically, it is also used for the specific political goal of isolating the denial of expectations (that the universal gun control bill should be passed) to one source, the Republicans, and in particular a subset of Republican senators.

This is just one brief example of one pragmatic marker in action, but it exemplifies the important fact that meanings are not always reflected in a simple "one word one meaning" equation. It is frequently the case that social and structural contexts interact with language to create specific interpretations and understandings, and these in turn are produced for specific communicative purposes.

Pragmatics is now central to any theory that attempts to explain human language (Huang, 2007), in particular the ways in which we understand and interpret the relationship between "what we say" and "what we mean." It is also central to our understanding of all aspects of everyday communication since our understanding of what is said in context draws on a wide range of knowledge types beyond the purely linguistic. Given the centrality of language in politics in general, and presidential politics in particular, it should not be surprising that pragmatics could provide insights into particular forms and use of presidential language—indeed, it is hard to see how one could explain presidential language without some recourse to how meaning is constructed in context, that is, without a consideration of pragmatics.

In general I will use the term "pragmatics" to refer to the analysis and description of meaning construction in social contexts of interaction, which is sometimes called "sociopragmatics" (Archer, 2005; Culpeper, 2009). Seen in this way, pragmatics is interactional and functional; it is the outcome of intentions and communicative goals. Such a perspective employs pragmatic tools from the intersection of a broad range of disciplinary positions, which would include inter alia sociolinguistics, discourse analysis, conversation analysis, discursive psychology, and the philosophy of language.

When one looks at work on presidential language, there is a significant and growing body of knowledge that includes a wide range of scholarship from a broad range of disciplines (see Medhurst, 2008). There are certainly texts on political discourse, and there is a virtual industry devoted to rhetorical studies of presidential communication—although the term "rhetoric" is used in several different (if related) ways, from the classical "persuasion and argumentation" perspective, through thematic or content-based analyses, to work that simply sees "rhetoric," "language," and "discourse" as synonymous (see Schroedel et al., 2013; Charteris-Black, 2014). There is, however, a more limited range of literature on the linguistic nature of presidential language, with almost no book-length studies focused specifically on this topic. There have recently been several texts linking cognitive linguistics, specifically through metaphor, to political understanding and interpretation in general (see, for example, Lakoff, 1987; Charteris-Black, 2014; Wodak, 2011), and there are also many texts that highlight, through chapters or themes, various linguistic aspects of political language; and, of course, one can find significant numbers of journal articles on politics, some of which focus on a specific president. However, there are few linguistically focused texts on presidential language, with fewer still concentrating only on the field of pragmatics, and almost none that offers a pragmatic analysis of several different presidents. Further, there is a core difference between the pragmatic approach and much of the other research noted above, in that pragmatics is at heart "inferential": meanings are worked out from evidence provided by an utterance in context. This goes beyond a general view that meanings can simply be read off the language as "signals" for comprehension or decoding (Sperber and Wilson, 1995); rather, sentences or utterances are the tools that speakers use in context to generate speaker intentions and speaker meanings.

Pragmatics and Presidential Language

During the initial development of modern pragmatics in the 1930s, scholars such as Morris, Carnap, and Peirce made a distinction between syntax (the relation of signs to one another), semantics (the relations of signs to what they denote), and pragmatics (the relation of signs to their users and interpreters). However, due to the influence of formal and abstract models of language research, which ignored language use and language users, there was not much progress on pragmatics until the 1960s and 1970s (see below). It is generally accepted now that pragmatics is required to explain a variety of problems within language theory, and that it is a significant component in understanding all forms of linguistic communication, and indeed miscommunication.

Centrally, pragmatics is concerned with the speaker, who she is and to whom she is speaking, what are her intentions and beliefs, and how what she says is affected by social circumstances, institutional structures, and social or cultural constraints. Within everyday interaction, pragmatics explains what people do with language and for what purpose, for example, being sarcastic or ironic, telling lies, making promises, telling jokes, or telling stories. Seen in this way, pragmatics underpins not only informal interaction but also institutional and formal behaviors, as in teaching, medicine, law, and, of course, politics.

Drawing upon pragmatic analysis, this book highlights the ways in which language is used in various contexts of presidential communication. The objective is not to claim that there is a specific pattern of linguistic use found within and across all presidential interaction; the aim is to reflect on how pragmatics assists us in understanding certain forms of communicative action adopted by several different presidents in dealing with a range of political problems and issues. In this way, while each chapter can be read independently, the development and application of a range of tools and theories serve to cumulatively advance the role of pragmatics in helping us understand and explain particular uses of presidential language. The term "presidential language" obviously suggests language as used by the "president," but in addition—and also presidential, I would argue— there are some examples of language used when a president may have been a presidential candidate (Kennedy and Obama), or examples of the language of a president when he has retired or resigned (Nixon).

As we will see, there are a range of pragmatic theories and pragmatic tools available for research. We will not be wedded to any specific theory and will adopt an ecological approach, drawing upon those tools that help explain the phenomenon at hand. It is not the job of this book to resolve disputes between particular theories, or to champion one specific type of analysis, or to satisfy all pragmatic tastes at the same time; the goal is to provide insights into particular examples of presidential language from a pragmatic perspective.

Of course, this will require some form of selection of both presidents and data. In the case of data, the aim was to select well-known, for positive or negative reasons, cases of presidential language, whether spoken or written or both. In the case of those presidents chosen, six have been selected: John F. Kennedy, Richard M. Nixon, Ronald W. Reagan, William F. Clinton, George W. Bush, and Barack H. Obama. These examples cover most of the last half of the twentieth century and the first decade of the twenty-first century, and each displays some specifically relevant communicative or other pragmatically interesting dimension. John F. Kennedy was famed for his quality of oratory, Nixon for his manipulative use of language, Reagan for his gift of telling stories, Clinton for his ability to engage the public and to linguistically turn arguments and descriptions in particular directions. Bush, on the other hand, was famed for his inability to use language appropriately, and Obama returns us to the rhetorical flourishes of early Kennedy. It is accepted that other presidents will also have reflected some similar communicative qualities (most presidents would have told stories, for example, and many were "economical with the truth," or lied); those presidents chosen, however, were particularly associated with the overall use of a particular pragmatic topic, for example, Reagan for storytelling or Nixon for lying.

These presidents are, therefore, an interesting group for the application of pragmatic analysis. It would not be possible, of course, to explore every pragmatic dimension of every speech, phrase, or word used by these presidents. Hence, for each president one or two interesting pragmatic phenomena are highlighted for analysis and are presented as evidence of the kinds of insights that pragmatics can provide in the study of presidential language.

Pragmatics: An Example

Consider the following question and answer:

(1)   Q. Has anyone seen John lately?
      A. I saw John with a woman last night.

What can we say about this answer? We have no idea who said it, when, where, or why. But we do know that it is a sentence of English. We also know that the pronoun "I" refers to a different person from John, and that it also refers to the speaker of the sentence. We know there is someone called John, and that he is the same John who appears in the question and the answer, and given the nature of names and naming, we will assume that John is male. We also know that the sentence is highlighting information from the past, "last night," and that there is also another person referred to, that is, "a woman." We know, of course, that the term "woman" is gender specific for a female, but also a female of a certain age, that is, not normally a girl or teenager. Given this, we can also infer that John is probably not a "boy" but a man, although this is not guaranteed. We have gleaned most of this information from the rules of syntax and semantics. But there is other information here that is not so easily classified. For example, we can infer that the woman John was with was not his wife, his mother, his sister, or his aunt. But where does this information come from? It is certainly not encoded in any of the words of the sentence. One of the major theorists of modern pragmatics, Paul H. Grice, sheds light on this question. Grice (1967) suggests that when we communicate with others our primary aim is to "be cooperative"; Grice referred to this as the "Cooperative Principle":

> Make your conversational contribution such as is required, at the stage at which it occurs, by the accepted purpose or direction of the talk exchange in which you are engaged. (1989, 26)

The principle is often interpreted in terms of a common-sense view of cooperation, suggesting a form of agreement and harmony in conversation or communication, but this is rarely the case. We lie, mislead, argue, speak metaphorically, and so on. Grice's primary aim was to distinguish between what we say and what we mean, and although the two may not always match, Grice believed that communicators tried to behave in a rational manner in an effort to produce successful communication. In considering how we could reconcile this "rational" process with the vagaries and indirectness of everyday talk, the Cooperative Principle provides the framework within which we "work out" meanings, as opposed to providing any guarantee that what we say is always the same as what we mean. In line with this, Grice provides a series of maxims underlying the Cooperative Principle:

Maxim of Quantity
Make your contribution to the conversation as informative as necessary.
Do not make your contribution to the conversation more informative than
    necessary.
Maxim of Quality
Do not say what you believe to be false.
Do not say that for which you lack adequate evidence.
Maxim of Relation
Be relevant.
Maxim of Manner
Avoid obscurity of expression.
Avoid ambiguity.
Be brief.
Be orderly.

As noted above, the Cooperative Principle and its maxims are invoked by Grice to explain one of the core issues of pragmatics, the difference between "what is said" and "what is meant." He notes that in some cases speakers seem to mean more than they say. Consider (2) and (3):

(2) Some the girls came to the party.
(3) Q: Where is John? A: The pubs are open.

In (2) we can infer that if some of the girls came to the party, then not all of the girls came to the party. This is because words like "all, some, many, most . . ." are said to form a scale where the use of one form will either confirm or negate the others. So if we say "all" of the girls came to the party, this entails (makes true in all circumstances) that "some of the girls came to the party." On the other hand, if we say "some of the girls came to the party," we infer that the speaker means "not all" of the girls came to the party. This inference is generated by what Grice calls a "conventional implicature," because it is based on the meanings of the words themselves. In (3), however, the answer implies (but does not state) that John is in the pub. This Grice calls a "conversational implicature" because it is worked out in the context of this specific conversational encounter. Assuming that the respondent is being cooperative, relevant, and informative, we can infer that he or she has reason to believe that "John is in the pub" (because that is where John goes when the pub is open). Though this is not known for certain, it is the best information available for answering the question.

Returning to example (1), because of the Cooperative Principle and its maxims we expect the speaker to say as much as required while being both relevant and informative. Since the speaker does not define the woman as John's wife or mother, we infer that the "woman" is not John's wife or mother. This type of meaning is pragmatic, because it is inferred from the language used in context.

We should also note that there is a sequential relationship between the question and answer. Questions and answers occur together, with the question delimiting the area of information being sought, and the answer usually providing such information. Conversation Analysis (a part of pragmatics according to Levinson, 2003) suggests that the words following a question are assessable as an answer, because the question provides a structural and interpretive constraint on the turn that follows. In this sense, "I saw John with a woman last night" may be seen as a response, and a specific type of response called an "answer." Answers form what conversation analysts call the second part of a paired structure, in which the first part is the question. Hence, questions/answers are referred to "adjacency pairs" (ten Have, 2007). We can say, then, that there is an interactional aspect to the response in (1) because its meaning is related, in part, to the question that has generated it as a response.

In assessing meaning we have sequential information as well as the information provided by Gricean implicatures, and we also have what we might think of as the "semantic" meaning of the sentence itself. Understanding all of this information requires consideration of human cognition and reasoning as well as social and cultural practices and behaviors. This is a complex task, and many linguists and philosophers try to keep semantics and pragmatics distinct so that one can consider the conventional meaning of language independent of context. Social psychologists, sociolinguists, sociologists, and others eschew such a distinction, and argue that all meaning arises in context and that a "null context" does not exist. Sociopragmatics acknowledges this issue and accepts that social context is central to understanding everyday meaning.

Consider the following political example from Governor Mitt Romney in the 2012 presidential campaign. He was interviewed on CNN and was asked about a secretly taped comment he made at a fundraising event: (http://www.huffingtonpost.com/2012/10/09/mitt-romney-cnn-interview_n_1952708.html):

> There are 47 percent of the people who will vote for the President no matter what. All right, there are 47 percent who are with him, who are dependent upon government, who believe that they are victims, who believe that the government has a responsibility to care for them. . . .

These claims caused outrage when the tape was released. At first Romney attempted to clarify his position to the media and public, but then opted to accept that what he said was wrong, and apologized.

> INTERVIEWER: You weren't exactly eloquently stating your position, later and more recently you said you were completely wrong. I'm curious Governor how did that evolution in your thinking go on from the initial reaction once that tape came out to what you said the other day that you were completely wrong.
> ROMNEY: Well, what I'm saying is that what the words that came out were not what I meant and what I mean I think ah people will understand that if I'm President I'll be President of 100% of the people.

Romney claims that what he said was not necessarily what he meant, and that because of this misunderstanding he has been interpreted in a very negative way. As he put it elsewhere:

> And, you know, now and then, things don't come out exactly the way you want them to come out. They don't sound the way you thought they sounded. . . . And now, with a good opposition campaign, they grab it, they blow it up, maybe they take it a bit out of context, maybe they don't, but, it obviously, is paraded in a way that you hadn't intended. (http://politicalticker.blogs.cnn.com/2013/06/06/romney-regrets-47-comments/)

We have all, of course, been in a similar position when we say, "that's not what I mean" or "that's not what I meant." Sometimes this may be a semantic issue—you have chosen the wrong words for the meaning you wanted to convey—or it may be a pragmatic issue—you have chosen the words you wanted to say, but you didn't realize the meaning they would convey in context.

Romney's original statement seemed pretty clear, but his answer in this interview may be less so. His argues that what he said was not what he meant, but in general terms his meaning seems clearly stated:

a. There are 47% a who will vote for the President—no matter what;
b. There are 47% who are with him;
c. (47%) Who are dependent on government;
d. (47%) Who believe they are victims;
e. (47%) Who believe that the government has a responsibility to care for them.

These statements can be assessed as true or false; they do not imply their meanings, they state them. But there is also a negative association here, specifically that Romney cannot change these peoples' minds, and that they will always want the state to look after them, and hence they are not relevant to his campaign or to his conservative aspirations.

In Romney's response to the interviewer's question, he tries to tell us what he meant, and then makes a claim that people understand that if he is president he will be president of 100% of the people. The relevance here is that since Romney will be responsible for all the people, this would have to include the 47% of the people he had previously criticized. Of course, this does not deny the set of statements in his taped claims about the 47%. He could still be president of 100% of the people, of whom 47% were exactly as he said. But here, however, Romney deals with the negative associations of his statement, as mentioned above. As president he will not abandon or ignore people simply because they disagree with him; as president he is responsible for everyone (100%).

The context of the interview is by its very nature "intertextual" (see Fairclough, 1984)—it contains explicit and implicit elements from other texts, such as what Romney said on tape as well as what was said by newspapers, other politicians, and the public. While the questions in this interview share elements with the question in example (1), specifically they both expect answers, there are also contextual differences: the questions to Romney arise as part of a televised interview, which means that answers can and will be followed up by other questions; interview questions have a number of levels or parts; and in the case of Romney, they contain social and structural presuppositions about his responsibility for what he said and whether he has really changed his mind; and questions to Romney act as much as challenges as requests for information.

It is clear from this example why some pragmatic analysts tend to disregard social context when discerning meaning; they argue that context conveys information that is too varied and unwieldy (see Huang, 2007). Other analysts counter that a study of meaning in context must include social, cultural, or cognitive issues. This is a core debate within pragmatics about how the study of meaning in context should proceed. In our consideration of presidential language, we will adopt a broad view of pragmatics, one that will initially define pragmatics in line with Lycan (1995), as expressed in the *Cambridge Dictionary of Philosophy*:

> Pragmatics studies the use of language in context, and the context-dependence of various aspects of linguistic interpretation.

How broad do we want to make "context"? If we want to make sense of natural language in communicative contexts, we must acknowledge that everyday interaction is full of all kinds of contextual information relevant to a pragmatic assessment. To understand this position, let me tell you a story.

A Short Story about Pragmatics: Part One

In the early part of the twentieth century, those studying linguistic meaning, particularly those within the philosophy of language, were influenced by the success of mathematics in bringing order to a significantly complex physical world. Deciphering linguistic meaning could be difficult because language is often confusing—it can be ambiguous, where one word or sentence has multiple meanings, or where more than one word or sentence mean the same thing (synonymy). Language can also contain irony and metaphor, where sentences can mean the opposite of what is said, or it can be used to talk about things that don't exist, as in fairy tales or mythology. In the seventeenth century the philosopher and mathematician Gottfried Leibniz argued that the confusions and inconsistencies of human language might reflect a confused mind (see Mates, 1986). What was needed, he argued, was a logically constructed language that would produce concise and ordered thought. He called for a more precise logical and mathematical meta-language to explain ordinary language; this meta-language would be a language that was different from the object language requiring explanation.

Gottlieb Frege (see Ricketts and Potter, 2010) and Bertrand Russell (1956) attempted to produce one of the first formal accounts of language meaning. They focused in particular on the meaning of reference in language—the referential relationship between words and sentences and objects and concepts. For instance, how does "London" refer to the capital of England? Or how does the definite description "the first man on the moon" designate a specific individual? Reference was seen as providing a description of specific objects, or in the case of proper names, abbreviated or associated descriptions. Problems arose almost immediately, many of which are still being worked out today (see Devitt, 2004; Campbell, 2002; Muller, 2013). Frege noted that there were sentences that had different meanings but referred to the same object. His famous example is that of "the evening star" and "the morning star." Although both terms refer to the planet Venus, they do so in different ways, which Frege referred to as "modes of presentation." To explain this, he introduced a distinction between the "sense" of a sentence (roughly the description) and its referent or reference (the object). There were many other problematic issues with reference, such as the use of sentences which refer to objects that do not exist, as in "Hercules was a great hero," or "the present king of France is bald." Commenting on such sentences, Russell noted, "logic . . . must not admit a unicorn any more than zoology can" (Russell, 1920: 169). Like Leibniz, Russell wanted to reconstruct natural human language as a "logically" formal system by avoiding any "obstinate addiction to ordinary language." This is an important claim, and one that still resonates throughout modern pragmatics, as we will see later. For the present, we will note that Russell's solution to nonexistent names, such as "Hercules" or "Pegasus," was that they were not logically proper names, which means, simply, that they can be understood in terms of their "disguised" descriptions:

Hercules was a hero of Greek mythology, said to be the son of Zeus.
Pegasus was the immortal winged horse of Bellerophon.

There are many other puzzles here, but it is fair to say that the Frege-Russell approach to reference was preferred until the late 1950s or early 1960s, when alternative approaches began to accept that in many cases it is not just language that refers, but also speakers who refer using language. To understand this, we need to note that for Russell (and philosophy in general at the time) sentences (or propositions) were assessed as either true or false. The statement "London is the capital of England" is true within our present system of knowledge, and the statement "Glasgow is the capital of England" is false. It also follows in a more systemic sense (logically) that if "London is the capital of England" is true, then a sentence such as "London is not the capital of England" is false. And, of course, if the sentence "London is the capital of England" is false, then the sentence "London is not the capital of England" would be true. In general terms this makes sense, but the philosopher P. F. Strawson challenged this Russellian view of sentences by arguing that in certain cases of negation one could not decide whether a sentence was true or false. Strawson gave examples of sentences that carry what are called "presuppositions," that is, types of information taken for granted. Consider the following two sentences:

John managed to stop in time.
John didn't manage to stop in time.

Both sentences contain the word "manage," which is a "factive verb," or a verb that presupposes the truth of its complement. So in these two sentences, what is presupposed is that John "tried to stop in time," succeeding in one case and failing in the other. But in both sentences, regardless of the outcome, it remains true that John did try to stop in time. Hence, argues Strawson, one cannot simply say that one sentence is true and the other false. This situation is further complicated by the fact that "presuppositions" can be canceled, as in the following:

John managed to stop in time even though he didn't try.
John didn't manage to stop in time and he didn't try.

There are many other issues surrounding "presuppositions," but they need not concern us now. We should just note that they created a problem for semantics where it had been assumed that a true sentence and its negation should produce a false sentence, and a false sentence and its negation should produce a true sentence. For those who preferred an organized and formal view of meaning, any talk of sentences that might be neither true nor false was heresy. However, Strawson drew attention to the idea that human language might be structured as it is for human communication, and this was an early indication of the emergence of "pragmatic meaning" (see also Peirce; discussed in Pietarinen, 2005). By the 1970s, Stalnaker (1972, 1973, 1974, 1998) was arguing for a "pragmatic" form of presupposition. He suggests that the object of focus is not what words or sentences presuppose, but rather what people presuppose. In certain cases of language use, it is "people" who presuppose information they assume to be "common ground" (shared information) among interlocutors.

John Austin was another philosopher who, like Strawson, was concerned about whether sentences were true or false. In his book *How to Do Things with Words* (1962), Austin distinguished between sentences that could be assessed as either true or false, which he called "constatives," and other sentences or utterances that are not necessarily true or false but are describing an action. These Austin referred to as "performative utterances," more generally known as "speech acts" (see Searle, 1969), and include the following:

I do (in a wedding ceremony).
I find you guilty (as pronounced by a judge).
Out! (as said by an umpire).
I promise to come to your party.

Austin suggested that "performative" utterances were marked by devices that indicated which action was taking place (such as "I ask" or "I order"); further, he noted that such acts would be successful only under certain conditions. For instance, if someone is declared "guilty," a judge or equivalent would normally make the pronouncement, in the correct circumstances, in a court, and at the correct time. Equally, walking up to a woman you like and saying "I do" does not constitute a marriage. A church minister or equivalent is required, vows have to be taken and witnessed, and so on. These relevant factors Austin called "felicity conditions," drawing an analogy with "truth conditions," the conditions for assessing a statement as true or false.

Austin began to compile a list of utterances that could be designated as "performatives"; as he did this, he realized that his constative/performative distinction might not be a distinction after all, since almost any utterance could be said to be performative in some way. Even statements are themselves performative in that they carry out the action of "stating," as in "I state that X." John Searle (1969) responded to this by arguing that all language was action-oriented and that most sentences could be said to have an implicit performative element, as in the following:

(I ask you) What's the time?
(I command you to) Stop doing that.
(I state that) I am hungry.

Searle also further developed Austin's distinction between the actual saying of something, a "locutionary act"; the action performed, an "illocutionary act" (promise, command, etc.); and the effect of the act, "the perlocutionary act."

With Speech Act Theory we have one of the first fully formed theories of language pragmatics. It is recognized that language not only describes but also acts on and constitutes the world of interaction and understanding. The focus shifts to what someone is doing by what they say: promising, commanding, excusing, and so on. In the performance of speech actions, different levels emerge, from articulation through recognition to reaction, and the question becomes, what are the cognitive, social, and linguistic mechanisms that allow us to interpret an utterance as a specific speech act? Speech Act Theory became bogged down, however, in logical or other formal delimitations of types and typologies of speech acts, and many feel that it failed to fulfill its original promise (see 1994;, 2001 and Kissine, 2013, for an alternative view). Nevertheless, Speech Act Theory remains a central tenet of pragmatics, and we consider its use in our analysis of Bill Clinton's language in Chapter 5.

Around the same time as the development of speech act theory, Paul Grice was formulating his theory of "conversation" based on the "Cooperative Principle" and its maxims of behavior. Grice, Strawson, and Austin were not seeking to explicitly construct a theory of pragmatics as such: they were working very much within the tradition of the philosophy of language. It became clear to all of them, however, that there were types of meaning that could not be easily dealt with in traditional models, since they were related to speaker intentions and language use in context. But it did not follow that all meaning was now "pragmatic" (sentences would continue to mean what they did semantically), but now we had to take account of other meanings that emerged explicitly or implicitly from the actual use of "sentences" in contexts of interaction (utterances).

From the story so far, we can see that from the beginning one of the aims in the study of meaning was to provide a formal, and hence logically consistent, account of the way in which language describes the world. It is now accepted that in understanding meaning there is much more involved than early philosophers thought. It is not just words or sentences that create meaning—speakers also create meaning through the use of words and sentences. This is speaker meaning, or pragmatics. Let's explore how some of these principles can be applied to presidential language.

First Interlude: Talking with the President

Most work on the formalization of semantics and its link or independence from pragmatics is based on constructed language examples. It is in the nature of the philosophy of language to create sample sentences or constructed scenarios, and modern linguistic approaches to semantics and pragmatics do the same. In many ways, both fields have not only converged on similar problems, but also adopted similar methods to explore these problems (see for example debates on "explicit communication": Carston, 2002; Bach, 1994, 1997; Horn, 2001; Levinson, 2000).

Recall, however, that one of the reasons it is difficult to produce a formal theory of language meaning is that natural language is full of inconsistencies and ambiguities. For example, take a sentence such as "he put it down and then picked it up again and threw at him." Who is being referred to, and what is the object that is thrown? Or consider the statement, "John went to the bank" (riverside or financial institution?), or finally, "John and Mary are married" (to each other or to different partners?). Such sentences undermined the effort to construct a precise theory that could explain how meaning worked. Of course, any formal theory must ultimately reflect the natural use of language, but even a cursory consideration of natural interaction reveals that the problem is not language's ambiguities, but rather the fact that these ambiguities pervade language use, and are quite normative. Given this, are they actually problematic, or are they naturally evolved functions of communication designed for particular objectives? Consider the following examples from Ronald Reagan:

(4) I have left orders to be awakened at any time in case of national emergency—even if I'm in a Cabinet meeting.

(5) I want you to know that also I will not make age an issue of this campaign. I am not going to exploit, for political purposes, my opponent's youth and inexperience. (during a 1984 presidential debate with Walter Mondale)

(6) I'm afraid I can't use a mule. I have several hundred up on Capitol Hill. (refusing the gift of a mule)

Most of us will have little difficulty in understanding these statements; we know they are not to be taken literally and that their aim is to be ironic and humorous. A cursory semantic analysis is unlikely to tell us much about what is going on here. But if we take Grice's view and assume that Reagan is being cooperative, we can look at his utterances with this principle in mind. We can see that Reagan may be intentionally flouting some maxims. For example, in (4) we have what is sometimes called a "garden path sentence" (Fodor and Ferreira, 1998; Pinker, 1995, where we process a sentence expecting/predicting a certain outcome or progression, only to be thrown off course. For example, "because he always jogs a mile seems a short distance to him" (Nordquist; About.com), or "Time flies like an arrow, fruit flies like a banana." Such forms lead us to reparse sentences to resolve a clash in meaning. Turning to (4), while it makes sense, that if there is a national emergency Reagan needs to be made aware of it, even if he is sleeping, as we process his comment and reach the term "even" we might predict other stronger examples where the president should be interrupted (even at my daughter's wedding, for example). Here our predictions clash with what seems to be an embedded presupposition that Reagan is asleep in cabinet meetings. Now of course this is odd: is Reagan really implying that he sleeps in cabinet meetings? Few of us would believe this is true, so Reagan might be saying something which is false. Now recall the maxim "Do not say what you believe to be false"; if we believe Reagan would not be asleep in cabinet meetings, but that he has said that he is asleep in cabinet meetings, then Reagan is flouting a Gricean maxim. Grice tells us that when maxims are flouted this very action can be contextually meaningful and generates what we noted above as "conversational implicatures." These inferences are calculated using contextual and other information to produce an alternative meaning or meanings. In this case, at least one meaning suggests that cabinet meetings are so boring that they put you to sleep. So it is not that Reagan is asleep in cabinet meetings, he only makes "as if to say" he is asleep in such meetings and by this to suggest such meetings are dry, overly formal, and boring. As most of us have access to everyday sayings that associate being bored with falling asleep and lack of interest or lethargy, (what they said put me to sleep; it was so boring I dozed off) we reach the conclusion that Reagan is being at least ironic, since he is saying that cabinet meetings are boring enough to put you to sleep.

Example (5) is similar, since it is false that Reagan has a number of "mules" on Capitol Hill. Here he is implying a contrast between the associated characteristics of the animal "mule" and members of Congress, specifically the trait of "stubbornness." By flouting the quality maxim he has focused our attention on the claim that he has several "mules" on Capital Hill. We know he does not have several animals (mules) on Capital Hill, so in order to maintain "Relevance" (see also Sperber and Wilson below) we can construct a metaphorical transfer between traits of the animal "mule" and members of Congress. Now there are a variety of possibilities here—the trait being implied could be big ears, the tendency to work hard, lack of intelligence—but in terms of relevance, the most likely candidate is "stubbornness," linked to such related concepts as difficult to work with or hard to convince.

Example (5) also seems to be ironic, but here we need to know that during Reagan's presidential campaign one of the criticisms of Reagan was that he was too "old" to be president. Given this, we can see that he has turned this argument around on his critics by focusing on age, in this case "youth," in order to indicate that age is a relative concept, and that being too young and inexperienced can be a problem as much as being too old.

These analyses are somewhat general at this stage, but they are generated for two reasons: first, to indicate how Reagan is utilizing pragmatics for political communication; second, although similar techniques occur in a range of talk types, they are particularly prevalent in political communication, indicating the ubiquity and relevance of pragmatics for analyzing political talk.

Turning now to a different example, consider the following interview involving John F. Kennedy:

KENNEDY. **Good morning**, Dave.
MR. GARROWAY: **Good morning**, Mr. President. **I suppose** those scenes of Mass. General look pretty familiar to you? You have been on the board of overseers since 1947, I believe?

KENNEDY: Yes, that's right. **I must say that I think** . . ., they perform a great public function. And **to think** that this hospital is celebrating its 150th anniversary. It was begun the year before the war of 1812, and yet there are two other American hospitals that are even older. When **we think** of the tremendous progress that has been made in medicine, yet even way back then, fellow citizens were concerned about caring for their neighbors . . .

MR. GARROWAY: They have put out, **I think**, $4 million a year, in this one hospital, into research. Is this enough, **I wonder**? Are we doing enough generally for research in this country?

KENNEDY. **I think** we can always do better . . . This center is going to begin building as soon as the snow is off the ground . . . **I think** this is one area where there has been inadequate research. . . . But **I do believe** that nearly every American family either has some member of its family or some friend who goes through the very harrowing experience of having a child in the family who suffers from mental retardation.

We have highlighted some phrases in bold, the first being an example of an adjacency pair. We discussed these above in the context of questions and answers, and here we have another type know as a "greeting."

KENNEDY: Good morning (Dave)
MR. GARROWAY: Good Morning (Mr. President)

The turns within such a greeting not only come in a specific order but their shape is symmetrically matched, as found in other greetings:

A: Hello
B: Hello
C: Hi there
D: Hi there

Such sequential organization contributes to the interaction and encodes meaning within turns. But such meaning is not semantic in any formal sense; it is rather "pragmatic" in that it assists in positioning the participants by providing a way into the interview, what is called an "opening" (Schegloff, 1968). Not surprisingly, as there are pairs that play a part on the opening of interaction, there are also pairs that play a part in "closing" interaction. For example:

A: Bye
B: Bye
C: See you
D: See You
E: Thank you Mr. President
F: Thank you Dave

In this last pair we have included the use of title and name, as happened in the opening of the actual interview. Here again, this "naming" process is contributing to interactional understanding. The president has called the interviewer by his "first" name, indicating a relaxed relationship. The interviewer refers to John Kennedy as Mr. President, and while this might suggest more formality, this is not necessarily the case since there are a limited number of ways to refer to the holder of the office of president, and this does not normally include first names.

Let us turn now to the other marked examples in the interview. Consider what happens if we remove some of the highlighted phrases, as seen in the (B) examples:

A: Mr. President. **I suppose** those scenes of Mass. General look pretty familiar to you? You have been on the board of overseers since 1947, **I believe**?

B: Mr. President. () those scenes of Mass. General look pretty familiar to you? You have been on the board of overseers since 1947, ()?

A: Yes, that's right. **I must say that I think** the work that Massachusetts General does and other similar hospitals around the country, they perform a great public function.

B: Yes, that's right. () the work that Massachusetts General does and other similar hospitals around the country, they perform a great public function.

A: Mr. Garroway: They have put out, **I think**, $4 million a year, in this one hospital, into research. Is this enough, **I wonder**?

B: Mr. Garroway: They have put out, (), $4 million a year, in this one hospital, into research. Is this enough, ()?

In (B) places indicated by () show where we have taken out the marked phrase. As you can see, when these phrases are deleted, what remains still makes perfect sense. So what are these phrases doing there in the first place? If they are not part of the core meaning, then they may be contributing in some way to "pragmatic meaning." These phrases are referred to as "pragmatic markers" (also known discourse markers: see Fraser, 1999; Schiffrin, 1987) and they form a diverse set of options with a wide range of functions. Most of those used in the interview are "cognitive verbs" ("think, believe, know, suppose"). These forms are thought of as "hedges" (Lakoff, 1972; Markkanen and Schröder, 2007), which are used to limit and control commitment to statements that are made:

(I think) it is measles (although it may not be).
(I believe) I am first (although I may not be).

"Hedges" allow us to modify our commitment to claims or statements and protect us should our claims or statements turn out to be wrong or not fully evidenced. For example. at one point in the interview Mr. Garroway says "They have put out, I think, $4 million a year. . . ." If it turns out that it was $2 million rather than $4 million, Mr. Garroway has covered himself since he did not make a bold assertion but rather "hedged" his claim. So if someone accuses Mr. Garroway of making a false statement, he can claim that he was stating what he thought (I think) was true at that time.

A Short Story about Pragmatics: Part Two

As we saw in our short story part one, major protagonists such as Frege and Russell wanted to develop formal theories of meaning that would bring some order and consistency to natural language. We noted that Strawson, Austin, Searle, and particularly Grice all offered arguments which suggested that there are a variety of aspects of meaning that might not be directly explained by the logical or propositional forms of sentences; these meanings were seen as belonging to pragmatics. All of those mentioned so far are philosophers, but linguists too, working on similar phenomena, also recognized the same issue (see Levinson, 2003; Huang, 2007). Most linguists and philosophers agree that there are forms of information conveyed in sentences that are underdetermined by linguistic semantics, and that these fall under the heading of pragmatics. How was this pragmatic material dealt with? There emerged what is known as the problem of the "semantic-pragmatic interface," the issue of what is semantic and what is pragmatic, and how these relate to each other in language processing or interactive communication. Kent Bach (2008: 1) argues that the semantics-pragmatics interface includes at least the following issues:

Indexicality
Ambiguity
Vagueness
Semantic underdetermination
Implicitness
Implicature
Non-literalness
Non truth-conditional content
Illocutionary force (speech acts).

While many analysts would agree with most of the above, how one actually tackles these leads to a variety of different formulations of the interface.

Those who directly follow Grice's original view, that an utterance is presented by the speaker for propositional decoding and that everything else is contextually or conversationally implicated, are referred to as neo-Griceans, or as "literalists" (see Recanati, 1998; 2007; Wilson and Sperber, 2012). Others have argued that this split between propositional meaning and implicit speaker meaning is not as straightforward as Grice envisaged, and there may be more going on at the level of propositional form than first thought. As Sperber and Wilson (2005: 3) put it:

> ... a major development in pragmatics over the past thirty years (going much further than Grice envisaged) has been to show that the explicit content of an utterance, like the implicit content, is largely underdetermined by the linguistically encoded meaning, and its recovery involves a substantial element of pragmatic inference.

This is what has been called the "contexualist view" (Recanati, 2007). Sperber and Wilson (1995) are not only the best-known proponents of this view, they are also the architects of one of the most significant developments within pragmatics since Grice. Sperber and Wilson developed what became known as Relevance Theory. As the title suggests, they are taking a lead from Grice's concept of relevance, but Sperber and Wilson develop this further by arguing that the very act of communication itself has an expectation of "relevance" built right into it, as opposed to being normatively assessed against social expectations:

> For relevance theorists, the very act of communicating raises precise and predictable expectations of relevance, which are enough on their own to guide the hearer towards the speaker's meaning. Speakers may fail to be relevant, but they cannot, if they are genuinely communicating (as opposed, say, to rehearsing a speech), produce utterances that do not convey a presumption of their own relevance. (Sperber and Wilson, 1995: 6)

While Relevance Theory (Sperber and Wilson, 1995; Carston 2002; Wilson and Sperber 2002, 2004), builds on original Gricean insights, it differs in that it emphasizes the inferential nature of explicit communication. The theory argues that sentence meaning is much more fragmented than Grice and others had believed. Sperber and Wilson (1995) introduce the term "explicature," for example, to reflect the way in which propositions may be filled out without reference to implicit or contextual inferences. An "explicature" is defined as:

> A proposition communicated by an utterance is an EXPLICATURE if and only if it is a development of a logical form encoded by the utterance. (Sperber and Wilson, 1995: 182)

And this is distinguished from an "implicature," which is a proposition expressed by an utterance "implicitly" not "explicitly." Sperber and Wilson (2005: 14) explain this difference in the following example:

ALAN JONES: Do you want to join us for supper?
LISA: No thanks. I've eaten.

Sperber and Wilson (2005) note that Griceans would treat Lisa's response as indicating she has eaten something at some time, though they suggest there is a much stronger explicit interpretation that she has eaten something that evening.

Thus, Lisa's meaning . . . might include the **explicature** that she has eaten supper on the evening of utterance and the **implicature** that she doesn't want to eat with the Joneses because she's already had supper that evening.

This explicit/implicit distinction raises a number of significant theoretical issues in semantics and pragmatics, but we will not consider these here (see Carston, 2002); we will instead focus on a perhaps even more significant consequence of Sperber and Wilson's theory of Relevance: its cognitive explanation of general pragmatic behavior. For Sperber and Wilson, the idea that speakers abide by a maxim of relevance is too vague and too weak (1995: 162):

Communicators do not 'follow' the principle of relevance, and they could not violate it even if they wanted to. The principle of relevance follows without exceptions.

"Relevance" is built into the very nature of communication and every utterance by dint of its production carries an assumption of relevance, which Sperber and Wilson call the "Presumption of Relevance." This is the second of two principles of relevance enunciated by Sperber and Wilson, specifically, "Every act of ostensive communication communicates a presumption of its own optimal relevance" (1985: 260). The first, or cognitive principle of Relevance Theory, suggests that "human cognition is geared to the maximization of relevance" (ibid.: 260). This maximization is the outcome of a processing balance between cognitive effort and information. So when a speaker produces an utterance the assumption is that it has been designed for optimal relevance, that is, that it is worth processing and that the effort expended in processing is balanced with the informational payoff returned.

Here is a simple example from Wilson (2010) where Relevance Theory is used to explain the use of metaphor. Wilson gives us an example from a line in an obituary about the novelist John Updike:

(6) Updike was a giant.

In processing lexical information for giants we might draw on encyclopedic information "that giants have extraordinary height, imposing presence, powers beyond those of ordinary humans, stand out from the crowd, and so on." While "giant" could be used in a number of these ways, Wilson suggests that:

. . . the expectations of relevance raised by an obituary of a public figure would lead the audience to look for implications having more to do with lifetime achievements than with physical properties. In this case, processing (6) in the context of easily accessible encyclopedic information about Updike's status as a novelist should yield enough implications to satisfy the audience's expectations of relevance without information about his physical stature being considered at all.

Context itself helps drive interpretation, but which context? Which aspects of our general knowledge—specific knowledge of the author, a knowledge of literature and the role of the novel, and so on—help us to interpret this statement? And how do our minds decide among these? This is where Relevance Theory plays its "trump card"—you know which context because it is the one that delivers the most effects for the least processing effort.

Second Interlude: Talking with the President Again

In this interlude we will discuss George H. W. Bush's use of metaphors in his inaugural speech of 1989. We want to consider what Relevance Theory might tell us here, and consider, once again, what happens when pragmatic theories, often built out of constructed single sentences or imagined utterances, come face to face with real world discourse.

In the opening of his speech Bush tells us that:

I come before you and assume the Presidency at a moment rich with promise.

The phrase "a moment rich with promise" is clearly metaphorical. In Relevance Theory terms, we should take account of the phrase as an input to optimal relevance, so that if we process the utterance we reach an optimal level of information that has been conveyed. As a first approximation we might paraphrase the metaphor as "the time is opportune for the people and for the country and things are looking good for the future." The lexical form "rich" is normally associated with "financial wealth," meaning that one has lots of money, or at least has much more than the average person. It is also assumed that being "rich" is something that is good and positive. There are also other domains where "rich" can be used; we might say "my family life is rich with the love of my family," or that "my dreams are rich with the hopes of the future," or that "my work life is rich with excitement and the unexpected." In each case the general understanding of wealth as "having a lot of money" is transferred, where "money" is replaced by other variables: love, dreams, work. When Bush says "this moment is rich with promise" it is "promise" which is conceptualized in the slot where money would normally be located. Hence, whatever we take "promise" to be, we know at this time we have more of it than might be expected. But in what sense can "promise" be "rich," or how can we have more than normal, more than the average of a promise? In a standard interpretation of "promise" we are looking at a commitment to some action in the future. So a "moment rich with promise" is a moment with more than expected opportunities to be returned or gained in the future. And given this statement occurs in an inaugural speech we won't be thinking directly of money, but rather of political issues such as employment, the economy, education, health, and so on. All of these become positively assessed as centers for future and "rich" returns.

Now all of this seems fine, but we could have done this analysis without Relevance Theory. What Relevance Theory brings for us, however, is an explanation of why we would accept the phrase "moment rich with promise" as an input for processing in the first place. We do so because we believe it contains within itself its own optimal relevance, and that this can be worked out with a communicative payoff in terms of information. Nevertheless, could Bush not simply have said, "I come at time when there are many opportunities for America and its people"? Of course he could, so it must be the case, if Relevance Theory is correct, that we gain more information, or more precise information, when the metaphor is used. Critics have argued that this is one of the problems for Relevance Theory in that it does not provide any clear process for measuring effort and information payoff, or how such effort may vary by context and individual (Cappelen and Lepore, 2007; Levinson, 1989). It is argued that relevance is also relevant to the context of the audience/hearer, because not everyone has the same encyclopedic knowledge or experiences, and some individuals might find the processing effort in interpreting a metaphor unnecessary, while others may extend the processing effort in terms of their own preferences. But of course either case would still be explained by Relevance Theory, and for critics this means it can never be wrong. To extend an example from Wilson and Carston (2006), consider the following:

A. Caroline is a princess.
B. You mean she is royalty and lives in a palace.
C. No, she is spoiled.
D. So why didn't you just say she is spoiled?

Of course, one can argue here that metaphors offer a much richer stylistic format full of potential, as opposed to a bald statement of facts. When Romeo says "Juliet is the sun" we don't try to interpret this as "she rises early in the morning" or that she is "hot stuff"; rather we consider the role of the sun as the center of the universe or that without it we would die. But as with Wilson's comments on the obituary above, we generate such options because of the context in which the phrase is being used, as within a play about lovers. Equally, to take Bush's comment out of the context of his speech as a whole will miss much, not only of where the phrase fits within the speech, but also how we might best understand the metaphor itself.

Most political speeches are not designed to be factual in any detailed sense; they are frequently filled with metaphors. This is in part because, as Lakoff has argued (Lakoff and Johnson, 1999; Lakoff, 1987; Lakoff, 2004), metaphorical representations are central to our conceptual organization of the world. But there are also core pragmatic reasons for the use of metaphors. For example, speeches are frequently presented to publics who are not always interested, or technically able, to follow difficult and detailed arguments (see Reid-Gold, 1988). For these reasons speeches also appeal to emotions desires and needs (see Chapter 7).

Consider the following selection of words from the opening lines of Bush's speech:

come, rich, before, live, time, new, blow(ing), free, fact, life, push,

Bush's aim in his speech was to present a "hymn to the triumph of democracy." As the ex-vice President to Ronald Reagan, one of his major aims was to indicate his own independence now that Reagan was gone; to make clear that what was to come in his period of office would not simply (or only) be more of the same. Consequently, a sense of change pervades the speech. The vocabulary selected, both through the use of set phrases created from basic elements (for example, the phrase "a new breeze is blowing" occurs several times) and through sets of lexical relations carefully structured to indicate change.

The general approach continues when we look at the following words, also used in this speech:

new/reborn/future/tomorrow/era/times/moment/passing
    breeze/leaves/ground(broken)/renew

Here there is a sense of changing time, both explicitly in the use of forms from a semantic field of time, that is, tomorrow, future, moment, and also through the invocation of nature. This is made clear in the indirect marking of the seasons, in particular the coming of spring after the old (dead) leaves have been blown away and the "broken ground" of winter has prepared for a new birth (reborn/new).

This concept of change and rebirth is particularly appropriate because it indicates the difference between Bush and Reagan. We are being informed that what is to come in the period of this administration will be new, but not completely or radically so. The process will be similar to the way in which, like nature, there is a development which draws on those positive aspects of the past while at the same time establishing something which is recognizably independent from that past. Consider the following:

A new breeze is blowing and the old . . . must be made new <u>again.</u>

The winds of autumn blow away the dead leaves to allow for new leaves in the spring. This does not mean we have a new tree, the foundations are solid, it is the foliage that is made new "again." Hence, with the administration the foundations are solid, it is old ideas that must swept away to make room for new concepts.

Bush develops this theme and across a few phrases he takes from America to the rest of the world.

For a new breeze is blowing, and a world refreshed by freedom seems reborn; for in man's heart, if not in fact, the day of the dictator is over. The totalitarian era is passing, its old ideas blown away like leaves from an ancient, lifeless tree. A new breeze is blowing, and a nation refreshed by freedom stands ready to push on. There is new ground to be broken, and new action to be taken.

Bush speaks of "a nation refreshed," "a world refreshed." Here we integrate the changes Bush will bring for America to the effects of America on the world. Although Bush refers several times to "freedom," and makes good use of the word "free" with reference to the (at that time) emerging democracies in Eastern Europe, any freedom is nevertheless of a particular type. This can be seen in the way that "freedom" as a concept is introduced. First, it is seen in a generic mode, as a general concept applicable without reservation, clarification or delimitation:

> . . . a world refreshed with freedom

Then we find that "freedom" becomes political in that it is linked to a specific political ideal (an implicit link between democracy and freedom):

> Great nations of the world are moving toward democracy through the door to freedom. Men and women of the world move toward free markets through the door to prosperity. The people of the world agitate for free expression and free thought through the door to the moral and intellectual satisfactions that only liberty allows.

Note how this is structured. First we have ". . . great nations of the world are moving toward democracy." Next we find "freedom" politically sub-categorized in terms of an economic principle: "Men and women of the world move toward free markets." And finally we have "freedom" focused in terms of a general belief in the freedom of individuals to speak and think as they wish: "The people of the world agitate for free expression and free thought."

We can see in these extracts that "freedom" is both an ideal and a specified concept. As an ideal it is what America stands for and has strived to assist others to achieve all over the world, particularly in those countries where "freedom" (in the sense that it is defined in America) is not readily available. But when we turn to such countries—in America's view the then communist countries of Eastern Europe—freedom becomes a specific concept. It is implied that these countries should not merely strive for "freedom," but freedom as defined by the capitalist West. Here it is more than simply freedom of speech, but free markets within a specific kind of capitalist democracy. This suggests that of the various forms a democracy could take, the democracy represented by the West, in particular as exemplified by the United States, is the one that provides for "freedom" in all its forms.

The combination of sets of words at various points throughout the speech reflects the combinatorial force of vocabulary in conveying both general points of change, and core ideological points regarding capitalism and democracy. On a specific point internal to the politics of the United States the pattern emerges again:

> . . . we must hope to give them a sense of what it means to be a loyal friend; a loving parent; a citizen who leaves his home, his neighborhood, his town, better than he found it.

Here we have a graded move from the general to the particular: "citizen," "friend," "parent," matched in a similar manner with "town," "neighborhood," "home." The selection of words here gathers together all Americans and locates them in relation to larger loyalties as well as local loyalties.

As we can see from this selective analysis of the opening sections of Bush's inaugural speech, the vocabulary is structurally distributed throughout, and speech functions in a highly organized way. The aims may be varied, from indicating change, to the ideologically controlled praise of American democracy, but Bush's manipulation of vocabulary for metaphorical effect remains constant.

This manipulation is used to generate a range of connected metaphors. Though each metaphor could be understood on its on its own, it is also the role of the set of metaphors to convey a higher level message, or even a higher level metaphor of political change as natural and progressive change. In this sense, "context" becomes significantly more complex when we try to understand actual communication in the real world of interaction and political interaction in particular. Nevertheless, pragmatics provides us with the tools to move forward our understanding of metaphors, first as relevance driven forms of communication and next as combinatorial elements of a higher ordered textual message.

Pragmatics: A Short Story: Part Three

In his paper on the "Semantics-Pragmatics Distinction," Kent Bach (2006) makes the following disclaimer:

> I will not use 'pragmatics' so broadly as to apply to the full range of phenomena falling under the heading of language use. That would take us too far afield into such areas as social psychology, sociolinguistics. Cultural anthropology, and rhetoric, I will restrict the discussion to those aspects of use that are directly related to acts of communication. . . .

Alternatively, other definitions of pragmatics (Leech, 1983; Thomas 1995, Verschueren et al, 1995; Huang; 2007) place much more emphasis on the speaker and the speech situation. Thomas (1995: 22) argues that meaning is an interactional outcome of a "dynamic process" involving both speaker and hearer and the "physical, social and linguistic" aspects of the context of utterance. Leech (1983: 11) also emphasizes the significance of social conditions in pragmatics and makes a distinction between "General Pragmatics" (the conditions of language use); "Pragmalinguistics" (the linguistics resources of a specific language: i.e., grammar) and "Sociopragmatics" (social and cultural conditions of use). Both Thomas and Leech would want to take us beyond the grammaticalization or formalization of context as it arises within language use. Mey (2001: 6) puts it that "pragmatics . . . cannot limit itself to the grammatically encoded aspects of contexts. . . ." All of these authors stress, to a greater or lesser degree, the potentially interdisciplinary nature of pragmatics and that it needs to include in, Verschueren's (1999) terms ". . . a general cognitive, social, and cultural perspective."

As Huang (2007) suggests, we seem to have two approaches to pragmatics, what is generally called "linguistic pragmatics" and the implicitly or explicitly more interdisciplinary oriented pragmatics, which links linguistics to other areas such as psychology, sociology, politics, and so on, which we have called "socio-pragmatics." Relevance Theory, for example, admits that it is openly "cognitive" in nature, and recently Dan Sperber has been actively exploring the cultural and experimental evidence for the efficacy of Relevance Theory (Sperber, 1996, 2009; Wilson and Sperber, 2012). On the other hand, some of the advocates for Relevance Theory, such as Robyn Carston (2002), are content to stress that their main interest is in the "sub-personal" level of pragmatic understanding, and to carry on the core traditions of linguistic pragmatics and the philosophy of language.

In modern linguistics, much time has been wasted on whether language can be studied as an abstract internal biological product accessed through underlying knowledge or intuitions (see Chomsky, 1996; Wilson and Henry, 2008), as opposed to the study of language as a socially designed communicative and interactional resource. The principle of abstracting linguistic knowledge away from its context of use has been presented, and justified, as a standard scientific procedure. Abstraction is not meant as form of control for constraining research behaviors, however. Einstein argued, for example, that as inductive exercises increase and our findings accumulate, we need to try to formulate a deductive program of thinking and a theory that goes beyond single or multiple instances of data that explains all the data. In contrast, the renowned mathematician von Newman suggests that those disciplines that become too deductive, focusing only on abstraction, will ultimately lose their way and will need to be returned to the actual data the theory was supposed to explain (cited in Wilson, 2003).

Modern pragmatics seems to take both routes at present, with some carrying on the underlying tradition enunciated by Leibniz and Russell, that semantics should be cleansed of the fuzziness of everyday use, and that where pragmatics enters at all, it should be delimited by linguistic constraints. Others argue for a "real" world view of pragmatics as the use of linguistic resources in context (Mey, 2001; Verschueren, 1998, not simply as they reflect context, but also how they help constitute that very context. But, of course, one can attempt to tread a middle way that recognizes the theoretical importance of formal theories as explanations of actual data, but also allows, ecologically, the use of other forms of social or cultural argument to supplement specific cases. Hence, in the rest of this book we will use pragmatic resources, in the broadest sense, in the explanation of selected examples of presidential language, where the assessment of the value of a pragmatic analysis is in terms of how it helps us understand the way in which presidents make use of language in the exercise of their role and their duties as "leaders of the free world."

In Chapter 2 we look at examples of John F. Kennedy's oratory drawing on some the core issues that arise from theories of reference both in semantics and pragmatics. In Chapter 3 we consider Richard Nixon's history of lying and consider the nature of lying as a speech action. In Chapter 4 we explore narrative pragmatics and Ronald Reagan's ability as a "storyteller," drawing on a range of social and cognitive theories that help explain how stories work for the president. Chapter 5 picks up again on some of the themes of Chapter 2 as we consider Bill Clinton's manipulation of language and issues of deception and what is now known as "stance" taking in linguistic interaction. In Chapter 6 we consider the problems and issues George W. Bush had in his use of language, and we reflect on whether these were pathological or reflective of a personal ideology that eschewed formality and intellectualism for simplicity and myth. And in our final chapter, Chapter 7, we consider both the strengths and weaknesses of Barack Obama as a public speaker, utilizing general pragmatics to explain both success and failure.

Throughout all of this, we explore what pragmatics brings to the study of presidential language and argue that not only does it offer original insights into linguistic manipulation, obfuscation, and political creativity, it also brings us closer to political leaders, as we understand that many of the things we criticize or praise in their language use are simply reflections of the same language system available to and used by everyone else. We are all equal when it comes to pragmatics.

2

Talking Pragmatics with the Best and the Brightest

JOHN F. KENNEDY

Introduction

John F. Kennedy is perhaps the best known of all US presidents, both at home and abroad. Surveys of the top-ranked US presidents consistently place him in the top four. In 1975, 52% of respondents in a Gallop poll rated Kennedy as the "greatest" president, ahead of Abraham Lincoln and Franklin Roosevelt. By the year 2000, nearly 40 years after his death, he topped the list again (see Dallek, 2003: 67). Yet Robert Dallek suggests that Kennedy's national record was far from significant. Dallek (2003) argues that on the historically important issue of "civil rights" he was a "cautious leader," and that of his major reform initiatives on tax, education, and Medicare ". . . none became law during his time in office" (see also Giglio, 2006). Within less than 100 days of taking office, Kennedy had ordered the disastrous "Bay of Pigs" invasion of Cuba, and he was outmaneuvered by the Russian leader Khrushchev in his meetings with him in Vienna. As Kennedy said of his experience in Vienna, it was ". . . the roughest thing in my life" (cited in Dallek, 2003: 40). Given all of this, why has Kennedy maintained such a positive profile in the minds of the American public?

The circumstances of his tragic death and the conspiracy theories surrounding who was actually responsible for his assassination contribute to an enduring mythology. But Kennedy's death may also offer a more mundane reason that he simply didn't get the chance of a second term in which to complete his main objectives. Indeed, Lyndon B. Johnson said he was completing Kennedy's work. But Dallek (2003; see also, Dallek and Golway 2007; Golway and Grantz, 2010) suggests that while Johnson agreed with Kennedy's political agenda, Johnson had his own particular strengths and a different set of social and political skills that allowed him to push through specific policies on the home front. Dallek goes further and argues that it is doubtful that Kennedy would have achieved the same results as Johnson. So is Kennedy's fame based mainly on his untimely and

Talking with the President. John Wilson. © Oxford University Press 2015.
Published 2015 by Oxford University Press

tragic death? In this context it is worth noting that President McKinley, who was also assassinated, served two full terms and was a particularly popular president, yet he does not appear anywhere as high on the polls of the most important US presidents.

It is true, of course, that Kennedy was one of the first presidents to take full benefit from, and indeed embrace, modern media communications. The John F. Kennedy Presidential Library and Museum says of his relations with television:

> John F. Kennedy was the first president to effectively use the new medium of television to speak directly to the American people. No other president had conducted live televised press conferences without delay or editing.

Kennedy was handsome, highly intelligent, articulate, and charismatic. He married one of the most photogenic and alluring women of the age, and he gathered around him some of the youngest and most intelligent people of the time—"the best and the brightest," to use Halberstram's now famous phrase (1972). Benson (2004) has argued that Kennedy was also one of the first modern presidents to cultivate and develop the politics of the personal, where "personification" becomes as central, if not more central, than the policies themselves. In this Kennedy explicitly courted the media, in particular the press media, and developed a model of speaking directly to the press, allowing them to deliver his message for him (see Schlesinger, 2002; Benson, 2004; Berry, 1987; Dallek and Golway, 2007). It is also now part of political and media folklore that Kennedy's media presence and performance in his debates with Richard Nixon in 1960 played a significant part in his becoming president (Druckman, 2003; Kraus, 2000; Stanton, 2000).

But we should also not forget the central role of Kennedy's foreign affairs policy, which he developed at a time of significant East-West tension, the development of the Peace Corps, his far-sightedness in supporting the Apollo space program, his concern with helping developing countries, and his balance of adopting a strong anti-communist stance alongside a strategic diplomatic position in dealing with the Soviet Union. This balancing act both allowed him to avoid a third world war as a consequence of the Cuban missile crisis, and to negotiate one of the first significant nuclear arms reduction treaties (Brinkly, 2012).

Throughout all his 1,000 days of political leadership as president, and indeed prior to this, the communication of his political views and actions was, of course, significant, and central to this was a heighted sense of the importance of language in all its aspects. Few political phrases are better known than "Ask not what your country can do for you, ask what you can do for your country," which formed part of one of the shortest yet one of the most memorable of presidential inaugural addresses. Perhaps less well known, according to one analyst, is that Kennedy took care in the delivery of that address so that his Boston accent did not interfere with the message. And during the Cuban missile crisis, Kennedy made efforts to draw a lexical distinction between "blockade" and "quarantine." In all things linguistic, the careful manipulation and organization of communication were uppermost in the minds of Kennedy and his political team.

In this chapter we will look at some of the ways in which pragmatic analysis may highlight aspects of Kennedy's linguistic communication. In order to do this, we will focus on two aspects of a single core issue, the fact that Kennedy was a Roman Catholic. We look first at how Kennedy himself dealt with the matter, drawing extensively on theoretical aspects of linguistic pragmatics. Next, we consider Sarah Palin's criticism of Kennedy's approach to his religion in her book *America by Heart*, published in 2010. In this she argues that Kennedy "denied his religion," and she compares Kennedy with the Republican presidential candidate Mitt Romney who, while facing a religious issue of his own (he is a Mormon), never denied his religion but, according to Palin, openly embraced it. Palin's intervention brings the issues Kennedy was dealing with in the 1960s into the twenty-first century, and in examining these issues we consider the nature of a pragmatic example as it is carried across time.

Can a Roman Catholic Be President?

In 1928 Alfred E. Smith ran for the office of president of the United States. He lost in a landside to Herbert Hoover. It is said that one of the main reasons he lost was that he was Roman Catholic. It was also said that many voters believed that to elect a Roman Catholic would be to allow the Pope an influence in the White House. Some 30 years later, so the story goes, in a conversation with his father in 1956, Senator Jack Kennedy said there were two main reasons why he could not seek the presidency of the United States of America in 1960; the first was that he was too young (he would only be 42), and the second reason was that he was a Roman Catholic (Shaw, 2011: 1).

When Kennedy decided to run for president, he and his supporters knew that his religion could be an issue. It was Kennedy's view, however, that if he stood on his own political record he could avoid any problems associated with religion. The challenge Kennedy faced was highlighted when he visited West Virginia, where only some 5% of the state were Catholic. The media response at the time was to highlight Kennedy's Catholicism. Kennedy responded by focusing on non-religious issues, such as his service to his country and his recognition as a war hero. Most important, Kennedy emphasized the political problems facing people in their everyday lives, and focused on how his political experience, not his religion, prepared him for the job of president. As one aide was said to have noted, "boys when you don't have enough food to eat, you don't care about a man's religion." Kennedy went on to win the Mountain State.

In September 1960, Norman Vincent Peale, author of the widely known book *The Power of Positive Thinking* (Peale, 1953), opposed the election of John F. Kennedy. He did so as the spokesperson of a group of 150 clergymen, and he declared, "Faced with the election of a Catholic, our culture is at stake." In a written manifesto he went on to argue that Kennedy would serve the goals of the Catholic Church rather than his country. While Peale's comments were condemned across the religious divide, Kennedy could not ignore the potential damage of such claims, and he was determined to deal with the matter "head-on." On September 12, 1960, Kennedy accepted an invitation to speak to the Greater Houston Ministerial Association (examples below are from the transcript of the speech in Flank, 2010). In that speech he focused directly on the issue of whether a Catholic could be president; in one of the most powerful and significant speeches of his career, he skillfully demarcates the difference between holding the office of president of the United States and an individual's private and religious beliefs. In the opening of his speech he states that he will talk about the "so called religious issue. . . ." This phrase forms part of an opening in which several pragmatic markers occur, but this single phrase, while simple in structure and content, is quite complex in its pragmatic orientation. The opening use of this phrase, along with the discursive organization and content of the speech that follows, indicates that "so called" is being used to question the assumption(s) behind a "religious issue," or whether there is an issue at all. Kennedy's use of "so called" is well known and well understood in an informal and everyday understanding of the phrase, that is, it provides a challenge to some previously presumed or claimed set of statements.

But how does this use of "so called" actually work? In Kennedy's speech we have access to historical and contextual information that religion is being made an electoral issue, in this case then the interpretation of "so called" is used to challenge the existence of a "religious issue." Yet the first thing to note is that this use of "so called" can only arise if there is something called the "religious issue." There first had to be a "calling" to attention by someone that there is something called X, and they will have offered a definition of what X is. This suggests that "so called" has a double meaning or function: (a) to note that there is something called X, and (b) to question whether that calling is appropriate or correct. This is not a case of ambiguity, however. In the context of the speech, "so called" means what it is supposed to mean—that is, that something has been called a "religious issue"—but also, in the context of a challenge, it indicates something more.

Let us begin at the beginning. "So called" is given a dictionary definition as an adjective, indicating "what has been called." The following examples exemplify this case.

(1) "US dollar bill," 1862, **so called** from the time of their introduction; 1860s.
(2) Mod.L. translation of Ger. *fingerhut*, the German name of "foxglove," lit. "thimble." Named by Fuchs (1542), and **so called** for its shape. The medicine (originally extracted from the plant) is **so called** from 1799. ink **had been called** this since 1778 (as opposed to *redbacks,* etc.).

(3) B movie 1930s, usually said to be **so called** from being the second, or support-ing, film in a double feature. But some film industry sources say it was **so called** for being the second of the two films major studios generally made in a year, and the one made with less headline talent and released with less promotion. (Online etymology dictionary, http://www.etymonline.com/index.php).

These examples refer to established forms of what we might describe as original "callings." Here "so called" would be equivalent to other uses such as "has been called," "was/is called," "was/is known," or even "so named/named," where the phrases function not only to say what something is called, but also to describe and refer to the process of the naming itself.

It is also claimed that "so called" can be used to "introduce a new word or phrase which is not yet known by many people."

(4) It isn't yet clear how destructive this so-called "super virus" is.
(from the *Cambridge Advanced Learner's Dictionary*)

And then there is the interpretation of "so called" we seem to be dealing with in Kennedy's speech, which challenges or questions that "calling." In this case, "so called" indicates that you think a word or phrase is being used incorrectly or inappropriately.

(5) It was one of his so-called friends who supplied him with the drugs that killed him.
(from the *Cambridge Advanced Learner's Dictionary*)

In this example, "so called" modifies the noun "friends" in terms of the action described in what follows in the rest of the sentence. The contrast is clear: by definition, "friends" are those we think of positively, and whom we do not expect to do us harm, so how could we call those who supplied the drugs that "killed him" "friends"?

Returning to John F. Kennedy's use of the phrase "so called religious issue," how do we decide from among the set of possible options the one that is intended? Theoretically, Kennedy could simply be referring to what an issue has been called, or highlighting the issue as something recently introduced, or as we sus-pect, he could be challenging the "something" that has been called a "religious issue." Or it is even possible that he intends to convey more than one or all of these potential interpretations. Whatever the case, it is not clear from the written text alone that we could easily decide which use of "so called" is the one meant.

If we look at the examples (1–3) above, which refer to the general and tradi-tional uses of "so called," we could suggest that in these cases there is a link to some previous reference: in (1) "dollar bill," (2) "foxglove," and (3) "B Movie." Indeed, Vandelanotte (2007) suggests phrases like "so called" "frame" some previous talk or text and embed it within present talk, a form of what is called "intertextuality" (see Chapter 1 of this volume; Bakhtin, 1981; Fairclough, 1984; Kristeva, 2002). In this sense, Vandelanotte argues that "so called" may be seen as a "framing adjective." This view would challenge example (4), which claimed that new terms could be introduced by "so called." According to Vandelanotte's view, "framing adjectives" make use of a previous text or texts, hence what they frame must have arisen before.

Consequently, while any "framed" term(s) may be new to a particular audience, there must have been some previous action of naming, and it is this previous action that is framed in (4). Although "so called" may act in this way, it may also have other different functions. Consider the following:

(6) The super virus, so called because of its destructive nature.

(7) It was his friends, so called, who supplied the drugs.

Example (6) seems plausible as the introduction of a new term, but it is also suggestive of an original naming. Example (7), however, seems slightly different; while it is grammatical, "so called" acts as a parenthetical, something which intrudes within the structure of the sentence. Parentheticals are normally defined as forms that interrupt the linear flow of sentences or utterances without necessarily having a core structural relationship within the syntax of the sentence. While it may be true that "so called" in (7) does not change the core syntactic structure of the sentence ("It was his friends who supplied the drugs"), the appearance of "so called" clearly affects the interpretation of (7), with "so called" challenging the use of the term "friends."

Could "so called," as used by Kennedy, be interpreted as a parenthetical? If so, then under the basic definition given above, it would be seen as incidental to the general structure of the host phrase:

(8)   a. I want to speak about the so-called religious issue.

b. I want to speak about the religious issue.

On this analysis, one could argue that "so called" does not contribute to the linear structure of Kennedy's claim, but, as with (7), it also remains clear that "so called" is playing some part in guiding audience interpretation.

One way to account for this is to recognize that our basic definition of parentheticals belies a complex phenomenon that can be realized in a variety of constructions with varying linguistic and social import. Some analysts refer to parentheticals as dysfluencies of speech (Clark, 1999; Wichmann, 2001), suggesting that online cognitive planning for both speech production and interactional maintenance drive a need to keep talking, hence such elements that break the flow of interaction are really "fillers," holding space until talk can continue. Yet this would not explain the varied ways in which parentheticals can reflect attitudes and emphasis in the production of turns, and hence their central role in situating and contextualizing meaning. On the other hand, syntacticians have difficulty in accommodating parenthetical forms since they do not, initially, seem to have a place in the hierarchical explanation of core grammatical structure; there are no clear rules that connect parentheticals to other syntactic elements within a sentence (see Potts, 2002; Thompson and Mulac,1991). Thus analysts have either attempted to extend syntactic analysis in order to accommodate parentheticals (Emonds, 1979; Espinal, 1991), or have moved the burden for their explanation away from standard syntactic theory to semantic theory (Potts, 2005, 2008). Whatever the case, Blakemore (2006) asks the obvious but significant question: If parentheticals are not central to X or Y theory of sentence/utterance construction, what are they doing there in the first place? Parentheticals, at whatever level of language, must be used for a reason. Blakemore (2009) notes an argument by Potts (2008) that various parentheticals may alter the context for interpretation; they "contextualize" "the main clauses' contribution to discourse." Taking this suggestion further, Blakemore tells us that parentheticals may play a number of contextualizing roles in terms of their relevance to their host clause, in particular what she calls the "conceptual content of the host." Blakemore develops this idea within a Relevance Theory model (Sperber and Wilson, 1995) and suggests that one can distinguish different ways in which parentheticals achieve what she calls "pragmatic integration." Specifically, there are those that directly affect the interpretation of the host, and those that affect interpretation at the level of implicit or explicit content.

To explain this, Blakemore gives the following examples (Blakemore, 2009: 11):

(8) The driver of Al-Kindi's only remaining ambulance—the other three had been stolen or looted—had disappeared. So the dangerously ill Mr. Khassem was bundled into a clapped-out rust-bitten Moskavich 408. (*The Independent*, May 16, 2003)
(9) A helicopter, a helicopter—and here was me who'd never even flown in an ordinary plane—would come and pick me up at. . . . (from reading of *Stargazing: Memoirs of a Young Lighthouse Keeper*, by Peter Hill, abridged by Laurence Waring, read for Radio 4 by David Tenant)

In the first of these examples, Blakemore (2009: 11) suggests that "[t]he parenthetical is pragmatically integrated with the host because . . . it provides an answer to a question raised by the host (Why was there only on ambulance?)." The integration here does not affect the content of the host, and both the host and the parenthetical have their own independent relevance. In the case of the second example, the "and" coordination has ". . . no relevance beyond the interpretation of the host, and thus it seems there is a sense in which the parenthetical plus host contribute to the recovery of a single proposition whose relevance is greater than the parenthetical or host taken individually."

There are some further technical issues linked to the recovery of explicit versus implicit content and the generation of contextual assumptions within relevance theory, but we will not concern ourselves with these at present. The main point is that parentheticals may act to contextualize interpretation in specific ways.

Returning to Kennedy's speech, we can ask in what way is his use of "so called" contextualizing the phrase "religious issue?" If we consider the phrase "religious issue," we could say it refers to an implicit statement that forms part of the background knowledge relevant to the context of the speech (an intertextual link; see Vandelanotte, 2007). Specifically, the Reverend Neale's previous statements provide an implicit propositional claim such as (10).

(10) A Roman Catholic President's decisions would be affected by their religious beliefs, specifically they must follow the edicts of the Roman Catholic church.

Hence, in the context of Kennedy's speech, the phrase "religious issue" and the statement given at (10) are topically equivalent. When "so called" is used by Kennedy can we say it acts to integrate with the host in Blakemore's terms, or to implicitly combine with the host in generating an extended set of contextual assumptions, or has it provided an explicit content at the level of "explicature" (see Chapter 1)?

First, "so called" is not independent from "religious issue" (syntactic modification). Second, as (10) suggests, "so called" may be highlighting a previous "calling," specifically that Kennedy's Catholicism may be problematic. In this case, "so called" acts to drive a set of assumptions from which we can infer that Kennedy would not accept (10), and hence not accept the "calling" in any previous text or discourse. Third, while the phrase "X is a religious issue" is an explicit statement and might be true or false, the "calling" of X as a religious issue is itself a type of "speech act," an act of calling, and hence is neither true nor false, but is constrained by performance issues rather than truth conditions (see Chapter 1). Therefore, Kennedy could be using the parenthetical in a speech act mode to say the calling of X as a religious issue is inappropriate or has "misfired" (see Austin, 1962; Searle, 1969). For example, the original speech act, which claims that one's religion controls all the decisions one makes, may be unsubstantiated or wrong, that is, the Pope dictates one's religious life and not one's political life.

Along similar lines, "so called" also draws attention to a contextual presupposition (see Levinson, 2003 that there is a "religious issue." Such a claim would be within what Stalnaker (1998, 2002) has called the "common ground," what everyone assumes to be the case. Within specific contexts, assertions are said to update the "common ground." Hence, while it is part of the common ground of this speech that someone has called into being a "religious issue," "so called" here cannot be referring to the naming of the issue or the issue itself, since it is already known by everyone; that is, it is a shared common ground. Rather, "so called" is parenthetically drawing attention to the religious issue to challenge what it is that is actually held as common ground, that is, to challenge those assumptions that underlie the calling of something a "religious issue."

And this is exactly what Kennedy proceeds to do. For example, having drawn attention to whether or not there is a "religious question" ("properly so called") he then proceeds by immediately using another pragmatic form, that of comparative contrasting, to move our assessment of the religious issue forward:

> I want to emphasize from the outset we have far more critical issues to face in the 1960 election; the spread of Communist influence until it festers 90 miles off the coast of Florida—the humiliating treatment of our President and Vice President by those who no longer respect power—the hungry children I saw in West Virginia, the old people who cannot pay doctor bills, the families forced to give up their farms—an America with too many slums, with too few schools . . .

It is quite clear what Kennedy is doing here; he initially states that the correct and proper "chief" topic of the talk tonight is the "religious issue," but then goes on to claim that there are more important issues—and here he looks like he is contradicting himself—"the religious issue is the most important issue but there are more important issues." Kennedy succeeds, however, by the use of quantified and comparative marking, that is, the use of "more" and "important." In pragmatics, "more" forms part of a comparative scale including such things as "most," "many" "all" (see Chapter 1). The term "important" may itself be quantified in selected ways, as in "all important," "less important," "more important," and of course "the most important." There is an inferred comparison between X and Y, where X is more important than Y—hence, the list of issues described by Kennedy's completion of the "more than" structure. However, if all these things are of more charged significance than the "religious issue," and if the very issue and its calling have been brought into question, why is it going to be the chief topic of the evening? The answer is that Kennedy is distinguishing between a present singular context marked in the present tense, "tonight," and beyond this singular context to more significant issues spreading out beyond a single evening or event. This both gives the "religious issue" a place while at the same time limiting that place/space of debate, and downgrading the significance of the issue against other issues. So in the first paragraph Kennedy manages to both give the "religious issue" a place/space for discussion, while at the same time questioning the appropriate calling of this issue, and the relative importance of this issue.

But Kennedy goes even further, and in the very next paragraph he states the following:

> These are the real issues that should decide this campaign. And they are not religious issues—for war and hunger and ignorance and despair know no religious boundaries.

We see here that there is a distinction made between "real" issues, of the type mentioned above, and other issues that are not as central. But Kennedy also does something even more important: he begins to make clear what the "real" issues are—"these are the real issues. . . . And they are not religious issues." As we will see in a moment, this will become the central pillar of Kennedy's argument against the prior claim of some "religious issue." Therefore, in this way, Kennedy has reinforced the challenge to any "calling" that makes religion an issue in politics.

We will consider now one or two of the ways in which Kennedy drives home this point, and we will look at the pragmatic implications of Kennedy's arguments.

Here are some core examples of the basic argument as defined and presented by Kennedy:

(11) It is apparently necessary for me to state once again—not what kind of church I believe in, for that should be important only to me—but what kind of America I believe in. I believe in an America that is officially neither Catholic, Protestant nor Jewish . . . where no religious body seeks to impose its will directly or indirectly upon the general populace. . . .

(12) . . . I believe in a great office that must be neither humbled by making it the instrument of any one religious group nor tarnished by arbitrarily withholding its occupancy from the members of any one religious group.

(13) I want a chief executive whose public acts are responsible to all groups and obligated to none.

(14) For side by side with Bowie and Crockett died McCafferty and Bailey and Carey—but no one knows whether they were Catholics or not. For there was no religious test at the Alamo.

(15) I am wholly opposed to the state being used by any religious group, Catholic or Protestant, to compel, prohibit or persecute the free exercise of any other religion.

(16) . . . contrary to common newspaper usage I am not the Catholic Candidate for President I am the Democratic Party's candidate for President who happens to be a Catholic. I do not speak for my Church on public matters and my Church does not speak for me.

These statements have a commonality that revolves around contrasting and separating out a number of things. The main distinction is about beliefs that individuals have about their country and beliefs they have about their religion. Presidents have responsibilities for all groups in society, not only selected groups; the state is separate from any individual religious group, hence Kennedy's Catholicism is separate from his Democratic Party affiliation, and it is his party's nomination that is central in determining his candidacy for president (exemplified in (16)).

We want to look at this last distinction in some detail, as it is the core point that Kennedy wants to make. He is not saying, of course, that either state or religious issues do not relate to each other, or that in some cases they may not collide or clash; rather, he is saying that they are independent in the sense that one does not necessarily drive the other. But how does his famous separation of Kennedy the Catholic and Kennedy the presidential candidate actually work? Can he, or indeed any individual, separate out parts of themselves, or their personalities, as if they are independent entities? Is our identity not tied to the sum of the parts that make us the individuals we are? Is it possible for something as central as our religion to be simply siphoned off as required?

Nearly 50 years after the death of John F. Kennedy, Sarah Palin, a past vice presidential candidate and governor of Alaska, tried to make this point in her book *America by Heart*. In the book, she reviews Kennedy's Houston speech, discussed above, and accuses him of rejecting or denying his religion. At the same time, she praises Mitt Romney, who was to become a presidential candidate for the 2012 presidential election. Romney was a Mormon and faced a similar problem: critics questioned his suitability as a presidential candidate, asking if a Mormon would let his church influence his presidency. According to Palin, while Kennedy sought to reject or downplay his religion, Romney positively embraced his religion and noted with pride and honesty his religious beliefs. Plain's comments raised a storm of controversy. John F. Kennedy's niece, Kathleen Kennedy, was angered by Palin's claims; writing in the *Washington Post*, December 3, 2010, she argues that Palin has misunderstood her uncle's goal of separating church and state, and that Palin's assessment of what John F. Kennedy said is just plain wrong. Despite this defense, the question Palin raised is at the core of explaining how Kennedy's arguments operated: How do we present ourselves as performing different roles or as reflecting different personas in different contexts?

Reference, Meaning, and the Divided Self

Here is a list of proper names and definite descriptions: John Wilson, Tony Blair, London, Paris, John Kennedy, the Queen of England, the capital of Italy, and the presidential candidate. But what do these actually mean? This may seem an odd question, and you might say that John Wilson is simply John Wilson, or that Paris is the capital of France.

Such an answer seems logical and it explains names and definite descriptions in terms of the how they designate or refer to some person, place, or concept. The president of the United States refers to the person who holds that position, and John Wilson refers to the person named as John Wilson. But there are all kinds of problems here, since at any point in time the president of the United States may refer to different individuals, and although John Wilson may designate John Wilson, there are many individuals now and in the past who have been called John Wilson. These problems are only the tip of the iceberg (see Devitt and Sterenly, 1999), and we need to briefly consider some of these issues before we explain how Kennedy manages to separate Kennedy the Catholic and Kennedy the presidential candidate.

In early work on names and definite descriptions, the meaning of a name or description was its "reference." As the German mathematician Gottlieb Frege (1892); cited in Geach and Black, 1980) famously noted, however, there are cases where one or more names or descriptions can refer to one and the same object but still have different meanings. We noted this in Chapter 1 with the example of "the morning star" and "the evening star," which both refer to the planet Venus. But let us now look at this in slightly more detail. Consider the following sentences:

(17)
   a. The morning star is the morning star.
   b. The evening star is the evening star.
   c. The morning star is the planet Venus.
   d. The evening star is the planet Venus.
   e. The morning star is the evening star.

We can see that while all these sentences may be true, a. and b. are only trivially so, while c., d., and e. provide us with some information, that is, they are meaningful.

Frege noted in such cases that two terms or descriptions could have the same reference, but they may also have different "senses," that is, each term or description has what he called a specific "mode of presentation." So the evening star refers to Venus as it as seen in the evening, while the morning star refers to Venus as it is seen in the morning. Although the morning star and the evening star refer to the same object, and hence have the same reference, they have different "senses" or "modes of presentation."

Following Frege, Bertrand Russell (1905; reprinted in 1973) attempted to make such referential issues clearer by using logical forms to describe definite descriptions (and names) in terms of the procedures used to designate a specific object, entity, or concept. In the case of "the president of the United States" the description acts as a "function" to pick out the object that is "the president of the United States." The term "function" is a formal one, but basically if you imagine a parking lot full of cars and you have a list of numbers that match the number plate of each car, each number, therefore, has a function, which picks out the car that matches the number on your list. Your list serves as a function to an object, that is, it is derived from the number of the matching car.

When we look at "the president of the United States," we can think of this as a description for locating a person. "The president of the United States" acts as a function to pick out that object which best fits the description. This is a purely objective function, and formally there are a number of ways of representing this, but for the present the following will do: $(\exists x)$ POU(x); this states that there is at least one x and x is the president of the United States. By reducing the interpretation of definite descriptions to a function, that is, a relationship between a description and its object, Russell removes many of the puzzles that had plagued reference and definite descriptions. For example, given that "Harry Potter" is a fictional character, in what sense can the name be said to refer? It can refer in this case if we treat "Harry Potter" as simply a function to an object, in this case a fictional one (see Chapter 1 on mythical characters).

Both Frege and Russell wanted to formalize the semantics of reference when used in sentences. Yet both also seem to recognize that there is some other level involved in determining meaning. Consider, for example, Frege's concept "mode of presentation," which suggests that some aspect of meaning is affected by the circumstances of a particular sentential use in context. Equally, Russell made a distinction between what he called knowing things in terms of ". . . such and such properties" and knowing things by "immediate acquaintance." Despite such other considerations, both Russell and Frege argued that meaning was limited to the confines of language as a formal system.

Keith Donnellan (1966) argues that Frege and Russell's position may have been too limited, and he suggests that they have failed to see that definite descriptions may have more than one function. Donnellan makes a distinction between what he called "attributive" and "referential" uses of definite descriptions. Imagine you are at a party and someone says to you, "The man with gray hair is drinking beer." Here, Russell would say this sentence states that there is one and only one man with gray hair and that he is drinking beer. But if we are wrong about one part of this, say that his hair is white not gray, or that he is drinking cider not beer, then the whole sentence fails to refer, and in this sense the sentence is false. For Donnellan, if someone says, "The man with gray hair is drinking beer" and intends that you, the listener, focus on that individual, that is, pick him out, then when you do pick out that individual, both the speaker and the listener have the same object/person in mind, even if the referent's hair is actually white and he is drinking cider. In this case the sentence successfully refers, even though it may be false.

For Donnellan, predicating that the "man has gray hair and he is drinking beer" are simply devices for referring to "the man" in order to bring him into shared focus. Alternatively, if you pick up a beer and discover a gray hair in it, you might say, "a gray-haired man has been drinking my beer," without knowing who that person was. Here, you predicate of "whoever" was drinking your beer that they have gray hair; in this case Donnellan says you are referring "attributively," predicating something of an individual "whoever they may be."

Donnellan offers us another example to explain these different ways of referring: "The murderer of Smith is insane." This could be said about a specific individual, say Tom, who is insane and who the speaker believes murdered Smith. In this case the sentence would be referential and it picks out an individual the speaker has in mind. But the sentence could also be used simply to comment upon the actions of the murderer of Smith who is not known to the speaker. In this case the sentence is being used "attributively" to assert of whoever murdered Smith that they are insane.

Some analysts have dismissed Donnellan's distinction because linking "referential use" to what the speaker has in mind takes us beyond the sentence, and hence we are outside semantics (Martin, 1987). For our purposes this is not necessarily a criticism, and this is summed up when Saul Kripke (1977) says that

Donnellan's focus on what a speaker wishes to convey about a particular object or entity makes it a pragmatic phenomenon.

If we accept Donnellan's approach, then speakers may use sentences in a number of ways to focus an interlocutor's attention, either attributively, whoever it may be, or referentially, with a specific object in mind. Thus, my use of "the president of the United States in 2013" could indicate that I have in mind Barack Obama. Alternatively, if I say, "the president of the United States is the leader of the free world," this may be used of whoever they may be, with no specific president in mind.

In real-world communication, picking out an object or entity is often for the purpose of commenting on that entity or object. In focusing on "the man with gray hair drinking beer," I may want to explain that his drinking has been the cause of premature graying. And as we saw in the case of "the murderer of Smith is insane," I may be explicitly commenting on the mental state of the murderer, either Tom (referential) or whoever they may be (attributive). In both cases the information may be expanded in various ways. Speaker/hearers may use general or shared knowledge to link aging to drinking alcohol, or the act of murder as an indication of insanity.

What to Believe and What Not to Believe, That's the Question?

Let us return to Kennedy's speech and consider how all of these generally abstract considerations help us understand and explain what Kennedy is doing. First, we should remind ourselves that Kennedy has a basic strategy to keep separate his beliefs about America, and specifically the role of an American president, and his beliefs about religion. He does this in the now famous and iconic statement:

(18) I am not the Catholic candidate for president. I am the Democratic Party's candidate for president who happens to be a Catholic.

This is two main statements with two definite descriptions, the first negative, and the other positive.

(19)   a. I am not the Catholic candidate for president.
        b. I am the Democratic Party's candidate for president.

As we saw above, such statements are said to refer when they pick out the referent, or entity, defined or denoted by the definite description. We can see this in (19b), which denotes that there is Democratic Party candidate for president, and that entity is indexed through the first person pronominal "I" to the speaker of the sentence. The claim can then be assessed against appropriate criteria (appropriate conditions for being the Democratic Party candidate) and we can judge the evidence for its validity or truth.

When we come to (19a), things do not seem as simple. If it was "I am the Catholic candidate for president," then it would have been assessed in the same way as (19b), but the problem is that this sentence carries a negative operator, that is, "not," and hence negates the claim that the speaker is "the Catholic candidate for president."

In presenting a version of this chapter at a number of US universities, it was put to me by some audience members that there is not a problem here. It was argued that the speaker deictically indexed at "I" is saying that in applying the criteria for denoting a Catholic candidate for president to a relevant entity, the person indexed at "I" does not fulfill that criteria. It is argued that the use of "the" suggests that there is a "Catholic candidate," that is, someone who represents Catholics, and this is not John F. Kennedy. This seems intuitively correct, although it doesn't actually explain how it works. Even if the argument were correct, this interpretation treats "Catholic candidate" above and beyond the critical debate in which Kennedy was involved. No one suggested that Kennedy represented Catholics in an electoral sense; what was suggested was that the Roman Catholic Church demands of Catholics that they see the Pope as the head of the church and that they obey the teachings of the church through him. In this context it really doesn't matter if Kennedy denies being a "Catholic candidate," because he is still a Catholic (as he emphasizes himself) who is the Democratic candidate, and this is where things seem a little odd. As we have seen in the examples above, Kennedy's main aim is to take religion, any religion, not only Catholicism, out of the equation. His core aim is to separate church and state. So what is going on then, when he states that he is a "Catholic" but not a "Catholic candidate"?

In (18) the two appearances of "I" are co-indexed to the same speaker, and that speaker is saying he is not the "Catholic candidate for president" but he is the "Democratic candidate for president." Processing the statement to this point could mean that the person is denying he is a Catholic—I am not the Catholic candidate, I am a Protestant. As we see, however, Kennedy blocks any such interpretation by adding that (he) "happens to be a Catholic." His statement makes all of the following claims true:

    a. Kennedy is a Catholic.
    b. Kenney is a presidential candidate.
    c. Kennedy is a Democratic Party candidate.

Commutatively, it would normally follow that if each of the above is true, then it must also be true that:

    d. Kennedy is a Catholic Democratic presidential candidate.

But d. is what Kennedy has explicitly denied. Was he therefore contradicting himself?

Semantically this could be said to be the case since if Kennedy is a Catholic, then one can descriptively append this to almost any other true sentence about

Kennedy: Kennedy was a Catholic senator, Kennedy was an America Catholic who fought in the war, or Kennedy was a Massachusetts Catholic. But are we exaggerating things here; after all, we all intuitively know what Kennedy was getting at in (18). Nevertheless, the point being made is that what Kennedy meant is not necessarily what he said, and the question is not whether we know what he means, but how does this work?

A potential solution leads us back to the problems of reference and the work of Russell, in particular the claim that definite descriptions presuppose the existence of their referent. A statement such as "the president of the United States is tired," presupposes there is an x, such that x is the president of the United States and x is tired. Russell asks us to consider a sentence such as "the king of France is bald." Here the presupposition seems to fail, as there is no king of France, and hence the statement is false. But what about the negation of this claim, as in "the king of France is not bald." Is the speaker saying that "there is a king of France but he is not bald," or that "there is no king of France and therefore he is neither bald nor has he a full head of hair"? In the first case, "the king of France is bald" is false, but in the second, "the king of France is not bald" could, on one level, be true and on another level false. In other words, there is more than one possible reading of the negated sentence. These alternative readings of negation are referred to as "wide scope" and "narrow scope." In the case of a "narrow scope" reading, "there is a king of France and he is not bald"; with a "wide scope" reading, "there is no king of France such that he is bald or not bald." In one case the focus of negation is on the "reference" (no king of France), and in the other on the predicate (bald).

Now if we return to Kennedy's statement "I am not the Catholic candidate for president," what he is trying to negate is the part of the sentence that is the phrase "Catholic candidate," not that he is not a Catholic. So on one reading the sentence could be: I am not the [Catholic candidate for president] (because I am not a Catholic and I am not a candidate for president). Or it could be read as "I am not the [Catholic candidate] for president" where it is "I am not a Catholic candidate," but "I am a candidate for president."

We can see that Kennedy is trying to separate his Catholicism from his candidacy; the issue is how he is doing this. How is it possible to believe two seemingly equivalent facts, that Kennedy is a Catholic and that Kennedy is the presidential candidate, but not what follows logically from this, that Kennedy is a Catholic presidential candidate?

Ferge's original analysis of definite descriptions as different "modes of presentation" might offer us a way out. As we saw, "the morning star" and "the evening star" are the same object, that is, the planet Venus, so they both refer to the same object, but they do not mean the same or have the same sense. Consequently, at the location and time of Kennedy's speech, and where the index of "I" is Kennedy himself, the "the Catholic candidate for president" and "The Democratic Party's candidate for president" both refer to the some entity, but may not mean the same thing in certain contexts, so they may be used in different ways. Nevertheless, whatever way we cut this one, we know there is a Democratic Party (presidential) candidate and that he is Catholic, so how can John F. Kennedy negate this description when in fact it is true in the actual world?

Once again, the puzzles that surround reference offer us another way of viewing this problem, one in which it may be possible to believe statement A and the negation of statement A, that is, not-A. But how can one believe A and its negation at the same time? Here we need to consider what are called "propositional attitude statements." Consider the following scenario:

(20) Bill believes that the planet Venus is very bright.
Bill believes that the morning star is not very bright.

Now let us we assume that Bill does not know that the planet Venus and the morning star refer to the same object. In the actual world, Bill ascribes to a belief that Venus is very bright and also ascribes to a belief that the morning star (Venus) is not very bright (both A and not-A). Now we can say, of course, that Bill is just mistaken since he doesn't know the two descriptions he has used refer to the same object. But this is the point, within Bill's beliefs the morning star and Venus refer to different objects, while in the other worlds or other sets of beliefs they refer to the same object. Imagine a scientist who knows that the morning star refers to the planet Venus; he meets Bill, and he says to Bill, "The morning star is my favorite star," and Bill says that "the morning star" is his favorite star as well. What they have said is semantically equivalent, and what they say references the same object, but there is a sense in which what Bill understands by the sentence is different from what the scientist understands. This is because the scientist believes that Venus is the same object as the morning star, while Bill does not.

In philosophy this debate revolves around the issue of whether meanings are individuated within individuals (individual minds) or whether meanings are externally given by the actual world (Martin, 1987). But there is another more pragmatic way one can view this, and this is the question of whether one can run different beliefs in different contexts, where those beliefs would clash in a single context. What we are suggesting is that it is not that an individual believes A and not-A, he only believes one or the other (either A or not-A) but he does this relative to a context. So Bill does not believe that Venus is the morning star, because his beliefs about the morning star do not include the belief that the morning star refers to the planet Venus. Hence, when Bill talks about the morning star there is no belief that it is the same object as the planet Venus. Similarly, when Bill talks of Venus, his beliefs about Venus do not contain the belief that it is the morning star. Consequently, Bill does not run beliefs that contain A and not-A. But when the scientist is talking with Bill, if the scientist knows what beliefs Bill has about both the planet Venus and the morning star, and what beliefs he (the scientist) has about the morning star and Venus, then the scientist knows that these different sets of beliefs clash on at least one level, where the morning star is believed to be the planet Venus and where it is believed to be a separate object. Now let us assume that the scientist does not want to correct Bill; it is still possible for them to communicate, as they both agree that the morning star is beautiful.

This may not be as convoluted as it sounds. Consider when you visit a doctor to complain about stomach pains. For most people, their common sense or folk beliefs about parts of their body tend to suggest that the stomach is much lower on their upper torso than it actually is. The doctor, on the other hand, has medical beliefs that indicate that the stomach is much higher than folk beliefs suggest. So the doctor has to translate your beliefs about where your pains are into his beliefs about where the pains would be if it is a stomach problem. In such cases the doctor has to run your beliefs about where internal organs are located alongside her own beliefs about where internal organs are located. So she may ask where in your stomach it hurts, and when you say "here," pointing lower than where the stomach is, the doctor will run your beliefs about where the stomach is located, then she may examine you in a different place, running her beliefs about where the stomach is located.

Now what is interesting here, in communication or pragmatic terms, is that communication can take place even when different belief sets are operating in different ways, and this is why those who argued that Kennedy simply negated "Catholic candidate" were both right and wrong at the same time. While they might be willing to read the sentence this way, the Reverend Peale could equally read it as a contradiction, that is, denying someone is a "Catholic" candidate when he admits that he is a "Catholic." Consider the possibilities for politicians. They can discuss issues having one set of beliefs, while knowing that their listeners have a different set of beliefs. The trick for politicians, then, is how to get voters/listeners to run messages/beliefs in the contexts they want.

To explain how this might work, we want look at the potential ways in which we could organize our beliefs about the world, and also how we organize our beliefs about other people's beliefs about the same world. There are a number of possible models available to us here, the concept of mental spaces outlined by Giles Fauconnier (1996; also Fauconnier and Turner, 2002; and Chapter 7 of this volume) or the mental models of Phil Johnson Laird (1983), both of which indicate that we process information in terms of organized mental spaces or models (doctor/patient models of the location of internal organs, for example). However, for our purposes we want to make use of the "belief ascription" model developed by Yorick Wilks and colleagues (Ballim and Wilks, 1991; Wilks and Bien, 1983). We focus on this model for three reasons. First, it is developed within artificial intelligence as a working model of computation; second, representations of beliefs within the model can be easily explained in graphic formats; and finally, Ballam and Wilks (see also Wilks, 1986) make use of the concept of "relevance" as a pragmatic tool in assessing competing or clashing beliefs, and hence provide a solution to how choices between beliefs and belief sets might be made.

JOHN
John is a Catholic
John is a Democrat
John is a Presidential Candidate

SYSTEM

FIGURE 1

Ballam and Wilks (1986) put together a model of belief ascription for an operative artificial system in the following way. The model for the beliefs begins with the system's beliefs and may be seen in Figure 1.

In Figure 1 we see the system has beliefs about John: that he is a Catholic, a Democrat, and a presidential candidate. From this the system could infer that John is a Catholic candidate; John is a Democratic candidate; and John is a Catholic Democratic presidential candidate.

The system's beliefs can also be about John's beliefs about John. We see this in Figure 2, where the system has beliefs both about John (the system's beliefs about John) and about John's beliefs about himself (the system's beliefs about John's belief's about John).

In this case they are exactly the same. So the system's beliefs about John's beliefs about John should allow for the same inferences the system made as a result of its beliefs about John in Figure 1.

In Figure 3 we have included the belief that follows from Kennedy's speech, that is, that he is not a Catholic candidate.

John

John
John is a Catholic
John is a Democrat
John is a Presidential Candidate

John is a Catholic
John is a Democrat
John is a Presidential Candidate

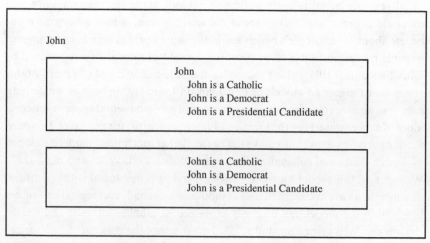

SYSTEM

FIGURE 2

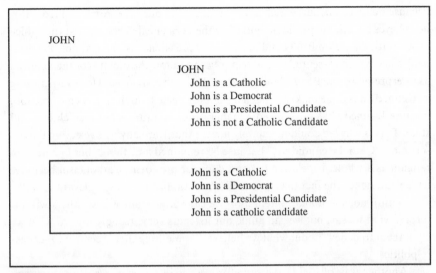

JOHN

> JOHN
> John is a Catholic
> John is a Democrat
> John is a Presidential Candidate
> John is not a Catholic Candidate

> John is a Catholic
> John is a Democrat
> John is a Presidential Candidate
> John is a catholic candidate

SYSTEM
FIGURE 3

Ballim and Wilks allow for the possibility of belief sets moving down or merging into each other for purposes of assessing any specific interpretive context. So if John's beliefs about himself are merged with the systems beliefs about John, as in Figures 1 and 2, we find that they match, so there is no problem. The system's beliefs about John are the same as the system's beliefs about John's beliefs. But when we come to Figure 3, if the system runs John's belief that he is not a Catholic candidate within existing belief environments, then this will clash with the beliefs the system is able to construct from the beliefs in Figures 1 and 2 that John is a Catholic candidate. What does the system do in such cases? It is here that the concept of "relevance" comes into play: the resolution of any clash is in terms of relevance to a context or environment. If the beliefs that the system is running are being created in the context of Kennedy's speech, and it is clear that he has added the belief that religion is not a criterion for candidacy for the presidency, it follows then, if a religion is not a criterion for presidential candidacy, and we know that religion in general would include Catholicism as a member of the set of religions, Catholicism is not a relevant criterion for candidacy for the presidency. If this is so, then in running the system's beliefs about John's beliefs, the commutative process of combining John's beliefs that he is a Catholic with John's beliefs that he is the presidential candidate is blocked by the further belief that religion (including therefore Catholicism) is not a criterion for presidential candidacy, and hence John is not a Catholic candidate makes sense in this context.

Now this is not to say that everyone listening to Kennedy will reach the same conclusions. Relevance is relevant to a context, and Kennedy's arch-critic Peale may run beliefs about John and beliefs about Catholicism in a different way, in this case blocking any separation of Catholicism from the job of president, because Peale has beliefs which say that Catholics obey the Pope, and from this he believes a Catholic president will obey the Pope. Peale believes that the choice of separating religion from candidacy for the presidency is not available for Kennedy since it is the essential role of Catholics to follow the dictates of their church as interpreted by the Pope. Hence, Peale will not be convinced. However, arguing as Kennedy has done makes it much harder for Peale to maintain such a position, because Kennedy has introduced a higher order separation between church and state. This is why we could not simply accept that Kennedy was rejecting the description "Catholic candidate," because he remained a Catholic; but by rejecting religion as a whole, in relation to candidacy for president, Catholicism becomes irrelevant, hence the fact that Kennedy is a Catholic becomes irrelevant as well.

Within normal human interaction we cannot guarantee how others will interpret what we say, but we can guide our listeners very strongly toward what we want them to believe about what we believe—something that is central to success in politics.

Another way of seeing the same process is in terms of what we discussed earlier as the distinction between "attributive" (whoever it may be) and referential description. Martin (1987) gives an example of a blind person A who asks someone B to hand him the red book from the shelf. B notices that there is only one book on the shelf and it is green, but he hands the book over anyway. A takes the book, which is in Braille, and begins to read, saying "thank you that is exactly the book I wanted." B now understands that A was mistaken about the color, the book was green not red, but B also understands that the book A wanted was the book handed to him from the shelf, the book they had in mind (this is somewhat similar to our doctor/patient example).

Now the analogy with Kennedy is that he is asking his audience to think about the presidential candidate he has in mind, that is, the Democratic Party nominee, that is, John F. Kennedy, not to think about him as candidate under other available descriptive categories, such as the Catholic candidate from Boston, or simply the Catholic candidate. It is the object/entity that Kennedy has in mind that he wants his audience to share, specifically John F. Kennedy as the Democratic Party nominee for president.

You Can't Fool All of the People All of the Time

As we noted, what Kennedy wants his audience to believe cannot be guaranteed, and those who want to offer alternative interpretations, given their own focus and their own sets of beliefs, are free do so. For example, in the book scenario given above, if B had said, "there is not a red book on the shelf," this would have been correct. However, in terms of general relevance, and since there is only one book on the shelf, the principle of charity might suggest that the actual entity which is "the book" is more relevant than "the color" of the book. Equally, while

Kennedy is a Catholic and while he is the presidential candidate, his religion is irrelevant compared not only to his candidacy in general but also his Democratic Party candidacy in particular.

In the end, of course, whatever the theoretical options and explanations, Kennedy's approach proved successful, and he was elected to the White House. Clearly, his separation of religion from politics worked, at least for most observers. However, as we noted earlier, many years after Kennedy's death, in 2010, Sarah Palin brought Kennedy's approach to dealing with the problem of his Catholicism back to public attention.

Sarah Palin criticized Kennedy for his stance on his religion. She notes that when she was growing up, JFK's speech was presented as an exemplar of the balance between public and religious allegiances. On re-reading the speech as an adult, she suggests that what Kennedy actually seemed to be claiming was that religion was such ". . . a private matter that it was irrelevant to what kind of country we are." She goes on to say that Kennedy's speech was "defensive . . . in tone and content" and does not reconcile faith and public duty but provides an "unequivocal divorce between the two." This is a clear example of the various ways in which belief ascriptions can be read differently in different belief environments. While Kennedy wanted us to run beliefs in one environment, individuals may run the same beliefs in alternative environments reaching alternative conclusions, as Palin seems to have done.

As we have argued, if one only looks at the statement, "I am not the Catholic candidate for president, I am the Democratic Party candidate for president, who happens to be a Catholic," there is a sense in which it is clearly correct to say that Kennedy is separating his political aspirations from religious affiliation. But whether this is "defensive" or "logical" depends on a variety of different issues. We began our analysis of Kennedy's speech by spending some time on the phrase "so called religious issue," and we did so because Kennedy's argument for the separation of religion from his presidential candidacy did not operate in a vacuum. We know he had been under attack for being a Catholic, and we know that there was a lobby that argued that a Catholic could not be president because his religion would influence the presidency. We also noted in our analysis that the use of "so called" could be seen as intertextual, linking material from previous texts or talk into present texts. In this sense we are not reading the speech and its goals completely independently of any prior contexts or topics, because by the use of "so called" Kennedy was explicitly telling us that he was drawing upon other texts and other voices. Indeed, we would suggest that to ignore these contexts might lead to skewed interpretations. In this section, therefore, we want to revisit, with Palin, John F. Kennedy's speech (along with our analysis so far), and consider it alongside the speech of a modern presidential candidate, Mitt Romney, who, as a Mormon, also faced criticism about the potential impact of his religion in running for president. While Palin was critical of Kennedy, she praised Romney for "embracing his religion." We want to consider this assessment in terms not of politics, or of any moral or other position, but purely in relation to pragmatic and linguistic issues.

We know that Kennedy wanted to make clear that religion is not and should not be considered a criterion for appointment as president of the United States of America. And he further notes that if it should arise that his own beliefs as a Catholic clashed with his duty as president, he would step aside from his presidential role. What concerns Palin is that if Kennedy's faith was part of his "makeup," part of his own sense of his identity, then he should be proud of that fact, and not suggest that it would have no role in his life as president. However, not only would this suggest that we cannot separate our religious beliefs from our political beliefs, but that even if we could, we should not do so. Kennedy's speech challenges this assessment, highlighting that there is no religious test for the presidency, and, therefore, private religious beliefs should not be part of the assessment for president. Many commentators have noted that this was enshrined in the political makeup of the United States and refer to Jefferson's letter to the Danbury Baptists (January:1802):

> Believing with you that religion is a matter which lies solely between Man & his God. That he owes account to none other for his faith or his worship, that the legitimate powers of Government reach actions only & not opinions, I contemplate with sovereign reverence that the act of the whole American people which declared that their legislature should 'make no law respecting an establishment of religion, or prohibiting the free exercise thereof,' **thus building a wall of separation between church & State.**
> (http://www.loc.gov/loc/lcib/9806/danpre.html)

Kennedy's position in his speech to the Houston Ministerial Council seems very much in line with Jefferson's argument. Why then does Palin claim that Kennedy made "religion irrelevant to the kind of country we are . . . ?" It seems that where Kennedy and Jefferson recognize the rights of individuals to hold their religious beliefs as individuals, but not to impose these through government on others, by turning religious belief into presidential action, Palin suggests that the country itself is affected by religious beliefs and therefore one cannot separate country and religion, nor president and religion.

In this regard she praises Mitt Romney for a speech he delivered as part of the Republican primary campaign (December 6, 2007, "Faith in America," mittromneycentral.com/speeches/). According to Palin, Romney gave a "thoughtful speech that eloquently and correctly described the role of faith in American public life." However, when one looks in detail at Romney's speech, he too makes clear that there is a separation between church and state; indeed, in one example Romney hints at his agreement with Kennedy's position on the separation of religion and state. Consider the following examples:

(20) Almost fifty years ago another candidate from Massachusetts explained that he was an American running for president, not a Catholic running for president. Like him I am an American running for president, I do not define my

candidacy by my religion. A person should not be elected because of his faith nor should they be rejected because of his faith.

(21) Let me assure you that no authorities of my church or of any other church for that matter will ever exert influence on presidential decisions. Their authority is theirs, within the province of church, and its ends where the affairs of the nation begin.

(22) As governor, I tried to do the right as best I knew it, serving the law and answering to the Constitution. I did not confuse the particular teachings of my church with the obligations of the office and of the constitution—and of course, I would not do so as president. I will put no doctrine of any church above the plain duties of the office and the sovereign authority of the law.

(23) If I am fortunate to become your president I will serve no one religion, no one group, no one cause, and no one interest. A president must serve only the common cause of the people of the United States.

On reading these statements, it seems clear that John F. Kennedy and Romney are in agreement on the separation of church and state. So what is it about Kennedy's position that Palin finds less worthy than that of Romney? Is it because Romney also goes out of his way to emphasize the importance and the right of individuals to have their own religious beliefs, and that these beliefs, similarly held among various religions, form the basis of the moral foundations of the American people? Consider the following:

(24) Today I will address a topic which I believe is fundamental to American greatness: our religious liberty. I will also offer a perspective on how my own faith will inform my presidency if elected.

Here Romney explicitly links his faith with the role of president, yet at the same time making clear, from the other examples above, that no one religion should influence the office of the president. And although he states that he will comment on how his faith will inform his presidency, he also criticizes those who ask for or demand an explanation of any individual's religious beliefs as a basis for considering them worthy of the office of president:

(25) There are some who would have a presidential candidate describe and explain his church's distinctive doctrines. To do so would enable the very religious test the founders prohibited in the Constitution. No candidate should become a spokesman for his faith. For if he becomes president he will need the prayers of the people of all faiths.

Here again, there are echoes of Kennedy, but Romney goes on to make a comment that perhaps brings us to the heart of the matter, and offers a guide to the core aims of his speech.

(26) We separate church and state affairs in this country, and for good reason. No religion should dictate to the state nor should the state interfere with the free

practice of religion. But in recent years the notion of a separation of church and state has been taken by some well beyond its original meaning. They seek to remove from the public domain any acknowledgment of God. Religion is seen as merely a private affair with no place in public life. It is as if they are intent on establishing a new religion in America—the religion of secularism. They are wrong.

So while Romney strongly endorses the separation of church and state, and emphasizes he will not let his church dictate his actions as president, at the same time he claims that religion is central to the public domain and to the nature of the American state and to American citizens.

(27) The founders proscribed the establishment of a state religion, but they did not countenance the elimination of religion from the public square. We are a nation under God and in God we do indeed trust.

He is arguing that it is in the nature of the American state, indeed American psyche, that religion, God, and American values coalesce; "Americans acknowledge that liberty is the gift of God, not an indulgence of Government." The important point here is that it is "religion" not "a single religion or faith" that underpins the American moral position: "These American values, this great moral heritage, is lived in my religion as it is in yours." Here is the core of the issue. Whatever Romney's individual religion, or his individual beliefs, or his values, they are shared, at a macro religious level, with all the religions of the United States, or at least those that endorse American values such as liberty, freedom, and equality.

Like Kennedy, Romney was under critical scrutiny because he was a Mormon. In Kennedy's day, some had feared that as a Catholic he would be influenced by his church's teaching, and in the twenty-first century there were those who feared what a Mormon might bring to the White House, and whether the Mormon church would influence Romney if he were elected president. While Kennedy separated religion (including Catholicism) from the post of president, Romney has invested religion in the presidency, but not any single religious creed; in this case Mormonism is simply one member of the set of religious options and, therefore, no different from any other religious option. Hence, in this way Romney seeks to allay any concerns about a Mormon candidate for presidency. Basically, then, while Kennedy sought to remove thoughts about him as a Catholic from the minds of voters, Romney does the same for Mormonism. In Kennedy's case, beliefs about him as a Catholic were not run in the same environment as beliefs about him as a candidate for president. In Romney's case, beliefs about him as a Christian are run alongside beliefs about him as a presidential candidate, but not specific beliefs about his beliefs about Mormonism.

So in many respects both Romney and Kennedy are doing something very similar. The difference of approach may not be, as Palin believes, because

Kennedy is being negative and Romney positive, but because they were responding to different, but related, intertextual positions. In explaining "intertextuality," Bakhtin (1981) introduced the concept of multi- or polyvocality, the idea
that in writing and other forms of communication the author or speaker uses
a number of voices. We have noted a similar version of this above in terms of
sets of different identities that we all hold. In a similar way, we have more than
one voice, both literally in terms of different accents, but also in terms of different styles, topics, or genres often associated with different contexts: everyday
conversation versus courtroom language, or medical style versus political style.
Further, in these styles, or genres, others' words or topics become integrated
and reformulated or rehearsed. As Bakhtin says, "Everyday conversation is full
of transmissions and interpretations of other people's words (1981: 338; cited in
Tannen, 2006: 599). In a similar manner, Kristeva (2002;1986) suggests that any
text contains elements of other texts. A simple example would be a direct quota-
tion of something someone said elsewhere, or a shift in style between a general
text and a technical text. Both Kristeva and Bakhtin acknowledge that all texts
are generated from or relate to other texts. Bakhtin argues that: ". . . when we
select words in the process of constructing an utterance we by no means take
them from the system of language in their neutral dictionary form. We usually
take them from other utterances. . ." (1986: 87; Tannen, 599).

According to Panagiotidou (2010), these words come loaded into an intertextual frame that provides a basis for cognitive processing. This frame contains
two types of knowledge, intertextual knowledge and textual knowledge, or more
simply, in Emmott's (1997) terms, "text specific" and "general knowledge." What
this means is that terms or phrases drawn from other texts carry information
from that text, but they also carry general knowledge or information not constrained by a specific text or contextual appearance. Consider the words "Catholic" and "Mormon"; each will carry its own general information about each
religion and each set of religious beliefs. The extent of this information will vary
for each individual, with Catholics and Mormons being able (in most cases) to
generate or process more information about Catholicism and Mormonism than
non-Catholics and non-Mormons.

Now consider again that the purpose of both Kennedy and Romney's
speeches was to respond to explicit or implicit criticisms of their candidature
for the presidency because they were both from specific religious backgrounds.
In Kennedy's case we know that the Reverend Peale had called into question the
potential impact of his Catholicism on the presidency. In this case, then, there
existed, at minimum, one prior text to which Kennedy was responding. In this
prior text, the term "Catholic" had been interpreted and treated in a specific
way, with the implication being that since any Catholic must obey the Pope, it
follows that any Catholic president must obey the Pope. In his speech Kennedy
uses that word "Catholic," echoing the prior text, but removes any link between
the term and the description "the president of the United States." Indeed, he

goes further and removes the link between any religion and the position of president of the United States. This was necessary not only because it broke the link between Catholicism and the presidency, but also because the removal of this link was not something specifically associated with Catholicism but with all religions. Equally, Romney is responding to prior texts that raised concerns about his Mormonism, and which had questioned whether this may impact upon his presidency. In this case, Romney reframes Mormonism as simply one form of Christianity, and using the general knowledge held by Americans which correlates Christian values—not any specific religion's values—with Constitutional values and beliefs, he makes clear that first and foremost he is a Christian with Christian values and beliefs. But he also makes clear that no one religion should dominate in the White House, and he rejects any notion that he would allow the head of his own Mormon church, or any church, to dictate to him. He does this while all the time reiterating that he remains a Christian, and that being a Christian is not incompatible with being president of the United States; indeed, historically and logically, given that the moral values of the United States were built on a Christian position, it follows that the president should reflect that position.

Both Kennedy and Romney separate church and state, both deny they would be controlled or influenced by any church leaders, and both merge their own faiths in belief sets where those faiths as individual faiths are not central to the presidency of the United States. In Kennedy's case Catholicism, or any specific religion, is not a requirement for being president. Romney agrees, and he argues that Mormonism is not a requirement and it is not linked to the presidency. In Romney's case, however, what is added is that he believes America is a Christian country and that Christian values are not incompatible with being president, and, as he says, he is a Christian. But Kennedy said he was a Catholic, and as a Catholic he is also a Christian, so here again both Romney and Kennedy are in agreement.

So what is Palin's concern? It seems that she has concentrated much more on Romney saying that he is a Christian, and that America is a Christian country, than on his clear separation of church and state. Where Kennedy was clear on this distinction, Romney is more ambiguous wherein he both claims that the presidency and the country are bound by Christian values and culture, but separated in terms of church and state. Romney suggests that whoever the president is, he should have Christian values, while Kennedy argues that whoever the president is, he must only have presidential values. It is not, as Palin suggests, that Romney embraces his religion, certainly not his specific religion as a Mormon. Indeed, he denies that his Mormonism or his church will influence him, but instead he embraces the correlation between Christian values and what he believes are constitutional values. It is this that Palin endorses. Nevertheless, to say that Kennedy would not agree with this because he made his argument in a different way would be wrong, and it would be to misunderstand him, and also to misunderstand Romney.

3

Lies, Truth, and Somewhere in Between

RICHARD M. NIXON

> Richard is a no good, lying bastard. He can lie out of both sides of his
> mouth at the same time, and if he ever caught himself telling the truth,
> he'd lie just to keep his hand in.
>
> Harry S. Truman

Introduction

In May 2011, only days after US Navy Seals killed Osama Bin Laden, it was alleged that Hussain Haggani, Pakistan's former ambassador to the United States,
sent a memo to Admiral Mike Mullan, US Chairman of the Joint Chiefs of Staff,
seeking assistance in stopping a military coup in Pakistan. Much controversy
followed when the leaked memo was published in its entirety on *Foreign Policy*'s website on November 17, 2011. The incident lead to resignations and judicial
reviews both in the United States and Pakistan, and the news story was called
"memogate."

The term "memogate" is based the original use of the term "Watergate" (see
below), one of the most infamous political scandals in American history. In February 2012, *Watergate Remembered: The Legacy for American Politics*, edited by
Michael A. Genovese and Iwan W. Morgan, was published by Palgrave Macmillan. An advertising blurb for the book read (Palgrave Macmillan Politics Cata-
logue, 2011):

> As the fortieth anniversary of the Nixon resignation approaches, it is time
> to take a fresh look at Watergate's impact on the American political system
> and to consider its significance for the historical reputation of the president
> indelibly associated [*with the scandal: my comment*].

That unnamed president was, of course, Richard M. Nixon, who will forever
be remembered for Watergate, and for the negative impact the event had on the

55

Talking with the President. John Wilson. © Oxford University Press 2015.
Published 2015 by Oxford University Press

image of the presidency and American politics in general. As a consequence of his actions in office, Nixon was to be impeached. The Articles of Impeachment stated:

> In his conduct of the office of President of the United States, Richard M. Nixon, in violation of his constitutional oath faithfully to execute the office of President of the United States and, to the best of his ability, preserve, protect, and defend the Constitution of the United States, and in violation of his constitutional duty to take care that the laws be faithfully executed, has prevented, obstructed, and impeded the administration of justice . . .

Nixon avoided impeachment by resigning as president. When Gerald Ford became president, Nixon was pardoned for any crimes he may have committed while in office. Some have made the pragmatic point that in accepting this pardon Nixon was also, indirectly, admitting his guilt. If, as Nixon argued, he did not commit any crimes, then he could not be pardoned for actions he didn't commit.

Here is Nixon in action, responding to David Frost in the famous Frost/Nixon interview of 1977.

> I didn't believe that we were covering-up any illegal activities . . . I was trying to contain it politically. And, that's a very different motive from the motive of covering-up criminal activities of an individual. And so there was no cover-up of any criminal activities; that was not my motive.

So Nixon will admit to a "cover-up" but only where that definition refers to "political containment," and not the cover-up of illegal activities (we look at this in detail later).

Throughout his career Nixon made good use of a full range of pragmatic tools and this contributed, in part, to his nickname "Tricky Dicky." When it comes to Watergate, the really interesting thing is that his guilt or innocence on various matters should have been straightforward; after all, much of the evidence that eventually emerged was based on secretly recorded tapes of White House conversations, what Nixon actually said! But even here, Nixon manages to argue that his words could be taken out of context, or where this tactic failed, that it was not the use of specific words or phrases that had to be assessed but the "intention" behind the use of those words. So if the speaker did not intend an illegal or negative interpretation, one should not interpret what they said in that way.

Paradoxically, pragmatics provides some support for Nixon's position. Pragmatics refers centrally to the role of context in interpreting specific utterances, and makes a clear distinction between what is said and what is meant. This does not mean the speaker controls interpretation; there are still standard semantic constraints, and also a range of pragmatic devices for explaining (not always categorically) what some utterance meant. Nevertheless, a judicious use of pragmatic tools can confuse, manipulate, and misdirect audiences, and this is why pragmatic analysis is so important in considering the language of the president.

Taping Language and the Language of Tapes

Following his election in 1968, Nixon had the taping system that Lyndon Johnson had installed in the White House taken out, and Nixon's own recording system, which was to be voice activated, installed. He had this set up in a number of places, including the Oval Office and also in his "hideaway" in the nearby Executive Building.

Nixon was not the only president to secretly record meetings in the White House; as noted above, Johnson also did this, as did Kennedy. But the breadth and scope of Nixon's recordings dwarfed anything previously envisaged. It was the transcripts of these tapes, as much as any other evidence, that condemned Nixon to his fate. While most people will be aware of the "Watergate Tapes," which became public knowledge in 1973, they may be less aware that those tapes were only a portion of the tapes actually made. The first set of tapes, released in 1974, totaled less than 40 hours, but there was enough in these tapes to indicate both abuse of power and presidential privilege.

There were, however, many more tapes in the Nixon archives, and Nixon spent the next 20 years trying to control access to these tapes. As Stanley I. Kutler (1998: xiv), who fought a legal case to have all the tapes released, describes it:

> He struggled so intensely, with such determination, because of his fear that the secret tapes would cripple his hopes for historical rehabilitation. In April 1996 twenty-two years after Congress had legislated the release of the tapes of Richard Nixon's presidential conversations "at the earliest reasonable date," nine years after the Supreme Court had upheld that law, nine years after the National Archives completed its processing and preparations for their public release, two years after Nixon's death, and after five years of litigation and mediation, the tapes were at last liberated from their archival purgatory.

And what a tale they tell: confirming Nixon's knowledge of a cover-up, hush money payments, and previous sanctioned illegal wire taps and break-ins. Even worse for Nixon, and his friends and supporters, was evidence of a foul-mouthed president and one who seemed anti-Semitic.

Given all this, and the voluminous scholarly and other works on Nixon and Watergate, what can we bring from our "pragmatic" or "sociopragmatic" perspective? We don't want to focus on the Watergate scandal directly, so much has already been written on the actions and consequences for those involved, and from every conceivable angle; rather, we will interrogate two core pragmatic sites where Nixon was questioned about both his general presidential behavior and his action during Watergate. The first is provided through the depositions he gave to the Grand Jury, taken in 1974 after he had resigned as president, but only released 40 years later in 2011. The second is the Frost/Nixon interview, which took place in 1977. Both are interviews, but of radically different types, and both offer a glimpse into the way in which Nixon "pragmatically" constructed himself, perhaps not so much either as the victim or as an innocent, but as someone whose actions were not unique to himself, either as an individual or as a president. Nixon believed that activities such as taping, lying, and carrying out covert actions for the benefit of the country, and indeed the presidency, had been going on for years, and had been carried out by other presidents, so what was it that he did wrong? Nixon's own answer is linked to his "loner paranoia," his insecurity, and his view that the establishment was always out to get him. For example, in the Frost/Nixon interview of 1977 (all examples from the Frost/Nixon interview are from are from Frost, 2007), Nixon seems to mix and match a conspiracy theory with individual responsibility, as he says:

> On the other hand there are some friends who say, "just face 'em down. There's a conspiracy to get you." There may have been. I don't know what the CIA had to do. Some of their shenanigans have yet to be told, according to a book I read recently. I don't know what was going on in some Republican, some Democratic circles as far as the so-called impeachment lobby was concerned. However, I don't go with the idea that there . . . that what brought me down was a coup, a conspiracy etc. I brought myself down. I gave them a sword, and they stuck it in and they twisted it with relish. And I guess if I had been in their position, I'd have done the same thing.

In this chapter it is taken for granted that by any normal criteria, or any standard legal criteria, Nixon lied, deceived, used executive privilege to wiretap and gather evidence on opponents, garnered money from a range of dubious sources, and sold political privilege for financial support (Summers, 2000). However, in his own mind, Nixon was not guilty simply because he carried out such actions (he believed other presidents had done similar things), he was guilty because he maybe went too far. For Nixon himself, he was guilty by the degree of his actions, rather than their kind.

He frequently commented, for example, on the importance and necessity of secrecy in the performance of the presidential role, and we will see this in a number of places in his depositions to the Grand Jury. Few commentators, or analysts, have been willing to accept such arguments, but why not? Do we really believe in the ultimate purity and sanctity of truth? Have none of us ever lied? And when we admit to lying, do most of us not seek to justify and then condone that action by some form of explanation, comparison, or utilitarian claim that it saved someone's embarrassment, or it stopped someone from worrying? This is hardly the same, you may say, as lying at the highest level of politics, where people's lives and careers are in the balance, and where the standards we might expect should be higher than those applied in everyday life. Well, yes and no. Is this very response not one of justification for different degrees of lying, in that some types of lies are acceptable while others are not, dependent, that is, on context—everyday life versus high office, for example? How are we to decide the issue? Given the general historical view of Nixon as someone who lied and deceived the American people, maybe we should consider this general issue further.

I'm the President, Trust Me

One of the ironies of the presidency of Richard M. Nixon is that almost no one remembers him for what were some quite significant political achievements, particularly in the international arena. He was central in opening up communist China to the West, he made progress on arms reductions and the development of détente, he made strides forward in beginning to bring down the Iron Curtain, and in the Paris Peace Agreement he oversaw an end to the Vietnam War. But all of this pales into insignificance when compared with the attempted cover-up of the Watergate break-in.

The details and the story behind Watergate have been told many times, both by observers, historians, and by those actually involved in the events (see Dean, 1976; Liddy, 1980). In brief, on June 17, 1972. five men were arrested for attempting to break into the Democratic National Headquarters that were located in the Watergate Building. The burglars included four Cubans and one G. Gordon Liddy, who was linked to the Committee for the Re-election of the President (CREEP). The FBI connected payments to the burglars back to CREEP, and questions began to emerge about the potential involvement of the White House and even the president himself. As Senate Committee investigations proceeded, it emerged that the president had been keeping tapes of conversations that took place in the White House. When these tapes were released, it became clear that there had been an attempt to cover up the links between the White House and Watergate, and that monies raised for the president's re-election campaign had been used in the form of payoffs to the burglars. As a result, impeachment proceedings were enacted against President Richard Nixon, who resigned before they could be completed.

In his book *When Presidents Lie* (2004: 1), Eric Alterman comments:

> In American politics today, the ability to lie convincingly has come to be considered an almost prima facie qualification for holding high office.

He then argues that Presidents Roosevelt, Truman, Kennedy, Johnson, Reagan, and George W. Bush may all have been lying about certain issues. Richard Nixon is not on this list because, Alterman argues, so much has already been written on Nixon, and it was quite clear he was lying. But Alterman's book is an endorsement of what Nixon claimed as part of his defense during and after Watergate: that he was not the only president who had lied.

While most people are aware of the Watergate scandal and Nixon's role in this, this was not the first break-in that he had sanctioned, nor the first case of misuse of wiretaps, nor the first case of misleading both the people and the government. One of the most glaring examples followed the publication of what became know as the "Pentagon Papers." These secret documents gave information on Lyndon Johnson's government's prosecution of the Vietnam War. A disaffected military analyst, Daniel Ellsberg, released them to the press. Although Nixon was furious about the release, in many ways it looked like the Pentagon Papers would be much more damaging for Johnson than they would for Nixon. But consider the following transcript of a conversation recorded just a few days after the release of the Pentagon papers (Kutler, 1998: 3):

> June 17th: The President, Haldeman, Ehrlichman and Kissinger, 5.17–6.13 pm Oval Office
>
> HALDEMAN: You maybe can blackmail [Lyndon B.] Johnson on this stuff [Pentagon Papers]
>
> PRESIDENT NIXON: What?
>
> HALDEMAN: You can blackmail Johnson on this stuff and it might be worth doing . . . The bombing halt stuff is all in that same file or in some of the same hands . . .
>
> PRESIDENT NIXON: Do we have it? I've asked for it. You said you didn't have it.
>
> HALDEMAN: We can't find it.
>
> KISSINGER: We have nothing here. Mr President.
>
> PRESIDENT NIXON: Well damit I asked for that because I need it.
>
> KISSINGER: But Bob and I have been trying to put the damn thing together.
>
> HALDEMAN: We have a basic history in constructing our own, but there is a file on it.
>
> PRESIDENT NIXON: Where?
>
> HALDEMAN: [Presidential aide Tom Charles] Huston swears to God there's a file on it and it's at Brookings [Institution, a centrist Washington "think tank"].
>
> PRESIDENT NIXON: . . . Bob? Bob? Do you remember Huston's plan [for White House-sponsored break-ins as part of domestic counterintelligence operations]? Implement it.
>
> KISSINGER: . . . Now Brookings have no right to have classified documents.
>
> KISSINGER: . . . Now Brookings have no right to have classified documents.
>
> PRESIDENT NIXON: . . . I want it implemented . . . Goddamit, get in and get those files. Blow the safe and get it.

On the tapes, Nixon does seem to encourage what looks like illegal activities, probably because he never believed anyone outside his circle would hear these tapes. This sets up a clash between what Nixon claimed in public and what can be evidenced from the tapes, and this is why Nixon, perhaps more than any other president, is so closely associated with lying and deception.

In his account of the political career of Richard Nixon, Antony Summers (2000: 2) notes that Nixon seemed unable to stop himself from lying, and that he had been lying from the very beginning of his political career.

Richard Nixon's life is shot through with lies great and small, whether out-right lying or skirting the truth, or embroidering it.

Summers also notes the comment of Nixon's own Watergate lawyer, Fred Bruzart, who said of the president that "he was the most transparent liar he had ever met" (ibid.: 2).

Summers comments, with some irony, that in his acceptance of the Republican nomination in 1968, Nixon said, "Let us begin by committing ourselves to the truth, to see it like it is, to find the truth, to speak the truth and to live with the truth, That's what we will do" (ibid.: 2). And earlier Nixon said, "All you have to do in this country of ours is just tell the people the truth, and not hide away from them" (Nixon, September 1952; cited in Summers, 2000: 116).

In discussing Nixon, Summers refers to different forms of telling or not telling the truth. He refers to those untruths "that mattered little": for instance, when Nixon was talking to a group of athletes, he claimed he met his wife at a football game, when on other accounts he met her as they both auditioned for a play. Or consider the example of Nixon talking to French reporters, when he claimed that he had "majored in French," whereas his college major had been in history (op. cit.: 3). As well as "untruths that mattered little," Summers considers what he calls other untruths or "deceptions" that "mattered greatly, whether or not they constituted outright lies." He notes the example of Nixon telling the American public there were no US troops in Laos, which Summers notes was simply a "lie," or consider Nixon's claim on national television that the United States was not bombing Cambodia—for Summers, another lie. In the case of Watergate, Summers notes that Nixon even lied to his own family, saying that he had no part in the Watergate cover-up. His daughter Tricia later told the press, "We have every reason to believe him because he has never lied, not even a white lie, to his family or the American people" (op. cit.: 3).

As we can see, "lies" are often contextualized and referred to in different ways. Nixon's daughter distinguishes between "lies" and "white lies." Summons uses "untruths" and "lies" seemingly synonymously, yet untruths are more associated with those "lies" that mattered little; when such untruths matter greatly, there seems to be less equivocation—they are "lies."

In a similar way, James Pfiffner (1999; 2006) asks the question "Do presidents lie?" He begins his answer by arguing that, in one sense, we all lie at one time or another. For example, we may lie when we offer flattery or compliments that are false, as in "you look lovely in that dress"; or "you have lost some weight." Or we may lie in order to maintain the smooth running of our personal or professional relationships: "Of course I'm glad your family are coming for Christmas"; "I really enjoyed your talk, so insightful." Thus, having established that lies are not unique to politicians and are freely used by all of us, Pfiffner goes on to discuss what he calls "serious lies," and introduces further distinctions such as temptations to "shade the truth." Finally, he states: "Just as people lie, so do most Presidents" (1999: 904).

In assessing presidential lies, Pfiffner introduces the concept of what he calls a "justifiable lie." For example, he discusses the situation that faced Richard Nixon during the 1960 campaign for the presidency when John F. Kennedy had been critical of the Eisenhower government for not providing enough support for those Cubans who were fighting against Fidel Castro. Nixon was aware, however, that the government was involved in covert support of Cuban exiles. Clearly, Nixon could not openly debate this issue with Kennedy; if he said that Kennedy was wrong and operations were already underway, Nixon would be revealing a secret action, placing individuals in danger. Instead, Nixon attacked Kennedy for being "reckless and irresponsible" (ibid.: 905). Pfiffner describes this as an example of Nixon ". . . telling a blatant lie." However, one could counter this in Pfiffner's own terms: the lie may also have been justifiable (a justifiable lie) since it is an example where ". . . a president might be obliged to lie in order to protect national security operations" (ibid.: 905). Pfiffner modifies this, however, and suggests (ibid.: 907):

> But this is not a blanket pass for Presidents to lie whenever national security is involved. The lies must be clearly justified by the circumstances and not merely used to avoid embarrassment.

But who decides what is "justified" or what is "embarrassing"? Pfiffner suggests that while lying to protect "covert operations" is justified, lying to conceal or support covert policies is not justified.

> Covert operations are secret actions meant to support legitimate, that is, constitutionally justified foreign policies. Covert policies, on the other hand, include instances when the President says the government is doing X when in fact it is doing Y. This type of lie breaks the bonds of accountability in democracy.

We can see where this argument is going, and it seems to suggest that you can lie all you want and do all you want in secret, as long as it is in the pursuit of policy aims that have already been explained to the public.

Pfiffner talks of the "minor lie" and "lies to avoid embarrassment" or such things as "lies of policy deception." The danger here, of course, is that the concept of "lying" or "telling lies" becomes affected by circumstance. And although Pfiffner, as with Summers above, wishes to distinguish between harmful deception as opposed to minor deception, this distinction can never be exact, as it becomes dependent on which principles, morals, or political theory you believe.

To see the problems here, let us look at some of the cases Pfiffner cites. Minor lies, he says, include Lyndon Johnson claiming his grandfather was at the Alamo, when he wasn't, or John F. Kennedy claiming he could speed-read through documents when he couldn't, or that he didn't have Addison's disease when he did. But consider that these are not dissimilar to the example above of Nixon claiming that he met his wife at a football game when he didn't, or that he majored in French when he didn't. However, Nixon's examples are used by Summers as examples of Nixon's propensity for lying, not merely minor lying. Also, given the fact that Kennedy actually had Addison's disease and that this could have had a serious impact on his ability to perform the job of president, is this really minor lying or something potentially more significant? On the other hand, we can look at this same point in a different way; given Kennedy's clear presidential abilities, is his denial of having Addison's disease an example of "justified" lying, where the benefit for the state outweighs any negative impact of lying?

In considering presidential lies, Pfiffner (1999) looks at two specific examples from Nixon. The first is that of Watergate, where Pfiffner claims, "Nixon lied numerous times concerning his knowledge of the Watergate Cover-up." For example, Nixon said that he had "no part in, nor was he aware of, subsequent efforts that may have been made to cover up Watergate." Yet when White House tapes became available there was clear evidence that Nixon ordered Bob Haldeman, his Chief of Staff, to have the CIA tell the FBI to stop investigating Watergate as it could impact CIA covert operations. Nixon not only lied, he asked the CIA to lie. The second example highlighted by Pfiffner is that of the secret bombing of Cambodia. In his efforts to end the war in Vietnam, Nixon decided to bomb North Vietnamese supply routes into Cambodia. To do this, he first told the US Ambassador to Vietnam, Elsworth Bunker, that discussions of bombing Cambodia were suspended, but at the same time he told the Commander of the American forces in Vietnam, General Creighton W. Abrams, to ignore the cable sent to the Ambassador, and to move forward on plans to bomb Cambodia.

Pfiffner argues that the secret bombing of Cambodia was based on lies: "the only implicated parties who did not know the bombing was taking place were the U.S. Congress and the American people" (1999: 913). According to Pfiffner, Nixon argued that ". . . if the bombing were acknowledged the Cambodian government might have felt compelled to protest or the North Vietnamese might have protested." Pfiffner goes on to suggest that the real reason was more likely revealed by Nixon in his memoirs when he claimed:

> Another reason for secrecy was the problem of domestic anti-war protest. My administration was only ten months old, and I wanted to provoke as little public outcry as possible at the outset.

In the end, whatever the reasons, Pfiffner (1999 914) concludes that the decision to bomb Cambodia was wrong because it:

> . . . was a significant (legally and militarily) expansion of the war into a neutral country. . . . Thus the lies and secrecy were intended to pursue a significant foreign policy change without the knowledge of Congress or the American people.

This may be true, but consider that if Nixon told the ambassador there has been a suspension of talks on bombing Cambodia, this could have been because there was no more talking since they were now bombing Cambodia. Also, Nixon could have argued that he didn't lie about bombing Cambodia if he said he was bombing North Vietnamese supply routes—they just happened to be in Cambodia! Now this is just playing with words, you might say; well, it's really playing with pragmatic inferences, and if, according to Pfiffner, the outcome is positive it may be justified, even if it was covert, since the policy was to end the war in Vietnam.

For instance, it is claimed that as the Paris peace talks were nearing their end, Nixon and Kissinger reflected on whether or not to stop the bombing in Cambodia. Nixon decided against this, and indeed he may have increased the bombing, believing that it was the bombing which, in part, was driving the progress of the peace talks. In this context, would lying be justified if one could argue that the bombing encouraged the North Vietnamese to agree to a peace deal? The question is, how does one deal with the potentially positive consequences of a negative act? If we follow Pfiffner or Summers, the question is not even do we lie or tell the truth, the question is what type of lie or what type of truth do we tell? But when we turn to pragmatics and introduce inferential manipulation, matters get even worse.

Political Lies, Truth, and Pragmatics

Much of what we have been discussing so far may look like it has moved beyond pragmatics, since both Summers and Pfiffner are concerned with political and moral issues rather than with linguistic ones. This is to some extent true, but we want to discuss here the way in which the manipulation of inferences cannot be excluded from either the social consideration of their impact or their close relationship to lies and lying. If we distinguish types of lies based on moral and political motivations, the same will be possible where inferences are used for deceptive purposes. Further, much of what has been referred to as "white" or "justified" lying is frequently based on the presentation of meaning in specific social contexts, one of the hallmarks of pragmatics, and certainly sociopragmatics. This is important because manipulating inferences may have evolved for specific social purposes (Hurford, 2007). Consider this example: a mother says to her four-year-old, "Did you eat some of the cookies from the cookie jar?" To which the reply is "no." Now imagine the mother presses further: "Well there are no cookies left in the jar," and this time the child says, "no I didn't eat some of the cookies, *I ate all of them*." Given this response, can we say that the child was lying, or even untruthful, in her initial response, when she simply said "no"? After all, if the child had eaten all of the cookies, she must have eaten some of them. On the other hand, the mother's initial question was about eating some, not all, of the biscuits, and in this sense the child's answer was honest. What has happened here is that at an early stage the child has understood the pragmatic principle of inference from quantification. In this case, when we say "some," we imply "not all." Gazdar (1979) argued that quantifiers such as "some" imply the negation of the next highest quantifier, in this case "all." On the other hand, when we choose "all," we entail the positive form of the next lowest quantifier (and subsequent lower quantifiers), in this case "some." For example, (a) would be a contradiction, while (b) is perfectly acceptable:

(a) I ate all but not some of the cookies.
(b) I ate some if not all of the cookies.

In this context, then, when the child is asked if she ate "some" of the cookies, if she had said "yes," this would have been propositionally true, but it might have also led the mother to believe that the child did not eat "all" of the cookies, which in this case is false. Hence, it seems there may be contexts where people infer something is true when it is not, or infer something is false when it is true. So the question is this: If a speaker intentionally allows a listener to draw inferences that create false beliefs, and the speaker knows that such beliefs are false, has the speaker lied?

Here is a different kind of example (see Wilson, 2004, for a more detailed analysis). Suppose someone you know (A), but whom you dislike, asks you: "Do you own a television, I want to watch the World Cup final and mine is broken?" You reply by saying, "No, I'm sorry I don't own a television." On the basis of this response, (A) may infer not only that you do you not own a television, but that you do not have access to one. This would be based on a Gricean view of "say as much as required for the purposes of the exchange." Now let us say it is true that you do not own a television, but that you do rent one. We know when (A) asked about ownership of the television he explicitly stated that he wanted to watch the World Cup final, and it was contextually implicit that his request was really "Do you have access to a television on which I could watch the World Cup final?" Since you dislike (A), you decide to make use of the way he has asked the question to your advantage, and you do this by stating that you do not own a television, but you also allow (A) to infer that you do not have access to a television. If (A) had asked "Do you have a television?" and you answered "no," would we not say in this case, since you rent a television, that you have lied? So what is the difference between allowing false beliefs from inferences to proceed and allowing false beliefs based on statements to proceed, since in both cases (A) ends up with the same erroneous understanding, that is, that you do not have access to a television.

You answered (A)'s original question truthfully, so why should you be held responsible for his faulty beliefs? Further, inferences, as we have seen, can be adjusted or canceled without contradiction, while statements cannot.

No I don't have a television, but I do have a television.
No I don't own a television, but I do rent one.

As we noted, the issue here comes back to Grice and the idea of cooperation. If someone says they do not own a television, why should we assume that they do not also have access to one, rented or borrowed, for example? The answer is linked to Gricean maxims; if the speaker was being truthful, relevant, and saying as much as required in the context, then if he had access to a television he would have said so.

Looking again at Nixon's claim that the US government was not bombing Cambodia, was he lying, or alternatively, was he allowing false beliefs based on manipulated inferences to proceed? After all, Nixon could claim that what he said was true on one level, since the government's primary objective was to bomb Vietnamese supply routes—they just happened to be in Cambodia. Is this not similar to our example above? If Nixon is lying, so is our friend who rents but doesn't own a television.

Reasonable Inferences and Unreasonable Politicians

We have considered two main issues in relation to lying and political lying specifically. First, many argue that there are different types of lies, and that how one describes the action of lying will vary with moral and other contexts of justification. Second, and related to the first, there are contexts in which speakers allow inferences to proceed knowing that such inferences will induce false beliefs, and in such contexts this may be similar to lying. We should take account of this level because it is rampant in politics. Consider the following examples from two British prime ministers and one US president.

During a political election campaign in the United Kingdom, the opposition Labour Party claimed that Margaret Thatcher intended to double Value Added Tax (VAT) from 8% to 16%. Thatcher said, "we will not double it." Not long after a Conservative victory, VAT was raised to 15%. While this is a significant rise, it is not double the original rate of 8%. The question is, what kind of number did voters infer when they were told that a figure of 8% would not be doubled? There are a range of arithmetical possibilities here, all the way from 8% to 15.9999 . . . %. But in terms of Gricean principles of cooperation, or any other pragmatic principles of cooperation, the voters' belief that Value Added Tax would not be doubled may also have included "they will not rise significantly beyond 8%, if they rise at all."

Here is a similar example from the 1992 Conservative campaign that returned Prime Minister John Major. During this campaign it was claimed, once again, that if the Conservatives won the election they would raise VAT. John major said, "I have no plans and see no need to increase VAT." Major's chancellor at that time was Norman Lamont, and he also stated in the House of Commons, "I have no need, no proposals and no plans to raise or to extend the scope of VAT" (examples cited in Oborne, 2005: 18). Oborne (2005: 18) says of these claims:

These pledges, were of course broken by the Tories, who soon raised VAT to . . . 17.5%. Unlucky John Major was driven towards falsehood, by his increasingly desperate attempt to sustain the pound within the exchange rate mechanism (ERM).

But in what sense are the claims of Major or Lamont pledges or indeed falsehoods? Both clearly state that at a point X in time they had "no plans" or "proposals" and saw no "need" to raise VAT. What they said at point X could be true. This makes such statements similar to the quantified forms we looked at above. When one says "at this time," any assessment of what follows is constrained by that phrase to that point in time. If things should change in the future, after that point in time, then what was said previously could still have been true. The phrases used by Major and Lamont may be referred to as "hedges," in this case a type of pragmatic marker that modifies claims as truth-bound at a point in time. But again, is this how voters would have understood what Major and Lamont said, or is Oborne correct that the voters would have seen such claims as pledges?

The final example occurred in 1988, when George H. W. Bush made his now famous statement, "Read my lips, no new taxes." This is an unequivocal statement, and while it may have helped Bush's successful election, it also became a significant "sound bite," and it was later used against Bush when he was forced to raise taxes. Some analysts have argued that while Bush did raise taxes, he didn't really introduce "new" taxes; but, once again, is this nuanced interpretation what voters understood from Bush's statement—that he would raise taxes but they would be existing taxes, not new ones? This doesn't really work anyway, since at least one dictionary includes a definition of "new" as "having lately come or been brought into being" (Disctionatu.com); used in this sense, when Bush raised taxes, even existing taxes, this could be thought of as "new tax rises." Here the lexical pragmatics of "new" allows an interpretation as "anything changed from the point of the statement."

In the case of Major, Thatcher, and Bush there is another important pragmatic issue in that what they said occurred in the specific circumstances of political electioneering. Within pragmatics, it is important that "context" is considered in interpretation. In Relevance Theory, for example, Sperber and Wilson (1995) refer to what they call "contextual assumptions," that is, information that is available through various sources for decoding a specific utterance. Such assumptions will vary with different utterances and different contexts (Sperber and Wilson, 1995: 181), and the trick is to know which are available at any point in time, particularly when dealing with real world utterances. In Relevance Theory, we know that of the many contextual assumptions we might invoke for any utterance, those which achieve the balance between cognitive processing effort and informational gain are the ones that meet the relevance threshold. In the examples given for Thatcher, Major, and Bush, there is one word or phrase that becomes important for assessing the deceptive or non-deceptive nature of what they said.

For Thatcher it is the word "double," particularly its mathematical sense of twice X. For Major it is ". . . we see no need" and "at this point in time," and for Bush it is "new," in the strict sense of something that did not exist prior to the statement.

In processing Thatcher's utterance, what she said remained true if VAT was not doubled. However, in the electioneering context, would the public have inferred that Thatcher does not intend to increase VAT to 16% (double), or that she does not intend to increase VAT significantly or at all? But why make this assumption? Simply because in an election, any increase in any tax is always problematic; hence if Thatcher is being relevant in this context the assumption most easily accessed would be that Thatcher is not going to raise VAT at all, or if so, not significantly. For voters processing both Major's and Bush's claims, the contextual assumption most easily accessed is that they will not raise VAT or taxes in general. This may seem counterintuitive in some ways, but as we will discuss in Chapter 7, different systems of thinking are accessed when processing information (see Kahneman, 1973, 2011; Kahneman and Tversky, 1973), and humans tend to use fast and automatic systems unless they are forced to do otherwise; hence in all the examples we are looking at, the assumption is that the claims are interpreted as no significant increase in VAT, no raising of VAT, and no tax rises.

The Truth, the Whole Truth, and Nothing but the Truth

From a general pragmatic perspective, we have seen that defining lies and the process of lying is not as simple as we might have first assumed, so when we consider whether Nixon was a liar, or say that he lied, we need to be clear in what sense we are using the terms. In the rest of this chapter we want to explore the pragmatics of Nixon's language in selected contexts; we will focus on what Nixon said about what many believe was his core lie, that he did not know about, nor was he involved in any "cover-up" of the Watergate break-in. We will pick this up, along with other relevant examples, when we look at the Frost/Nixon interview. We begin, however, by focusing on selected materials from Nixon's Grand Jury depositions in 1975. The aim here is to show the way in which Nixon's language reflects a range of contextualization patterns that go beyond lying; we will do this by considering how meaning is framed in specific epistemic and situational formats where what is true or what is false is not only difficult to unpack, it is, in many ways, not even relevant.

The depositions were taken over a period of two days, June 23 and June 24, and the testimony was part of various investigations being conducted by the January 7, 1974, Grand Jury for the District of Columbia (the third Watergate Grand Jury). It was agreed that the sworn deposition of Nixon would be taken in California, with two members of the Grand Jury present. The deposition was taken in California because Nixon's doctor had confirmed that he was unable to travel to Washington, D.C., for health reasons. While the Watergate Special Prosecutions

Force had agreed with Nixon's lawyers on several areas of inquiry, we want to focus specifically on the opening issue, which questions whether Nixon awarded ambassadorships in return for donations to his campaign fund. We look at this example because it contains all of the main linguistic ingredients that Nixon uses throughout the depositions.

A deposition is the testimony of a witness taken out of court. It is written down and used, or may be used, later in court. It generally involves the lawyers for both sides, who may have met before the deposition, to agree on the general principles for the deposition. Thus, the deposition is highly formalized, with specific roles being designated and clearly defined in the process. Depositions allow both sides to explore what each other knows, what concerns they have, and what they may intend to bring to the attention of a jury. This is why they are seen as forms of "discovery," or more informally they are sometimes referred to as "fishing trips."

While the formal nature of depositions is well understood within the legal profession, this was the first time that a deposition of this type involved a former president of the United States. It is also worth noting that Nixon was, of course, trained as a lawyer himself, something he hints at on several occasions throughout the depositions. We begin with the legal and core basis of a deposition, where all answers and information provided are given under oath. We would also note at the start that it is quite clear that Nixon and his lawyers wanted to emphasize that his evidence is being given voluntarily, and the information provided should only be read by members of the Grand Jury. It is for this latter reason that for almost 40 years these depositions had remained secret; even now, many sections of the transcripts remain redacted for various legal purposes (all examples are taken from the US Government Printing Office online; for clarity we use "Nixon" as opposed to "witness").

The opening section of the depositions begins with the "swearing in" of Nixon, followed by the naming and professional designation of those present, an outline of the specific aims of the deposition, and an explanation of the core type of information being sought through depositional questioning. We include this lengthy section because it is important in exploring Nixon's response, which, as we will see, sets an interactional and pragmatic tone for much of the rest of the depositions.

Schwartz: Do you solemnly swear that the testimony you are about to give in this deposition proceeding shall be the truth, the whole truth and nothing but the truth, so help you God?

Nixon: I do.

Mr. Ruth: Sir, I just want to make an introductory statement. My name is Henry Ruth, and with me is Tom McBride and Richard Davis, and we are representatives of the Watergate Special Prosecution Force. During the course of this deposition, as you know, other attorneys from this office will be present at different times to ask questions on different matters. Before we begin, though, I want to outline the nature of the proceedings and just advise you of your rights and obligations here. This deposition is part of various investigations being conducted by the January 7, 1974, Grand Jury for the District of Columbia. In order to assist them with various investigations that body authorized us, as their counsel, after a series of meetings with your counsel, to arrange for the taking of your sworn deposition here in California in the presence of two representatives of the Grand Jury. In order to allow the deposition to go forth in this manner, Chief Judge Hart in the District of Columbia signed an order authorizing the presence of these two members of the Grand Jury at a deposition in California conducted ancillary to the Grand Jury investigation. Therefore, present here today are Mr. (redacted) both members of the January 7, 1974 Grand Jury. Additionally, the transcript of the proceedings will be read to the Grand Jury back in the District of Columbia.

There follows a list of topics:

1. The circumstances surrounding the eighteen and a half minute gap in the tape of the meeting between you and Haldeman on June 20, 1972.

2. Aspects of alleged receipt of large amounts of cash by Charles Rebozo or Rose Mary Woods on your behalf, and financial transactions or aspects thereof between Mr. Rebozo and you.

3. Attempts to prevent the disclosure of the existence of the National Security Council wire tap program through removal of the records from the FBI, matters dealing with threats to reveal the existence of such records, and the testimony of L. Patrick Gray at his confirmation hearings in the U.S. Senate upon his nomination to be permanent Director of the FBI.

4. Any relationship between campaign contributions and the consideration of ambassadorships for five persons: Ruth Farkas, J. Fife Symington, Jr., Vincent deRoulet, Cornelius V. Whitney and Kingdon Gould, Jr.

5. The obtaining and release of information by the White House concerning Lawrence O'Brien through use of the Internal Revenue Service.

As we understand it, sir, you are appearing here to respond voluntarily to questions in this area. Your counsel, Herbert J. Hiller, Jr. and R. Hortenson are present in the room and, naturally, you may consult with them at any time during the questioning. If you want to interrupt the questioning for that purpose, please so indicate at any time. However, neither Hr. Hiller nor Mr. Mortenson may make any statement or perform any other role during this deposition, although, of course, we are available to consult with your counsel outside the hearing room if that becomes necessary. Finally, since this deposition is being conducted ancillary to the Grand Jury, fairness requires the advice to you that the making of any false material declaration during this deposition would be a violation of Title 18, U.S. Code, Section 1623, which makes it a crime to make such a false statement. I want to make sure you understand everything I have said, sir.

Nixon: Yes, I understand everything you have said, Mr. Ruth. I understand your statement and I particularly understand the last part of your statement which dealt with the fact of any false statement was one that would make whoever was a witness liable to criminal prosecution. Needless to say, I am here, as I indicated in taking the oath, to make true statements and while, of course, I suppose it is your obligation to warn witnesses, I did not feel that it was particularly necessary for you to warn me in this instance, although I accept it and I appreciate the advice.

As we see, the deposition's "opening" reflects the formal organization of the event. What is said is, in a sense, addressed to an unseen legal audience, and it acts to confirm that all procedures are in accordance with legal expectations for the opening of such an event. Like other formulaic interview contexts, this is essential in that it makes clear what kind of speech event is in progress. In legal terms, of course, this opening is also central in that if it should stray from its formalized format, one might not only be breaking the structural rules of the discursive event, one might also be breaking the law, or ruling certain information and evidence as legally inadmissible.

Hence, there is little room for flexibility in deposition openings. In this legal sense, Mr. Ruth acts as what Goffman (1974, 1981) calls an "animator," someone who speaks the words that are required by the social situation, in this case a spokesperson for the social and legal context of the deposition. Given this point, Nixon's reaction to the way Mr. Ruth has "animated" the legal context of the deposition seems one of "hurt" or "annoyance"; Nixon seems offended by the process and what has just been said.

Nixon accepts that it is Mr. Ruth's "obligation to warn witnesses" that they are under oath, and in such a context if they do not tell the truth are liable for legal prosecution. Nevertheless, in this case Nixon challenges this obligation in the case of Nixon himself, since he did not feel it was necessary that he should be warned of his legal responsibilities. This seems an odd position for a trained lawyer to adopt; Nixon must know that Ruth has to follow procedure.

For Nixon there seems to be some connection between his appearing "voluntarily" and the expectation that he is there to "make true statements." Nixon suggests that if one appears "voluntarily," then it is assumed one wants to tell the truth. There may be a legal point that Nixon is trying to make between witnesses who have to be subpoenaed (legally required to appear and give evidence) and those who appear voluntarily, where courts may take a positive view of the latter and a negative view of the former. In this sense, "voluntarily" is being read in the legal context, not in a general semantic sense. It seems that Nixon does not feel he is being given credit for voluntarily coming forward to give evidence to the Grand Jury; indeed, he may feel he is being treated in the same way as he would have been had he been subpoenaed. But how could Mr. Ruth have played it otherwise?

The answer is that not only has Nixon voluntarily agreed to give evidence, he is doing so as a former president of the United States; hence for Nixon this is no ordinary deposition. Nixon has not been charged or convicted of any crime, nor, in his own mind, has it been proven that he told lies in any context. Therefore, to be asked to confirm that he will tell the truth rankles Nixon. It is almost as if we are to construct a syllogism of the form:

a. If an ex-president voluntarily agrees to give evidence then he will tell the truth.
b. Ex-president Nixon has voluntarily agreed to give evidence.
c. Therefore ex-president Nixon will tell the truth.

Given this logic, why should Mr. Ruth require Nixon to confirm he will tell the truth?

Responding to Nixon's comments, Mr. Ruth makes it clear he is acting within the structural frame of the deposition; he had no other choice.

Mr. Ruth: Under our Grand Jury proceedings, it would have been derelict not to read that, sir.

In his response Nixon says "I understand," and "I accept it, and I appreciate the advice" and that seems the end of the matter; but there may more going on here.

Erving Goffman (1959; 1974) has argued that everyday encounters consist of a variety of structural techniques that maintain interactional equilibrium; three particularly relevant here are "framing," "footing," and "alignment." Framing involves the use of interactional resources to manage engagements. In the deposition Mr. Ruth is performing a framing action in his opening by setting out the context within the "legal" structure of the deposition. The framing sets out structural expectations (Bateson, 2000; Goffman, 1974; Tannen, 1993) for the process. Part of this, of course, relates to the roles and responsibilities of the participants, and how those roles "align" to each other. But as Goffman (1974) points out, interaction contexts also allow for shifts in "frames" (some more than others), and a reframing of role relationships. This reframing may be done by changing the "footing" of the interaction, or by implying a change in alignment for interactional participants. For example, a doctor's diagnosis is framed within a set of assumptions about the patient's role and the doctor's role. If in this process the doctor discovers that the patient is a qualified doctor, this may shift the footing of the interactional language and reframe the interaction away from simply giving information on what the patient should do, to discussing options about what the patient might do given a shared and technical knowledge of the illness.

If we look at Nixon's actions in this way, he may be seen to be asserting that he is appearing voluntarily, reminding everyone of his status as a past president, and highlighting his qualifications as a lawyer, and he may be using these claims to shift the "footing," and in so doing he is attempting to reframe the event such that he has a different status within the interaction from that of a simple deponent or witness. Such a shift in footing would present a challenge to the procedural norms, and challenge the way in which Mr. Ruth intends to treat Nixon. This may be why Mr. Ruth is almost "apologetic" in explaining how his role is formally constrained within depositions.

Another and related way of viewing this is in terms of "stance," wherein language is used to position participants in relation to a specific object, event, or individual (Du Bois, 2007: see Chapter 5). In this case, Nixon's challenge reveals that the stance he intends to adopt is not simply as a witness, or as just any old witness; his "stance" is that he is an ex-president of the United States. This is sociopragmatically important because the meanings of words like "truth" and "deposition," or at least the contextual assumptions based on these, may vary between the participants, given the different "stances" being taken (see also Chapter 5).

The concepts of "reframing," "footing," or "stance taking," are further utilized when Nixon requests the right to provide an opening statement himself:

> Nixon: I understand. I would like to respond briefly to your statement so we will have a meeting of the minds as to what I understand the proceeding is.

Nixon's use of a "meeting of minds" reflects a "stance" issue, an explicit claim that the event may be viewed in different ways, and that Nixon, through his own statement, will make clear the "position" he will take in the event. For Nixon, this is not simply a deposition, and he wants Ruth to understand he is dealing with an ex-president of the United States.

In his statement Nixon notes several things:

> Nixon: First, it is important to note that my appearance is voluntary, that I am here on my own volition to answer the questions in the areas that you worked out with our counsel, as those that you feel my testimony will be helpful in concluding your investigation. Second, it should be noted that your investigation has been going on I hadn't realized it was quite this long— for almost two years, and I realize that you, naturally have a great desire to get everything you possibly can together so that at the end you can say that you have explored every avenue possible. That is the reason I am here, in addition to the fact that you asked me to come, which, of course, was a factor that weighed in my decision.

Nixon's first point revives the issue of his voluntary appearance as a witness. The second point, however, is a bit more puzzling; surely the investigators will know how long the investigation has been going on, although whether they want to get it over with is another matter, but we will assume that is correct. The investigators will also know they invited Nixon to give testimony. But who does the second person pronoun "you" refer to? Is it the Grand Jury, the investigating counsel, Mr. Ruth himself, or all of the above? The ambiguity of reference here allows for an interpretation that, along with the voluntary nature of Nixon's attendance, suggests that his actions reflect some form of respect for the investigators, and he indicates his wish to assist, acknowledging the importance of the investigation, and, indirectly, his sympathy for those who have been toiling for so long on this investigation. This is a form of ingratiation; it is as if Nixon is doing the deposing committee a favor out of his concern for the length of time they have been working on this problem—a problem that Nixon created.

The next section is important in that it indirectly introduces an issue which Nixon raises on a regular basis, that of presidential confidentiality.

Nixon: Now in making this appearance, however, I should point out that I am taking into consideration a very profound belief, that I have expressed publicly on many occasions, in the vital necessity for the confidentiality of presidential communications. It seems to me today that when you pick up the papers, and particularly in recent weeks, and read of former presidents, President Kennedy, for example, President Johnson, even President Eisenhower, being accused of approving or participating in discussions in which there was approval of assassination of other people is very much not in the national interest, and probably it is, of course, not true. Nevertheless it makes the point very strongly that I am going to make right now, and that is that in the Office of the Presidency . . . it is necessary for the president to have no holds-barred conversations with his advisers. It is necessary for his advisers to believe that they can give him their unvarnished opinions without regard and without fear of the possibility that those opinions are going to be spread in the public print. It is necessary for them to feel, in other words, that they are talking to the President and that they are not going to the press and that is the reason why confidentiality, which I know, not perhaps you gentlemen, but some of the members of your staff, and certainly some of the members of the House and Senate, and most of the members of the press think is not important.

We see here how Nixon draws on the perceived or real actions of other presidents and the behavior of the press, and he uses both of these to implicitly support his own position on the centrality of confidentiality. In doing this, he may also be doing several other things at the same time: first, justifying any previous withholding or manipulation of information; second, indicating how the press can misrepresent the facts; third, providing justification for keeping his evidence secret; and finally, targeting the counsels, as opposed to those who work for them, as people who understand Nixon's arguments and who agree with him.

There have been a number of examples in the actions of Nixon so far which, as we will see again in the Frost/Nixon interview, display Nixon's efforts to make use of what we will call a "pragmatics of empathy." In general terms, empathy is the ability to imagine oneself in another's place and in doing so to reflect on and understand another's feelings and concerns. (cf. Encyclopedia Britannica Online, 2005). There is general agreement, particularly within therapeutic contexts (see Bachelor, 1988; Wynn and Wynn, 2006), that empathy is something interactionally achieved through interlocutors aligning with and acknowledging another's trouble or issues. In Nixon's statements he has hinted at the concerns and problems of others, particularly those sent to depose him. For example, he drew attention to the length of the investigation, suggesting that he would be able to help to get this completed and hence solve a problem; he suggests that he agreed to be deposed out of respect for those who requested it; and, as we have just seen, he now draws this group within his field of concerns, implying they agree with his emphasis on "Presidential confidentiality."

Nixon must know that counsels have to abide by rules in gathering information, and that they were not there to take anyone's side. So why did Nixon act as he did? One reason is that it keeps shifting the "footing" of the event and hence the balance of the interaction, and the other is that while counsels may not explicitly state their agreement with Nixon, he may indirectly influence their thinking, and, therefore, the direction and tone of their questioning.

A further possibility, linked to our discussion of "stance" above, is that Nixon is not operating with one "stance" but shifts between an open friendly empathic style and a more formal and potentially aggressive legal style, and this may further challenge the interactional equilibrium of the deposition in his favor. Consider the following example:

> Nixon: And I also must say, and it will probably not occur today in our discussion of Ambassadors, but it may occur tomorrow in our discussion of wire taps, that only if there is an absolute guarantee that there will not be disclosure of what I say, I will reveal for the first time information with regard to why wire taps were proposed, information which, if it is made public, will be terribly damaging to the United States.

Notice how Nixon calls for an "absolute guarantee" of confidentiality if he is to give appropriate information in his deposition. This is basically the speech act of a "threat." If the guarantee is not equivocal, Nixon may refuse to provide certain information. We have here a form of what is known as an invited inference (Geis and Zwicky, 1971). If I say to someone, "I will give you five dollars if you mow the lawn," I imply the negative form, "if you do not mow the lawn I will not give you five dollars." In Nixon's case he is saying, "If there is an absolute guarantee I will reveal information," and this invites the inference, "if there is not an absolute guarantee I will not supply the information."

Now contrast this implied threat with the following example:

> Nixon: So in emphasizing that these presidential privileged communications will be discussed in this instance, I do want to make it clear that I do not consider that to be a waiver of my privilege for the future. Of course a privilege cannot be waived of this sort, as you are well aware, unless expressly waived for the future. It is made solely for the purposes of this Grand Jury's investigation, solely for your purposes, gentlemen, and for no other purpose.

Here we are back to a seemingly more reasonable Nixon.

In the end, however, Mr. Ruth confirms what Nixon would probably have believed from the start.

> Mr. Ruth: On the secrecy, I just want to say since this is ancillary to the Grand Jury investigation, it will be read to the Grand Jury.
>
> Nixon: I understand.
>
> Mr. Ruth: It will be subject to the non-disclosure rule, Rule 6 of the Federal Criminal Procedures, and we will take that position, that it is Grand Jury material and not subject to disclosure.

The opening of the depositions has set the tone for the rest of what is to follow, with Nixon shifting stance and footing on issues of empathy and procedure, mixed in with reminders of the decisions all presidents have to make, the complexity and breadth of the job, and hence the limitations of what evidence Nixon can give on past activities. And to make the limitations linguistically clear, Nixon says he can only say what he remembers, that is, he will use "hedges" when he is not sure. For example:

> Nixon: I **think** it is at least helpful for us to be quite frank about how I shall answer the questions and I shall attempt to be as cooperative **as possible** and to remember everything that I **possibly** can. If **I don' t remember**, I am going to say so. If I do remember, I will tell you **what I remember**. If **I am not sure**, I am going to say **"to the best of my recollection"** and so with that, gentlemen, proceed with any questions you like.

Money for Ambassadors

One of the core reasons for the deposition was to explore whether Nixon had been awarding ambassadorships in return for fiscal or other donations, and transcripts of a number of the White House tapes had suggested this was case. The deposition therefore focused on the details of the appointment of several ambassadors:

> Mr. Ruth: Sir, the questioning in this area of ambassadors will focus on five individuals: Vincent deRoulet, J. Fife Symington, Jr., Kingdom Gould, Cornelius V. Whitney and Ruth Farkas and, insofar as possible, I will attempt to have the questioning proceed in that order . . . Now my question is do you recall Mr. deRoulet's appointment in 1969, his nomination and confirmation as Ambassador to Jamaica?

We do not need to explore each ambassadorial case that was presented to Nixon, since in response to this first example Nixon more or less summarizes the strategy he will adopt throughout.

Nixon: Well, I think it would be helpful, Mr. McBride, if I were to tell you how I handled ambassadors and how such a document would come to me so that you can be absolutely certain as to what I do recall and what I don't and *why* I do not recall.

Mr. Ruth: Very well.

Nixon: First, noting this date, it was a rather busy time. That was the time we were in the midst of the, one of the great Tet offensives, as you recall. There had been one in '68 and then despite our peace overtures in early '69—there was one that was just coming to conclusion then and Dr. Kissinger and I were developing strategy for his secret meetings which began in August. I laid the groundwork on it because it will indicate to you the basis for the statement I am now going to make with regard to papers like this and others that came across my desk. As far as ambassadors were concerned, I had certain guidelines that I laid down when I became President. One, that the number of non-career ambassadors should be no higher, the percentage thereof, than that in previous administrations and, if possible, lower. That was no reflection on non-career ambassadors, but in the past there had been in some administrations a tendency to appoint to highly important posts incompetent non-career people and, in my view, the important thing, if it was an important post, was an individual who was totally and highly qualified. In some instances he might be a very wealthy individual, in other instances he might not, but the most important point to me was that he had to be qualified.

The first thing to note is that the original question Nixon was asked was a yes/no question, "Do you recall. . . ." But the question had a number of elements over which a negative or positive response would have ranged (recollection; nomination; appointment), a simple "yes" or "no" would indicate a positive or negative agreement with all the parts. Nixon avoids this issue by performing a pre-move (pre-answer) which indicates that a simple "yes" or "no" would not be helpful. This further endorses Nixon's role as the constructive witness. But Nixon also does something else, he adds that the information he is about to give, about how ambassadors were appointed, will provide justification for both the information he can supply as well as the information he can't supply. Here he is already doing preparatory work just in case there may be information he doesn't remember from 1969. This pre-move helps us understand what seems to be a rambling response from Nixon. What he says about the date and the Tet offensive seems to have nothing to do with appointing ambassadors, let alone the specific case of Mr. de Roulet. However, although we said Mr. Ruth's question had a simple yes/no structure, this is a deposition, and questions are asked for specific reasons related to specific topics. Hence, Nixon already knows what is coming is an exploration of how and why ambassadors were appointed, and in this sense Nixon is not really responding to the question asked, but to other broader questions contextually presupposed such as: How were ambassadors appointed? And did appointments involve any payment of funds? Nixon understands this and he is beginning to offer a response to the first part of the broader question, that is an "explanation" of how ambassadors are appointed. But he goes further and constructs his response as a specific type of explanation, what sociologists call an "account." Scott and Lyman (1968: 46) say:

> An account is a linguistic device employed whenever an action is subjected to evaluative inquiry . . . they prevent conflicts from arising [*or smooth them out once they have arisen*] by verbally bridging the gap between action and expectation [*or, between action and puzzlement*] [*my comments in italics*].

Such accounts include factors such as status and power differences, the formal or informal nature of the interaction, and the consequences of providing such accounts. There are two main types of accounts, "excuses" and "justifications," and both occur when people are accused of doing something wrong or bad. For example, "I'm late because my alarm didn't go off," or "I'm late because I stopped to help an old lady who had slipped in the snow." The first example is an "excuse" because it recognizes responsibility for a bad or inappropriate behavior, although an effort is also made to explain and mitigate responsibility through factors beyond individual control. The second example is a "justification," because the person accepts responsibility for the act, but suggests that in the circumstances it was justified.

If we treat Nixon's response as an "account," then the first part begins to make more sense. The opening mentions important matters of state, some of the most significant during Nixon's time in the White House, and this is what Nixon refers to as keeping him busy. But what has this to do with the appointment of ambassadors? Well, if we refer again to Sperber and Wilson's (1995) Relevance Theory, we know that we will try to make sense of what Nixon is saying by drawing upon contextual assumptions. In this case assumptions that could be drawn would be that events such as the Tet offensive would have been much more significant than appointing the ambassador to Jamaica. In this sense Nixon's opening provides a contextualization to the appointment, which lowers such appointments on the scale of significance of affairs of state. Nixon then adds to this point by noting how ambassadorial appointments were based on procedural "guidelines." These might vary from career to non-career appointments, but in the process money would have been an incidental issue. Nixon also tells us how he was bringing order and structure to a random procedure as exercised by other presidents (once more raising himself positively against others).

Nixon is not simply explaining how ambassadors were appointed in his administration, he is setting up a situational background for a cognitive account of deniability ("I don't remember because I was very busy at that time with many, perhaps, more, important things"); and he is responding within the general framework of ambassadorial appointments to any accusation that such appointments were on the basis of an ambassador giving funds to support Nixon's campaign—how could this be so since qualifications came first, wealth was incidental.

As Nixon continues, he builds on the rhetorical moves we have outlined; for example, he goes on to rank ambassadorships in terms of importance.

> Nixon: The second point is that insofar as the nations are concerned, where a major post was involved, I insisted that that be discussed as a priority item. For example, ambassador to France, ambassador to Great Britain, to any of the major NATO countries, ambassador to Japan, ambassador to the Soviet Union, these were the major posts. I don't mean to reflect, incidentally, on the third world and the others, but they were not at that time major, except, of course, for the ambassador to South Vietnam, which was major because of the fact we were involved in a war, and in those instances, those posts were brought to my attention and they would be discussed by Dr. Kissinger, by the Secretary of State, sometimes by other members of my staff, in terms of is this individual qualified to handle this job.

Nixon is ranking the significance of ambassadors and linking this to how much attention they may or may not have been given, but this isn't relevant given Nixon's comments on suitability in terms of qualifications or background as opposed to how much money a candidate has; it shouldn't really matter whether the state is considered "minor," as long as the ambassador has been assessed as appropriately qualified for the position. However, consider how Nixon expands on his point.

> Nixon: **As far as other ambassadorial assignments were concerned, ambassador to Luxembourg or El Salvador or Trinidad, et cetera, it was not vitally important, as far as the national interest was concerned, to have in that post an individual whose qualifications were extraordinary**. It didn't mean that we wanted to send somebody down who would disgrace the United States or who couldn't do an adequate job, but whether it was a non-career person or a career person—there were just certain posts that I did not consider important enough and **I told my staff as far as these posts that are not major, don't bring them to my attention, bring me recommendations—check them out and bring me a check list and tell me what everybody says on them and then I will make the final decision because, of course, ambassadors are appointed by the President**. Many think they are appointed by the Secretary of State, and, incidentally, most of them believe they serve the Secretary of State and him only. That is particularly true of the non-career ones—of the career ones, I should say—but they are appointed by the President. Now I will bring this to a conclusion quite hurriedly so you can go on with the questioning. Where the post, therefore, was not in the, **what I considered the priority classification, all I wanted was a piece of paper indicating to me that there was unanimous agreement on the staff and also indicating to me if there was not unanimous agreement,** who disagreed,

so that I could, of course, talk to that individual. Sometimes the Secretary of State wouldn't agree with Kissinger and so forth. Also, as far as those ambassadors were concerned where certain non-career appointments were to be made, a notation would be made as to not only that it had been approved by all of the people in the Administration Secretary of State, Kissinger, et al—but who was approving it insofar as people who were outside the Administration, in the area, for example, of working in political campaigns or contribution political campaigns in this case, like Mr. Stans—and then with all of that material before me, I would make a final decision.

We have highlighted in bold the cores issues that Nixon wants to get across. The appointment of ambassadors to minor states was assessed by the President's staff, Nixon didn't even have this process brought to his "attention," he wanted the staff to present their assessment and their agreement or disagreement for the president's consent—or in exceptional circumstances for his further consideration. So summing up, what we have the following Nixon claims:

1. Ambassadors were appointed only if they had the appropriate qualifications.
2. Where minor states are involved the qualifications did not need to be extraordinary.
3. If minor states required appointments I did not give them attention and left it to my staff.
4. At the time Mr. de Roulet was appointed to Jamaica I was very busy with major issues.

From these it follows that given Mr. de Roulet was appointed to Jamaica, a minor state, and given that Nixon was involved with the Tet offensive, he was probably not involved in the appointment process (2 and 3). The ambassador's qualifications and background would not have been given the same attention as in the appointment of major state ambassador (1 and 2), and even if Nixon had been involved in assessing the candidate in 1969 he would probably remember very little about this (4).

Although the president made the final decision on any appointments, many other people were involved in the recommendation, and for minor state appointments, if everyone agreed, Nixon just signed things off. There is one further important point, almost made in passing at the end of Nixon's response, that is when some non-career appointments were considered the list of those agreeing to the appointment would have included individuals outside the administration; those ". . . working on political campaigns," and this could/would have included fundraisers. This is clearly significant in that if those in charge of raising funds had a say in who gets certain ambassadorships, this suggests that money may have been an issue in such cases. But, of course, even if it was, how could Nixon have known since money was not within the guidelines for appointment.

There is one final point I want to mention before leaving the issue of ambassadorships, and this is outlined in Nixon's comments as follows.

> Nixon: Then I will add one other point and then I am through. One of the reasons why you see so few on this list and on the list than you generally do, ambassadors that were appointed who had made contributions was that I felt that the previous administrations, and this was particularly true of the State Department in its recommendations, had not adequately represented all of America. I felt that all of America should be represented, and I said, for example, I wanted two black ambassadors appointed, not to black countries, where they had always been before, but to white countries where they would be accepted. I asked for two Latin Americans, Mexicans, for example, or some Latin Americans who were living in the United States and had become citizens of the United States. I asked for at least two Italians. We've had some we should have more. I also asked for representatives for one or two who might be of Polish background. That, therefore cut down the number that were available for appointment based on whatever recommendation in the non-career area, a recommendation that might be made by Mr. Stans or Mr. Kalmbach or anybody else who had contacted the ambassador—I mean the applicant for the ambassadorship for a contribution.

Unpacking this argument is difficult. Clearly, we see again how Nixon wants to highlight his own positive behavior in seeking to appoint members of minority groups who have been underrepresented. Hence, the number of appointed ambassadorships within his term may seem lower compared to other regimes. Yet, while this might be good, or indeed true, perhaps what Nixon is really doing is pre-empting any inference from the number of appointments to the process of paying for appointments; that is, the number is lower because fewer people were willing to pay to be appointed. But most important, he admits that members of his political campaign team would indeed, in some cases, ask for a contribution to Nixon's political campaign fund, but only after they have been selected, not before the selection.

Nixon's tactics, as analyzed above, are repeated throughout the depositions and on all topics. He continually draws on an image of the difficult role of the president, and that people should be grateful for what he achieved, that he had many complex tasks and decisions to make and many tasks had to be delegated, and that, most of all, much of what is being discussed should not be in the public domain because discussions within the presidency must remain confidential for the job to work. In other words, Nixon admits no wrongdoing in any direct sense. He does, however, lay down a framework of "explanatory" accounts of the operation of the presidency in the area of appointing ambassadors which would not exclude donations, should they have been offered, as this was not a sine qua non for the position. Further, Nixon admits that sometimes members of the advisory group could include those involved in political campaigns, and this would include fundraisers like Mr. Stans. The problem is that there is no direct link between giving funds, or even being asked for funds, and appointments. Any connection is said to be after the fact, after the appointment.

Frost/Nixon

The Frost/Nixon interviews were a milestone in the history of political interviewing. In 2008 they became the basis of a major motion picture, and a number of books by those involved in the making of the interview series (Frost himself, and James Reston, Jr. [2007], for example). The film, and the books, introduced a new generation to both Watergate and its impact and consequences for the American presidency. The interviews ranged over a number of days, but it was the interview that focused on the Watergate break-in which drew most audience attention—it is said some 45 million Americans tuned in. In what follows we will consider only the main sections of the Watergate interview, making use of the transcript provided in Frost's (2007) book *Frost—Nixon*.

The interview opens innocently enough with a general question from Frost on the importance of looking at the various issues, events, and elements of Watergate so that the audience may gain a clear picture of what took place. But Frost adds a specific question at the end of his initial remarks which is much more pointed (Frost, 2007: 207):

> Mr. President. . . . But just one brief, preliminary question: reviewing now your conduct over the whole Watergate period, with the additional perspective now of three years out of office and so on, do you feel that you ever obstructed justice or were part of a conspiracy to obstruct justice?

In his study of journalistic interviews, Clayman (2002) suggests that journalists as interviewers act as what he calls "a tribune for the people," a rhetorical surrogate for the audience, asking the questions they want answered on their behalf. Clayman draws on the concept of "footing," which we discussed earlier, and argues that the interviewer's questions align in different ways in terms of where the responsibility for the question comes from. The interviewer may ask a question on his or her own initiative, or align with a third party "such as a government official, expert or other elite source" (2002: 3); for example, "The Financial Secretary has suggested that . . . do you agree"; or "The *Washington Post* reported today that. . . . Would you like to comment on this." The interviewer may also align with the larger and more amorphous group known as "the public" and ask a question on their behalf; as in "what the public wants to know is. . . . ." However, if Clayman is correct, since media interviews are for the public, it is they who watch them, then, on one level, the questions must also be for the public. Questions may or may not have different relevance for subsets of the public, but that is a different point. Whatever the case, it is useful here to see Frost as a tribune for everyone who wanted to understand Watergate.

Of course, if we accept this, Frost's questions also become important for the interviewee in a similar public sense. The interviewee's responses, in turn, will not be directly targeted at the individual interviewer, with his own interests or concerns, but to a broader public, which for a politician contains voters, and those who would judge the words, promises, and legacy of the politician, and in, this case, the ex-president.

Looking at Frost's opening question(s) in this way, both he and Nixon, and the public, will have a set of contextual assumptions that "obstruction of justice" was one of the core elements in the impeachment of Nixon. They will also be aware that Nixon rejected accusations that he broke the law, so Frost's question goes to the heart of Watergate and its legacy, and it is cleverly structured to pragmatically frustrate the interviewee.

While it looks like Frost has asked two linked yes/no questions, they are not necessarily mutually exclusive, giving a positive response to one or the other produces the same result as giving a positive response to both, specifically that Nixon was involved in obstruction of justice. The style of questioning is not unlike the example, "When did you stop beating your dog?" which presupposes the action has happened, that (you) have been beating your dog. This inference can be canceled by saying, "I haven't beaten my dog, because I have never beaten my dog/I don't have a dog" (see Chapter 1). Frost's questions are not directly presuppositional in this sense, but they carry a constraint in that a negative response "no" may still leave behind a possibility that the respondent is still responsible for an action which is an obstruction of justice.

When Frost asks, "do you feel that you ever obstructed justice?" if Nixon says "no," to which part of the question is he offering a negative response, the "feeling" that he obstructed justice, or that he obstructed justice. Nixon could say "I never felt like I was obstructing justice, but clearly I was." Hence, only the "feeling" is denied. Equally, in the question "were (you) part of a conspiracy to obstruct justice?" Nixon could say "no, I wasn't part of a conspiracy, but I did obstruct justice." By asking the questions in this way, Frost directs his audience to infer contextual presuppositions or assumptions that there was a conspiracy to obstruct justice and this is taken for granted. This is further enhanced by the repetition of the phrase "obstruction of justice," where such repetition can confirm in the public's mind that something is true by virtue of the repetition. For example, in the run-up to the Iraq War, George W. Bush made several speeches in which he repeatedly linked Iraq, Al Qaeda, and weapons of mass destruction (WMD). Bush's use of repetition proved so successful that even today, despite evidence that Iraq did not have WMD (evidence that Bush now accepts), many Americans continue to believe that Iraq had WMDs (we discuss this in more detail in Chapter 6).

Nixon's response attends to Frost's opening remark and uses this as a basis for dealing with questions about an obstruction of justice (ibid.: 208):

> Nixon: Well, in answer to that question, I think that the best procedure would be for us to do exactly what you are going to do in this program; ah, to go through the whole record in which I will, ah say what I did; ah what my motives were; ah and ah then I will give you my evaluation as to, ah. Whether those actions or, ah anything I said for that matter, ah amounted to what you have called an "obstruction, ah of justice." Ah I will express an opinion on it but I think what we should do is go over it, ah, the whole matter, so that ah, our viewers will have an opportunity to know what we are talking about. Ah, ah, so that in effect, as they listen, ah, will be able to hear the facts, ah, make up their own minds. I'll express an opinion. They may have a different opinion. Ah but that is really the best way to do it, rather than to preclude it in advance and maybe prejudice their viewpoint.

This response turns the table on Frost as it downgrades the appropriateness of the questions about "obstruction of justice" in terms of the aims of the interview, which, as Frost himself admits, is to ". . . press first of all through the sort of factual record and the sequence of events as precisely as we can. . . ." Further, Nixon manages to challenge the interviewer's role as a "tribune for the people," implicitly criticizing Frost's attempt to ask loaded yes/no questions. Nixon argues that, as Frost agrees, they should "go through the whole record . . . so that ah, our viewers will have an opportunity to know what we are talking about . . . ah make up their own minds." It is interesting that Nixon makes use of "our" as in "our viewers." This binds not only Frost and Nixon together, but allows Nixon to align himself with the audience, once again potentially disrupting the role of the interviewer as a "tribune for the people."

Frost is forced, in a way, to accept Nixon's counter-offense and he moves directly to one of the most controversial elements of the Watergate investigation—that on June 20, 1972, Nixon had a meeting with his Chief of Staff Bob Haldeman. This meeting became significant because when the tape of this conversation was played, part of it was erased—what became known as the missing 18½ minutes. Nixon had previously argued that he had no clear knowledge of how or why part of the tape had been erased and maintained it must have been an accident, suggesting that his secretary may have done this in error. Nixon further argued that he did not recall anything of significance in that morning's conversation with Haldeman, and that the main point of discussion was about a public relations offensive against others who may have been trying to wiretap the Nixon administration. Frost, however, challenges Nixon to tell us what happened in the missing 18½ minutes (ibid.: 208):

> Frost: . . . So beginning June 20th then, what did Haldeman tell you during the 18½ minute gap?

Nixon: Haldeman's notes are the only recollection I have of what he told me. Haldeman was a very good note taker, ah, because of course, we've had other opportunities to look at the notes and he was very . . .

Frost: PR offensive.

Nixon: That's right.

So the only evidence Nixon claims to have of what was said is Haldeman's notes. This is a fairly weak response, of course, so Nixon embellishes this slightly by adding that Haldeman was a good note taker, implying that these would be an accurate representation of what was said. By placing the emphasis on Haldeman's notes, Nixon also, however, is protecting himself in that such notes are secondhand evidence of what was said. In theories of "evidentiality" (see Chafe and Nichols, 1986; Aikhenvald, 2004), it is claimed that we linguistically mark commitment to types of evidence, as in "I believe, I know I saw"; different types of evidence are rated in terms of validity, with personal experience being more credible than information gained secondhand. Haldeman's notes are not only secondhand, they are Haldeman's interpretations and recollections, which, no matter how good they are, could be challenged on a number of levels. Hence, should any of these notes have proved problematic for Nixon, he could always challenge their veracity.

Frost's next move is particularly interesting. At the time of the interviews, Frost's research team managed to uncover a number of tapes that had been previously unheard. These tapes where provided by Charles Coulson, who had been a presidential aide in the Nixon administration. It was agreed that information from these tapes would be used in the interviews, but that Nixon would not be informed of the research team's access to the tapes.

One of the tapes provided by Coulson was dated June 20, 1972, where there is a conversation between Nixon and Coulson on the evening of that day, and in the conversation Nixon says he is aware of several of the participants involved in the break-in at Watergate, including Howard Hunt (who had recruited the burglars for Watergate). The issue for Frost and his team was how could Nixon be so well informed on the evening of June 20 if Haldeman, Nixon's main source of information on Watergate, had not discussed the matter earlier that day—was this what was on the missing 18½ minutes? (op. cit.: 209)

Frost: But as far as the general state of your knowledge that evening, ah, when you were talking to Chuck Coulson on the evening of the 20th, it suggests that, from somewhere, your knowledge had gone much further. You say, 'If we didn't know better, we'd have thought the whole thing had been deliberately botched.' Coulson tells you, 'Bob is pulling it all together. Thus far, I think we've done the right things to date.' And you say, 'Ba . . . ah, basic . . .' He says, basically, they're all pretty hard line guys.' And you say, 'of course, we're just gonna leave this where is with the Cubans. At times I just Stonewall it' And, you also say, 'We gotta have the lawyers smart enough to have our people delay.' Now, somewhere you were pretty well informed by that conversation on June 20th.

We can see on the videotape of the Frost/Nixon interview that the introduction and reference to the Coulson conversation was a shock to Nixon (see Reston, 2007). When we look at the tape we see that Nixon's eyes begin a rapid movement back and forth, indicating his nonverbal reaction to what Frost said. Nixon can be said to be "giving off cues" (Goffman, 1981), that is, failing to control bodily information about his mental or emotional state. Such cues may be seen when our feet nervously tap, or when we start to sweat, or our face turns red.

> Nixon: As far as my information on June 20th is concerned, ah, I had been informed ah, by . . . with regard to the possibility of Hunt's involvement, ah, whether I knew on 20th or 21st or 22nd, I knew something . . . I learned in the period about the possibility of Liddy's involvement. Of course I knew about the Cubans and McCord, who were all picked up at the scene of the crime. Ah, no, ah you have read here, ah, excerpts out of a conversation with Coulson. Ah, and let me say, as far as my motive was concerned—and that's the important thing—my motive was, in everything I was saying or certainly thinking at the time, ah, ah, was not to try to cover up a criminal action. But, to be sure, that as far as any slip over, or should I say, 'slop-over' I think would be a better word, any slop-over that, ah, ah, damage innocent people, or blow it into political proportions . . . it was that that I certainly wanted to avoid. (op. cit.: 210)

This makes clear that Nixon had not been expecting Frost's revelation about the Coulson tape. When Nixon says, "As far as my information is concerned, ah, I had been informed ah, by . . ." it looks as if he is about to tell us who had given him the information, but there is a significant pause here, and he changes tack. He lists a set of dates about when he might have known about Hunt. In doing this, he accomplishes two things. First, by listing dates he creates an ambiguity about which date it was, and second, he downplays both the ambiguity and the relevance of an exact date by accepting that yes he "knew something . . .," although exactly what that is he doesn't say. He also admits that somewhere around those dates, or even more ambiguously ". . . in that period," he learns ". . . about the possibility of Liddy's involvement." Having said this much, he fully recovers his control and goes back on a standard form of defense between actions and motives and intentions for those actions. Frost comments on this in his notes that:

> Once again Nixon will incorrectly offer the purity of his motives as a defense to conduct that is clearly criminal. (Frost, 2007: 210)

This refers of course to a legal argument, whatever your intentions may have been if you cover up a criminal act that is itself a criminal offense. Now the most significant of Nixon's actions at the time of Watergate, which could fall into this category, was his attempt to get the CIA to tell the FBI to "back off" the investigation into the Watergate break-in, as it might compromise certain ongoing CIA operations. This was just not true; there were no such CIA operations. For many looking at Nixon's behavior, this action alone would indicate criminal intent (op. cit.: 201).

> Frost: So, you invented the CIA thing on the 23rd as a cover?
>
> Nixon: No. Now let's . . . lets use the word 'cover-up' in the sense that it had . . . should be used and should not be used. If a cover-up is for the purpose of covering up criminal activities, it is illegal. If however, a cover-up, as you have called it, is a motive that is not criminal, that is something else again. And, my motive was not criminal. I didn't believe that we were covering-up any illegal activities. Ah, I didn't believe that John Mitchell was involved. Ah I didn't believe. Ah, that, for that matter, anybody else was. I was trying to contain it politically. And, that's a very different motive from the motive of covering-up criminal activities of an individual. And so there was no cover-up of any criminal activities; that was not my motive.

Nixon has moved into a specific linguistic and legal mode as he sets out how the term "cover-up" should be used. If it is used in connection with illegal activities it is criminal; if it is used generally it is not criminal. The default definition of the term "cover-up" would be, for most people, an illegal cover-up, but Nixon is right in that one can cover up a multitude of issues, many not illegal. We are to infer from this distinction that what Nixon believed he was involved in was possibly a cover-up, but not of illegal activities, rather political mistakes or political embarrassment. Nixon also adds a couple of epistemic claims about his knowledge at that time such as "I did not believe . . . ," and as we have seen these may act as "hedges" should what they refer to turn out to be factually incorrect. Finally, and importantly, Nixon suggests that if you are involved in a cover-up, it is only illegal if your motive was to cover up what you knew were illegal activities.

As the interview continues, Frost and Nixon clash over "cover-up" and "motive," but also "motive" and "obstruction of justice," at one point debating the legal statue on the matter (214–215), and here again Nixon makes "motive" the issue:

> Nixon: a con. . . . a con . . . all right, we'll . . . a conduct endeavour. Corrupt intent. But it must be corrupt and that gets to the point of motive. One must have a corrupt motive. Now I did not have a corrupt motive.
>
> Frost: You. . . . were . . .
>
> Nixon: My motive was pure political containment. And, political containment is not a corrupt motive. If so, for example, we . . . President Truman would have been impeached.

At this point Frost changes direction and drops "motive" for "intent" (ibid.: 215):

> Frost: Your motive can be helpful when your intent is not clear. Your intent is absolutely clear . . .

But this change doesn't really help as Nixon can play with intent as well:

> Nixon: I didn't think of it as a cover-up. I didn't intend it to cover up. Let me say, if I intended to cover up, believe me, I'd have done it. You know how I could have done it?

This reminds us of the distinction between simply making a false statement and doing so intentionally, that is with the explicit goal of lying. Nixon's defense here, and elsewhere, is that whatever his actions they cannot be labeled criminal, or lying or deception, since he did not have the appropriate motives or the appropriate intentions. Consider here how Speech Act Theory argued that in the performance of a particular act, promising, threatening, or lying, the speaker should have the appropriate intentions to perform the act. Nixon argues he did not have specific intentions in any illegal cover-up, so in an extended sense of the speech act argument he did not perform, or correctly perform, the action of cover-up.

Further, he argues that terms such as "cover-up" do not automatically indicate criminality, since what is covered-up may not be illegal. So while the historical legacy of Nixon is that he lied and broke the law by trying to cover up Watergate, Nixon suggests many people have only given "cover-up" a default interpretation, as something illegal, and here they would be wrong. If Nixon is correct that any cover-up was for political purposes, this could also bring such an action within the scope of Pfiffner's arguments about "justifiable lies" since the purpose of the cover-up was for positive political reasons.

So what are we to make of all this from a pragmatic perspective. Was Nixon lying? Did he attempt to have Watergate covered up? Did he try to interfere with a federal investigation? The answer to all these questions would seem to be yes and no. The problem is that once contextual information is introduced through such things as political actions verses criminal actions, stating untruths as opposed to inferring what is false, it becomes difficult to define things in exact terms. Clearly, Nixon is arguing that what he did was for the political good, and not for the expediency of covering up, or directly protecting, individual criminals. However, one could argue that whatever the motive, what happened, or what was intended to happen, led to an attempt to cover up the criminal activities of certain individuals. Frost takes this basic logic and runs with it:

> Frost: But surely, in all you've said, you have proved exactly that that was the case; that there was a cover-up of criminal activity because you have already said, and the record shows, that you knew that Hunt and Libby were involved. At the moment you told the CIA to tell the FBI to 'Stop period' as you put it. At that point, only five people had been arrested. Liddy was not even under suspicion, and so you knew, in terms of intent, and you knew in terms of foreseeable consequence, ah, that the result would be that, in fact, criminals would be protected. Hunt and Liddy, who were criminally liable would be protected.

Frost gives further quotes from Nixon, most significantly Nixon's comment: "Tell them don't go any further into this case, Period."

Nixon responded (as he had done previously) by quoting a conversation he had with acting FBI director Patrick Gray in which he encouraged a full investigation of Watergate. How could he want a cover-up, while at the same time encouraging an investigation of the very thing he was accused of covering up? Reasonable and logical as this may be, Frost correctly points out that the conversation with Patrick Gray was on July 6, well after the president's clear injunction to his aides to get the CIA to have the FBI stop their investigation. As Frost notes (213):

> Nixon used this July 6th conversation with acting FBI Director L. Patrick Gray to purge himself of any culpability for the criminal cover-up.

In his notes Frost is quite clear and calls Nixon's actions a "criminal cover-up"; both Frost and his team already had a view who was, legally and or otherwise, responsible. But it was always Nixon's lament, that others were out to get him. As we have seen, he frequently referred to other presidents and their wrongdoing—recall that Alterman (2004) accused Roosevelt, Truman, Kennedy, Johnson, Reagan, and George W. Bush of lying to the people of the United States. Pfiffner (2007) might say here that some of these presidents' actions represented "justifiable lies," but who is the ultimate arbiter of what is an acceptable or unacceptable lie for the sake of the country. One response might be that it's not just that Nixon lied about many things, it is that he took part in illegal activities. But this is the point; some of the lies that Alterman and Pfiffner discuss could also be seen as illegal, not only in terms of US law but also international law. So are we attempting to defend Nixon? No, the aim is only to make clear that his use of pragmatics to defend himself is a reflection of the possibilities available to him (and all of us). Yes, it looks very much like he used language to create excuses, justifications, and defenses of some questionable behaviors, but is this just an extreme or heightened example of what we ourselves often do? Maybe this is the point—a little linguistic manipulation is OK as long as you are not the president of the United States, or at least as long as you don't get caught.

4

The Narrative Presidency

RONALD REAGAN AND STORIES FROM THE WHITE HOUSE

Introduction

On March 30, 1981, President Ronald Reagan put on a brand new blue suit and made his way to the Washington Hilton Hotel in Washington, D.C., where he was due to make a speech to the Construction Trades Council. He later recalled that the speech was not "riotously received," which he explained by observing, "I think most of the audience were Democrats." After the speech, as Reagan was leaving the hotel, John Hinckley Jr. approached the president and his entourage and shot the president and three others. President Reagan was rushed to the George Washington University Hospital and it was clear that he was seriously wounded, and perhaps close to death. Initial medical actions did not stem the bleeding, and the chief of thoracic surgery decided to operate. In the operating room Reagan is said to have quipped, "Please, tell me you are all Republicans."

Reagan recalled later that when he first entered the hospital he was lying on a gurney and was only "half conscious," but then he

> . . . realized that someone was holding my hand. It was a soft feminine hand. I felt it come up and touch mine and then hold on tight to it. It gave me a wonderful feeling. Even now I find it difficult to explain how reassuring, how wonderful, it felt. It must have been the hand of a nurse kneeling very close to the gurney, but I couldn't see her. I started asking, "Who's holding my hand? Who's holding my hand? When I didn't hear any response I said, "Does Nancy know about us?" Although I tried afterward to learn who the nurse was, I was never able to find her. I had wanted to tell her how much the touch of her hand had meant to me, but I was never able to do that. Once I opened my eyes I saw Nancy looking down at me. "Honey," I said, "I forgot to duck."

In this brief account of the shooting of Ronald Reagan, we see the classic Reagan style, joking that a less than interested audience must be Democrats, or that he

90

Talking with the President. John Wilson. © Oxford University Press 2015.
Published 2015 by Oxford University Press

hoped the operating room staff who were about to cut him open were Republicans, or offering us the pathos of a small vignette about a caring nurse, an angel who seems to have been there when needed but who mysteriously could not be found afterward; and finally, the line which is probably the most quoted of the story, "Honey, I forgot to duck," a line that was not actually Reagan's own, having originally been used by the heavyweight boxing champion, Jack Dempsey, speaking to his wife on the night he was beaten by Gene Turney.

In lines such as "I think most of the audience were Democrats," "Please, tell me you are all Republicans" and "Honey, I forgot to duck," we have jocular forms of linguistic irony (see Gibbs, 2002). As with most ironic forms, these lines have a pragmatically driven meaning beyond their literal meaning and rely on processes of contextual and linguistic inference to produce speaker-intended meaning: for example, "Democrats don't have a sense of humor"; "Would Democrats save a Republican President?"; and "I didn't stand a chance but I'm OK." We can see, on one level, these forms have an underlying humor and informality and, given the seriousness of the situation in which some of them were uttered, they also carry social implications of courage. After all, Reagan had just been shot, he was in mortal danger, yet he still took the time to joke with those around him, to create a relaxed atmosphere for the medical staff, and, as some more cynical have argued, to play his part, even potentially at the end, of the mythical American hero.

In the example of the nurse holding Reagan's hand we have something slightly different. Here we have a narrative form, a structured story of past personal experience (Labov and Waletsky, 1967). As with all stories, this structure is created for a purpose or point, or several points. In this case, the story not only invokes the cultural stereotype of the nurse as a ministering angel, but Reagan's claim that he could not find her later has echoes of the humble American hero/ heroine. As we will see later, Reagan was often accused of living his life as if it were a movie, and while it may well have been true that he couldn't find the nurse to thank her, it is hard to imagine that a nurse who had been involved in the care of a president could not be found. Yet the claim that she could not be found serves the story at another level. Here, we can invoke the guardian angel, that there is someone "up there" looking out for you. We can imagine the scene found in many movies where someone saves an individual in danger or close to death, and only later do we find out that that very someone, the savior, was never officially there, or cannot be found, or most dramatically of all, was already dead! The drama here, the added mystery, is redolent of the movies, but perhaps no less powerful for that, particularly in an American society where life is still heavily influenced by media such as movies.

All of these examples are filled with pragmatic implication and orientation, and it is through Reagan's mastery of such forms—and certainly through his mastery of delivering such forms—that he became known as the "Great Communicator," or as we will consider him in this chapter, the "Great Storyteller."

The Political Story

Stories are central to our lives, we understand the world through them and the way in which they can be shared, repeated, and embellished. As Sartre (1965: 126) notes, "a man is always a teller of tales, he sees everything that happens to him through them; and he tries to live his own life as if he were telling a story." Storytelling is an essentially human process. As children, we learn to verbalize our experiences and to become "narrated selves." We learn, in turn, to understand others and to distinguish our own experiences from other shared experiences through forms of narration, or telling stories (Bruner, 1986). Within our "lifeworlds" (Husserl, 1936) stories help to shape an understanding of our shared sociocultural experience, and through stories we understand the intricate connection between language, culture, society, and power (Bakhtin, 1981).

The analysis of stories, or narratives, has a long history dating back to Aristotle, but it is in the last 30–40 years that there has been an explosion of interest in narrative work within the social and human sciences, sometimes referred to as the "narrative turn" (see Chase, 1995; Riessman, 2008). This "turn" represents the realization that narratives operate in a much wider sphere than written or oral texts. Narrative is much more fragmented than previous structural analysis suggests (Rumelhart, 1975; Mandler and Johnson, 1977).

Obviously, scholars interested in the literary genre have given specific attention to the structure of narrative, and terms like "narratology" and, interestingly, "narrative pragmatics" (see Prince, 1983; Bal, 1997) have been introduced to designate the way in which particular structural processes or routines exemplify and explain narrative practices. However, an interest in narrative has also attracted the attention of a myriad of disciplines with seemingly diverse motivations, including, among others, history, psychology, sociology, and sociolinguistics (see Polkinghorne, 1988; Bruner, 1990; Gee, 1991; Linde, 1993; Capps and Ochs, 1995; Bell, 2000; Mishler, 1999; Schiffrin, 2003; Phoenix and Sparkes, 2009). And even beyond such core academic disciplines we find narrative used as an explanatory tool in studies of occupational conflict, medical encounters, legal matters, and therapies and counseling (Sarbin, 1986; Kleinman, 1988; White and Epson, 1990; Rosenwald and Ochberg, 1992; Joffe, 1997; Greenhalgh and Hurwitz, 1998; Ryan, 2003).

Yet perhaps the most significant development in recent years has been a recognition of the core role played by narrative in everyday talk. De Fina and Georgakopoulou (2008) suggest that this shift has been marked in three main ways: first, by an increasing use of such areas as Conversational Analysis; second, an emphasis on the contextualizing aspect of narrative—that is, its role in constructing rather than reflecting the context of talk; and third, an increasing concentration on the use of social theory in explaining the processes and structure of talk in social interaction.

Despite the growth of interest in narratives, we are still no closer to an agreed-upon definition of narrative itself, or how it is distinct from a story. Indeed, some analysts have given up on this debate and treat the two as equivalent (see Ochs and Capps, 2001). One way to view the link between narrative and story is Hinchman and Hinchman's (1997) view, as described by Riessman (2004), that narratives are "storied ways of knowing and communicating." Taking this lead, this chapter concentrates on political narrative as a storied form of communication, that is, quite simply, the "political story."

As ways of knowing and communicating, stories offer particular opportunities to politicians. Through stories, politicians can provide glimpses of their own lives to the audience, they can use stories to indicate they understand the concerns and issues of the voters, and through stories they can generate audience emotions such as fear, excitement, apprehension, and enthusiasm. In the 2008 US presidential election campaign, Sarah Palin famously made use of her "hockey mom" story, utilizing the memorable sound bite: "What's the difference between a hockey mom and a pitbull? Lipstick." In her first address as the nominated vice presidential candidate, she also utilized the story of her own family and its members and linked them to the "American story." Hence, she invokes a son about to go off to war, loving and loyal daughters, and reflects on the care and pride shown to her child who has special needs. Here she relates her own experiences to the ordinary life, real or imagined, of many Americans:

> Our family has the same ups and downs as any other . . . the same challenges and the same joys. Sometimes even the greatest joys bring challenge. And children with special needs inspire a special love" (Sarah Palin, 2008 *RNC Convention Speech*).

Equally, her presidential running mate, John McCain, used his status as a war hero to exemplify the story of the stoic American soldier, willing to offer the ultimate sacrifice in defense of his country, while the Democratic presidential candidate, Barack Obama, made use of his own life experiences as evidence of the success that could be achieved by those less privileged sections of the community, and also, to affirm that that success comes through the values of hard work and education, and that these override or transcend race or class.

We find something similar in the British election of 2010, where we could see how the main protagonists drew on stories in similar ways. During that election, Britain had its first run of televised debates involving the leaders of the three main parties, Conservative, Labour, and Liberal-Democrat. All three leaders drew on stories in various ways, from the personal experience they had of poverty, crime, or tragic family health circumstances, to the use of stories relayed to them by constituents or people that they had met, people who had tales suited to exemplifying specific political claims or points. For example, on the issue of immigration, David Cameron, leader of the Conservative Party, told of his personal experience of meeting a Black man in Plymouth who was ashamed of Britain's "out-of-control immigration system"; Nick Clegg, leader of the Liberal Democrats, told of meeting a nurse at a Cardiff hospital who claimed that her ward was empty due to new rules preventing the National Health Service from employing sufficient numbers of foreign workers (both examples are from *The Guardian*, April 16, 2010).

But of all politicians in modern times, few exemplify the role of stories and their political potential as well as Ronald Reagan. In what follows, we want to show how Reagan makes use of a range of forms of storytelling, and we want to unpack these to highlight the underlying pragmatic force of such stories within the context of presidential communication. In doing this, we will argue that the "point"-based nature of stories (that is, they have a specific communicative goal; see Vipond and Hunt, 1984) generates pragmatic implications just as much as specific lexical items, phrases, or sentences.

The Storyteller from the White House

When Reagan first began making political speeches, he prepared all the materials himself, and in later years he was always sensitive to the need for the inclusion of certain content, or for the presentation of specified content in selected ways. One of his preferred ways of presenting sets of facts was in a narrative form. Reid Gold (1988: 163) cites the example of how Reagan revised the following information from a 1964 *Human Events* article by Rogers entitled "Welfare: $4,000 per poor family."

- There are 47 million families in America.
- One-fifth . . . are living in poverty because they have family incomes of $3,000 a year or less.
- Welfare officials [at all levels] spent $44 billion in 1962.
- If one-fifth of 47 million families are impoverished, that's 9.3 million poor families.
- If $44 billion was spent . . . it comes out to be more than $4,000 per family. . . .
- Direct relief to the poor comes only a bit more than $500 per year. . . .
- The balance of the welfare program is diverted to those who have less actual need for the money.

The reworked version of this became an integrated narrative that Reagan used on several occasions:

> Welfare spending is ten times greater than in the dark depths of the depression [a startling if unverified statement]. We are spending 45 billion dollars on welfare. Now do a little arithmetic and you will find that if we divided 45 billion dollars . . . we would be able to give each family $4,600 a year. . . . Direct aid to the poor, however, is running only about $600 per family, it seems that someplace there must be some overhead. (Ronald Reagan, quoted in Reid Gold, 1988: 164)

Reagan's sensitivity to linguistic presentation manifested itself in other similar and related ways that also enhance the structural and relational aspects of telling stories. Lawrence and Carpenter (2007) argue, for example, that much can be learned about Reagan's style from a review of his emendations in early drafts of speeches given to him by speechwriters. They note that Reagan would often add long handwritten comments, or modify and simplify words or phrases. One of the most prominent of these was the use of informal "contractions" and "qualifiers" (2007: 4). Reagan would often simplify forms through contraction as in "it's," "can't," "that's," "they're," and "we're." Such contractions enhance informality, and may assist in enhancing the communicative relationship with an audience. Reagan would also commonly make use of forms such as "Well," "Now," "So," and "But" at the start of sentences, along with others such as "anyway," "because," "oh," and "you know." These types of constructions are called "pragmatic markers" (or "discourse markers"; see Schiffrin, 1987, 2001; Fraser, 1999; Schourup, 1999; also Chapter 1 of this volume).

Pragmatic markers (PMs) function in variety of ways, for instance, marking causality or sequentiality, maintaining discourse coherence, and suggesting shifts in topic direction or expected outcomes. There is a large and expanding body of research on PMs (see, for example, Schiffrin, 1987, 2001; Lenk, 1997; Fraser, 1999; Norrick, 2001), ranging across issues such as their prosodic and grammatical status and their various functions in conversation, narrative, and other speech events. But according to Fraser (1999: 938) there is one thing all PMs have in common, which is that "they impose a relationship between some aspect of the discourse segment they are part of . . . and some aspect of the prior discourse segment." Consider the following:

John likes tea **but** Ronald likes coffee.
Fred bought the buns **so** Jim bought the ice cream.
We will not get there until eight, **anyway** the movie doesn't start until nine.
Well, you can eat the cake **but** I'm not going to.
Thelma left the party **because** she was unwell.

In these examples, PMs mark some aspect of the relationship between the parts, contrast (but), causality (so, because), reflection (anyway), shift in direction (well). This may frequently occur initially in the sentence, as suggested by Lawrence and Carpenter (2007 see above), but PMs may also perform similar functions in other sentential and discourse positions.

Reagan frequently made use of pragmatic markers such as those noted above. Consider the following uses of "so" (both examples from *Our Noble Vision*, March 2, 1984).

(1) Just as America has always been synonymous with freedom, **so,** too, should we become the symbol of peace across the Earth. I'm confident we can keep faith with that mission.

(2) **So**, our first responsibility is to keep America strong enough to remain free, secure, and at peace, and I intend to make sure that we do just that.

In the first case, **"so"** is marking an inference between a present state and a linked causal process with a future state. In the second, we see again a discourse link between what has been said and the connection to what comes next.

We can also see many examples of **"well"** in Reagan speeches (as in 3–5 below; all examples from his *Inaugural Address, 1981*).

(3) **Well**, this administration's objective will be a healthy, vigorous, growing economy that provides equal opportunity for all Americans, with no barriers born of bigotry or discrimination. Putting America back to work means putting all Americans back to work

(4) **Well**, the answer is an unequivocal and emphatic "yes." To paraphrase Winston Churchill, I did not take the oath.

(5) **Well**, I believe we, the Americans of today, are ready to act worthy of ourselves, ready to do what must be done to ensure happiness and liberty for ourselves, our children and our children's children.

Reagan makes use of these markers in a fairly standard sense, that is, as almost anyone, or any president, would use them, and there is nothing to suggest they are particularly suited for informal usage. For example, in a brief review of three randomly selected speeches from Bill Clinton and John F. Kennedy, there was a similar use of PMs. So Lawrence and Carpenter assumption that the use of these PMs set out some rhetorically informal pattern does not necessarily follow, since the forms they mention are classic universal pragmatic markers utilized by most people, including presidents, in most speech events.

However, when it comes to grammatical contraction, Lawerence and Carpenter (2007) may be on to something. Forms simplified through contraction such as "they're" or "can't" are the stylistic variants one would predict in more informal spoken styles (although there are also many other complicating linguistic factors: see Zwicky, 1970; Hiller, 1983; Kjeilmer, 1998). Indeed, as early as 1940, C. C. Fries commented:

> The language practices of conversation differ in many subtle ways from those used in formal writing. Most apparent is the abundance of contractions in the language of conversation. Thoroughly unnatural would sound the speech of those who in conversation did not constantly use *I'm, you'll, isn't, don't, aren't, they'd better, we've,* instead of the fully expanded *I am, you will, is not, do not, are not, they had better, we have.* And in similar fashion the formal writing that habitually employed such contractions would seem equally unnatural because of the impression of very informal familiarity which they would create. (Fries, 1940: 8)

It is not that contractions cannot be found in writing or in political speeches, but the choice is clearly a stylistic one. Consider the following variants of Winston Churchill's famous speech;

(a) We shall fight them on the beaches, we shall fight them on the landing ground, we shall fight in the fields and the streets, we shall fight in the hills; we shall never surrender.

(b) We'll fight them on the beaches, we'll fight them on the landing ground, we'll fight in the fields and streets, we'll fight in the hills, we'll never surrender.

In (a), of course, we also have the more old fashioned use of "shall" as opposed to "will," which we contracted in (b), although in modern English usage "will" and "shall" are now seen as equivalent. One could make a case that "shall" was more dramatic for Churchill's purposes, but the important thing to note is that the meaning of both (a) and (b) is the equivalent, so why contract, or why not contract? Some scholars have argued that "emphasis" is more easily maintained in non-contracted forms. But Nik Coupland points out in his book *Style* (2007) that linguistic differences are not just structural, they are also social markers. They are used, that is, to signal social facts such as gender, status, age, education, and, of course, formality and informality. In (a) and (b) we have a two sets of possibilities: "shall" versus "will" and "contracted" versus "non-contracted." In the original in this case a more formal choice of style was adopted.

Consider (c) and (d) from Reagan (*Noble Vision* 1984):

(c) **I'll** admit our critics are worried sick about the future of the economy. **They're** worried it might keep getting better and better.

(d) **I will** admit our critics are worried sick about the future of the economy. **They are** worried it might keep getting better and better.

Consider also (e) and (f) (*Noble Vision*, 1984):

(e) **It's** time to try again. We also seek a line-item veto to prevent pork barrel projects from passing just because **they're** attached to otherwise good legislation. **I'm** sure **we're** united by one goal.

(f) **It is** time to try again. We also seek a line-item veto to prevent pork barrel projects from passing just because **they are** attached to otherwise good legislation. **I am** sure **we are** united by one goal.

As with Churchill, the semantics of those sentences containing contracted and non-contracted forms are equivalent. The fact that Reagan has made changes to his speeches to signal contraction is therefore the most important point. When we reshape our language in such ways, we are performing what sociolinguists such as Allan Bell (1984) call "audience design," that is, designing language for an audience in terms of how the speaker wants them to understand the social dimensions of the message, or how he wants them to perceive the speaker himself, and this includes whether one wants to accentuate formality or informality. The fact that Reagan has been making specific changes in his texts to make them more informal, plus his propensity for storytelling in general, both serve to highlight the image he wants to display to the general public, that is, that he is a straight-forward man, not focused on the complicated formal processes of politics, but rather the simple process of getting things done, and getting them done right!

A similar point can be made for Reagan's famous use of a range of ironic comments. Most of these comments were constructed with the objective of engendering humor, as we have seen above (see also Chapter 1), and here are some more (see Kurtzman, Ronald Reagan quotes, About.com: political humor; http// political humor/about.com):

- ¤ Honey I'm not worried about the deficit. It is big enough to take care of itself.
- ¤ I want you to know that also I will not be making age an issue of this campaign. I am not going to exploit, for political purposes, my opponent's youth and inexperience. (debating with Walter Mondale in the 1984 campaign)
- ¤ I notice that everyone who is for abortion has already been born.
- ¤ I'm afraid I can't use a mule. I have several hundred up on Capitol Hill.
- ¤ The nine most terrifying words in the English language: "I'm from the government and I'm here to help."
- ¤ Politics is supposed to be the second oldest profession. I've come to realize that it bears a resemblance to the first.

Part of Reagan's legacy, however, is that some intentional and ironic humor gets lost among the many similarly humorous comments that seem to be mistakes, or errors in logic.

- ¤ Trees cause more pollution than automobiles.
- ¤ All the waste in a year from a nuclear plant can be stored under a desk.
- ¤ The state of California has no business subsidizing intellectual curiosity.
- ¤ We are trying to get unemployment to go up, and I think we are going to succeed.

Despite any errors, Reagan's use of humor clearly contributes to the informal nature of Reagan's style. It is not simply the use of irony, since this may have many functions, but rather it is the playful manipulation of language that is important. Irony has been given significant attention in recent years (see review in Gibbs and Colston, 2007, 2012), with increasing effort expended on explaining how irony is cognitively processed during comprehension. Originally it was assumed that ironic utterances simply functioned to generate an inference that was the opposite of what was said. So a golfer missing an important putt might hear his opponent or partner saying "nice putt," while meaning exactly the opposite, that is, that it was a bad or terrible putt. It was soon realized, however, that ironic utterances could function in a host of ways, and today there are several different theories which attempt to explain how irony works (see, for example, Clark and Gerrig, 1984; Wilson and Sperber, 1992; Kumon-Nakamura et al., 1995).

More important from our perspective has been recent interest in the social nature of irony (see, for example, Gibbs, 2002). While it is important that we understand the underlying cognitive and pragmatic processes of irony, the question is, why be ironic in the first place? Given that ironic utterances are not interpreted literally, and that they are often used to make negative comments, they carry not only the risk of misinterpretation but also disapproval. However, counter to this, it has been argued that because irony involves both literal and non-literal meanings it may act to attenuate the social negativity of an ironic comment (see Dews et al., 1995). Alternatively, the "contrast theory" of ironic utterances (see Gibbs and Colston, 2007) suggests that in some cases the literal/non-literal contrast can actually be used to enhance negativity. While there are different views here, regarding the potential risk in using irony, if the intention is to be humorous, this may militate any negative outcomes (see Gibbs, 2002; Goffman, 1955; Haig, 1988; Rogan and Hammer, 1994). Humor within social interaction tends to create and maintain a relaxed informality, and it is in this sense that Reagan makes use of irony. So the combination of Reagan's use of irony, selected PMs, and grammatically contracted forms assists in generating informal contexts suitable for telling a story.

There is a downside to this, however. As noted by Lewis (1987), among others, Reagan had many critics, both during and after his presidency, who deplored his level of rhetorical skill precisely because of his informal style. Yet as we noted above, many of these critics failed to see that Reagan's success was not one, or only one, of logical debate or formal argumentation, it was one of *communication as narrative*. From the perspective of rhetorical studies, Lewis's analysis of Reagan's narrative reveals that he utilized a number of thematics around which he told stories: the myth of the American nation, the role of the individual (including Reagan himself), the importance of the moral view, and a belief that Americans and American history reflect the natural and successful outcome of various struggles. It is certainly correct, as Fisher (1987) has asserted, that everyday life is not always about the rational coordination and solution of problems in a logical and organized manner, but rather about sharing our experience through stories, and through these stories, to also clarify and resolve issues (see also Bruner, 1986, 1990), on narrative and logic as the two core forms of human knowing). However, the question is, how is all this actually achieved? What is it about stories that allows us to get things done, to have things believed, and to create personal and shared relationships across social divides such as social class, age, and gender?

There have been a significant number of rhetorical studies of Reagan's style, and while insightful, they often provide labels for linguistic output rather than a core linguistic analysis. For example, suggesting that Reagan has a propensity for "anecdote," or that he uses stories to exemplify the "jeremiad," gives a name or names to the sermon style or the simplified, often amusing, story form, but it doesn't tell us *how* these are produced, and still less how they might be processed (see Wilson and Sperber, 2012). We have seen some structural and pragmatic alternative explanations above in the form of PMs, irony, and grammatical contraction, and we believe that these, operating alongside Reagan's greatest tool, the use of storytelling, reflect specific audience design sensitivity, which, while not "high rhetoric," is functionally successful.

What's the Story?

It has been noted that Reagan would often make use of the phrase, "There's a story," and on several occasions it was said that he told a story about storytelling (see Reid Gold, 1988). In *Reagan Speaks*, Erickson (1985) discusses the full range of Reagan's storytelling and provides an excellent analysis of how Reagan makes use of analogies, allegories, homilies, stock characters, quotations, and imagery. The following are selected examples from this range: the first links two stories, one about an American who receives the Congressional Medal of Honor, and the other is about a Soviet citizen who received an equivalent honor in his own country. The next two are examples of the use of analogy and homily. All of these examples provide instances of the Reagan storytelling style (these examples are taken from *Reagan Speaks*: 5–6):

> (6) (a) A B-17 coming back across the Channel from a raid over Europe was badly shot up by anti-aircraft, the ball turret that hung underneath the belly of the plane had taken a hit. The young ball-turret gunner was wounded, and they couldn't get him out of the turret while they were flying. But over the Channel, the plane began to lose altitude, and the commander had to order "Bail Out." And as the men started to leave the plane, the last one to leave—the boy, understandably, knowing he was left behind to go down with the plane, cried out in terror. The last man to leave the plane saw the Commander sit down on the floor. He took the boy's hand and said, "Never mind, son, we'll ride it down together." Congressional Medal of Honor posthumously awarded.
>
> (b) The second part, or related story, is told because Reagan claimed that he had read that the Soviet Union had awarded its highest medal of honor to a man without explaining why. Intrigued, Reagan enlisted the help of a journalist and discovered that the man was a Spaniard, who had lived in Moscow, Mexico, and Cuba, and who had spent 23 years in a Mexican jail. "Finally, the truth came out. He was the man who buried that ice axe mountaineers [*sic*] mountain climbers carry in the head of Leon Trotsky . . . they in another society gave their highest honor to a political assassin. We gave ours to a man who would sacrifice his life simply to bring comfort to a boy who had to die. . . . I think that explains the great difference between our

societies. . . . The bedrock of our strength is America's moral and spiritual character."

(7) Example (a) here was given in a speech to the Building and Construction Trades Department of the AFL-C10 in 1981. The point being made by the story will be obvious enough. Example (b) is a classic of its kind, and exemplifies graphically Reagan's ability to manipulate the emotional states of his audience. This story is about American GIs in Great Britain during World War II, and relates to the principle of American family values.

(a) I've told before, I have a neighbor out in my neighborhood in California who was building his own home. And he got so fed up with all the paper work and the regulations required that he pasted them all together into one strip of paper, put up two poles in front of the half finished house, and strung them up across there. The strip of paper was 250 feet long.

(b) Driving around the English countryside after a day of filming, Reagan stopped at a pub run by "an elderly couple, very tiny." As her husband hovered in the background, "the rather motherly looking lady," who served Reagan, recalled the American GIs who had been stationed down the road during the war: "She said, 'they used to come in here all the time in the evenings and have songfests.' She said, 'They called me Mom and the old man Pop.' And as she went on her voice was softening and she wasn't looking at me anymore; she was looking kind of beyond into her memories. Her eyes were beginning to fill. And then she said, 'It was Christmas Eve. The old man and me were here all alone. And all of a sudden the door burst open, and in they came with presents for the both of us.' And the tears now had overflowed and were on her cheeks. And she said, 'Big strappin' lads they was from a place called Ioway.' By this time my eyes were a little filled also."

This last example is one that many might find melodramatic, particularly as it is coming from a politician who held the highest political office in the world. The problem is that the accentuated melodrama seems at times overly contrived, resonant of the movie world rather than the real world. Frequently, however, the intellectualism of commentators gets in the way of recognizing the ability Reagan had to relate to his audience, and to touch emotions as well as minds (see Lewis, 1987). This is what made him the "Great Communicator."

Analysts may also fail to fully appreciate what this epithet indicates. In a direct analysis of Reagan's language, Geis (1987), for example, raises doubts as to whether Reagan fully deserved the description of the "Great Communicator." It is not that Geis does not recognize Reagan's considerable ability as a speaker, but he was concerned with Reagan's difficulties with "extemporaneous responses" (1987: 169). In analyzing a number of press conferences, Geis shows how Reagan would continually interrupt both himself, and the flow of his answers, in an effort to add further information and particularize specific points. This is a legitimate criticism, but it doesn't completely attend to the question (contradiction) that

Geis is highlighting, that is, how anyone who is a "great communicator" could often fail to communicate. There are, of course, many different levels and layers of communication. Geis is focusing on the interaction of politicians and journalists in the professional and technical political forum of press conferences. Here, the politician is dealing with policies rather than ideals, with bold facts rather than the images constructed by stories. If we shift the communicative context to one in which Reagan operates with a real audience, the public, then a different picture emerges. Here Reagan is playing to the crowd—playing a role and performing it well.

It is for this reason that Reid Gold (1988) is much nearer to the truth when she points out that Reagan's success as a communicator was dependent on his adaptation of the principles of an "oral tradition," for example, the use of formulae, mythical presentations, metaphorical hyperbole, enthymematic argument, thematic simplicity, and, of course, the telling of stories. Within this tradition, the literal expectation of accuracy highlighted by Geis disappears as the audience becomes enlivened with the ebb and flow of a dramatic presentation. Reagan ". . . learned that abstract and recondite arguments left audiences sitting on their hands, unmoved, while well timed stories and cleverly phrased anecdotes attracted the attention-and applause- of audiences . . . Reagan's ability to articulate the thinking of his audiences in aurally attractive forms has been one of the most important components of his success. More than many contemporary political figures, Ronald Reagan has achieved his current status through oral discourse" (Reid Gold, 1988: 162).

Telling the Story

There are many ways in which one can consider the linguistic production of stories. One can focus on their internal structure and organization, the thematic roles of phrase and clause types, the use of cohesive devices, the distribution of structural forms (verbs, nouns, adjectives, etc.), the use of free and narrative clauses, and so on (see Labov, 1972, 1997; also essays in Thornborrow and Coates, 2005). One specific approach to the analysis of storytelling relevant here may be found in the work of Livia Polyani (1985), as presented in her book *Telling the American Story*. Polyani is one of a respected line of scholars who have been developing ways of analyzing the structural organization of narratives in general and stories in particular. Polyani defines stories as a type of narrative activity: "stories along with plans, simultaneous 'blow by blow' descriptions, generic narratives about 'the way it used to be' or 'what usually happens,' and reports of past activities are all narratives" (Polyani, 1985: 9). On stories she says, "Stories . . . are specific affirmative, past time narratives which tell about a series of events (i.e. more than one) which did take place at specific unique moments in a unique past time world" (Polyani, 1985: 10). We have already encountered several stories of this kind above. A slightly different type, but for us clearly still a story, is the following reported event (taken from a speech by Ronald Reagan; see Balitzer and Bonetto 1983: 47):

> Recently a judge told me of an incident in his court. A fairly young woman with six children, pregnant with her seventh, came to him for a divorce. Under his questioning it became apparent her husband did not share this desire. Then the whole story came out. Her husband was a labourer earning $250 a month. By divorcing him she could get an $80 dollar raise. She was eligible for $350 dollars a month from the Aid to Dependent Children Program. She had been talked into divorce by two friends who had already done this very kind of thing.

This example is one we want to consider in some detail, but let us first note why this is a story. One might argue, for example, that this is a report of a story and not a story itself. Such taxonomic refinements are not of interest or of specific relevance here. In general terms, this is a story about a young woman who attempted to get a divorce for very specific reasons. It is told in the affirmative past tense (event) manner as outlined by Polyani, and it is the kind of example that one might find in a variety of speech event types, from informal conversation to political speeches.

One of the points of presenting a story, according to Polyani, is to have the story evaluated in relation to its relevance within a speech event (debate, speech, conversation, etc.; a point also made by Labov, 1972). Polyani argues that participants have a shared worldview and that "[t]he narrator relies upon this common understanding to constrain the interlocutors to infer the same point from the goings on in the story world which he himself infers" (Polyani, 1985: 13). If we refer back to Reagan's story in (6a), for example, the inferences Reagan draws as a result of this story are that heroism and morality are viewed radically differently in democratic as opposed to communist societies. He relies on his audience to distinguish, as he does, the difference between a commander who offers his own life to help comfort a young soldier who is about to die, and a representative of a communist state who murders an individual simply because that individual may have had a disagreement with the aims of the state. Further, on the basis of this information, other inferences may follow: that communist states cannot be trusted, that they are evil, that democratic states offer freedom, produce people of character and heroism, and basically that democracy is good and communism is bad. This information is not generated by the story alone, however, but is shaped by the total framework of the discourse within which the story is embedded (and, of course, by each individual's own stock of experiences and knowledge in interpreting the story). A story's relevance within a political speech is revealed not only within the individual story world, but also within the world being constructed by the speech, a schematic world within which certain actions have inferred consequences of both a cultural and political nature.

Let us return, then, to the Reagan's story of *the judge and the divorce*, presented above. This story forms part of Reagan's famous 1964 address "A Time for Choosing." Within this speech, Reagan covered a variety of his favorite themes, such as the threat of communism to the democratic ideals of America and Americans, and the freedom of the individual in the face of government control. Interestingly, in this speech, his phrase "the most dangerous enemy known to man?" (referring to the communist threat to the US), was echoed in later years by the now infamous "evil empire" statement used with reference to the Soviet Union. However, our story is targeted to another Reagan concern—housing and welfare.

To remind ourselves of the story let us first present it as a series of individual statements:

1. (Recently) A judge told me of an incident in his court.
2. A (fairly young) woman (with six children, pregnant with her seventh) came to him for a divorce.
3. (Under his questioning, it became apparent) her husband did not share this desire.
4. (Then the story came out)
5. Her husband was a laborer.
6. ((her husband was)) earning $250 a month
7. By divorcing him she could get an $80 raise.
8. She was eligible for $350 a month from the Aid to Dependent Children program.
9. She had been talked into divorce by two friends (who had already done this very thing).

This breakdown of the story has reduced it to its basic propositional form, those phrases in brackets being seen as modifying elements (but no less meaningful for that; see below), which do not affect the general propositional claims of the total story. Taking our lead from the general principle of a *story paraphrase*, as suggested by Polyani (1985), but in this case reducing the story to its base propositional form, we would have something like the following:

A judge told me of an incident in his court. A woman came to him for a divorce. Her husband did not share this desire. Her husband was a laborer earning $250 a month. By divorcing him she could get an $80 raise. She was eligible for $350 a month from the Aid to Dependent Children Program. She had been talked into divorce by two friends.

By reducing the story in this way, we may highlight a number of interesting issues. First, in a number of ways the story will not make sense in its base form without the inclusion of selected aspects of general knowledge about the world and general assumptions about discourse organization. The first three sentences are perfectly acceptable on their own, and introduce the basic theme of the story, which is about a woman who wants a divorce, and a husband who does not. We are next told that the husband earns $250 a month, and that through divorce the wife will receive an $80 raise. The result of this is that the wife will receive $350 from the Aid to Dependent Children program. This generates a number of questions. What is the relationship between this $80 raise and the divorce? And what has this got to do with the $350 from the Aid to Dependent Children program?

To understand what is going on, and to answer these questions, listeners (readers) would require further background information, or a set of general assumptions (see previous discussions on shared knowledge/assumption). For example, if we add the following piece of information: "A wife with X number of children receives aid for dependent children when divorced," we can make use of this to construct a set of general input statements something like:

(a) The wife receives $X while she remains married.
(b) If she is divorced she will receive $Y.
(c) Therefore if $Y is greater than $X the wife would be financially better off if divorced.

Statement (c) follows where $Y is greater than $X, which is, of course, the case in our example story. The general process represented by (a), (b), and (c) is essentially one of natural deduction (see Sperber and Wilson, 1995). It should be noted, in this context, that there are many deductions one might make from the premises supplied above, but in a simple truth-based context, if (a) and (b) are both true, then (c) must be true (since $Y is greater than $X: as indicated by the figures in the story). These premises and conclusion do not present a case for divorce per se, but merely highlight one factual result in this particular example. The syllogism is certainly not a formal argument in favor of divorce, only a description from one state of affairs to another state of affairs, where one state of affairs may be shown to be logically dependent on the other.

Financial issues will certainly play a part in influencing an individual's judgment about whether she should remain married, or whether she should sue for divorce, but the financial context is only one element in making such judgments. Nevertheless, since we have no further information in this story, it is the only detail we have on which to base our judgments. This is an important fact in the presentation of the story, but in order to fully understand what is taking place, we need to explore in more detail the overall nature of the story, and the broader cultural and political inferences that this organization produces.

As we have a noted previously, individual sentences may carry inferences of different types. For example, a sentence such as "I'll give you $5 if you mow the lawn" invites the inference "if you don't mow the lawn I won't give you $5"; and a sentence like "some of the boys enjoyed the party" implies that "not all of the boys enjoyed the party" (see Chapter 1; also Lycan,1991; Levinson, 2000; Carston, 2002; Recanati, 2010). Green (1989) argues that similar inferential processes may also be applied beyond sentences to texts. She suggests that when we are provided with a text, we assume the author has some plan or strategy that he/she wants listeners to access. Further, we are also to assume that this strategy or plan operates beyond the internal structure of the text (as in cohesion, for example). Green (1989: 101–102) provides us with the following examples to clarify her point:

> (a) The following days were unlike any that had gone before. There wasn't a man on the ranch who didn't know of Saturday's race and the conditions under which it would be run. They gave any excuses to get near the black stallion's corral. [Walter Farley, The Black Stallion, p. 199, New York: Random House]
>
>   (b) The sun climbed higher, and with its ascent the desert changed. There was nothing Lucy liked so much as the smell and feel of fur. One evening, after dark, she crept away and tried to open the first gate, but swing and tug as she might she could not budge the pin.

Green suggests that text (b) has a similar type of cohesive structure to that found in (a), but that it is not possible to make sense of (b) because:

> Coherence . . . depends not on the properties of the text components themselves, either individually, or in relation to each other, but on the extent to which effort is required to construct a reasonable plan to attribute to the text producer in producing the text. (1989: 102–103)

The problem with (b), then, is that there is no clear connection between the propositions, and this makes it difficult for us to construct a world or mental model within which the total text makes sense; or in Green's terms, there is no way one can interpret the author's goal or plan from the text as presented.

The point of all this is that in attempting to understand a text, we search not only for surface cohesion, but also for rational coherence, and we will use all the means of understanding at our disposal to make any presented discourse meaningful. Only when we cannot do so do we say that the text doesn't make any sense (or that it fails to be relevant, in Sperber and Wilson's (1995) terms).

Bearing these general comments in mind, let us return to both our propositionally reduced version of Reagan's story, and to the original and full version of the story. In looking at both of these, it is quite clear that the internal coherence of both is sound. The move from one proposition to the next is logical and forms a coherent discourse type. But there is one element in the structure of the full story that is left open, the point of the story itself; the reasoning that takes the audience from the wife who wants a divorce for monetary gain to the relevance of this within the political speech. Any listener who achieves a general understanding of the story will also attempt to place the story within some larger and relevant context that allows her to understand the *point* of the story (similar to Sperber and Wilson's [1995] *Relevance Theory*). It is here that it seems legitimate to draw upon other information that will assist us in discovering the speaker's goal in telling this story. In doing this, we can look at the positioning of the story within the overall speech, along with its function as a real world critique of those government welfare plans that encourage people to abandon their marriages for financial gain.

The logic is something like this: If this wife only wants a divorce in order to achieve monetary profit, and this profit has only been made possible by a government plan, then it is this very government plan which is the cause (at one level) of the divorce. Since the activity of divorce is not generally viewed as something positive, then we can further infer that a government plan is having specific negative effects on society. Clearly, most members of society would not wish this to be the case and would, therefore, want such plans changed or removed. And this is exactly Reagan's point: he too wants such plans removed because he sees them as socially divisive, and this is, in fact, the point of the story. In achieving his general goal, however, Reagan has also included in his story a series of other cultural assumptions which reflect more than a simple logic about the effects of government plans.

Ideologies and Stories

In the previous section we looked at the propositional basis of the story about *the judge and the divorce*, and argued that it contained an underlying logic linking the wife's actions with their financial consequences. There are many other aspects of the presentation of this story that we have ignored, and in order to make sense of these, we must go beyond the simple propositional form. But first let us remind ourselves of what our earlier analysis revealed by repeating the syllogism constructed above:

(a) The wife receives $X while she remains married.
(b) If she is divorced she will receive $Y.
(c) Therefore the wife would be financially better off if divorced.

Now if we accept that premise (b) is only possible where the government provides financial aid, and that the interaction of (b) and (c) only leads to the consideration of divorce where the levels of government support are greater than the income already received, then it becomes obvious that the issue of divorce would not arise for the wife (in financial terms) where (b) and (c) are affected by the government either removing aid, or adjusting the level of that aid. If $Y is less than $X, for example, then in purely financial terms the wife would be better off staying married.

(a) The wife receives $X while she remains married.
(b) If she is divorced she will receive $Y.
(c) Therefore* the wife would be financially better off staying married.

*remember that in this case $Y is less than $X

The argument grounded within Reagan's story presents a classic conservative case for less government interference (and it is an argument that has been echoed in the UK and many other countries, particularly in relation to unemployment). The argument is, basically, that governments should not encourage, through financial incentives, certain types of social behavior like unemployment, divorce, or single-parent families. But the problem of course is that individuals making a choice about whether they should stay married do not always see this as only a financial matter.

But sometimes there are other cases where providing financial support for divorce or separation would actually be positive. Consider that a liberal counter-argument to Reagan's position would consider those women who are mistreated by their husbands but yet are forced to stay married because they cannot afford to get divorced.

Let us explore more closely some of the real world implications of Reagan's story. In particular, we will examine how these are revealed through the way in which the propositional base, delimited above, is modified by various linguistic forms. We will be interested, initially, in how the language reveals an ideological loading, that is, in how the linguistic selection provides a particular ideological context within which to interpret the story.

The term "ideology" is difficult to pin down in exact terms (see, for example, van Dijk, 1998). It is a word that (paradoxically) often carries political connotations, but it is also a term that may be used to reflect a particular life view. In his text on the subject, Thompson (1990) discusses the disparate nature of ideology under such headings as "Ideology as belief" and "Ideology as rationality." Thompson notes in general terms, however, that ". . . the theory of ideology has commonly sought to examine the ways in which 'meanings' or 'ideas' affect the conceptions or activities of the individuals and groups which make up the social world" (1984: 73). We are interested in ideology here, because of the central relationship between ideology and language, a relationship summed up by Thompson's claim that:

> . . . to study language is, in some part, and in some way, to study language in the social world. . . . The theory of ideology, thus enriched and elaborated through a reflection on language, enriches our view of language. (1984: 3)

In looking at ideological construction within Reagan's story, we should begin by considering the general ideological context of the story. From the beginning, it is made clear that this is not just an example of the effects that arise when the government interferes in people's lives, but a statement of specific social roles within society, and the part these roles play in affirming particular ideological forms of life.

For example, the story is introduced as one that has been told to Reagan by a *judge*, a legal guardian of the state—but more important in the political context, someone whose job it is to uphold the law independently of political concerns (although how far the American system of appointments allows this is a matter of debate). In this sense, this is not a story from someone who has a biased view, but someone whose job it is to decide that which is legal and acceptable to society. In this sense, Reagan has generated a story told to him by an individual who has a significant degree of social credibility, and also someone who is assumed to be politically neutral, at least in making legal decisions.

Having established the social and political credibility of his source at the outset, Reagan next contrasts this source with the main character of the story, "the woman." In the propositionally reduced version of the story "the woman" is presented as a simple noun phrase, and while this was useful as a first step in understanding the story, it masks the potential stylistic versatility of noun phrases for expansiveness and complexity One can talk about "the tall woman, the tall beautiful woman, the tall beautiful young woman." In each of these cases, what grammarians refer to as the head of the phrase (in this example "the woman") is modified in some way; first, in terms of height (tall), then in terms of appearance (beautiful), and then in relation to age (young). Modifying the head of the noun phrase in this way is referred to as *premodification*; thus "tall," "beautiful," and "young" act as premodifiers. Not surprisingly, perhaps, the head of the noun phrase may also be postmodified, as in "the tall beautiful woman with the strange and mysterious eyes."

In Reagan's introduction of "the woman," he makes use of expansion through both pre- and post-modification, we are introduced not simply to "a woman" but to "a fairly young woman." In this expansion, adverbial premodification emphasizes the relative importance of age in the description of this woman. The phrase is then further expanded through postmodification to produce: "A fairly young woman with six children, pregnant with her seventh." Such noun phrase modifications are clearly not stylistic accidents. It is Reagan's goal to provide us with characterizations that we may utilize in constructing an interpretation of the story.

One way in which these modifications operate is to direct how we construct our mental picture of the central character of the story. First we are presented with an indefinite noun phrase, "a woman"; as a result, we have very little information to go on, and any initial characterization is constrained within a generic framework for *women*, within which we are being asked to consider a single example. We next discover that this woman is "fairly young"; this allows us at least to delimit a specific subset from the total set of *women*. This subset may be further delimited following postmodification, "with six children, pregnant with her seventh." The number six is not neutral, however, and we must ask why this numerical value is meaningful in this context? When numbers are attached to certain activities, they affect interpretation in either a positive or negative direction (see Potter et al., 1991) . For example, it may be more negative to drink 10 pints of beer as opposed to one, but, in health terms, it is more positive to run three miles regularly as opposed to running one hundred yards regularly. In relation to the number of children a woman has, we must bear in mind two points. First, in the West the number of children per family has been falling; second, this fall in numbers is relative to the socioeconomic class of the family, with lower socioeconomic groups tending to have larger families.

In one direction, then, the number of children becomes important in generating selected social interpretations. But it also becomes important within the basic form of the story, where monetary issues are involved. Remember we noted that the woman would be financially better off if divorced, because she would get funds from the Aid for Dependent Children Program. She would receive such funds because she would be divorced and the children would be dependent on her. But the actual amount she would receive would be affected by the number of children she has. A woman with six children (and a seventh on the way) would clearly gain more from the system than a woman with fewer children.

The social impact of this purely economic fact is brought out as the story proceeds. After we have been introduced to the woman, we are then told she approached a judge for divorce: "(she) came to him (the judge) for a divorce." The use of "came" indicates an intentional directionality, that is, the woman has been active in seeking out the judge, and therefore active in seeking the divorce. This is contrasted with the position of her husband: "Under his (the judge's) questioning it became apparent her husband did not share this desire."

There are a number of interesting issues here. First, the husband's views on the divorce only emerge under questioning by the judge. The positional preposition "under" may be collocated in certain contexts with negative outcomes: *under cross-examination; under stress; under pressure; under scrutiny; undernourished; under fire; underclass.* As Lakoff and Johnson (1980) have noted, we tend to understand our world within the frame of guiding metaphors (see also Lakoff, 2002, 2008; Gibbs, 2008; Semino, 2008). Hence, many of our social, moral, and political beliefs are shaped by such guiding metaphors. One of these metaphors is *argument as war* (Lakoff and Johnson, 1980), with associated concepts such as "attacking the argument," "a weak argument," and an "indefensible argument." Lakoff's recent research on metaphor and politics (Lakoff, 2002) has examined conservative American rhetoric versus liberal American rhetoric, within the core frame of *nation as a family*, with contrasting models of strict parent (conservative) versus family as "nutrient" (liberal) and associated values and policies, such as approaches to taxation. From this perspective, we can also apply the metaphorical frame in which *up* is positive and *down* is negative; and in relation to the present example, *under* falls within the metaphorical frame of *down is bad* (see also Stapleton and Wilson, 2010). In this sense, then, it is the judge, as the legal guardian, who discovers through his scrutiny that this divorce may not be as straightforward as the woman claims. This claim is further validated in the next sentence of the story: "Then the whole story came out." It is the judge's questions that have forced the woman to tell the truth, to provide, that is, the real reason behind her request for a divorce. This reason, as we have discussed, is purely financial: the purpose of the divorce is to gain further money under the Aid to Dependent Children Program.

The stylistic modifications and choices Reagan makes are clearly selected to confirm a conservative ideology of the poor as lazy and intent on manipulating the system for their own gain, as opposed to working to solve their own problems. Although Reagan's story is told in 1964, the very same ideological points were raised again in the 1980s, and have become relevant again in 2012 in both the United States, Britain, and Europe, all of which faced major financial difficulties and were forced to reduce the extent of state support to the unemployed, the single parent, and the immigrant. Within Britain in the 1980s the term "spongers" was used to designate individuals who lived off the state without making any attempt to support themselves or their families. The use of this term caused a heated debate between conservative and socialist politicians. The Labour Party argued that the term was one of approbation, and noted that many of those claiming state benefits were forced to do so through no fault of their own; they did not deny, however, that one would always find a minority who will attempt to manipulate the system. The Conservatives, while never claiming that the majority of claimants were simply "sponging" from the state, nevertheless expended a great deal of energy in attempting to make sure that only those most in need would receive the necessary help, and that those capable of looking after themselves should be encouraged to do so.

Interestingly, the 1980s Conservative government in Britain, and more recently in the Conservative/Lib-Dem coalition of 2013, became concerned with exactly the same problem that Reagan's story was constructed to highlight. In this case, however, there were stories of young women who became pregnant outside marriage in order to make gains from single parent allowances (an issue that also arose in the mid-1990s under a Labour government). Such views of women in general, and in particular the woman in Reagan's story, may seem harsh and uncaring. In this sense it is particularly appropriate that the story of the *judge and the divorce* should end as it does. At the end of the story we are told of the woman that "She had been talked into divorce by two friends who had already done this very kind of thing." In story terms, this represents a form of *resolution* (Labov and Waletzky, 1967), where potential conflicts and confusions are reconciled. It now seems that the wife is not necessarily to blame for her actions. She had been goaded into the divorce by friends, and tempted by a system that makes people financially better off (in certain circumstances) when they are divorced. Reagan's aim was to highlight the limitations of a particular government scheme, not to attack the character of this particular woman. By providing the final resolution in the form he does, Reagan makes sure that any negative reaction is reserved for the system and not for the individual woman herself.

Myths, Schemas, and Stories

There are a couple of questions raised by our analysis of Reagan's story. Why should anyone go beyond a set of basic propositional facts? And how do the stylistic and structural selections generate a specific view of a political world operating beyond the confines of the story—a world in which the poor may be lazy, manipulative, greedy, misguided, and easily influenced, and in which women abandon husbands and destroy families for monetary gain? Such a world, if it exists, only exists where governments are so tardy as to tempt the weak into negative actions, as opposed to encouraging them to adopt correct practices of honesty and hard work. So goes the conservative ideology. But why should hearers construct such a world? And in what way(s) does the story play a part in both the creation and maintenance of such worlds?

One way in which we may understand the political function of stories is through the formulation of what Geis (1987) and Edelman (1988) refer to as "political myths." The term "myth" is used here not to evoke fiction, but rather to indicate a set of beliefs (see also Gamson, 1996 on "frames"). Edelman suggests that political language may serve to evoke particular myths that function as explanatory frameworks for political action. Edelman distinguishes the following myths (adapted from Geis, 1987: 21):

i. The Conspiratorial Enemy: "the myth of a hostile outgroup plotting to commit harmful acts," which is perceived as "different, homogeneous, highly potent or omnipotent, and conspiring to harm the in group"

ii. The Valiant Leader: "the view that the political leader is benevolent and effective in saving people from danger," and that he or she exhibits the qualities of courage, aggressiveness and ability to cope

iii. United we stand: the belief that a group-nation, a state, a party, can achieve victory over its enemies if it will only work, sacrifice, and obey its leaders.

The argument is that certain linguistic features, or selections, within political language operationalize these myths, for instance, the use of what Edelman calls "the grandiloquent speech." This may be seen in Kennedy's famous phrase, "Ask not what your country can do for you; ask what you can do for your country." According to Edelman, this statement may be explained in that "we normally associate the usual deployment of adverb and accusative pronoun with Biblical and with eloquent oratory of the past, and we respond to the poetry of these associations."

However, we may not always require grand or archaic language to generate mythic worlds. Different styles will operate equally well within their own domains. Consider the following two extracts from the speeches of John F. Kennedy and Lyndon Johnson.

REMARKS IN SEATTLE AT THE SILVER ANNIVERSARY DINNER HONORING SENATOR WARREN MAGNUNSON

This state was half sagebrush. The Columbia River ran unharnessed to the sea. There was no atomic energy plant at Hanford, no aluminum plants, no dams or locks, no up river navigation. Today there are more than a million acres of new fertile farmland, more than fifty thousand men working in the aluminium plants, millions of kilowatts of electrical energy are produced by a vast complex of hydro-electric power plants—the Columbia has been tamed and great ships sail its waters. (cited in Hart, 1987: 22)

REMARKS AT THE SWEARING IN OF HOMER THORNBERRY

This is a very happy occasion for and Ladybird and me and all the members of our family. We are so pleased we could be honored with the presence of Judge Brown this morning, Judge Spears and Judge Jones, who is a long time personal friend of Judge Thornberry and a former partner of his. Homer and Eloise have been with us the last few days while they went through the necessary constitutional requirements of getting confirmed, and we have enjoyed their presence so much.

I don't know of anyone that is missed more from Washington than this wonderful Thornberry family. But I know, too, that the people that they serve in this are of the United States are very happy that they could be here. . . . So, it is a peculiar delight for us to come back here to the porch of our little home and ask the Thornberry family, and the Engles, and the Thornberry children, to come here to see Homer administered the oath as circuit judge of the Fifth Judicial District, in the Fifth Circuit Court, in the presence of his neighbors, here, and some of the best friends he has in the world. (cited in Hart, 1987: 27)

In the Kennedy extract, we have the dramatic and heightened tone of "the grandiloquent speech." One cannot doubt the poetic associations in phrases such as: "the Columbia has been tamed and great ships sail its waters"; or "This state was half sagebrush. The Columbia River ran unharnessed to the sea." In Johnson's case we have the common everyday tone of sentimentality. There is simplicity and homeliness about what Johnson says. Whereas Kennedy creates grand and heroic images, Johnson paints pictures of the local scene with family and relational values at the core. In both cases, although styles may differ, myths are being maintained and constructed. Kennedy gives us the valiant leader, the brave and true nation; and Johnson gives us the homeliness and friendliness of the people, the core values of American family life.

It is not only style that may be used in myth or frame creation; the very nature of argument structure itself may also be utilized. Consider the use of historical analogy in the build-up to the invasion of Iraq in 2003. One argument

compared Saddam Hussein to Hitler and the used the generic myth that all dictators behave in exactly the same way.

The use of a "Nazi analogy" by pro-war advocates can be reformulated as
a "symptomatic argumentation": Saddam is like Hitler (he gassed his people; he
waged war against Iran; he invaded Kuwait; he fired SCUD missiles at Israel).
Hitler could not be contained peacefully [an assumption and not a "historical"
fact], therefore, Saddam can't be contained peacefully (all dictators cannot be
appeased) (adapted from Kornprobst, 2007: 29). This conclusion is then used as
justification for military action (see Wilson et al., 2012).

Reagan's style was no less concerned with myth making. Although many of
his speeches and stories were often anecdotal in both content and delivery, there
was also a hint of the grand and heroic.

[George] Washington was gifted with the vision of the future. He dreamed
America could be a great, prosperous and peaceful nation, stretching from
ocean to ocean. He hoped the deliberations at Philadelphia would end with
a declaration of our independence . . .

When the war was going badly, his courage and leadership turned the tide
of history our way. On our first Christmas as a nation in 1776, he led his
band of ragged citizen soldiers across the Delaware River through the driving snow to a victory that saved the cause of American independence. (cited
in Hart, 1987: 37)

This type of language does not have the poetic imagery of Kennedy; the tone is
more resonant of the dramatic, of the constructed story. In order to understand
the reasoning behind this style, consider, again, Reagan's story of the commander
who offered his life for the sake of the young ball-turret gunner:

A B-17 coming back across the Channel from a raid over Europe, was badly
shot up by anti-aircraft, the ball turret that hung underneath the belly of
the plane had taken a hit. The young ball-turret gunner was wounded, and
they couldn't get him out of the turret while they were flying. But over the
Channel, the plane began to lose altitude, and the commander had to order
"Bail Out." And as the men started to leave the plane, the last one to leave—
the boy, understandably, knowing he was left behind to go down with the
plane, cried out in terror. The last man to leave the plane saw the commander
sit down on the floor. He took the boy's hand and said, "Never mind, son,
we'll ride it down together." Congressional Medal of Honor posthumously
awarded.

Although the commander is not himself a political leader, he is certainly displaying benevolence and courage, and, in this sense, this story may be related to the
valiant leader myth. But of course it is more than this, it is a myth of the American hero told in the style of one of the greatest of all American myth-making
forms, "the movie." One could imagine one of Reagan's own friends and heroes,

John Wayne, in the role of the commander (indeed, it has been suggested that this story was not in fact taken from real life, but represents a scene from the movies). The utterance "never mind, son, we'll ride it down together" echoes the heroic statements of so many of Reagan's movie contemporaries. The paternalistic use of the word "son," the euphemistic comparison of the approaching crash with a fairground ride (or another non-threatening activity to which "ride" might refer) all display the mythic qualities of the American hero.

Or consider again Reagan's story of the old English couple who ran a pub during World War II, and who recalled their experiences with American GIs:

> She said, "they used to come in here all the time in the evenings and have songfests." She said, "They called me Mom and the old man Pop." And as she went on her voice was softening and she wasn't looking at me anymore; she was looking kind of beyond into her memories. Her eyes were beginning to fill. And then she said, "It was Christmas Eve. The old man and me were here all alone. And all of a sudden the door burst open, and in they came with presents for the both of us." And the tears now had overflowed and were on her cheeks. And she said, "Big strappin' lads they was from a place called Ioway." By this time my eyes were a little filled also.

A major mythic theme displayed here is that of American family and moral values. These were soldiers sent to war, miles from their home and possibly facing death, yet when they went to the pub it was for a "songfest." They called the elderly couple "Mom" and "Pop." And when Reagan refers to the generosity of the GIs in giving this old couple presents, it is situated in the context of Christmas Eve, one of the most emotional and mythic of all days within Western society.

The influence of the movies on Reagan's style cannot be doubted, but this was more than the adoption of a particular myth-making form, it was almost as if the movie world and the real world intermingled in Reagan's understanding of his own experiences.

> And I remember April '45 I remember seeing the first film that came in when the war was still on, but our troops had come upon the first camps and had entered those camps. And you saw unretouched—no way that it could ever have been rehearsed—what they saw, the horror they saw. I felt the pride when, in one of those camps, there was a nearby town, and the people were ordered to come and look at what had been going on, and to see them. And the reaction of horror on their faces was the greatest proof that they had not been conscious of what had been happening to them.
>
> And that film still, I know must exist in the military, and there it is, living motion pictures, for anyone to see, and I won't go into the horrible scenes that we saw. But it remains with me as of our right to rekindle these memories, because we need always to guard against that kind of tyranny and inhumanity. Our spirit is strengthened by remembering, and our hope is in our strength.

Now, if I don't watch out, this may turn out to be less of a commence-ment than a warm bath in nostalgic memories. Growing up in Illinois, I was influenced by a sports legend so national in scope, it was almost mystical. It is based on a combination of three elements: a game, football; a University, Notre Dame; and a man, Knute Rockne. I must confess that I had someone in mind to play the Gipper. On one of my sportscasts before going to Hol-lywood, I had told the story of his career and tragic death. I didn't have very many words on paper when I learned that the studio that employed me was already preparing a story treatment for that film. And that brings me to the theme of my remarks. (cited in Hart, 1987: 57)

As Hart (1987: 57) comments:

It is interesting to note that in neither excerpt was Mr. Reagan sharing *actual experiences* he had had with the victims of death camps or with Knute Rockne. In both cases, *he was responding to films he had seen* [italics added].

While one might be accused of a certain cynicism in considering the above sto-ries, it should be borne in mind that mythic constructions serve as a background for audiences in understanding the world. In this sense, stories as political myths can be manipulative of perceptions, and indeed can play a role in the creation of specific beliefs. The problem is, however, that myths represent constructions, not reality. As Geis suggests, mythic formations allow politicians to present alterna-tive sets of myths that may themselves be seen as competitive interpretations of the same set of facts. Geis (1987: 28) explains this last point by summarizing two basic mythic themes related to poverty as:

    i. The poor are victims: the poor are poor because they are victims of economic, social, ethnic, racial, etc., justice.
    ii. The lazy poor: the poor are poor because they do not take advantage of the opportunities the society makes available to them all.

These mythic themes have been condensed from a longer description provided by Edelman. Geis invites us to consider how these themes might be invoked where we (the audience) are made aware of an incident where an unemployed Black man has been killed in a robbery. Clearly, depending on which mythic theme (i or ii) we cognitively invoke, our interpretations will vary. Relativity in interpretation is never the result of an explicit process, however, and is based on each individual's own beliefs and experiences as they become indirectly initiated through political language. Nevertheless, this very indirectness makes these myths just as strong and as real as any explicitly and rationally fashioned arguments (see Geis, 1982; Wilson, 1990).

Seen in this way, mythic constructions, created through stories or otherwise, act to causally generate potential sets of beliefs. If we refer again to the story of *the judge and the divorce*, we might argue that the outcome of this story relates to the myth of the "lazy poor." Within this mythic context, the actions of the wife indicate that she would much rather manipulate her personal circumstances in order to access more money from the state, than to go out and work for that money herself. Here, the cause of her actions is greed born of laziness. If this were true, then any government would be expected to deal with this problem. One might cut benefits, for example, or provide tougher guidelines for access to state monies. In either case, the actions would be justified in relation to the causal myth which presents certain types of people as living off the state, not because they are in need, but because they are "lazy." Such arguments were applied during the Reagan administration.

At this level, the story may be seen as contributing to a specific conservative ideological position, or to a particular political myth, that is, that certain groups will live off the system when this is easier and more lucrative than working, or than remaining married. Here we can see the strong link between myth, language, and beliefs about the world, something which is far from new. As Max Muller put it as long ago as 1873: "Mythology . . . is an inherent necessity of language. . . . Mythology in its highest sense is the power exercised by language on thought in every possible sphere of mental activity" (quoted in Cassier, 1954: 5).

In this strong sense, myth becomes part of our lives, not only within political presentations, but also within the broad frame of our cultural existence. Both Margaret Thatcher and Ronald Reagan might be seen in this way. Cassier (1954) has argued that one of the stages of mythic construction is a spiritual or other experience, which one then uses as a basis for explaining other aspects of life (as noted above). In the case of Margaret Thatcher, we had what we might call the "housewife myth" created from her experiences as a housewife and mother. It has long been clear, and Thatcher herself has supported such an interpretation through a variety of domestic stories, that being a housewife and mother helped guide some of the thinking that went into her policies. Her experiences on the domestic front left an impact on her interpretation of life in general, and may be specifically seen in the form of what became known as "kitchen sink economics," that is, the notion that every housewife knows that you cannot spend more money than you have, a lesson Thatcher stressed over and over again as a principle that governments should also keep in mind. In Reagan's case, one might point (as he did himself) to his period of time as the chairman of the Screen Actors Guild, a time when he clearly formulated his "fifth column" view of communism, leading over time to his "evil empire" perspective.

The claims we have been making for the role of myth and myth-making in the construction of reality receives further confirmation from work on cognition, in particular, how human beings organize and represent the knowledge they have of their world. Work on what have been referred to as "schemas" seems particularly appropriate here. The term "schema," along with related terms like "frame," "script," "plans," "scenes," among others (see Minsky, 1975; Schank, 1975; Schank and Abelson, 1977), is used to indicate the ways in which knowledge may be organized into specific structures: ". . . a schema refers to an organized structure that captures our knowledge and expectations of some part of the world" (Baddeley, 1990). Within a schema for young women with six children, one might locate such features as poor, lower socioeconomic class, lack of education, and so on. These are, of course, stereotypes, but they can be clear conservative stereotypes, and it is a conservative viewpoint (argument) that Reagan is constructing (see Greenwald and Banaji, 1995; Kunda, 1999). Although an audience may choose from a range of schematic frames within which to interpret Reagan's story, it does not seem unreasonable that he would like the interpretation to operate within a conservative (Republican) dominated schema. Within this schema we might suggest that there are two groupings: one group (generally the middle class) are hard-working and the creators of wealth, that is, the taxpayers who provide the funds necessary to support the state, and through the state, those in need. The second group (generally the lower classes) attempt to manipulate the state system for their own ends, and they do so as part of a cultural form of behavior. By this, we mean that this group actively encourages its members to "play the system," and that within the boundaries of the group this kind of behavior is acceptable.

These are generalizations, of course, or stereotypes, in a more technical sense. Reagan's story, then, contains elements from a specific schematic description; we have the judge as an exemplar of the state; with the woman, youthful, yet with six children and pregnant again, we have the attempt to manipulate the state for gain; and we have the cultural support, the encouragement of friends who have behaved in a similar way. But we also have one other element, a moral element, the consequences of the action of divorce. In this case a divorced husband, a separated family, and a culture of deceit, all of which have been generated by a far too generous state system. In political terms, this story is not simply a "verbal support" (in the sense of rhetoric or public speaking skills; see above), but rather an attempt to selectively focus the audience's minds in a specific schematic direction. The story fulfills the myths, or schematic expectations of a particular political ideology. But even outside this ideology, these myths, or schemas, are often accepted (even by those who reject the conservative perspective) as having some grain of truth. This is a consequence of the fact that the story itself is stereotypical, or contains stereotypical constructs.

To explain this stereotyped effect, consider that defining the meaning of words in any precise sense is difficult, if not impossible: the edges of any set of meanings can always be shown to be fuzzy (see Putnam, 1975). If we attempt to define the meaning of the word "dog," for example, we might include the feature four-legged, but does this mean that a dog who has had a leg amputated is no longer a dog? What about two legs, or an ear, or . . . Somewhat gruesomely you can see it is not easy to reduce a dog, or other objects, to a core semantic essence. As a consequence, some scholars argue that rather than exact meanings we only have stereotyped sets of elements that delineate particular objects, and that to assist us in understanding meaning we make use of exemplars, or *prototypes* (see Hurford and Heasley, 1983) of those objects which display these features. An Alsatian, for example, is a prototypical dog, displaying stereotyped features of recognition (four-legged, tail, canine, etc.).

Now, with the concept of a stereotyped view of meaning in mind, we can explain (to some extent) both how we learn meaning in general, and how we come to extrapolate from sample cases (prototypes) to generalizations across a range of objects (and vice versa). This is relevant in the case of the Reagan story. Although it is presented as a single case, the story contains stereotypical qualities that allow for generalization from one woman (wife), or one form of state benefit, to a specific social group and the whole principle of state support. This process of extrapolation is quite normal within human processing and learning (see Greenwald and Banaji, 1995).

By presenting the story within this stereotyped frame, in the hope that it will be understood under the correct schematic representation, the story also comes to represent an example of politics as culture—in this case, the elements of American culture concerned with hard work, fairness, the role of the family, and the functioning of the law. All of these elements are also revealed in the story. The role of the law in the story seems obvious enough. This is not simply, or only, as represented by the judge or the courtroom context, but also its protective quality. After all, it was the judge's questioning that brought the whole situation to light—a situation in which a family would be broken up for the sake of financial temptation, a temptation which was unnecessary and unfair. The real force behind the generation of wealth in America is hard work (stereotype?).

We can see that a story presented within a political speech can be a very powerful tool for conveying a specific message. But because the message is in the form of a story, presented for audience assessment, it allows the audience to bring its own assumptions and knowledge to bear in understanding and assessing the story. In this way, stories can generate a range of beliefs without being seen to do so explicitly. By this we mean that in no explicit sense has Reagan explicitly stated any of the things that we have suggested are embedded within his story. Therefore, he cannot be held responsible for some of the interpretations we have presented, a particularly useful fact for a politician. Also particularly useful is the fact that stories are often based on real experiences of either the speaker or someone else, and are, therefore, often given greater credibility by listeners. In this sense, Reagan's use of stories allowed him to form not only a relationship with his audience, but also allowed him to present his case convincingly, even though, in reality, he was only telling them a story.

5

It's Language, Jim, but Not as We Know It

WILLIAM JEFFERSON CLINTON

Introduction

Like Richard Nixon before him, Bill Clinton faced the prospect of impeachment. While Nixon resigned before he could be impeached, Clinton's impeachment articles were sent from the House of Representatives to the Senate, and it was the vote of the Senate that saved Clinton. There have been three US presidents who faced impeachment: Andrew Johnson in 1868, Richard Nixon in 1974, and Bill Clinton in 1998. Arthur Schlesinger Jr. suggested that following Johnson's impeachment the presidency was weakened for many years afterward, and he predicted the same for Clinton's impeachment (see Wittington, 2000: 424). In the case of Nixon and Clinton, there were a number of similarities in the process of impeachment, but specifically interesting from our viewpoint is that they were both accused of lying under oath and obstruction of justice. For both presidents, language became central to their explanations, their defense, and the justification of their behavior. We saw in Chapter 3 that Nixon frequently challenged the linguistic formulation of questions put to him during depositions, and also how he would prevaricate and articulate various alternative interpretations of contexts and situations that could provide non-threatening or even positive political readings of his own or others' actions. We also saw how Nixon's circumlocutions could be interpreted as stalling at best and at worst as self-delusion. Nixon often noted in his depositions that he understood the aims and goals of the deposers; after all he was a trained lawyer himself, and so too was Bill Clinton. Like Nixon, Clinton faced a number of Grand Jury depositions, and he understood exactly what his deposers were after, and, as he would argue as justification for his evidence under oath, he did not see it as his job to provide his deposers with information that suited their purposes; rather, his job was to make life difficult for his questioners, while not, at the same time, lying or being seen to lie. There is still continuing debate as to how successful Clinton was in his efforts here, but clearly

Talking with the President. John Wilson. © Oxford University Press 2015.
Published 2015 by Oxford University Press

Clinton could draw upon both his legal training and his considerable political skills to sidetrack, challenge, or reinterpret any accusations put to him. However, for the general public listening to or reading about Clinton's responses, it often looked like nothing more than pedantry, obfuscation, and delaying tactics.

Consider for example one famous Clinton response: "It depends on what the meaning of the word *is* is." During depositions given in the Paula Jones case (see below), Clinton's lawyer responded to a suggestion that Clinton had had sex with a young intern named Monica Lewinsky and said that there ". . . is absolutely no sex of any kind in any manner shape or form between Clinton and Lewinsky" (Baker, 2000: 29). When it emerged that Clinton did have a relationship with Lewinsky, it was put to him that his lawyer's claim was "an utterly false statement. Is that correct?" Clinton's response was:

> It depends what the meaning of the word *is* is? If the—if he—if *is* means is and never has been, that is not, that is one thing. If it means there is none, that is [a] completely true statement.

Reading this several times, one can unpack the import of Clinton's statement, but in the flow of questioning Baker (2000, 29) says that all Clinton really does is "reinforce the public criticism of his slippery style with words"; but for us it is that very "slippery style" that intrigues. In this chapter we will look at two things: first, a range of examples that display the pragmatics utilized by Clinton; second, we consider a more a more general question, where is the linguistic, not moral or legal, line between defending one's self and one's family, and performing one's professional and public duty as president of the United States?

Impeachment

The story of Bill Clinton's impeachment has been told many times and from many angles (see the excellent account in Posner, 2000). Nevertheless, it may be useful to review the basics. The story begins with the filing of a lawsuit in Arkansas on May 6, 1994, by Paula Corbin Jones. Ms. Jones claimed that in 1991, when Clinton was governor of Arkansas, he invited her to his hotel, where he made sexual advances toward her, which she rejected. This, she claimed, was a violation of her civil rights as a state employee.

President Clinton denied the allegations and legally questioned whether such a private litigation could be brought against a sitting president of the United States. He argued that under the Constitution, the case should be delayed until the end of his term as president. In 1997 the Supreme Court rejected the president's claim, arguing that Ms. Jones had the same rights as every other citizen who invokes the court's jurisdiction to have her case heard. Following the Supreme Court's decision, a process of "pre-trial discovery" began, and this was to include other alleged cases of President Clinton's sexual behavior toward other women. Clinton legally challenged any requirement that he should provide information about alleged sexual relationships with other women, but in 1997 Judge Susan Webber ruled that such information was relevant to the case against the president.

The initial questions on this topic were presented to the president as "written discovery questions." In December 1997 when asked to "identify all women who were state or federal employees and with whom he had 'sexual relations' since 1986" the president answered, "None." At this point the term "sexual relations" was not defined.

A list of potential witnesses had been prepared by Jones's attorneys and most were referred to as Jane Doe, 1, 2, and so on. Jane Doe number 6 turned out to be a young woman who had worked as an intern in the White House in 1995; she was called Monica Lewinsky. A former White House employee, Linda Tripp, who had befriended Lewinsky when she was at the White House, gave Monica Lewinsky's name to Jones. Tripp and Lewinsky had frequent telephone conversations in which Lewinsky told Tripp of her sexual encounters with President Clinton. Tripp had secretly recorded these conversations, and on January 12, 1998, Tripp provided these conversations to Kenneth Starr, who had been appointed independent counsel in the investigation of the Whitewater real estate venture in Arkansas, which involved President and Mrs. Clinton. At the same time, Ms. Lewinsky was providing a sworn affidavit to Jones's lawyers in which she claimed:

> I have never had a sexual relationship with the President, he did not propose that we have a sexual relationship, he did not offer me employment or other benefits in exchange for a sexual relationship, he did not deny me employment or other benefits for rejecting a sexual relationship.

Following this, Starr convinced Attorney General Janet Reno that his investigation into Whitewater should be expanded to include the recent allegations that had emerged in the Jones case.

After accessing a court order, the FBI secretly recorded a meeting between Ms. Lewinsky and Ms. Tripp. Following this, FBI agents threatened Ms. Lewinsky with charges of perjury and demanded that she cooperate in providing evidence against the president. Ms. Lewinsky initially rejected this demand and claimed that much of what she had told Ms. Tripp was false.

On January 17, 1998, President Clinton was questioned in the Jones lawsuit. According to the Starr Report (Factual Background: accessed at www.cnn.com/starr.report/-united states):

> President Clinton was questioned under oath about his relationships with other women in the workplace. . . . The President was asked numerous questions about his relationship with Monica Lewinsky. . . . Under oath and in the presence of Judge Wright, the President denied that he had engaged in a "sexual affair," a "sexual relationship," or "sexual relations"

with Ms. Lewinsky. The President also stated that he had no specific memory of having been alone with Ms. Lewinsky, that he remembered few details of any gifts they might have exchanged, and indicated that no one except his attorneys had kept him informed of Ms. Lewinsky's status as a potential witness in the *Jones's* case.

On January 21, The *Washington Post*, the *Los Angeles Times*, and ABC News reported that Starr had expanded his investigation of the president to include the allegations related to Lewinsky. In a media appearance on January 26, President Clinton made his now (in)famous assertion, "I did not have sexual relations with that woman, Miss Lewinsky," and he vehemently denied ever having encouraged her to lie about the affair.

Starr's expansion of his investigation now included the question of whether the president himself had lied under oath in his own deposition in the Paula Jones case. In July 1998, Starr gave Ms. Lewinsky immunity from prosecution and she admitted that she had had a sexual relationship with the president, but noted that it did not include sexual intercourse. She denied, however, that she had ever been asked to lie about the relationship with the president, either by Clinton himself or by any of those around him.

On August 17, 1998, the president appeared before a federal Grand Jury that was called to consider whether he committed perjury, or otherwise obstructed justice, in the Paula Jones case. He agreed that he had adopted some very specific definitions of words and terms during the deposition, but argued that he had every right to do so. He noted, for example, that "oral sex" was not, in his view, subsumed under the court's definition of "sexual relations" that had been drafted by the court and provided to Clinton (more on this below). He did not accept that fondling Lewinsky could be defined as "sexual relations" and, therefore, indirectly rejected Lewinsky's claim that he had fondled her breasts and genitalia a number of times. On the issue of whether he had been involved in trying to get Lewinsky to give false information under oath, or that he had played a key role in trying to get Lewinsky favorable treatment in accessing federal employment, there was evidence that Clinton had had conversations with his secretary regarding whether he was ever fully alone with Lewinsky, and also evidence that a friend of Clinton's, Vernon Jordan, had made efforts to assist Ms. Lewinsky find other employment. Clinton claimed that such conversations represented an innocent attempt to check his recollection of facts against Ms. Lewinsky's, and he denied that Vernon Jordan's job-hunting efforts were in any way tied to Lewinsky's decision to file an affidavit falsely denying a sexual relationship with the president.

Following his Grand Jury deposition, Clinton appeared on television that evening. In his statement, he admitted, "I did have a relationship with Miss Lewinsky that was not appropriate." However, he also claimed that the process of trying to find out what he and Ms. Lewinsky did or did not do was irrelevant to the real needs of government, that it was a personal attack by Kenneth Starr on his private life, and he should be allowed to keep his private and political lives separate.

After Clinton's admission, many Americans were shocked, friends and supporters of the president felt particularly let down, and talk of impeachment began to surface.

On September 9, 1998, Starr submitted a detailed report to Congress in which he claimed there was "substantial and credible information that President William Jefferson Clinton committed acts that may constitute grounds for an impeachment." Starr put forward 11 counts against Clinton, including perjury in his Jones and Grand Jury depositions, obstruction of justice, and one count asserting abuse of the office the presidency. Congress eventually voted for impeachment, approving two of the four impeachment articles sent up by the Judiciary Committee. This led to an impeachment trial by the Senate. On Friday, February 12, 1999, Clinton was found not guilty.

The Truth, Nothing but the Truth, and Pragmatics

In this section we want to consider the way in which language is used as the basis for pragmatic interpretation, first in Clinton's deposition in the Paula Jones case, and then in the context of the Grand Jury deposition.

The study and assessment of language use in the courtroom is covered in several different disciplines, including, of course, law itself. The role of language has always been central to any consideration of courtroom interaction and in recent times the sub- (or applied) discipline of "forensic linguistics" has emerged (see Shuy, 1996, 1998; Olsson, 2004); the term covers a broad range of topics, including police interrogations, witness statements, cross examinations, judges' language, jury assessment, and so on. Central here, of course, is the use of linguistic techniques to provide explanatory accounts of such issues as, did the police interpret a witness statement for their own purposes? Did the witness fully understand the questions put to her? Did the judge, by implication, lead the jury to a particular verdict? And central to our interests, can we define specific witness responses as lies as opposed to attempts to mislead or misdirect, and in either case, can such responses be deemed perjury?

For most of us, we understand perjury as meaning the intentional telling of a lie under oath. Doyle (2010:1) states that the definition of perjury has ". . . not changed a great deal since the framing of the constitution." The relevant legal article states that:

> Whoever—
>
> (1) . . . having taken an oath before a competent tribunal, officer, or person, in any case in which a law of the United States authorizes an oath to be administered, that he will testify, declare, depose, or certify truly, or that any

written testimony, declaration, deposition, or certificate by him subscribed, is true, willfully and contrary to such oath states or subscribes any material matter which he does not believe to be true; or

(2) in any declaration, certificate, verification, or statement under penalty of perjury as permitted under section 1746 of title 28, United States Code, willfully subscribes as true any material matter which he does not believe to be true. (18 USC 1621)

The action of perjury and the procurement of another person to commit perjury were central to Starr's case against Clinton. Given the legal definition described above, let us look at what was actually said using a number of core examples.

The transcripts of the various depositions are available from a range of online sources and we will be drawing on a small sample of these in the next section, although we will also look at a broader range of the materials when we come to consider issues of pragmatic marking, evidentiality, and "stance taking." To begin, consider this example which appeared in President Clinton's deposition in the Paula Jones case; it occurs in the opening phase of questioning on Monica Lewinsky (Attorney: Mr. Fisher).

> FISHER: Is it true that when she worked at the White House she met with you several times?
>
> CLINTON: I don't know about several times. There was a period when the, when the Republican Congress shut the government down that the whole White House was being run by interns, and she was assigned to work back in the chief of staff's office, and we were all working there, and so I saw her on two or three occasions then, and then when she worked at the White House, I think there was one or two other times when she brought some documents to me.

Research on the language of the courtroom has drawn attention to the way in which questions and answers are negotiated within lawyer and witness interaction. It is generally agreed that the question/answer context is an asymmetric one with the main power and control residing on the side of the lawyer (Atkinson and Drew, 1979; O'Barr, 1982; Danet, 1984; Woodbury, 1984; Philips, 1987; Walker, 1987; Luchjenbroers, 1997). This control resides partly in the very social and legal context itself, which has already pre-allocated turns in a Q/A format as part of the courtroom practice. However, lawyers do have flexible options as to how and in what way they structure and organize their questions. They may use a series of simple yes/no questions, or more open-ended *wh*-format questions; they may use negative and positive tag questions, which presuppose in some cases the truth of their answer; or they may use statements with questioning intonation. Whatever range of techniques they adopt, they are attempting to control the situation and derive information useful for their case. It is not just the organization and structure of the questions that lawyers control, they also control the very "narrative" structure of the unfolding event itself (Cotterill, 2004).

Of course the witness also has options available to him or her. When Richard Nixon was advising some of his aides on how to deal with cross-examination, he told them to make liberal use of such phrases as "as I recall" or "to the best of my memory" (what we have been calling "hedging"). Such phrases modify or mitigate the content of responses such that if specific claims should prove false, one can always say that it was a slip of memory, not an intention to lie.

Consider the opening interrogative mode adopted by Mr. Fisher, "Isn't it true that . . ." This is a negative yes/no question which marks out the "that" complement as either "true or not true." Yes/no questions with negative or positive polarity can act in a number of ways, and one of the most significant is that negative preposed questions tend to assume a positive epistemic implicature (Han and Romero, 2002: see also Ladd, 1981; Buring and Gunlogson, 2000); this means that the speaker believes the answer is positive. So in (a) and (b) the speaker indicates his or her belief that the answer is in the affirmative.

(a) Doesn't Jim look big for his age? (Jim is big for his age)
(b) Isn't Jim coming to the party? (I believed (or expected) Jim was coming to the party)

We can see, then, that Mr. Fisher has phrased the question so that he is placing an emphasis on the positive belief that the complement is true. In this sense, a negative response becomes unexpected, or marked, and is hence highlighted, which is exactly what Fisher was attempting to achieve.

But there is also more to the question than this: it presents us with an assumption that not only has President Clinton "met" Monica Lewinsky before, but that he has done so on "several" occasions. "Met" is the past tense of "meet," and "meet" and "meet with" are said to be synonymous. Hence, when you say that you will "meet" with someone or you have "met" with someone, there is an assumption that it was by "arrangement." One can also use "met," however, to refer to an accidental encounter, as in "guess who I met yesterday." In such cases, of course, there is the assumption that both the speaker and interlocutor have knowledge of who X is.

Guess who I met yesterday, my ex-husband.

With the use of "meet" we are guided toward "intentionality," as in arrangements, meetings, appointments, and so on, as opposed to say simply being "aware of" "seeing someone." So "meet" is being used to indicate arrangement, planning, and hence a reasonable level of knowledge of the person one is meeting.

This point is further supported by the use of the word "several." The dictionary definition of "several" is often somewhat imprecise, and is presented as meaning generally more than two or three, but less than many. But what number is that? "Several," then, is a vague quantifier. But despite the dictionary claim of "more than two or three" many people put several at around four to seven, partly induced by the homophonous relation between "seven" and "several."

We can see from the beginning that Fisher wants to establish Clinton's knowledge of Lewinsky as going beyond someone who might have simply worked in the White House, or someone whom he may have seen around the White House but whom he did not know personally. This is perfectly legitimate, and what we would expect in the examination of witnesses. But what does this mean from the perspective of the witness? In the case of someone as knowledgeable and as legally experienced as Clinton, he would predict such question types, and as he would later comment, in response to accusations that he was less than truthful in his deposition, that his job was not to help those questioning him, but in fact to make it difficult for them while at the same time maintaining his legal oath to give truthful responses.

In light of Clinton's "stance" (see below), consider his response to Fisher: first he challenges the phrase "several times," although he does so by marking his assessment of "several" with the comment, "I don't know about several." Here Clinton does at least two things: first, he negates Fisher's claim about "several" meetings; second, although he suggests it was not several, he epistemically marks the negation using "know" (I don't know about . . .), and in this sense he "hedges" against any number that might emerge, should it approach the definition of "several." He does this because he is going to argue for a lower order number, but in case there is evidence to the contrary, and the number he gives was wrong, he will be covered by his "hedge."

In line with this, Clinton quantitatively marks those encounters with Lewinsky as:

(a) I saw her on **two** or **three** occasions then . . .
(b) I think there was **one** or **two** other times when she brought some documents to me.

So Clinton counters "several" with "two or three" and "one or two"; in both cases, these are within the lower limits that could exclude the use of "several."

Also note that Clinton counters the use of "meet" or "meet with," along with any intentional connotations associated with this term, with the more neutral "I saw her," and the equally neutral "there was." In both cases, the encounters with Lewinsky are "work" bound and simply encounters—not "meetings."

Clinton also does something else in his response. He provides a "narrative" that contextualizes the encounters, that is, he sets the scene noting that any encounters that occurred only arose because of the impact of external circumstances, which meant that "interns" would be more active in the White House and more likely, therefore, to be "encountered." This narrative provides a justification for not only seeing or encountering interns such as Monica Lewinsky, but for seeing them more regularly, because the working context was not normal, "the Republican Congress shut the government down. . . ."

The purpose in looking at this initial example is to highlight how Clinton is countering any contextual meanings generated by Fisher's questions. While this might be expected, Clinton was criticized for his delaying, avoidance, and obfuscation tactics, both in his Paula Jones deposition and in his Grand Jury testimony. The question is, what are the boundaries of what is to be expected of a witness in both cases? If, as Clinton claims, he always stayed within the bounds of his oath and always endeavored to tell the truth, then what is the problem? Is it that Clinton pushed the role of recalcitrant but truthful witness too far? But who gets to decide what is too far? As long as the rules of the legal speech event are not broken, there would be significant flexibility in responses. So what is it that Clinton is doing, and how far does he succeed, or exceed, in framing his responses? To decide this we need to look at several further examples from the Paula Jones deposition and then compare these both with the Grand Jury testimony and with Clinton's confessions of what he and Monica Lewinsky actually did do. Whatever we decide, we will see that Clinton pushes the pragmatics of language as far as he can.

Consider, for example, the following exchanges:

FRASER: Mr. President, before the break, we were talking about Monica Lewinsky. At any time were you and Monica Lewinsky alone together in the Oval Office?

CLINTON: I don't recall, but as I said, when she worked at the legislative affairs office, they always had somebody there on the weekends. I typically worked some on the weekends. Sometimes they'd bring me things on the weekends. She—it seems to me she brought things to me once or twice on the weekends. In that case, whatever time she would be in there, drop it off, exchange a few words and go, she was there. I don't have any specific recollections of what the issues were, what was going on, but when the Congress is there, we're working all the time, and typically I would do some work on one of the days of the weekends in the afternoon.

FRASER: So I understand, your testimony is that it was possible, then, that you were alone with her, but you have no specific recollection of that ever happening?

CLINTON: Yes, that's correct. It's possible that she, in, while she was working there, brought something to me and that at the time she brought it to me, she was the only person there. That's possible.

FRASER: Did it ever happen that you and she went down the hallway from the Oval Office to the private kitchen?

MR. BENNETT (CLINTON'S LAWYER): Your Honor, excuse me, Mr. President, I need some guidance from the Court at this point. I'm going to object to the innuendo. I'm afraid, as I say, that this will leak. I don't question the predicates here. I question the good faith of counsel, the innuendo in the question. Counsel is fully aware that Ms. Jane Doe 6 has filed, has an affidavit which they are in possession of saying that there is absolutely no sex of any kind in any manner, shape or form, with President Clinton, and yet listening to the innuendo in the questions. . .

From our present historical perspective, and indeed with information available to the Jones inquiry at the time, we know what President Clinton was doing with and to Miss Lewinsky, but as we know, Clinton did not believe it was his job to give his inquisitors what they wanted. In his first answer, Clinton makes use again of "evidential weakening" in his responses, and draws, again, on a situational narrative to create a "scenario" within which, given the natural flow of work at the White House, it is possible Lewinsky delivered papers to the president—as did many others—and if there was no one else in the president's office, then, theoretically, they would be "alone." But here is one of those words again. If you are "alone," no one is with you, but if you are said to be "alone with X," then there is only you and X. But so what? Consider the following:

I saw John with a woman last night, they went into his office and they were alone for 30 minutes.

In the first part of this sentence we have a classic Gricean implicature of the type discussed in Chapter 1. According to the general principle of "say as much as you can for the purposes of the exchange," we assume that the "woman" was not John's wife, mother, or sister, for example. If the speaker had such further detail then he would have been expected to provide it. So we know John was with a woman who we believe is not his wife, mother, sister, and so forth. But what does this tell us? This just means the woman could have all kinds of different identities: John's boss, an interviewee for a job, the cleaner, and so on. However, most people draw a cultural inference, or a contextual assumption, that John might also be up to something with the woman, having an affair for example. When we add that they went into the office "alone," we further have to consider why we are being told this, and if one runs the cultural assumption that John may be having an affair, then people who have affairs like to be alone with those they are having the affair with.

This seems to be in line with Fisher's objectives, as we can see within the rest of the exchange. First, Fisher explains, for the record, that the president says he could have alone with Miss Lewinsky, but without recollection of this. This seems to be aimed at turning President Clinton's use of evidential weakening (the use of "it's possible") into a negative assessment of the president's memory. But then Fisher asks what seems to be an innocent question:

FISHER: Did it ever happen that you and she went down the hallway from the Oval Office to the private kitchen?

On the surface, this seems like an ordinary question, but then something interesting happens. Clinton's own attorney, Mr. Bennett, draws attention to possible inferences he believes are generated by Fisher's question, and thus makes explicit what he believes is the core aim of the question: ". . . there is absolutely no sex of any kind in any manner shape or form" between Clinton and Lewinsky. But where is this inference or "innuendo," as Mr. Bennett calls it, coming from? There are no generic terms like "woman" that could have been more explicit, or no lexically coded cultural assumptions about two people being "alone." What is it, therefore, that is driving this possible inference? One way of explaining this is through Relevance Theory. Recall that with every utterance there is a communicative assumption of "relevance" that makes the utterance worth processing, and a further assumption that processing the sentence will produce information output which is in balance with the processing effort (see Chapter 1). Given that President Clinton has spent some time outlining that Miss Lewinsky operated as an intern, among many other interns, and that he would have seen her, or even been briefly alone with her when she delivered papers as part of her duties, why would he and Miss Lewinsky be "heading down," not just to the "kitchen," but the "private kitchen." If, as Sperber and Wilson suggest, we try to understand utterances in terms of a "payoff" between the effort to process an utterance and the information we construct, and if, again to use a Sperber and Wilson term, that it is "mutually manifest" (speaker and hearer[s] can cognitively access the same information and know that each of them can) to the parties in this interaction that Miss Lewinsky has already given information about her relationship with the president, including whether or not they had sex, then the relevance of the question could be to suggest that they intentionally went to the private kitchen to be "alone" for sex. In this case, we would have a reconstruction of our sentence above as:

The President would go to the private kitchen with a woman to be alone.
Why?
To have sex

But what is also very important here for what follows is Mr. Bennett's claim that:

. . . there is absolutely **no sex of any kind in any manner, shape or form**, with President Clinton. . . .

Mr. Bennett has mentioned the activity of having sex in order to deny it; that is, he has drawn attention to Clinton and Lewinsky having sex whereas Fisher only implied it. By doing this, Bennett allows listeners to draw on other cognitive frames and inferences, and not always ones he may have intended (Lakoff, 2004). In many ways, therefore, Mr. Bennett's intervention may not have been very helpful for Clinton. This example is similar to the case of Richard Nixon when he said, "I am not a crook." Nixon invoked the term in order to deny it, but in doing this he highlighted the conceptual possibility that he was a crook. Similarly, Bennett may have explicitly drawn attention to the possibility of Clinton and Lewinsky having sex, which was the very thing Clinton wanted to avoid.

After some further debate between the lawyers and the judge about the acceptability and aims of Fisher's question, Clinton answers the question as follows:

CLINTON: Well, let me try to describe the facts first, because you keep talking about this private kitchen. The private kitchen is staffed by two naval aides. They have total, unrestricted access to my dining room, to that hallway, to coming into the Oval Office. The people who are in the outer office of the Oval Office can also enter at any time.

I was, after I went through a presidential campaign in which the far right tried to convince the American people I had committed murder, run drugs, slept in my mother's bed with four prostitutes, and done numerous other things, I had a high level of paranoia.

There are no curtains on the Oval Office, there are no curtains on my private office, there are no curtains or blinds that can close the windows in my private dining room. The naval aides come and go at will. There is a peephole on the office that George Stephanopoulos first and then Rahm Emanuel occupied that looks back down that corridor. I have done everything I could to avoid the kind of questions you are asking me here today, so to talk about this kitchen as if it is a private kitchen, it's a little cubbyhole, and these guys keep the door open. They come and go at will. Now that's the factual background here.

Now, to go back to your question, my recollection is that, that at some point during the government shutdown, when Ms. Lewinsky was still an intern but was working the chief staff's office because all the employees had to go home, that she was back there with a pizza that she brought to me and to others. I do not believe she was there alone, however. I don't think she was. And my recollection is that on a couple of occasions after that she was there but my secretary Betty Currie was there with her. She and Betty are friends. That's my, that's my recollection. And I have no other recollection of that.

Most important here is the famous description of the Oval office without curtains and so on. This is a narrative related to what Clinton calls his "paranoia." His enemies seek to create all kinds of negative images of his behavior, but he describes the office without curtains to indirectly suggest he is not attempting to "hide" anything. Why would Clinton have an office where everyone can see what is going on if he wanted to indulge in clandestine activities? He goes on:

That I have done everything I could to avoid the kind of questions you are asking me here today, so to talk about this kitchen as if it is a private kitchen, it's a little cubbyhole, and these guys keep the door open. They come and go at will. Now that's the factual background here.

The culturally constructed inferences here are clear: if you wanted to hide something, or if you wanted to have an affair or a secret meeting, you wouldn't do it in an environment where everyone can see what you are doing. Hence, it follows that there is very little that is "private" in this context; therefore Clinton challenges any description of the kitchen as a "private kitchen." This is both a semantic and pragmatic challenge: semantic in that if something is private it would not be open to everyone, consequently if the kitchen is part of open environment to call it "private" could be a contradiction; pragmatically, if one were having a clandestine affair one would seek to hide this, and carrying on such activities in an open environment would be contrary to this.

There then follows a further exchange on those meetings with Ms. Lewinsky and whether he can, for example, recall his secretary meeting with Lewinsky, or whether he or she discussed with Lewinsky that she might be asked to testify, or whether he had bought Lewinsky gifts and so on. Clinton's response to such questions is similar to the examples discussed above. He makes frequent use of various forms of limiting evidential marking (hedging: see Markkanen and Schröder, 1997), along with an account that any "meetings" were part of normal procedures in the White House, but most significant is the following exchange:

FRASER: Did you have an extramarital sexual affair with Monica
    Lewinsky?
CLINTON: No.
FRASER: If she told someone that she had a sexual affair with you
    beginning in November of 1995, would that be a lie?
CLINTON: It's certainly not the truth. It would not be the truth.
FRASER: I think I used the term "sexual affair." And so the record is
    completely clear, have you ever had sexual relations with Monica Lewinsky,
    as that term is defined in Deposition Exhibit 1, as modified by the Court.
MR. BENNETT: I object because I don't know that he can remember.
JUDGE WRIGHT: Well, it's real short. He can—I will permit the question
    and you may show the witness definition number one.
CLINTON: I have never had sexual relations with Monica Lewinsky. I've
    never had an affair with her.

Clinton is quite unequivocal in his answers to these questions. And he denies ever having "sexual relations" or having "an affair" with Ms. Lewinsky. Reference is also made to the definition of "sexual relations" as determined by the court, "deposition number 1." This definition had been agreed upon by the parties involved in the deposition. It states as follows:

For the purposes of this deposition, a person engages in "sexual relations" when the person knowingly engages in or causes

(1) contact with the genitalia, anus, groin, breast, inner thigh, or buttocks of any person with an intent to arouse or gratify the sexual desire of any person;

(2) contact between any part of the person's body or an object and the genitals or anus of another person; or

(3) contact between the genitals or anus of the person and any part of another person's body. "Contact" means intentional touching, either directly
or through clothing.

As noted, Clinton denies having had "sexual relations" with Miss Lewinsky, but
by the time the Grand Jury testimony was to take place, it had become known
that Clinton and Ms. Lewinsky had been involved in forms of sexual activity. In
this case, did Clinton lie and therefore perjure himself in the Paula Jones deposition? Let's see what happened next.

The Grand Jury

During his evidence to the Grand Jury, Clinton began with the following opening
statement:

> CLINTON: When I was alone with Ms. Lewinsky on certain occasions in
> early 1996 and once in early 1997, I engaged in conduct that was wrong.
> These encounters did not consist of sexual intercourse. They did not
> constitute sexual relations as I understood that term to be defined at
> my January 17th, 1998 deposition. But they did involve inappropriate
> intimate contact.

These inappropriate encounters ended, at my insistence, in early 1997. I also
had occasional telephone conversations with Ms. Lewinsky that included
inappropriate sexual banter.

I regret that what began as a friendship came to include this conduct, and
I take full responsibility for my actions.

While I will provide the grand jury whatever other information I can, because of privacy considerations affecting my family, myself, and others, and
in an effort to preserve the dignity of the office I hold, this is all I will say
about the specifics of these particular matters.

I will try to answer, to the best of my ability, other questions including questions about my relationship with Ms. Lewinsky; questions about
my understanding of the term "sexual relations," as I understood it to be
defined at my January 17th, 1998 deposition; and questions concerning alleged subornation of perjury, obstruction of justice, and intimidation of
witnesses.

That, Mr. Bittman, is my statement.

When one looks at this statement, its looks like Clinton has not been truthful in his deposition to the Paula Jones inquiry, and indeed it looked like Monica
Lewinsky had also been lying in her statement to the inquiry. It was such facts
that formed the basis for impeachment, specifically that the president had lied

and perjured himself, and that he had encouraged others to lie and perjure themselves. But had Clinton lied and encouraged others to do the same? At the Grand Jury he was specifically asked about this:

Q: And you remember that Ms. Lewinsky's affidavit said that she had had no sexual relationship with you. Do you remember that?

CLINTON: I do.

Q: And do you remember in the deposition that Mr. Bennett asked you about that. This is at the end of the—towards the end of the deposition. And you indicated, he asked you whether the statement that Ms. Lewinsky made in her affidavit was -

CLINTON: Truthful.

Q:—true. And you indicated that it was absolutely correct.

CLINTON: I did. And at the time that she made the statement, and indeed to the present day because, as far as I know, she was never deposed since the Judge ruled she would not be permitted to testify in a case the Judge ruled had no merit; that is, this case we're talking about.

I believe at the time that she filled out this affidavit, if she believed that the definition of sexual relationship was two people having intercourse, then this is accurate. And I believe that is the definition that most ordinary Americans would give it.

If you said Jane and Harry have a sexual relationship, and you're not talking about people being drawn into a lawsuit and being given definitions, and then a great effort to trick them in some way, but you are just talking about people in ordinary conversations, I'll bet the grand jurors, if they were talking about two people they know, and said they have a sexual relationship, they meant they were sleeping together; they meant they were having intercourse together.

So, I'm not at all sure that this affidavit is not true and was not true in Ms. Lewinsky's mind at the time she swore it out.

Q: Did you talk with Ms. Lewinsky about what she meant to write in her affidavit?

CLINTON: I didn't talk to her about her definition. I did not know what was in this affidavit before it was filled out specifically. I did not know what words were used specifically before it was filled out, or what meaning she gave to them.But I'm just telling you that it's certainly true what she says here, that we didn't have—there was no employment, no benefit in exchange, there was nothing having anything to do with sexual harassment. And if she defined sexual relationship in the way I think most Americans do, meaning intercourse, then she told the truth.

Q: My question -

CLINTON: And that depends on what was in her mind. I don't know what was in her mind. You'll have to ask her that.

Q: But you indicated before that you were aware of what she intended by the term "sexual relationship."

CLINTON: No, sir. I said I thought that this could be a truthful affidavit. And when I read it, since that's the way I would define it, since—keep in mind, she was not, she was not bound by this sexual relations definition, which is highly unusual; I think anybody would admit that. When she used a different term, sexual relationship, if she meant by that what most people mean by it, then that is not an untruthful statement.

Q: So, your definition of sexual relationship is intercourse only, is that correct?

CLINTON: No, not necessarily intercourse only. But it would include intercourse. I believe, I believe that the common understanding of the term . . .

The apparent conflict between what Clinton said at the Paula Jones deposition, and what he then said subsequently at the Grand Jury, and afterward, have been at the center of various heated legal and other debates. For some, including Kenneth Starr, Clinton had given false testimony and therefore perjured himself; for others this was simply lying (see Hitchens, 1999), and for most, even some of his supporters, whatever the legal merits of Clinton's approach he was at least being unhelpful and surely deceptive.

We discussed in Chapter 3 how determining what is and what is not a lie is not always a straightforward matter. We noted how some scholars and people in general treat lies as different points on a scale, with "white lies" or "justified lies" at one end and "bald-faced lies" at the other. We also considered that when a speaker intentionally produced pragmatic inferences that were known to be false, where they were intentionally generated to deceive listeners into believing they were true, this might also be seen as a form of lying.

So where do Clinton's claims sit on a scale of lies and lying? To answer this, we first need to assess what Clinton was trying to do both in his deposition in the Paula Jones case, and in giving evidence to the Grand Jury. Consider the following:

Q: Was it your responsibility to answers those questions truthfully, Mr. President?

CLINTON: It was. But it was not my responsibility, in the face of repeated illegal leaking, it was not my responsibility to volunteer a lot of information.

Clinton's answers are guided by his view that it was his job to be truthful, but not necessarily to be compliant. Basically, Clinton set out to be linguistically awkward. While he may have viewed this as his right, as a lawyer he would also have been aware that such "awkwardness" and "lack of compliance" might be legally defined as "obstructive."

Indeed, the complex pragmatics of what Clinton said was often so convoluted that it seems to have misled pragmatic analysts themselves. Solan (2002) says the following of Clinton:

> In some instances, he admitted to the grand jury that the substance of what he said at the deposition was not the truth. For example, at his deposition he was asked whether he had ever been alone with Lewinsky. He answered:
>
> I don't recall. She—it seems to me she brought me things to me once or twice on the weekends. In that case, whatever time she would be there, drop off, exchange a few words and go, she was there.
>
> To the grand jury he conceded the following:
>
> Q: Let me ask you, Mr. President, you indicate in your statement that you were alone with Ms. Lewinsky is that right?
>
> Clinton: Yes sir.

Solan says nothing more on this, leaving the inconsistency to stand for itself, that is, that in one case Clinton says he can't recall if he was "alone" with Ms. Lewinsky, yet in another case, asked if he had ever been alone with Ms. Lewinsky, he says "yes sir." This certainly seems damning and contradictory. But there are a couple of points one could make. First, one could argue that in the Grand Jury example Clinton is saying: Yes Sir—**it is correct that I said in my statement that I was alone with Miss Lewinsky**. Here his response is a "meta" comment on his own comment, as opposed to an admission. And, if we look at a fuller account of what Clinton said in the Paula Jones deposition another explanation emerges:

> Q: Mr. President, before the break, we were talking about Monica Lewinsky. At any time were you and Monica Lewinsky alone together in the Oval Office?
>
> CLINTON: I don't recall, but as I said, when she worked at the legislative affairs office, they always had somebody there on the weekends. I typically worked some on the weekends. Sometimes they'd bring me things on the weekends. She—it seems to me she brought things to me once or twice on the weekends. In that case, whatever time she would be in there, drop it off, exchange a few words and go, she was there. I don't have any specific recollections of what the issues were, what was going on, but when the Congress is there, we're working all the time, and typically I would do some work on one of the days of the weekends in the afternoon.
>
> Q: So I understand, your testimony is that it was possible, then, that you were alone with her, but you have no specific recollection of that ever happening?
>
> CLINTON: Yes, that's correct. It's possible that she, in, while she was working there, brought something to me and that at the time she brought it to me, she was the only person there. That's possible.

We see here that after "I don't recall" Clinton adds, "but as I said . . ." reiterating again that since many interns came and went through his office it is logically possible that at one point he and the intern Monica Lewinsky were alone in the office, and in this case one could say that he was alone with her. The contrastive "but as I said" is used to refer to what Clinton said previously, and Counsel understands this and summarizes Clinton's statement for confirmation, specifically noting the possibility that Clinton was alone with Lewinsky, and Clinton also takes the opportunity to reconfirm this possibility. Now if we look at what Clinton said in the Paula Jones case, it may not be as contradictory as Solan believes. What Clinton claims when he says "I don't recall" in the Jones testimony is:

(a) It is possible that he was alone with Ms. Lewinsky, but at this time, Clinton cannot recall if this was the case of if this was not the case.
(b) Further, being "alone" in this context, should it have occurred, would be purely functional as opposed to intentional. Since it was part of an intern's function at the time to bring papers to Clinton, if no one else was in the room when an intern entered then technically she would have been alone with Clinton.

If this is correct then, when Clinton later admits to the Grand Jury that he was alone with Lewinsky he could argue that his recollection is now much clearer than it was in the previous Jones deposition. If this is so, then when he says "yes sir" he could be comparing one claim with another previous claim, having had the chance to reflect on previous responses. Of course, in the Jones inquiry, had Clinton fully recalled being alone with Lewinsky and then denied this, he would have been misleading the jury, or indeed lying. We might question, since we later learn that Clinton had been alone with Lewinsky on several occasions, how likely would it be that he could not recall this at the time of the Jones deposition? While this is very unlikely, this is not the same as proof of lying.

This kind of pragmatic argument may seem somewhat contrived in terms of our normal intuitions about interactions, but it is exactly the kind of pragmatic thinking that Clinton would continually draw upon, and, further, it is not as circuitous as it may seem, since we must also allow for the fact that we are comparing two forms of testimony that were given in legal contexts and under judicial rules. As most of us know, if only from our experiences of legal-speak in the movies, it is in the nature of legal language in such contexts to be very limited and constrained (see Shuy, 1996).

Solan (ibid.: 182) takes up this point and explores the concept of perjury under American Law. We have briefly described perjury above, but here is Solan's summary:

The federal perjury statute is:
  Whoever-having taken an oath . . . that he will testify, declare, depose, or certify truly, or that any written testimony, declaration, deposition, or

certificate by him subscribed is true, willfully and contrary to such oath states or subscribes any material matter which he does not believe to be true . . . is guilty of perjury and shall, except as otherwise expressly provided by law, be fined under this title or imprisoned not more than five years, or both. . . . (cited in Solan, 2003: 184)

Solan notes that: "nothing in the perjury statute requires a statement to be literally false." Nonetheless, the Supreme Court in a unanimous decision held that perjury does require proof of a "false statement."

The Supreme Court decision arose in the case of *Bronston v. the United States*. Bronston's prosecution was based, in part, on the following exchange (Solan, 2003: 184):

Q. Do you have any bank accounts in Swiss banks, Mr. Bronston?
A. No Sir.
Q. Have you ever?
A. The company had an account there for about six months, in Zurich.

Apparently it was the case that Bronston also had, at an earlier point in time, a personal Swiss bank account. In this context, Bronston was judged as having lied in his first response and he was convicted of perjury. The Supreme Court later overturned this conviction, arguing that in answering the questions put by the prosecution Bronston was telling the truth, since at the time of the question he didn't have a Swiss bank account.

The problem was the first question. In its present tense form it referred to Bronston having/not having an account now, not whether he had ever at any time had an account. While the prosecution tries to correct this in a follow-up question, directly asking Bronston if he had ever had any Swiss bank accounts, Bronston's response provided an answer to a different question, one that had not been asked, something like "has the company ever had a Swiss bank account?" Although Bronston was not asked this question, had he been asked such a question, his answer would have been truthful. Hence, while Bronston may have been misleading in his evidence, he was telling the truth, or at least he answered truthfully.

Solan notes that various scholars (for example, Tiersma, 1990) have criticized the Bronston decision because it fails to see that "lying should be seen as a special case of the act of deception," where deception is seen as a speech act (Austin, 1962; Searle, 1969) with a specific "perlocutionary" effect (Chapter 1), in this case using a speech act with the intention of having others believe something that is false. So while Bronston's answers were truthful, that is, that he did not have a Swiss bank account, such an answer can also lead some people to infer a stronger version of his response, specifically that he has "never" had a bank account in Switzerland. The problem is that in terms of shared information, it would have been clear to Bronston that the first question meant "did he **ever** have a Swiss back account," and this is confirmed by the second question. In this context, and within a Gricean frame of cooperation, Bronston could be said to say less than required for the purposes of the exchange. This assumes, of course, that such a principle of cooperation applies in all contexts in the same way and at the same level—which it does not. Hence, like Clinton, since Bronston is in a court of law he is being careful in what in he says, knowing that to admit to certain facts would be problematic for him; the trick is to be truthful without giving the exact information the attorney seeks for the prosecution's purposes. It is this type of pragmatic behavior, I would suggest, that Tiersma (1990) and Winter (2001) are defining as "lying" (see Chapter 4).

But is this reasonable? Consider the view of Richard Posner, a judge and senior law lecturer at the Chicago Law School (2000: 49):

> The defendant was asked "Do you have" any Swiss bank accounts? He answered no. The follow-up question was, "Have you ever?" To that he answered, "The company had an account there about six months." The truth was that he had had Swiss bank account for five years, but did not have any at the time of trial, and so his first answer is correct. Had he said "no" to the follow-up question, he would have been guilty of perjury. Instead, he gave an answer (a truthful one) to a question that had not been asked, whether not he but his company had ever had a Swiss bank account. The answer was misleading but not false.

In this case, then, the "speech act" argument would not apply in law since at no point did Bronston say anything which was "materially" false. If the perlocutionary effect of his answers led some jurors to believe more than he said (based on inference or "unstated premises"), Bronston cannot be held legally responsibly for this, since what he said was "literally true."

Posner (2000) also gives us another and similar legal example known as the DeZarn case, where the outcome of the "literal truth" defense comes out slightly differently; in this case a charge of perjury is upheld. DeZarn was questioned about illegal political fundraising; one question put to him was whether there had been fundraising taking place at a party he attended in 1991. In his answer De Zarn argued that he had not seen any fundraising activity or been aware of any. The problem was that the party in question occurred in 1990, not 1991, so in this sense one might say that what DeZarn said was truthful. Since there was no party in 1991, he could not have seen or been aware of any fundraising. This argument was rejected by the courts; it was argued that at the time the question was asked DeZarn was fully aware that the question was referring to the party that occurred in 1990, and not a fictitious party of 1991. Posner argues that this is a "sound" decision. If we apply this position to Clinton, in many of his answers he clearly knew what his questioners were getting at; his very avoidance tactics, if they "materially" affected the case, would be indicative of perjury. Certainly this is what Posner argues, suggesting that Clinton lied on several different issues and at several different times.

Part of the problem here is that within the legal context debates are not only about language, but also about what is "reasonable." The decision to uphold the charge of perjury in the DeZarn case assumes that the attorney made a mistake with the date and that this could have, indeed should have, been understood by DeZarn. Consequently, his answer should have been adjusted in the light of this mistake, and since it was not, what he said was untrue. This sets a very strong standard for what is "reasonable." It seems, in courts, if some aspect of knowledge could be made "mutually manifest" (Sperber and Wilson, 1995) then it should be. But this means that any form of linguistic manipulation could become "unreasonable." Does this make sarcasm or irony potentially illegal, for example?

a. Did you have a few drinks at the party last Saturday?
b. No.
c. What, you went to the party and didn't have a drink?
d. Yes I had lots of drinks at the party.
e. You just said you didn't have any drinks at the party.
f. No, I said I didn't have any drinks at the party on Saturday, there was no party on Saturday, the party was on Friday night.

Or consider how our previous discussion about scalar implicatures and how they might play out in court (see Chapter 3).

Q. How many children does John have?
A. Three.
Q. That is not true, John has four children.
A. Well when I said three, I meant at least three.

Posner's arguments raise some interesting pragmatic as well as legal issues, but the court's decision in the DeZarn case also seems to deny a witness the opportunity to intentionally obfuscate to protect himself. Of course, as Posner points out, it is only where such obfuscation "materially" affects the case that is it an obstruction of justice. We will consider this point further below, but for now let us return to Clinton's evidence.

If we look closely at the terms "sexual relations" and "sexual relationship," what is central for Clinton is that these terms imply or include in their meaning "sexual intercourse."

Q: So, your definition of sexual relationship is intercourse only, is that correct?
CLINTON: No, not necessarily intercourse only. But it would include intercourse. I believe, I believe that the common understanding of the term, if you say two people are having a sexual relationship, most people believe that includes intercourse. So, if that's what Ms. Lewinsky thought, then this is a truthful affidavit. I don't know what was in her mind. But if that's what she thought, the affidavit is true.

Many people do think that "sexual relations" would include intercourse, and indeed if that was what Ms. Lewinsky had in mind at the time of her affidavit, when she said she did not have sexual relations with Clinton, it would be true. But if one invokes "what most or many people" would believe or would commonly believe, then one would have to ask, given the definition of "sexual relations" in the Paula Jones case, how could Clinton claim that he was not having "sexual relations" with Ms. Lewinsky when he admits to fondling her breasts, touching her genitals, and allowing her to perform oral sex on him, all of which seem to be covered by the agreed court definition outlined above?

The encounter with the Grand Jury on this issue is worth citing in some detail, beginning where Clinton is pushed to explain for the Grand Jury what he meant when he said he had an "inappropriate relationship" with Miss Lewinsky.

A . . . What I meant was, and what they can infer that I meant was, that I did things that were—when I was alone with her, that were inappropriate and wrong. But that they did not include any activity that was within the definition of sexual relations that I was given by Judge Wright in the deposition. I said that I did not do those things that were in that, within that definition, and I testified truthfully to that. And that's all I can say about it.

Given that the definition given by Judge Wright (see above) included touching part of another person's body and genitalia, it seems difficult to see how Clinton squares this circle—and it seems to get worse.

Q: Well, I have a question regarding your definition then. And my question is, is oral sex performed on you within that definition as you understood it, the definition in the Jones.

CLINTON: As I understood it, it was not, no.

Clinton has indicated that he will not go into detail regarding why he believes much of what he was doing with Monica Lewinsky was not covered by the description of "sexual relations" in definition 1, because he believes it is not necessary.

CLINTON . . . Now, respectfully, I believe the grand jurors can ask me if I believe—just like that grand juror did—could ask me, do you believe that this conduct falls within that definition. If it does, then you are free to conclude, that my testimony is that I didn't do that. And I believe that you can achieve that without requiring me to say and do things that I don't think are necessary and that I think, frankly, go too far in trying to criminalize my private life.

The questioning continues in an attempt to get a clearer view of what it is that Clinton does agree would be covered by "sexual relations" in definition 1, and how the elements of this definition map or match in any way with what he was doing with Miss Lewinsky.

> Q: If a person touched another person, if you touched another person on the breast, would that be, in your view, and was it within your view, when you took the deposition, within the definition of sexual relations?
>
> CLINTON: If the person being deposed -
>
> Q: Yes.
>
> CLINTON:—in this case, me, directly touched the breast of another person, with the purpose to arouse or gratify, under that definition that would be included.
>
> Q. Only directly, sir, or would it be directly or through clothing?
>
> CLINTON: Well, I would—I think the common sense definition would be directly. That's how I would infer what it means.
>
> Q. If the person being deposed kissed the breast of another person, would that be in the definition of sexual relations as you understood it when you were under oath in the Jones case?
>
> CLINTON: Yes, that would constitute contact. I think that would. If it were direct contact, I believe it would. I—maybe I should read it again, just to make sure.
>
> Q. Because this basically says if there was any direct contact with an intent to arouse or gratify, if that was the intent of the contact, then that would fall within the definition.
>
> CLINTON: That's correct.
>
> Q. So, touching, in your view then and now—the person being deposed touching or kissing the breast of another person would fall within the definition?
>
> CLINTON: That's correct, sir.
>
> Q. And you testified that you didn't have sexual relations with Monica Lewinsky in the Jones deposition, under that definition, correct?
>
> CLINTON: That's correct, sir.

The questioning carries on in this manner for some considerable time, but perhaps it is best summed up in this last example:

> CLINTON: You are free to infer that my testimony is that I did not have sexual relations, as I understood this term to be defined.
>
> Q. Including touching her breast, kissing her breast, or touching her genitalia?
>
> CLINTON: That's correct.

The issue here is how Clinton interprets the concept of "intention" as used in definition 1 (see also Chapter 3). It can be accepted that touching may have taken place, but this only becomes defined as sexual relations if one accepts that there was an intention to arouse. If Clinton did touch Miss Lewinsky's breasts but did not intend to arouse her, or indeed himself, then such touching might fall outside definition 1. Clinton later stated, "I thought the definition included any activity by [me], where [I] was the actor and came in contact with those parts of the body which had been explicitly listed," and "with an **intent** to gratify or arouse the sexual desire of any person." Consequently, Clinton denies that he ever touched, as an intentional actor, Lewinsky's "genitalia, anus, groin, breast, inner thigh, or buttocks," and thus in terms of the definition 1 he did not have sexual relations with Miss Lewinsky. But there is more; following a similar logic, Clinton could also claim that there is a distinction between receiving and giving oral sex. Those receiving oral sex are in a different intentional mode to those giving such sex, since the performance of fellatio would seem to be with the intention to arouse; however, even if the receiver became aroused, this may not have been intentional on their part. Further, Clinton argued that fellatio is in itself not covered by definition 1 since the person who is the receiver would be causing contact ". . . with the lips of the fellator rather than any of the body parts listed in the definition" (Posner, 2000: 29).

In many ways this seems an absurd interpretation of "sexual relations," but as several legal commentators have pointed out, Clinton's manipulation of the definition would never have been made possible had the court not tried to agree to a form of words for a definition of "sexual relations" in the first place. Once given such a definition, Clinton sees it as his right, under the law, to interpret this as he sees relevant for his case.

Clearly, Clinton is involved in several levels of pragmatic manipulation, but is this something negative, or something you shouldn't do? Grice's "Cooperative Principle" assists us in making interpretations both when it is obeyed and when it is flouted; the general "principle of relevance" still applies even when one is being deceptive (otherwise the deception might not work). One cannot be arrested for making pragmatic selections as such, but clearly such selections, however structurally appropriate, may be contextually illegal in some cases, and this should be a legal judgment, not a linguistic one. As I have suggested above and elsewhere in this book, it is an open question as to where one draws the line between lying, deception, interpersonal sensitivity, persuasion, and so on. Are there social contexts where one must only ever say what is true, what can be semantically assessed as factual, or what can be evidenced or objectively assessed? Or is it simply in the nature of language that it is used for different purposes, in different contexts, and at different times? Whether such uses are illegal, immoral, unjustified, or whatever, are social and ethical assessments, not necessarily linguistic or pragmatic ones. The issue is that language has always been shot through with indirectness, ambiguity, and confusion.

In a study carried out after Clinton's impeachment, Sanders and Reinisch (1999; cited in Tiersma, 2004:943), surveyed 600 undergraduates and asked them what they would define as "having sex." Specifically, the students were asked to determine if someone could be said to have "had sex with someone else if they . . ." and here a variety of options were given, such as kissing, touching, penetration, and so on. In the case of "French kissing," only 2% would see this as fulfilling the criteria for having "had sex." If oral sex was involved, this figure rose to 40%. But, of course, when we come to full sexual intercourse involving penetration the figure is 99.5%. Sexual intercourse is the clear "prototype" of having sex with someone else, and it doesn't seem unreasonable to define full "sexual intercourse" as also the "prototype" of "sexual relations," and this is exactly what Clinton was claiming.

Humpty Dumpty on the Ropes: Intentions, Semantic Underdetermination, and Pragmatics

In a well-known example from Lewis Carroll's *Alice Through the Looking Glass*, Alice has an exchange with Humpty Dumpty:

> "And only *one* for birthday presents, you know. There's glory for you!"
>
> "I don't know what you mean by 'glory,'" Alice said.
>
> Humpty Dumpty smiled contemptuously. "Of course you don't—till I tell you. I meant 'there's a nice knock-down argument for you!'"
>
> "But 'glory' doesn't mean 'a nice knock-down argument,'" Alice objected.
>
> "When *I* use a word," Humpty Dumpty said, in rather a scornful tone, "it means just what I choose it to mean—neither more nor less."
>
> "The question is," said Alice, "whether you *can* make words mean so many different things."
>
> "The question is," said Humpty Dumpty, "which is to be master—that's all."

In chapter 2 of Book 10 of Carroll's work *Symbolic Logic*, he says (cited by Malcolm Chilsom: March 2012; blog):

> . . . I maintain that any writer of a book is fully authorized in attaching any meaning he likes to any word he intends to use. If I find an author saying at the beginning of his book, 'Let it be understood that by the word *white* I shall always mean *black*' I meekly accept his ruling, however injudicious I may think it.

Is this Humpty Dumpty's linguistic free-for-all? Not really; the issue is one of consistency in language use. But the question is, whose or which "consistency" are we talking about? Clinton was given a court-agreed definition of "sexual relations" in the Paula Jones case, and that was the court's definition, not Clinton's definition. When he said he understood the definition he had been given by the court, he was telling the truth, something like, "I understand the court's definition of sexual relations." This is not the same as saying either he agreed with the definition, or thought it a fair and reasonable definition of sexual relations. Clinton had his own definition of "sexual relations," which differed from that of the court; in Clinton's definition, sexual intercourse was included within "sexual

relations." One might ask why the court constructed a definition of "sexual relations" as they did. Ironically, one reason might be that since the prosecution
already had information of what had taken place between Lewinsky and Clinton,
and it was known that it did not involve sexual intercourse, they may have assumed there was no need to place this center. But by including almost everything
but "sexual intercourse" under the definition of "sexual relations," this allowed
Clinton to say he understood the definition, yet at the same time reject it as a
description of his inappropriate behavior with Miss Lewinsky because his own
definition of "sexual relations" included "sexual intercourse," while the definition offered by the courts did not.

We see here that Clinton is behaving like Nixon, making use of the alternative ways in which words or phrases may be understood in different contexts. But
does this mean that Humpty Dumpty wins—that because meaning is slippery
and underdetermined that we can create meanings at will? Part of the problem
lies in the view that meanings can be easily formalized, and therefore made precise. It is not that we don't have agreed-upon definitions of what words or sentences mean; rather, this agreement is often not as formally precise when we come
to look at the real world use of language in context. We tend to operate with what
are called "stereotypes" (what we might expect) and "prototypes" (exemplars of
phenomena) (see Geeraerts, 2008, who discusses these concepts in relation to
Clinton).

Technically, strawberries are not a fruit, but many people do not know this,
and therefore strawberries are often thought of as fruit. If I had some strawberries for lunch and someone asked if I had fruit today, I could say yes and this
would be a prototypical use, or I could say no, and go "all technical" and argue
that strawberries are not fruit. But who says what is and what is not a fruit? This is
what the philosopher Hilary Putnam (1975) calls a "linguistic division of labor."
Putnam says if we look at a tree, most of us might not be able to say much about
it other than that it's a tree. An arborist (tree expert), however, will see a specific
tree, an oak, ash, or whatever. But this does not mean that the arborist will not
understand what we mean when we say, "I ate my strawberries under a tree."

One of the problems with establishing an agreed-upon theory of semantics
is that "meaning" is not merely imprecise, it is worse—as Quine (1960) argues,
meanings are underdetermined, that is, for any word given to us at a specific
point in time, we will never have enough evidence to determine its exact meaning.
In Quine's famous example, if we hear members of a an exotic tribe shout "Gav-
agai" when a rabbit runs past, we might be tempted to translate this as "rabbit."
But Quine argues that we can't know whether it means rabbit, part of a rabbit,
rabbit state, or whatever, since the reaction to the stimuli would be the same in
each case. This argument goes much deeper than the issue of whether we understand the same words differently; it challenges the very nature of an objective
level of meaning. However, as Searle (1987) and others have pointed out (and as
Quine himself concedes), the strong indeterminacy thesis could not exist unless

there was some level of agreed-upon meaning and understanding between the writer and reader in which to assess, agree, or refute the thesis of indeterminacy (Searle, 1987).

In this context, analysts still strive, as Grice did, to keep distinct "what is said" (linguistic meaning) and "what is meant" (speaker meaning). The original aim had been to create a level where linguistic meaning focused on "propositions," the underlying core meanings of words and sentences, and everything that fell outside this was pragmatics. Two problems ensue here; the first is that many ordinary sentences seem propositionally incomplete, and hence require some addition or filling in, independently of context. Bach (1994: 268) suggests that following sentences seem problematic in this sense:

(a) You are going to die.
(b) I haven't eaten.
(c) Everyone must wear a costume.
(d) Steel isn't strong enough.

Example (a) leaves an open question, die from what? Die naturally, or die from injuries or disease or whatever? Again with (b) we would want to know something about when and why? With (c) we might need some constraint on the quantification "everyone" and in (d) once again we might ask "strong enough for what?" The "filling in" or "out" of these propositions creates what Bach calls "implicitures" and what Sperber and Wilson call "explicatures" (see Chapter 1). Explicatures and implicitures are very similar, the main differences being in terms of the theoretical models within which they are explained—Bach preferring to work within a Gricean framework and Sperber and Wilson adopting the cognitive frame of Relevance Theory. For our purposes, however, the main point is that such elements of meaning become available for manipulation within real world interaction.

Consider a well-known example form Sperber and Wilson (1995): "It will take some time to fix this watch." It is argued that this sentence is underdetermined in that all actions will take some amount of time. The expansion required here is that the process of fixing the "watch" will take some "significant" time. After all, watches are complex objects. On the other hand, the term "fix" in this context could also be ambiguous; it might simply refer to "replace a battery," which in modern watches would take a short amount of time. It is not suggested that Sperber and Wilson's example sentence does not require completion; rather, that completion may be used in context for different purposes. Let's say, for example, that the watch is brought to a jeweler by someone who doesn't understand watches; he only knows it has stopped working. The jeweler may be unscrupulous and try to take advantage of the customer. The jeweler may realize, for example, that all that is required is a replacement battery, which might take two minutes and cost very little. If the jeweler says, "It will take some time to fix this watch," she will be telling the truth, but if the customer assumes she means (via an explicature) that it will take some significant time, he may expect to pay more for the process. Hence, the jeweler may say, "Come back tomorrow," and then charge a price well beyond the time spent on the watch.

If we produce a sentence such as "I have had sexual relations," one might argue that this is incomplete, in that we need to assign an identity to the first person pronoun, we need to consider "with whom," and we may also need to consider why or for what purposes. But at the level of completion, would we need to fill in "sexual relations," and if we did try to do this, how would we do it? If we look to semantics and try to assess a set of all and only those truth conditions for sexual relations, we would find this very difficult to complete. However, as the student study above suggests, if we look at the prototype of "sexual relations," this would imply the inclusion of "sexual intercourse." And this is exactly Clinton's point; hence if you ask him if he has had sexual relations with Miss Lewinsky, he will say no.

Clinton Takes a Stand: The Presidential Stance

As we have noted, Clinton has made clear that he did not see it as his responsibility to assist those prying into his private life. In this context he saw himself as defending both his rights as president and his rights to a private life. He believed the depositions were unnecessary and went beyond the brief that Starr had originally been given. Clinton approached the depositions as a "hostile witness"; he was not there to be helpful. The very nature of this hostility is calibrated through his pragmatic motivation and manipulation of such things as the definition of "sexual relations" and his frequent use of hedges and epistemic markers of evidentiality such as "I believe," "I think," "as I remember," "its possible that," and so on. Hence, Clinton's pragmatic style indicates his positioning, or as it has become known in recent years, his "stance."

One of the main proponents of the concept of "stance" is John Du Bois (2004, 2007, who argues that "stance" is not something you do, it is something you take with respect to other participants, objects, and topics. As Du Bois states:

> I define stance as a public act by a social actor, achieved dialogically through overt communicative means (language, gesture, and other symbolic forms), through which social actors simultaneously evaluate objects, position subjects (themselves and others), and align with other subjects, with respect to any salient dimension of value in the sociocultural field. (Du Bois, 2007: 32)

The process of stance taking involves three core elements: evaluation, positioning, and alignment. Simply put, a speaker evaluates an "object," positions himself relative to that object, and aligns with other subjects relative to that object. This is a "dialogical" process in that it is built upon the words of the stance-taker as he himself relates to the words of others. Du Bois suggests that there may be what he calls a "dialogic syntax" such that speakers may use the utterances of others to build their own utterances (not unlike intertextuality: see Chapter 2).

Given the question/answer structure of depositions, they present themselves as "stance"-oriented environments. The actions of rejecting, modifying, or marking questions reflects the way the respondent is evaluating the question, its content, and its contextual operation within delimited sociocultural environments. In doing this, respondents are involved in the action of "positioning," defined by Du Bois as

> ... the act of situating a social actor with respect to responsibility for stance and for invoking a sociocultural value. (Du Bois 2007: 140)

The general process of stance taking is represented by Du Bois within what he calls "The Stance Triangle (see figure 4, adapted from Du Bois, 2007)."

Because of the dialogical nature of "stance taking," and its intersubjective construction, it is an interactionally iterative process that is open to continuous change and development. But it is possible to read "stances" off linguistic frames, and this seems certainly available from Clinton's "stance taking" and "stance construction" in his depositions. One major "object," or "topic," under view in the Paula Jones case, and in the depositions to the Grand Jury, is Clinton's relationship with Monica Lewinsky. This relationship dialogically links previous testimony in the Paula Jones case and the depositions of the Grand Jury.

In the Paula Jones case, Clinton takes the "stance" that he does not see the object or topic the prosecution wishes to explore as fit or relevant to the needs of the Paula Jones inquiry, hence his pragmatic marking of evidence, and his delimitation, or manipulation, of the definition of "sexual relations." In the case of the Grand Jury, Clinton carries forward a similar "stance," but this is also interactively and intersubjectively enjoined with his positioning in his Grand Jury opening statement and his previous deposition in the Paula Jones case. Here the node of "the stance triangle" as "object" is Clinton's "stance" on two sets of

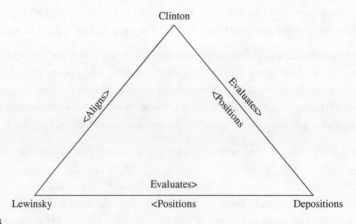

FIGURE 4

information or evidence: what he has said previously to the Paula Jones inquiry, and his deposition to the Grand Jury. For the Grand Jury Clinton will focus on the consistency of evidence in this object node, that is, evidence P (Paula Jones) and evidence G (Grand Jury). Clinton's stance on this is that P and G are consistent, or at least not intentionally inconsistent, in that they both contain truthful responses.

In order to maintain this "stance," Clinton must draw upon evidential resources, his own definition of sexual relations, and also, in this case, what we might call a "blocking" stance (see Wilson and Stapleton, 2007: see also Chapter 7). What we mean here is that Clinton refuses to assess, confirm, or comment on what the Grand Jury or any others might infer from what he has said, placing responsibility for any such inferences with members of the jury themselves.

Such "stance taking" and the production of the opening statement to the Grand Jury, in which Clinton admits an inappropriate relationship with Miss Lewinsky, and in which he also explains his "stance taking" in his Jones deposition, are produced directly for the Grand Jury. However, what Clinton says also becomes available directly and indirectly for the public. In this case, the public are what Goffman (1974, 1981) refers to as "overhearers." They are not directly involved in the dialogical processes involving the Grand Jury and Clinton, but they can access what is said as "overhearers" and can make an assessment of those "stances" that have or are being adopted by the parties to the interaction. As Clinton is first and foremost a politician, he is fully aware of the access the public would have through various sources (newspapers, radio, television, etc.) to not only what he said to the Grand Jury, but also how this fits with what he said previously in the Paula Jones case. It is for this reason that Clinton decides to speak to the nation immediately following his Grand Jury testimony, and here, at least initially, he becomes involved in another pragmatic process of stance taking, involving the speech actions associated with "apologizing."

You Call That an Apology?

As we have discussed at some length, many of the core issues in the Clinton/Lewinsky case involve a variety of linguistically driven concerns. We also noted that following his statement to the Grand Jury, Clinton went on national television and made a statement to the nation:

> Good evening.
>
> This afternoon in this room, from this chair, I testified before the Office of Independent Counsel and the grand jury. I answered their questions truthfully, including questions about my private life, questions no American citizen would ever want to answer. Still, I must take complete responsibility for all my actions, both public and private. And that is why I am speaking to you tonight.

As you know, in a deposition in January, I was asked questions about my relationship with Monica Lewinsky. While my answers were legally accurate, I did not volunteer information.

Indeed, I did have a relationship with Ms. Lewinsky that was not appropriate. In fact, it was wrong. It constituted a critical lapse in judgment and a personal failure on my part for which I am solely and completely responsible.

But I told the grand jury today and I say to you now that at no time did I ask anyone to lie, to hide or destroy evidence or to take any other unlawful action.

I know that my public comments and my silence about this matter gave a false impression. I misled people, including even my wife. I deeply regret that. I can only tell you I was motivated by many factors. First, by a desire to protect myself from the embarrassment of my own conduct.

I was also very concerned about protecting my family. The fact that these questions were being asked in a politically inspired lawsuit, which has since been dismissed, was a consideration, too.

In addition, I had real and serious concerns about an independent counsel investigation that began with private business dealings 20 years ago—dealings, I might add, about which an independent federal agency found no evidence of any wrongdoing by me or my wife over two years ago. The independent counsel investigation moved on to my staff and friends, then into my private life. And now the investigation itself is under investigation.

This has gone on too long, cost too much and hurt too many innocent people.

Now, this matter is between me, the two people I love most—my wife and our daughter—and our God. I must put it right, and I am prepared to do whatever it takes to do so.

Nothing is more important to me personally. But it is private, and I intend to reclaim my family life for my family. It's nobody's business but ours. Even presidents have private lives. It is time to stop the pursuit of personal destruction and the prying into private lives and get on with our national life.

Our country has been distracted by this matter for too long, and I take my responsibility for my part in all of this. That is all I can do.

Now it is time—in fact, it is past time—to move on.

We have important work to do—real opportunities to seize, real problems to solve, real security matters to face.

And so tonight, I ask you to turn away from the spectacle of the past seven months, to repair the fabric of our national discourse, and to return our attention to all the challenges and all the promise of the next American century.

Thank you for watching. And good night.

President Bill Clinton, August 17, 1998

In her chapter "The Semantics of an Impeachment: Meanings and Models in a Political Conflict," Pamela S. Morgan considers the Clinton/Lewinsky scandal and claims that at ". . . every point in the events of the scandal the issues were centered around the meanings of words" (Morgan, 2001: 77). In her analysis she focuses on a number of issues similar to those we have discussed above; for example, did Clinton lie? But she also draws attention to Clinton's public address to the nation just cited, which she claims was described by Clinton's ". . . adherents as an apology." As Morgan correctly points out, "apologies" are "speech acts" and calls these core "pragmatic" phenomena. It is somewhat confusing, then, that Morgan refers to Clinton's statement to the nation as raising ". . . questions of semantics in the definitions of speech acts" (Morgan, 2001: 80), by which I think she simply means whether or not Clinton has in fact fulfilled a number of the conditions required for the correct performance of an apology. Austin (1962) and Searle (1969) defined speech acts in relation to what Austin originally called "felicity conditions" and which are now just generally known as "speech act conditions," those conditions which should be in place if the act is to be successfully performed. These conditions fall under a number of core headings: "essential conditions," "sincerity conditions," and "preparatory conditions." Applying these to apologies, Owen (1983) suggests the following:

Preparatory condition:

> Rule (1). The act A specified in the propositional content is an offense against the addressee H.
> Rule (2). H would have preferred S's not doing A to S's doing A and S believes H would have preferred S's not doing A to his doing A.
> Rule (3). A does not benefit H and S believes A does not benefit H.

Sincerity condition:
S regrets (is sorry for) having done A.
Essential condition:
The proposition counts as an expression of regret by S for having done A.

So if one is to produce an apology, one must have something to apologize for, and one must then sincerely produce an utterance that counts as an "apology," the most obvious being "I apologize." But how does one confirm that something is or is not an apology if various forms may be used directly or indirectly, and how does one assess the degree of sincerity or insincerity within a speaker's expression of an apology?

Apologies have received significant academic attention in recent years, studies have ranged from a focus on apologies within a single language to a comparison of apologies across one or more languages (Bharuthram, 2003; Butler, 2001; Deutschmann, 2003; Holmes, 1990; Risen and Gilovich, 2007; Cohen and Shively, 2007; Jebahi, 2011; Guan, Park, and Lee, 2009). Such research has emphasized the role of linguistic structure in the performance of apologies. Searle (1969) reminds us, however, that apologies are also socially constructed (see also

Kissine, 2013). For example, while apologies have the core aim of expressing "regret," they also express that "regret" toward some end or objective. Since such ends or objectives will be socially, individually, and culturally variable, focusing mainly on the linguistically constitutive nature of apologies may miss the related and important functional and social nature of apologies. In this sense, Meier (1998: 227) calls for a shift in focus away from the "how" to the "why" of apologies, that is, a shift toward understanding the cultural and contextual production of actions that become interactionally understood as apologies.

For example, a distinction has been made between "private" and "public" apologies. Public apologies are increasingly found within politics and other forms of public life (see Funk-Unrau, 2004; Cunningham, 1999; Hargie, Stapleton, and Tourish, 2010). Cunningham (1999) notes that within public apologies the issue of "sincerity" has become central. This is not surprising in that public figures may be called upon to apologize for historic actions for which they are not individually responsible; thus genuine regret may be less obvious in public apologies (see O'Neill, 1999). Equally, when the actions of large corporations negatively impact on society, CEOs may feel that they should not be singled out and made to apologize because responsibility operates at various levels of management within large multinational corporations.

Harris et al. (2006) have attempted to distinguish several components within political apologies. They note four main dimensions (721–723):

(1) Political apologies are in the public domain and . . . are highly mediated.
(2) Political apologies are often generated by (and further generate) conflict and controversy.
(3) Both an explicit IFID (illocutionary force indicating device) and a form of words which indicates the acceptance of responsibility and/or blame for the "offense" by the apologizer appear to be crucial component parts of political apologies in order for the media and viewers to perceive them as apologies.
(4) Because they are usually in the public domain and they are highly mediated, as well as often involving substantial differences in status and power between the apologizer and the "victim," it is rare for the response to the political apology to contain an explicit form of absolution.

Harris et al. also make the point that one of the most important factors in a political apology is the relative seriousness of the offense, and this can range from "social gaffes" to "leading a country to war." There is also the issue that many recent political apologies have been for actions that are historically distant, and politicians may be apologizing on behalf of a previous administration, for instance Prime Minister Tony Blair apologized for the Irish famine, and Bill Clinton apologized for America's role in the slave trade (Harris et al., 2006: 725).

But such apologies may also be politically problematic. In 1997 Australian Prime Minister John Howard spoke to a Reconciliation Convention about the relationship between "indigenous" and "white" Australians. In an analysis of Howard's presentation, Augoustinos, Le Couteur, and Fogarty (2007: 97) note that:

> . . . by constructing apologizing to mean an admission of guilt, the Prime Minister was able to make a national apology seem wrong and unfair to present generations of 'white' Australians. Constructing apologizing as an admission of guilt also enabled the Prime Minister to contest and undermine versions of history that give weight to the suffering experienced by Australia's indigenous peoples at the hands of past generations of 'white' Australians.

Howard claimed, for example, that:

> Reconciliation will not work if it puts a higher value on symbolic gestures and overblown promises rather than the practical needs of Aboriginal and Torres Straight Island people in areas like health, housing, education and employment.
>
> It will not work if it is premised solely on a sense of national guilt and shame. Rather we should acknowledge past injustices and focus our energies on addressing the root causes of current and future disadvantage among our Indigenous people.
>
> (examples from Augoustinos, Le Couteur, and Fogarty (2007: 98)

Here Howard downplays the need for the performative action of apologizing for past deeds—which most modern Australians were not part of—in favor of concentrating on the needs of the present.

Returning now to Clinton's statement to the nation, it certainly looks like an apology. According to Harris et al.'s analysis above, Clinton's statement (a) has been explicitly produced so that it would be distributed across the media, (b) it has occurred as the result of controversy, (c) there is an acceptance of blame and there is the use of selected forms of words relevant to the illocutionary performance of an apology (for example, "regret"), and (d) there is clearly an issue of power differential in the apologizing process. However, Clinton's apology does create problems for (c) and (d). In (d), for example, Clinton may be apologizing to several groups or individuals simultaneously, each with their own differential levels of power. Compare, for example, the difference between Monica Lewinsky and Hilary Clinton, or the Senate and Congress and the judiciary, and consider, in terms of power, that Clinton is also apologizing to the American people. Further, with (c), although we find the use of the word "regret," we also find an explanation or justification for actions, so it becomes unclear whether we have an "account" or a "justification," or an "apology," or all three.

Was Clinton's statement to the nation an apology, or did it at least contain an apology, as well as several other speech acts? As noted above, Morgan (2001 has been critical of the claim that Clinton's statement was an apology. Murata (1998: 502) cautions us, however, that we mustn't judge apologies only in relation to an abstract set of conditions, we must also draw upon social and interactional information, and look at data that arises in "real life incidents." In other words, we can't just line up theory alongside Clinton's apology, we must take some account of the apology as a public event, and we must try to assess Clinton's own goals and aspirations in making his statement.

The View from Clinton's Window

In this section I consider some technical issues in deciding whether Clinton's statement to the nation was or was not an apology. In doing so, we will also consider Clinton's own view of what it is he thought he was doing. We are not claiming some special insight into Clinton's mind, but are merely taking account of what we know with hindsight; for example, we know that Clinton's advisors were quite clear what the goals of the statement should be, that Clinton should "apologize." According to Baker (2000: 32), Clinton seemed to agree with his advisors when he stated, "I was wrong I have to apologize to the American people," but then he added, "But this is outrageous what Starr has done. If I don't say that, no one else will. I can't just let it go." And Clinton wouldn't let it go, insisting and including in his statement his view that Starr was acting inappropriately and that he (Clinton) had to defend himself and his family. Erskine Bowles, Clinton's Chief of Staff, made his view clear on Clinton's strategy: "This is crazy: This is stupid and wrong" (cited in Baker, 2000: 33).

As we noted above, apologies are not only based on a set of performative conditions, but also the operation of those conditions in context and with an specific objective in mind (Searle, 1969; Kissine, 2013). Further, Tavuchis (1991) argues that we need to keep clear the distinction between an "account" and an "apology." Tavuchis says that apologies are different from accounts since an apology indicates that there is no excuse, justification, or defense for actions— hence the need for an apology. In terms of Searle's comment, that apologies are targeted to an end, Tavuchis constrains all apologies to a single end, a restorative one in which the apology transforms negative actions in an effort to restore social harmony.

If we adopt Tavuchis's view of apologies, there can be no excuse or explanation for the action, it is or was wrong and the responsible person should apologize. This would seem to be in line with the approach that Clinton's advisors wanted him to adopt, and which Clinton chose to ignore. Rahm Emanuel told Clinton, "People aren't going to hang with you because you are opposed to Starr. They're going to hang with you because of what you are doing for them" (Baker, 2000: 32). Other advisors and friends agreed, but Clinton would not be moved. "I did wrong and so did he. Damn it, somebody has to say these things. I don't care if I'm impeached, it's the right thing to do." And so with both the aim of apologizing, but also with the aim of challenging Starr's actions, Clinton faced the nation and gave them the televised speech noted above.

So was it an apology? As we said, it has the "conditions" of an apology. Clinton has met a number of Owen's (2003) conditions (see above). He meets the preparatory condition when he says (a) and (b):

(a) Indeed, I did have a relationship with Miss Lewinsky that was not appropriate. In fact, it was wrong. It constituted a critical lapse in judgment and a personal failure on my part for which I am solely and completely responsible.

(b) I know that my public comments and my silence about this matter gave a false impression. I misled people, including even my wife. I deeply regret that.

These include an admission of wrongdoing, acceptance of responsibility, and an indication of regret. If we treat this as a public apology, then Clinton also admits that he has propositionally committed act A which is wrong, and he knows that the nation would have preferred him not to have committed Act A, since it does not benefit them in any way. Clinton would also seem to have met the "sincerity condition," as he explicitly says, "I deeply regret. . . ."; this also suggests that Clinton meets the "essential condition," since he regrets having done Act A. Apart from these technical claims, most people who saw or heard Clinton's statement thought of it as an apology. If you type the words "Clinton and apology" into Google, many of the sites call up Clinton's 1998 statement to the nation. Further, while the public may not have been wholly convinced by Clinton's speech, a majority saw the statement as an apology. In a *New York Times*/CBS News Poll conducted immediately after the speech, 63 percent of the public felt that the nation should move beyond the scandal, 18 percent felt that Clinton should resign as president, and 12 percent felt that he should be impeached. According to the post-speech poll, the majority of the public accepted the proposal of "forgive and forget," which again suggests that Clinton's statement was seen as an apology.

Academics who focused on Clinton's statement explored it from various different perspectives, including its rhetorical display of "atonement" and its positioning within the framework of "apologia" (see Koesten and Rowland, 2004; Simons, 2000). The concept of "apologia" comes from the original Greek legal system, where to deliver an *apologia* meant making a formal speech or giving an explanation in order to rebut charges. It is was also used to refer to early Christians' defense of their religion, in which they were "apologists" for their faith. Of course the modern term "apology" has changed, and focuses now on the process and procedures of forgiveness.

It is in this sense that some critics question the semantic/pragmatic nature of the apology (Morgan, 2002). Others complain that Clinton fails to "amplify" his emotional regret, and spends rather more time on "excusing" or justifying his behavior (his apologia). Part of the problem here is that critics sometimes confuse the reception or interactional aspect of "apologizing" with its execution as a speech act (apology).

For example, in Austin's (1962) original analysis he made a distinction between what he called "constatives," statements that are "true" or "false," and "performatives," those utterances which by their very expression perform an action. So one could say "I'm sorry" but not mean it, but one could not say "I apologize" but not have "apologized." As the study of speech acts developed, it was recognized that all utterances are forms of action. Hence, one finds analysts treating "I'm sorry" or "I apologize" as roughly the same thing (Robinson, 2004). Janet Holmes (1990) says that the majority of the apologies in everyday talk use some form of the word "sorry." As we noted above, however, other conditions indicating that an apology was taking place are associated with evidence that the speaker had done something wrong, and they have expressed regret for this. Harris Grainger and Mullany (2006) note that studies which produce taxonomies of apologies focus on two "compulsory elements": some form of illocutionary force indicating device (IFID, I apologize), and an explicit indication and acceptance of responsibility (X was wrong). Along with such compulsory elements, Harris et al. (721) also note three other features that have proved prominent in describing apologies:

   a. an explanation or account
   b. an offer of reparation
   c. a promise of future forbearance

Note that the first one on the list runs counter to Tavuchis's claim that apologies should not contain an account, but this is perhaps a "moral" rather than a structural judgment. Interestingly, if political apologies also tend to occur with some form of account or explanation, then they seem to have a dual function: combining the act of apology with the rhetorical process of apologia.

We noted that the Clinton statement seems to fulfill the conditions for performing an apology, and it could be argued that he also draws upon other elements found within apologies as defined by Harris et al.; he offers some form of explanation for his behavior, for example. He also offers reparation when he says:

> I must put it right, and I am prepared to do whatever it takes to do so.
> Nothing is more important to me personally. But it is private, and I intend to reclaim my family life for my family. It's nobody's business but ours.

Finally, one might argue there is an element of "forbearance" here, as Clinton says:

> Our country has been distracted by this matter for too long, and I take my responsibility for my part in all of this. That is all I can do.

In several different senses, then, one could argue Clinton has apologized. Of course, some people may want more contrition, some may doubt his sincerity (a subjective opinion), some may be unclear to whom he is apologizing (the country, his family, his advisors and friends, Monica Lewinsky, or indeed all of them); but whatever the case, surely we can say he has performed the act of "apology" in that he seems to meet a range of the conditions demanded by, or described by, analysts.

But there is also a structural issue here in that we have been treating the recognition of negative action, regret for that action, and the explanation or justification of that action(s) as naturally connected—and, of course, they normally would be. But in Clinton's statement there are two negative actions and explanation components, and the question is, can they both be assessed as apologies? The first contains the negative action (a) having an inappropriate relationship with Monica Lewinsky, which Clinton explains as (b) that it was "wrong," indicating a "moral lapse" on his part. So we may see this as "negative action 1" and account/explanation 1. Negative action 2 is (c) while the information Clinton gave in his depositions was "legally accurate" it could also have been more informative, that is, he may have misled people, and he tells us that he regrets this, and explains (d) his behavior as one of personal protection in a context where his privacy and status are challenged by counsel; this is explanation/account 2. Here is the relevant section again.

> As you know, in a deposition in January, I was asked questions about my relationship with Monica Lewinsky. While my answers were legally accurate, I did not volunteer information.
>
> Indeed, I did have a relationship with Miss Lewinsky that was not appropriate. In fact, it was wrong. It constituted a critical lapse in judgment and a personal failure on my part for which I am solely and completely responsible.
>
> But I told the grand jury today and I say to you now that at no time did I ask anyone to lie, to hide or destroy evidence or to take any other unlawful action.
>
> I know that my public comments and my silence about this matter gave a false impression. I misled people, including even my wife. I deeply regret that.

Here Clinton admits the inappropriate relationship, and that his comments on this relationship have been misleading to a range of audiences. So when he says I deeply regret "that," what is "that" referring to? Is it the inappropriate relationship or the misleading comments or both? The most likely candidate is that Clinton regrets misleading people, in which case the expression of "regret" refers to the offense of misleading people, and the admission of "wrong" and "inappropriate" behavior. So in terms of the two compulsory elements for apology given by Harris et al., how do they stack up in terms of the examples of negative action/explanation account we have just outlined?

In terms of "misleading remarks," Clinton admits these, and accepts responsibility and regret. Let us give this a charitable interpretation and treat "regret" as indicative of apology (although not guaranteed, since it could have a number of functions), and let us treat "I misled people" and his admission that he gave a "false impression," as acceptance of responsibility. Under our charitable interpretation this is an apology for Clinton's actions in his deposition.

Now in the case of his "inappropriate" behavior with Monica Lewinsky, what do we have? First, he admits that he had a "relationship," accepts it was inappropriate and that it was wrong. So the acceptance of responsibility is covered. But is there an IFID, some word or indirect sign that an apology had been performed? The main thing Clinton says on this matter is this:

> Indeed, I did have a relationship with Miss Lewinsky that was not appropriate. In fact, it was wrong. It constituted a critical lapse in judgment and a personal failure on my part for which I am solely and completely responsible.

Is this an implicit apology or possibly an indirect apology, or an admission that an action that was committed was wrong? It is difficult to claim it is an explicit apology in any sense, and some might say it is not really an apology at all, and for those who claim that Clinton didn't apologize, they may be thinking that he has not apologized for his inappropriate behavior with Miss Lewinsky. Looking back, we know that in later statements and speeches Clinton does explicitly apologize for his "inappropriate behavior"; in fact, he does it all over the world. For example, on 12, 1998, in a speech to an audience of clergy he said:

> I agree with those who have said that in my first statement after I testified I was not contrite enough. I don't think there is a fancy way to say that I have sinned.
>
> It is important to me that everybody who has been hurt know that the sorrow I feel is genuine: first and most important, my family; also my friends, my staff, my Cabinet, Monica Lewinsky and her family, and the American people. I have asked all for their forgiveness.

Here Clinton even refers to the critics of his first statement that he was not contrite enough, and he admits he has "sinned," and has asked for "forgiveness." Clinton was given an ovation during this speech, and the speech was touted around the world as an "apology." Here he does talk about "the sorrow" he feels, and that he has asked for forgiveness. This speech is directly targeted at the issue of Monica Lewinsky, whereas the first statement to the nation was targeted directly at the issue of perjury and the Starr investigation. Both speeches are "apologies," or contain "apologies"; we just need to be careful unpacking the core targets of these apologies.

So are critics right that Clinton's statement to the nation was not an apology? No, there is clearly enough evidence on both "inappropriate behavior" and Clinton's acceptance that he misled people to indicate both his recognition of wrongdoing and his regret. If evidence of these conditions is not enough for some critics, then I suggest they are looking in the wrong place. It is true that research on apologies emphasizes the centrality of both an IFID and acceptance of responsibility, but in some cases it may be enough that the acceptance of responsibility on its own could be construed as an apology. Even when apologies are expressed using both an IFID and acceptance of responsibility, they may be interpreted differently depending on the position from which they are observed. Further, depending on the elaboration of the apology, audiences give differential responses on how willing they are to forgive. It is clear that a range of situational, cultural, and other factors affects apologies.

Interestingly, the integration of intentions, motivations, and goals, as well as degrees of responsibility and the severity of the offense, are things that are learned at an early stage of our social development (see Darby and Schlenker, 1982). Also the degree to which we will accept something as an apology is determined by whether the offense and the apology relate directly to ourselves or to others. Risen and Gilovich (2007) note that those who personally receive apologies, as opposed to those who observe them being given, are more tolerant of the efforts of the apologizer and more willing to accept the apology. This may explain why critics, as observers, are less convinced by Clinton's speech as apologetic, as opposed to those who saw themselves as being directly addressed by Clinton and who wanted to accept the statement as an apology and move on, and, I think, so should we.

6

Bring 'em on! The Empire Strikes Back

GEORGE W. BUSH

Introduction

George W. Bush's early life gave no indication of an interest in politics, or any indication of a significant awareness of policy issues or practical political involvement. There are no clues suggesting an underlying ambition to enter politics and to become the president of the United States; as Bush himself put it, "I was apolitical." Even in his autobiography, *Decision Points*, Bush seems unsure why he ended up running for president. He explains that at various times in his life he was concerned about different things: the way small businesses were treated, or his growing awareness of the importance of state education for the children of America (see also Bush 1999). There is also some suggestion that, ultimately, Bush had a calling from a higher authority (God) to take on the job of president, a point we will discuss in more detail later. But it has been noted frequently that there was an imbalance between Bush the easygoing, fun-loving rabble-rouser of his younger years and the teetotal career politician concerned with developing a caring conservatism. This disjunction fueled the belief that Bush was simply a representative for neoconservative forces, and that the power behind the presidency resided in the likes of Chief of Staff Karl Rove or Vice President Dick Cheney (Buchanan, 2005; Hamn, 2005). There has never been any agreement, or undisputed evidence, that this was the case. Insiders, and Bush himself, have pointed to the way he took individual responsibility for his actions both as governor of Texas and as president of the United States. However, responsibility involves more than making decisions; it also relates to the processes underlying those decisions: how one tests and considers the arguments, how one sifts evidence for specific choices, how far and how wide one listens to alternative positions.

In personal, scholarly, and other assessments of Bush, it is often stated that he had a low boredom threshold: Bush. ". . . needed to know the point of things

160

Talking with the President. John Wilson. © Oxford University Press 2015.
Published 2015 by Oxford University Press

not the details" (Draper, 2007: 12). Bush wanted cases made within a ten- to fifteen-minute frame, and his stubborn streak meant that he would not be easily shifted or side-tracked once a decision was made, and Bush would have to make some of the most significant decisions of any president. In this chapter we what to consider what we can learn about Bush and his political message(s) by applying a pragmatic focus to what he says and what he does. First, we will consider his language directly and focus on his particular penchant for making linguistic errors. Second, and more substantially, we will consider his language use and its inferential content in both explaining why he became president and why he went to war in Iraq.

Problems at the Ranch: Bush Speak?

The first issue, for critics in particular, is that it is difficult to assess what Bush wants to talk about since pundits and journalists have highlighted Bush's tendency to produce a variety of speech errors. These have ranged across the full gamut of what linguists call "levels of language": errors in sound production (phonetics/phonology), use of words (lexis/morphology), sentence structure (syntax), meaning (semantics), and meaning in context (pragmatics). Bush's opponents have delighted in poking fun at his mistakes, and they have introduced terms into the political lexicon to describe his errors: Bushisms, Dubyaspeak, and Bushlexia. But it wasn't just that Bush produced speech errors; it was the extent and range of these errors that led commentators, both seriously and tongue in cheek, to suggest that Bush may have a real speech disorder. As one pundit put it:

> It doesn't take a brain surgeon to be president, but do we really want a President who appears to need the services of one? (The Amateur Pundit, Things Fall Apart: Bush Takes Aim at the Language and Shoots it Dead, http://amateurpundit.com)

Jacob Weisberg, who published two volumes of "Bushisms," speculated that Bush may suffer from a "genetic disorder" directly linked to language. He was referring to work by Myrna Gopnik, as reported by Stephen Pinker in his book *The Language Instinct* (1995). Gopnik (1990; see also Gopnik and Crago, 1991) studied a large family across several generations and discovered that about half the members suffered from what is referred to as "specific language impairment," or SLI (Leonard, 2000; Bishop and Leonard, 2000). This term refers to a range of language disorders not easily attributed to other general causes, such as deafness or autism, for example. The assessment of SLI within the family suggested that it might be linked to a set of genetic dispositions, and research highlighted a specific gene, FOXP2, as the potential cause of SLI in the family (Fisher et al., 1998; Lai et al., 2001).

This discovery generated a debate about whether a "grammar gene" had been discovered (Pinker, 1995). The claim that there might be a "grammar gene" was taken up with interest and enthusiasm by the media, but the claim may have been premature. MacAndrew (2012) notes that there is less debate today; as evidence emerged about the actions and interactions of FOXP2, it became clear that the picture was much more complicated than journalists and some academics had believed. While the FOXP2 gene does indeed have some impact on speech articulation, MacAndrew notes that:

> The key point, that all the popular reports missed, is that FOXP2 is a transcription factor—in other words it has the potential to affect the expression of an unknown, but potentially large number of other genes. No wonder the syndrome presents in such a diffuse way. We know now that a FOXP2 homologue is strongly expressed in the development of the mouse brain. So not only does it potentially affect many other genes, but it is known to be important in the development of the brain (by being strongly expressed in the brain of the mouse embryo). I expect that breaking FOXP2 in mice would result in some compromises to brain structure and function—an experiment that someone is sure to do. (http://www.pnas.org/cgi/reprint/0503739102v1.pdf)

While it would have been interesting to claim that Bush's errors in sentences like "Is our children learning" were caused by a genetically based grammar disorder, both the scientific evidence and the variety of Bush's errors suggest that the answer lies elsewhere.

Equally, attempts to suggest that Bush suffered from dyslexia fare little better. In an article in *Vanity Fair*, several experts were quoted by writer Gail Sheey (2000) as suggesting that Bush's linguistic errors were consistent with indications of dyslexia. In an interview on ABC's *Good Morning America*, Bush dismissed the claims as false. He noted that he had not seen the article but stated quite clearly: "I am not dyslexic, that's all I can tell you." He added: "This is a case where fiction is greater than fact."

Not everyone who makes grammatical or other linguistic errors is necessarily suffering from a biological or clinically recognized language disorder. Most of us make linguistic errors of one kind or another. Victoria Fromkin (1973) notes that interest in speech errors has a long and varied history. She quotes Henry Peacham's "Compleat Gentleman," written in 1622, when a "melancholy Gentleman" says: "I must go dye a beggar," meaning "I must go buy a dagger." Fromkin has compiled a website at: http://www.mpi.nl/cgi-bin/sedb/sperco_form4.pl where one can find every imaginable form of speech error, and many are produced by normal speakers.

In defining "speech errors," most analysts agree that they are involuntary accidental variations within a speaker's linguistic output. Analysts also agree that speech errors are "regular," indicating the way in which speech is patterned and made up of discrete units. What this means is that we can recognize the type of error because we can recognize or predict the linguistic target. For example, if I said, "I want to cry a new drink," we can see that I have substituted one sound for another in the word "cry," which should have been "try." Now the fact is that we all make mistakes, and these mistakes indicate the regular structure of language, so why has George W. Bush been vilified for making speech errors? What exactly has Bush been doing that marks him out for particular critical attention, and is this, as some of Bush's supporters would argue, just one form of opposition criticism, or is it something more significant both in terms of language production and the way that language output is being understood in context? And what, if anything, can this range of errors at tell us about the pragmatics of George Bush's presidential language?

"Did I just say those words": George W. Bush

Let us begin by looking at the range of errors Bush has made in a variety of different contexts and on a variety of different topics. The examples below at are taken, in the main, from Weisberg, *Bushisms* (2001, 2004).

(1) If terriers and barriffs are torn down, this economy will grow.
(2) You cannot lead if you send mexed missages.
(3) My pan plays down a significant amount of debt.

Examples (1), (2), and (3) are commonly known as "spoonerisms." The term refers to the Reverend William Spooner, who is famously associated with producing words where consonants, vowels, or morphemes are switched. A well-known example is Spooner toasting Queen Victoria and saying: "Give three cheers for our queer old Dean." Of course, what he meant was "our dear old Queen." Similarly, in (1) Bush intended "tariffs" and "barriers" but it came out as "terriers and barriffs." In (2) Bush has exchanged vowels in the last two words (it should have been "mixed messages" and not "mexed missages"), and in (3) the consonant "l" of the word "play" is transposed to the word "pay," producing "plays." So instead of "My plan pays" we get "my pan plays."
Next consider (4) and (5).

(4) Is our children learning?
(5) Laura and I don't realize how bright our children is.

In (4) and (5) we have problems of subject-verb agreement. Bush is mixing up plural verbs with singular subjects.
For another type of error, consider (6) and (7):

(6) I know it is hard to put food on your family.
(7) We ought to make the pie higher.

In both these cases, Bush seems to have selected a word or phrase from a different but related semantic set. In (6) the form he intends is "feed," but he selects a word/phrase from a related semantic set, which in this context is inappropriate. The phrase "put food on the table" means to feed, and more generally, "look after" your family. So "put food on the table" and "feed your family" mean essentially the same thing. From this we can see that Bush has mixed and matched these alternatives to produce the phrase "put food on your family." Although the phrases "put food on the table" and "feed your family" may be used to mean the same thing, "put food on the table" is metaphoric and more general in the sense that it also relates to working for money to feed/clothe/look after your family. But there is clear a connection between "put food on the table" and "feed your family" and it is this connection that leads Bush to transpose words to generate the odd, and comic, sentence "put food on your family."

In (7) the intended form is the comparative adjective "bigger"; Bush has selected a related but inappropriate comparative "higher." The problem is that while both "higher" and "bigger" are comparative adjectives, they are from different sets or dimensions, one referring to volume/size, the other height, although it is also true that we sometimes use "bigger" for height, as one might say on seeing a child, "look how big he has gotten." But this can also be ambiguous between height and bulk, for example.

Consider some other related cases:

(8) I want to remind you all that in order to fight and win wars it requires an expenditure of money that is commiserate with keeping a promise to our troops to make sure they are well paid well trained and well equipped.
(9) We cannot let terrorists and rogue nations hold this nation hostile or hold our allies hostile.
(10) When Iraq is liberated you will be treated tried and persecuted as a war criminal.
(11) A tax cut is really one of the anecdotes to coming out of a recession.

Examples (8) through (11) are called "malapropisms." This refers to the incorrect use of a word in the place of one it resembles. In (8) "commiserate" is substituted for "commensurate," in (9) "hostile" is used instead of "hostage," in (10) "persecuted" is substituted for "prosecuted," and in (11) "anecdotes" is used instead of "antidote."

There are other examples of error types that seem to have less to do with basic linguistic processing and more to do with logic and general discourse structure. Consider the following:

(12) Tide turning, see as I remember—I was raised in the desert,—but tides kin-a its easy to see a tide turn (pause) did I say those words.
(13) No question that the enemy has tried to spread sectarian violence and they use violence as a tool to do that.
(14) Our enemies are innovative and resourceful, and so are we. They never stop thinking about new ways to harm our country and our people and neither do we.
(15) I'm the decider and I decide what is best.

(16) They misundestimated the . . . compassion of our country and they misun-derestimated the Commander in Chief too.

(17) If you don't stand for anything you don't stand for anything.

(18) I know that human being and fish can co-exist peacefully.

(19) Fool me once shame . . . shame on you . . . it fool me . . . can't get fooled again.

We see in (12) that Bush has a problem with how he interprets "tide," as he seems to have mixed up both a metaphorical and literal use of the term. The phrase "the tide has turned" once referred to the literal fact of a change in sea tides. Now it is a standard metaphor for any change, as in "we were winning" but the tide has turned against us. The parenthetical comment, "I was raised in a desert," is presented almost as an excuse to explain why Bush cannot comment on actual "sea tides." Someone raised in a desert would be unlikely to see tides turning since there would be no seas. This suggests that at some point in his cognitive processing of "the tide turning" Bush has given the phrase a literal interpretation. In one view of how we cognitively process "metaphors," we begin by processing the literal meaning and only when this does not make sense in context do we reprocess the utterance as a metaphor in line with communicative intentions (dual processing). The alternative position is that there is a unitary processing mechanism that operates directly on the metaphor (for a general account of metaphor, see Gibbs, 2008; Kövescses, 2010). In the example of "turning tides," it looks like Bush has processed the phrase literally and only when this fails does he understand it was meant as a metaphor. While this may look like dual processing, it is more of a reprocessing following a discourse error. It is only when we get his final phrase "did I just say those words" that we can see that Bush has, through this meta-assessment, realized the problem was that he has given a literal interpretation to a phrase intended metaphorically.

Example (13) is odd but in a some ways it almost works. It may be possible to spread sectarian violence by a number of methods which are not themselves violent—the use of propaganda or brainwashing, for example—but in the end most people will hear what Bush has said as a tautology, something like "violence is being spread by the use of violence."

Example (14) indicates a problem of linguistic processing at the level of what is referred to as "cohesion." Cohesion describes those lexical and grammatical processes that help bind or hold a text together. In a sentence such as "John took out five cigarettes and gave them to me" we know that "them" refers back to the "five cigarettes"; this is known as anaphora, or referring backward. Or consider the frequent use of what is known as "ellipsis," where words are elided or omitted because they are already understood from a previous mention. This can be seen in the following:

A: Would you like an ice cream?
B: Yes.

We know from the question that the answer has elided the fuller form "yes (I would like an ice cream)." The form "I would like an ice cream" is elided because it can be "read off" the discourse context in terms of sequential and grammatical expectations.

Similar discursive and cohesive considerations may also explain what is happening in the first part of (14). When the phrase "and so are we" occurs, we know that the full form would be "and so are we (innovative and resourceful)." But Bush's use of this elliptical technique in the second part of the example is at best ambiguous between something like (a) ". . . and neither do we stop thinking about the ways our enemies are thinking of harming our people and our country", and (b) "and neither do we stop thinking about new ways to harm our country and our people." It is (b), of course, that leads to the inclusion of the example as a Bush error. While (a) has some plausibility, it is a "meta" form that may extend beyond the more available limits of ellipsis, and it is certainly convoluted. If (a) is a more plausible candidate, any misuse is not in terms of the technique of ellipsis itself, that is, referring back to a previous mention, since it is perfectly possible for Bush to say what he did. Although pragmatically it would be very odd for the president of the United States to say that he and his government ". . . never stop thinking about new ways to harm our country and our people," the problem is that Bush intends the opposite of this, something like "we never stop thinking of ways to protect our people." Bush's problem is one of symmetry and contrast. In the first part of (14) his use of ellipsis provides symmetry between the statement and the ellipsis, with the shifts being between the different referents "enemies" and "the United States." He is saying that while the "enemy" is innovative and resourceful, so too is the United States. In the second part of (14) Bush wants to contrast the thoughts and actions of the terrorists with those of the US government, because the meaning of "harm our people" is, of course, negative. Consequently, Bush wants to set this against some alternative and positive US position. However, because he simply repeats the same elliptical technique, as in the first part of his claim, he fails to achieve his goal. In fact, it is much worse than this; not only does he not achieve his goal, he produces a potentially absurd inference, that is, that the United States never stops thinking of ways to harm its people.

In terms of the kinds of pragmatic processing we have been discussing within this book, it is quite clear that Bush's audience will be able to re-evaluate what he has said in (14). We know that he could be said to have claimed that "the United States never stops thinking of ways to harms its people," but placing this alongside all that we know about Bush, the United States, and the war on terror, we don't have to process this information too far to recognize that something is wrong, and since we know Bush does not believe what he has said or implied, we know that he has made a mistake. In this case, although we could say that Bush has said that which is false, he has not done so intending us to infer other relevant information, it is simply a mistake that one we can correct by making use of our knowledge of ellipsis for the context and the meaning Bush intended.

Example (15) raises a language issue related to creativity and productivity. We all understand that there is a basic stock of English words, but we also know that new words enter the English lexicon all the time. This is not a random process, however, and there are a number of different ways in which it can take place. New words may be required to describe previously unknown events or objects. Well-known examples include the emergence of acronyms that become words in their own right:

RADAR: Radio Detection and Ranging
SCUBA: Self-Contained Underwater Breathing Apparatus
LASER: Light Amplification by the Stimulated Emission of Radiation

Other examples would be words originally coined to refer to a company brand name but that come to stand for the product as a whole: Hoover, Xerox, Kleenex, or Google, which now means to look something up, whether one is using the "Google" search engine or not.

New words may also be also created by the application of linguistic rules; for example, what are known as agentive nouns are generally created by the addition of "er" to verbs. Examples would be:

To run: runner
To win: winner
To sing: singer
someone or something that does X.

It is this rule that Bush is applying when he used the term "decider." He seems to be following the principle that one adds "er" to indicate someone who does something, and as he is someone who makes decisions he is a "decider," someone who decides. This seems perfectly logical, and some commentators have suggested that Bush's errors are, on some occasions, linguistically creative. The principle of adding "er" is a rule for creating agentive nouns and Bush has applied that rule. But that, in itself, does not make it creative. There should be some level of awareness that one is intentionally using a rule where it has not been applied before. For example, in 2012 some high-profile media and political personalities were using the word "chillax." "Chillax" has been constructed by combining the terms "chill" and "relax" to create something that means approximately both resting and being calm.

The creation of words such as "chillax" is different, however, from creating words by mistake and then attempting to deflect criticism by suggesting that because the outcome may be linked to a rule or pattern that it could be called creative. Consider the case of Sarah Palin, the ex-governor of Alaska and former vice presidential candidate. Like Bush, Palin has been criticized for her linguistic errors. In one interview she used the term "refudiate," and it was assumed that the target word was "repudiate." However, in response to criticism, Palin argued that she might be bringing a new word into the English lexicon, something she noted that Shakespeare had done, and she suggested that we should "celebrate the invention of new words." The argument is that "refudiate" could be seen as a combination of the terms "refute and repudiate." This seems to be an ex post facto argument; it does not provide an explanation for the introduction of such a new word or indicate what job it would do that isn't already being done by other existing forms.

English (as with many other languages) has constraints of different types that block rule applications in all cases. Consider a child acquiring English; he or she may learn that in order to create a plural one adds an "s," so we get dog-dogs, cat-cats, and so on. But when the child encounters mouse and says mouses, this may be logical, but we correct this to "mice." The irregular plural form "mice" may be an odd historical legacy from the development of the English language, and it may fly in the face of logic, but we tend to adhere to what is known as the irregular form (where the standard rule doesn't work) because normative social behaviors are also rule based.

Similarly, while Bush does apply the rule for creating agentive nouns correctly, the use of "decider" in English does not normally mean "someone who decides." There is a word "decider" in English, but this term is used as a noun and has a very restricted domain, generally that of sports or games, where a "decider" is the goal or point that decides the winner of a game.

In creating new words there is a general constraint that one should not create a word where one already exists. If one were to create a word "decider" as meaning "someone who decides" then one could generate confusion between how the term "decider" is being used, the winning goal or point or someone making decisions. More important, since we can simply say "the person who decides or makes the decisions," we may not need a new word, particularly where it will be a homophone of one that already exists.

The application of a standard rule in contexts where an irregular form is normative may be in some cases creative, reflect independence, or even be constructed for amusement, but where such an application is uncontrolled, or unreflective, it may be just an error, and in some cases this can be embarrassing and in others it may even be seen as insulting. When we describe the world's languages we tend to refer to them in different morphological ways. So in China we have Chinese; in Japan we have Japanese; in Taiwan, Taiwanese; and as a result we might say the rule for forming the word for the language of a country is to add "ese." But what about American; African; and Mexican; here the rule seems to be add "an." On the other hand we also have Irish; English; Flemish; and Polish, which would seem to have the rule of adding "ish." Where patterns and rules already exist we should not thoughtlessly mix and match these, since this may be socially inappropriate or cause offense. Consider the following Bush statements:

> If the East Timorians decide to revolt, I'm sure I'll have a statement. (*New York Times*, June 16, 1999)
>
> Keep good relations with the Grecians. (*The Economist*, June 12, 1999)
>
> Kosovians can move back. (CNN *Inside Politics*, April 9, 1999)

Bush understands that when one refers to the language or the people of a state certain morphological changes are required. The problem is that he is using the wrong morphemes. Surely we would not want to call this creativity.

There is a similar creative issue with example (16), in which Bush famously coined the term "misunderestimate." Once again, Bush has again got something right, but also something wrong. He clearly understands combinatorial principles, as in the use of "under" or "over": understand, overrate, or the use of "mis-" as in "misunderstand," "misunderstood," "mistake," and "mistaken." While one can combine morphemes in various ways, the most important constraint is that if there is another or already accepted way of saying what you want to say, that is, there is no gap in the language for the meaning you want to convey, then there is no need to be creative with morphology. So while "misunderestimate" seems theoretically possible, in simple combinatorial terms its semantic definition would be "someone has failed to underestimate someone else." But we already have a scale with "estimate" at the midpoint, "overestimate-estimate-underestimate." If one fails to estimate someone correctly, they can only either overestimate them, or underestimate them, hence there is no need to add a further morpheme suggesting an error in estimation, since the forms exist that actually do this. Further, since "mis-" is essentially a negative marker, if one were to say "they misunderestimate me," this could be taken to mean **they have not** "underestimated me," which, of course, is the opposite of what Bush intends to say.

Let us quickly complete the analysis of the other examples: (17) is a simple and straightforward tautology; (18) seems bizarre, and requires the context that Bush is defending a dam project and trying to argue that nature's needs and the needs of humans can be made compatible. In the case of (19) this is just a failure of memory processing in that Bush is trying to access an old saying, which may be "fool me once, shame on you, fool me twice, shame on me." The addition of "won't get fooled again" is more difficult explain. A Google search returns the phrase as the title of a song written by the rock group "The Who." It may be, of course, that in trying to process the second part of the saying, "fool me twice shame on me," Bush has reached what is the conclusion or aim of the saying, that once you have been fooled once you should not be fooled again. Bush mixes up the aim of the saying and the saying itself. This is a bit like the "turning tide" example, as Bush seems to be processing two separate things, the adage and the interpretation of the adage.

As we can see from this discussion, whether one is a Bush supporter or critic, there is little doubt that both the range and extent of Bush's errors do draw specific attention to them. Indeed, several of the examples just discussed were used in an NBC current affairs debate on the topic "Is Bush an idiot?" But is this fair? We have noted that the types of errors are regular and similar to those many of us make. But perhaps it is not so much the speech errors, their range, volume, or type, that is the problem, but rather who is producing them, that is, the president of the United States. While most of us may make similar mistakes, we would surely try to avoid these in public speaking, and we would surely expect professional public speakers, such as politicians, to make an even greater effort to avoid such errors. Any politician who frequently makes such mistakes stands out, and a politician at the level of the president of the United States who makes such mistakes on a regular basis stands out even more than most.

On the other hand, if one of your main goals is not to be a "run of the mill" formal and boring politician, but to be your informal and relaxed self, then it may not be surprising that you might make more mistakes in formal speaking situations because you are not trying to be formal. It is well known that George W. Bush did not like "stuffy formality." Draper (2007: 9) notes the way in which he distributed nicknames to people no matter what their standing or rank. He comments:

> He dispensed nicknames the way his attentive young bodyman, Logan Walters whipped out the canister of hand spray after a round of gripping and grinning. "Hey, Barberini! To field director Barbara Russell. "Things okay Robbyboy?" to state co-chair Robb Thompson. Local ad-maker Pat Griffen was Griffey, a U.S Congressman Charlie Bass the Bassmaster . . . In this way the Texan closed the distance and his Granite State hired hands instantly became towel snapping teammates.

Even on the international stage Bush would take the same approach. At one international summit of major nations Bush was heard to shout at the approaching British Prime Minister Tony Blair, "yo Blair."

So when Bush made speech errors, this was just evidence that, as Draper (ibid.: 10) puts it, "Good ol George he is one of us." In this sense, when we consider Bush's errors, maybe we are applying the wrong standards. We are assuming that he should be judged by the formal and rhetorical expectations of high office politics. But Bush did not accept those standards or those rules; hence if we judge him on a more informal basis of "back-slapping" informality, the number and range of errors may seem less difficult to explain.

There is an interesting paradox here; after all, most of us understand the basics of style, and the concept of cultural and situational variation in both behavior and language use. Indeed, it is where social pragmatics and sociolinguistics meet that we understand how and why people make linguistic choices to indicate solidarity, gender, age, status, politeness, and so on. Social psychological and other research has shown for many years that the way we speak generates audience perceptions of us that go well beyond the content of what we say. One would have thought politicians in particular would have understood the sociolinguist Allan Bell's (1984) principle of "audience design," that we construct our writing, talk, or whatever in terms of the audience who will receive the message. But for Bush, it seems that he was determined to be simply who he was, and in his case it really was a case of "what you heard was what you got."

What Has Pragmatics Got to Do with It?

The errors noted above display a range of linguistic features, misplaced sounds, syntactic errors, errors in word selection, or word substitution, and errors in meaning, but in what way are these related to pragmatics? There is one sense in which one could say some of these are not specifically pragmatic, as they may be seen as errors at specific points in speech or language production that are related to other linguistic levels. However, pragmatics is often defined as "interactionist" (Craig, 1995; McTear and Conti-Ramsden, 1992; Penn, 1999; Wilson and Sperber, 1991; Bates and MacWhinney, 1982) where the term can refer to the interactional domain within which sensorimotor, memory, cognition, and grammar operate in order to generate specific outputs. The term may also refer to a more common-sense view of interaction, in this case "communicative interaction" wherein speakers and hearers utilize the available internal systems of language in jointly constructing and negotiating the production of meaning and understanding (Clark, 1996; ten Have, 2007). Successful communication involves the synchronization of both these interactional levels. Clearly, if at the level of language production one fails to produce comprehensible sentences or utterances, communication may fail.

But is this too general? Consider what we might do when confronted with errors such as:

a. . . . . it requires an expenditure of money that is **commiserate** with keeping a promise to our troops to make sure they are well paid well trained and well equipped.

b. I know it is hard **to put food on your family**.

We will be able to re-analyze these as (a) an error in word selection and (b) an error either in word selection (food for feed) with a knock-on prepositional effect (food on vs. feed your), or alternatively we could also see this as a mistake mixing a "formulaic" or standard metaphorical selection "put food on the table," with a syntactic error of prepositional completion "on your family." Either way, both are plausible re-analyses of what Bush has said, and this would allow for pragmatic completion, that is, a recognition of what Bush intended to say, and more important, intended to mean.

An interesting pragmatic question here is not so much why would anyone carry out such re-analyses, but how they would do this, given that the input for analysis does not conform to the internal "language" system as we understand it, that is, we do not have in our mental lexicon any acquired reading of "commiserate" as being the same as "commensurate," because, quite simply, in the English lexicon there is no slot where "commiserate" and "commensurate" are displayed as meaning the same thing.

In a paper entitled "A Nice Derangement of Epitaphs" the philosopher Donald Davidson raises a complex question about the interpretation of speech errors such as "malapropisms." He argues that while we understand malapropisms are based on errors or mistakes in word selection, he claims that they raise quite significant issues about what it is to know a language.

The title of Davidson's paper is taken from Mrs. Malaprop herself, the humorous Aunt in Sheridan's play *The Rivals*. Mrs. Malaprop was prone to using the wrong word in a sentence, but one that sounded similar to the target word. In the sentence "A nice derangement of epitaphs," "derangement" should be "arrangement" and "epitaphs" should be epithets; hence, the correct interpretation of the sentence is "a nice arrangement of epithets." The fact that Mrs. Malaprop uses words in a non-standard way is not a problem in itself, nor, essentially, is the process by which a hearer reaches the intended interpretation—which Donaldson concedes could be explained in a standard Gricean manner. The problem is that if Mrs. Malaprop actually does mean, literally, "a nice derangement of epitaphs" then the hearer needs some equivalent theory of language to that of Mrs. Malaprop herself. However, one would be unlikely to have heard Mrs. Malaprop's sentence before, and it is equally unlikely that any prior theory of language the hearer knows could account for the literal meaning of what Mrs. Malaprop actually said. What this means is that any theory which is used to interpret what Mrs. Malaprop literally meant would be what Davidson calls a "passing theory"—basically a theory needed to explain the statement as it has been produced. It is a "passing theory" because no prior theory of language as we currently describe it could account for the literal meaning of Mrs. Malaprop's sentence; hence in interpreting what she has said, a listener must construct a "passing theory" that on this occasion allows them to process "derangement" as meaning "arrangement" and "epitaph" as meaning "epithet." Thus, at the point of interpretation—the passing theory—neither the speaker nor the hearer is using language as it is normally explained and understood within any linguistic available theory. As Davidson (1986: 446) has put it, "There is therefore no such thing as a language, not if language is anything like what philosophers and linguists have supposed."

If we accept what Davidson claims, standard theories of language break down and thus we might say Mrs. Malaprop is not speaking English—as conventionally understood. Given this account, then, in the case of malapropisms at least, critics of Bush could claim that he is not having difficulty speaking English, because he is not speaking English at all, and, indeed, for those theories of language we have, he may not be speaking any language as we know it. Of course, the same criticism would apply to all of us when we utter our own malapropisms. In this case, distinguishing "what is meant" from "what is said" takes on a new form in terms of the "passing theory," which must be, as it is contextualized, a pragmatic theory.

Pragmatics, Explanation, and Accounts of Action?

In an ABC news interview Vice President Dick Cheney (ABC news.com; 2008) argued that America's intervention in Iraq had been a success. The interviewer quoted figures to Cheney indicating that two-thirds of Americans did not think the war in Iraq was worth it. Following a short pause, Cheney simply says "So!" "So" is a well-known pragmatic marker (see Chapter 5), which has a number of structural functions, from continuation ("so next I went to . . .") to causality ("so it was the spice in the soup that made me sick"). Cheney uses "so" elliptically as a version of "so what!" a marker used to indicate the speaker's dismissal of a prior claim or comment. This implies that a previous comment is not only potentially irrelevant, but also that the respondent doesn't care about the comment or it's content, or indeed those who may have made it. While it is true that politicians often dismiss polls, particularly when their findings do not align with the politician's policy or needs, it is rare to see the views of the public dismissed so blatantly, and, indeed, the interviewer challenges Cheney on this: "You don't care what the American people think." Cheney, however, attempts to recover from his first response by returning to a fairly standard reaction to such polls; he argues that in the mid-term of any administration the polls are generally low. He further suggests that the government is in a phase where very difficult and tough decisions have to be made, and it is his job to make those decisions, and if that makes him unpopular, so be it. In this way Cheney manages to "realign" his dismissive use of the marker "so," bringing it under two related arguments:

a. Mid-terms polls are often negative.
b. Polls are negative when the government has to make tough decisions.

If one has to make tough decisions at mid-term then the polls will be negative; hence the use of "so" is not dismissive, but simply stresses that there is nothing surprising in the poll's findings. In this way, Cheney provides an explanation of his initial dismissive response.

"Explanations" are a central facet of social interaction in general, and they are a central plank in the link between politicians' actions and the public's understanding of specific policies and government behaviors. We have already discussed "explanations" as part of the theory of "accounts" (see Chapter 5), but here we want to further explore the general pragmatics of political explanation and its various related manifestations as "accounts," "excuses," and "justifications" (see Antaki, 1994). To do so we will look at a number of examples of major political decisions made by Bush and how they were justified, explained, or accounted for, both at the time the decisions were made and later, when the consequences of those decisions had become clear. While attention will be given to areas such as 9/11 and the Iraq War, we will also consider a more general question related to Bush's actions overall, specifically, why did George W. Bush enter politics and why did he want to become president?

What Is an Explanation?

Within the philosophy of natural science a number of scholars, encouraged by the original work of Hempel (1962), have attempted to construct a formal description of "explanations." This is done by viewing an explanation as an answer to a *wh-* question, such as (ironically) "What is an explanation?" Sintonen (1993) suggests that questions such as "What is the color of copper?" and "Who authorized the arms deal?" may be formally seen as:

(18) (?x) (x is the color of copper)
(19) (?x) (x authorized the arms deal)

Questions provide an empty variable (x), which the answer completes. In (18) x is the variable and it is replaced by "brown" as being the color of copper, or John Doe in (19) as the identity of the person who authorized the arms deal. This works pretty well with most *wh-* questions, but "why" questions raise a host of different issues. Consider questions such as "Why is my car not working?" "Why does it snow?" "Why is it dark at night?" The problem with these questions is that the detail of any response could be lengthy, or even indeterminate. Sintonen (1993) notes of such "why" questions that it is difficult to decide when the information provided for any missing variable is complete. But this becomes even more complex in the field of human interaction since any answer to "Why did John go to the store?" could introduce an indeterminate variety of "intentions" and goal-directed actions. An answer could be "to buy some milk," or further, "to buy some milk to feed the baby," or again, "to buy some milk, to feed the baby, because his wife has left him," and so on. Hence, questions such as "Why did George W. Bush become president?" or "Why did America go to war with Iraq?" will have many possible answers, and not only within purely formal systems, but also within political, social, or economic systems.

The difficulties faced in delimiting explanations is noted by Antaki (1988), but as he says, despite any difficulty in circumscribing "explanations" we tend to know one when we see it. Antaki (1988) further comments that not only are explanations difficult to delimit in all cases, but they tend to be constrained by the theoretical perspective brought to bear on their analysis. For social psychologists, explanations can be accounted for in terms of "attributions," that is the reason "why" X does "Y" may be a result of certain psychological attributions utilized by "Y" such that it "yields" X: Tom threw a brick at the policeman because he does not like the police. For other analysts, such as conversation analysts, explanations are jointly constructed turn by turn, and explanations may be jointly produced recognitions of participants' "in turn" accounts for actions. And for narrative analysts, explanations are like stories; they are set out with beginnings, go through structural stages, and reach some form of conclusion. However, whichever approach one adopts, perhaps the main difficulty in defining explanations is that they occur in many various formats, for a host of different reasons and causes, and with many different surface cues (Draper, 1988).

Consider, for example, explanations that arise from problematic interactional behavior, that is, where a speaker has said or done something unexpected or untoward, these are generally know as "accounts." As we noted previously, an "account" may be described as "a linguistic device employed whenever an action is subjected to a 'valuative inquiry'" (Scott and Lyman, 1968: 46). The purpose of these devices is to deal with problematic aspects of interaction by offering such things as "justifications" and "excuses." "Justifications" are used when the actor wants to accept responsibility for an action, but also wants to deny the negative associations of the action. An "excuse" is used when one admits that the act in question is wrong, but nevertheless denies full responsibility. Actors carry out such actions to maintain order within social interactions; they do this by managing their own self-esteem, and providing recognition of the social concerns and needs of others.

There is a sense in which "accounts" could be seen as specific forms of "explanation," a point noted by Garfinkel (1956, 1967), who argued that "accounts" are structural elements found in all kinds and levels of social interaction, since the primary purpose of such interaction is to make jointly constructed behaviors "accountable" for oneself and others. Garfinkel does not deny, of course, that forms of "accountability" may have different sets of classifications, and that "accounts" which arise from problematic behaviors may be different from other more general accounts (explanations?). However, Garfinkel's point is well taken, and in more recent work on "accounts" they have become closely aligned with the performance of narratives of individual lives (Bochner et al., 1997; Harvey et al., 1990, Brice-Heath, 1983; Maines, 1993; Orbuch et al., 1993, 1994), and occasionally explanations, accounts, and stories become blended within a single broad analysis. There is nothing wrong with this, and what tools one uses depends very much on the question one asks, and in the case of politicians this becomes a significant point.

When one asks a politician why he or she did X or Y, it is very rarely for the simple purpose of gaining an explanation in the scientific manner noted above. Most questions asked of politicians are explicitly or implicitly accusatory or adversarial in some sense (see Chapter 3; Clayman and Heritage, 2002), and one could suggest that most politicians' responses are, by their very nature, "accounts." This is because there is almost always someone or some group that finds political actions wrong, unacceptable, biased, or whatever. Consequently, for many politicians, statements are "justifications" for actions taken, and often for actions to be taken. Politicians tend to avoid "excuses," and only draw on these when they have no other options. For politicians, "excuses" place them in a negative light, since an excuse is often associated with a loss of control, and this places the politician in a weak position. For this reason, politicians' excuses frequently occur along with apologies (see Benoit, 1995), hence when a politician explains what he or she did or did not do, it is generally in the form of a "justification."

"Justifications" call upon a variety of contents, formats, and reasoning modalities. They may be emotional, practical, or logical. But they will always take place in a complex environment of interacting needs, desires, and motivations, both on the part of the politician, their audience(s), and their interrogators (the press, for example). Consider the following example from Bush's early campaigns for the republican nomination for the presidency. In New Hampshire, Bush suffered an early defeat to the then relatively unknown and financially much weaker John McCain. There were many reasons that Bush lost New Hampshire, but one reason included his inability to respond to a series of questions in a media interview. On November 1, 1999, Andy Hiller from Boston News 7 was given the opportunity to interview Bush. As Robert Draper (2007: 10) notes ". . . Hiller began innocently enough, asking if the Governor believed himself weak on foreign policy." Bush responded: "No I've got a clear vision of where I want to lead America." So if one were to ask the question "Why is Bush strong on foreign policy?" the answer would be "because he has a clear vision of where he wants to lead America." This causal claim suggests that Bush's "clear vision" is an explanation for his strength. Now, of course, we do not know what that vision is in detail, but we can infer that "clear vision" is a kind of metaphor for a view of where Bush wants not only to position foreign policy, but also the steps he will take to achieve his policy, when and where he will take such steps, and how he will assess his progress in delivering his vision. Now look at what happens following Bush's "clear vision" comment (adapted form Draper, 2007: 10–11):

HILLER: Can you name the President of Chechnya?

BUSH: No can you?

HILLER: Can you name the President of Taiwan?

BUSH: Yeah Lee, wait a minute—is this Fifty questions?

HILLER: No. It's four questions of four leaders of four hot spots. The leader of Pakistan?

BUSH: The new Pakistani General—Just been elected—he's not been elected. The guy took over office . . . it appears he is going to bring stability to the country, and I think that is good news for the subcontinent.

HILLER: And can you name him?

BUSH: General—I can name the General . . .

HILLER: And it's . . .

BUSH: General

HILLER: Finally, how about the Prime Minister of India?

BUSH: Uh . . . no . . . Can you name the foreign minister of Mexico?

HILLER: No sir, but I would say to that I'm not running for President.

Not surprisingly, Bush was furious that he had been ambushed in this way, but what this shows is that in answering questions, the provision of information or the lack of it involves more than the completion of a missing variable. While many of the questions above are prefaced with "Can," such questions may be easily paraphrased as *wh-* questions. For example, "Who is the prime minster of X?" "What is the name of the president of X?" and so on. There are two problems facing Bush here. First, he is unable to complete any missing variable as set up by the questions; he clearly does not have the information. But why is this a problem? The answer relates to the second issue: Hiller created a context where Bush, in his own words, indicated that he would be a strong leader on foreign policy, yet how can you lead on foreign policy when you do not have the knowledge of certain relevant issues or people in the foreign policy arena?

As we noted in Chapter 2, dealing with questions in news interviews forms part of a modern politician's everyday life. From an interviewer's point of view, it is also a core context where they get to interrogate politicians, both for themselves and as an advocate for their audiences (see Chapter 3; also Clayman and Heritage, 2002). Journalistic questioning is generally adversarial and challenges the claims of politicians. In this sense, both the politician and the interviewer go into interviews sensitive to the organizational structure of the question/answer process, each prepared and monitoring the other in terms of their own goals and objectives. We can see this in the above example, when Bush answers the first question with a return question, "Do you?" Politicians also have a number of techniques for not answering questions; they may challenge them or reformulate them. For example, they may say "well let me put your question in perspective . . . ," "I think you have asked that question out of context," "I have said that I cannot answer such questions at this time," and so on. In Bush's first response he answers the question but then challenges the interviewer by offering, or returning, the question back to him. While in various everyday contexts this is a tried and tested technique for offsetting a challenge to one's interactional "face" or self-esteem (Brown and Levinson, 1978), it is less successful in those contexts where the interviewee, and not the interviewer, is considered to be someone with a level of expertise, experience, or specialized knowledge. Remember that the context for the series of questions we are considering is Bush's ability in the area of foreign policy, not the interviewer's knowledge of foreign policy.

Bush's responds to the second question, "Can you name the President of Taiwan?" With "Yeah Lee, wait a minute—is this Fifty questions?" This is interesting in several respects. First, he seems to have answered the question in that he has named the president of Taiwan as "Lee." But, of course, we know this is not a correct answer; indeed, although it is meant as flippant, perhaps even as sarcasm, it borders on "racism," suggesting that all the Chinese are called "Lee." This is equivalent to the visually racist version of "you all look the same to me."

Within the question/answer format the structural assumption is that answers follow questions in a pair-wise format (see Chapter 1). What this means is that in the turn following the question we look for information that the turn is structurally coordinated with the question. However, there is also an assumption within any context that the questioner will ask a question for a reason (Wilson, 1980), and when that reason is not clear the respondent is entitled either to delay an answer with something like "Why do you want to know?" or to provide an answer with the addition of "Why do you want to know?" In some cases, when questions attend to socially sensitive issues, the question may be rejected altogether: "Mind your own business" or "What has it got to do with you?" In Bush's case his flippant response is followed by "is this fifty questions." This phrase refers to a form of quiz type interaction, and not an interview process. So this phrase is implicitly challenging both the question type and the question process.

Hiller recognizes this challenge to both his question and his questioning procedure, and when he says: "No. It's four questions of four leaders of four hot spots. The leader of Pakistan?" What he does is to recycle Bush's challenge (is this fifty questions) by treating Bush's ironic remark as if it were a real question. In doing this, Hiller is able to highlight a numerical issue germane to his main goal, and he then makes use of the repetition of the much smaller number "four" to drive home not simply the limits and reasonableness of his questioning, but also the importance of knowledge of foreign affairs in a small and selected (hot) number of areas of the world.

Hiller then tags this process with a further question about Bush's knowledge of world leaders, in this case the "leader of Pakistan." In what follows, it is hard to understand Bush's goals. He seems clearly aware now what Hiller is trying to do, and it also becomes clear that he does not know the name of Pakistan's leader. His response seems to be linked to identity and referential issues of the type we discussed in Chapter 2, specifically, that a number of different referential tags may be used to identify the same object or individual. So Bush seems to be aware that Pakistan has a new leader and that he is a general, and goes further, stating that the general's policies may be a good thing for Pakistan. Here Bush is perhaps trying to redirect the interview in terms of broader policy issues, rather than epistemic assessments of his personal knowledge of leader's names. But this fails badly when the interviewer redirects Bush back to the question, ". . . and can you name him?" Bush's response "General . . . I can name the general" seems to confirm that his mode of thinking is around the one referential type, the leader of Pakistan is "a general," and this may be true, but while "general" is a generic name for the holder of a senior position in the army, it is not a "given" birth name, which is clearly what the question is about. Unfortunately, by taking this route, Bush is forced either to admit, again, that he does not know the name, or worse, as he does, to repeat once again the title "general," which only seems to exacerbate the issue of Bush's ignorance in this area.

In the last question-answer about the leader of India, Bush responds to the question by once again challenging the interviewer on his own knowledge. This might work in some political interviews since one could suggest that the journalist should have a knowledge of the area he is asking questions about, but as we noted above, this is not a requirement, since it is the politicians who presents themselves as knowledgeable in selected political areas—it is partly on the basis of being knowledgeable in selected areas that the politicians are asking the electorate to vote for them. But Bush's attempt to challenge the interviewer's knowledge base is not only risky, it looks like he is trying to avoid the issue and redirect the focus away from himself. After all, even if we think the journalist should have some knowledge of foreign affairs if he is going to ask questions on this topic, how much more knowledgeable should a presidential hopeful be? And this is exactly what follows with Hiller's final comment, which is pragmatically laden with the logic that even if he does not know the name of the "foreign minister of Mexico" this is not relevant to his general role as a journalist, but it might be important (along with answers to the other questions) if you are running for president.

The discussion of this extract highlights the way in which a formal view of questions and answers as the process of completing or not completing a missing variable is inadequate for explaining what takes place in interaction. The process provides a starting point for considering the guiding rules of the process, but sequential and contextual expectations operating alongside this offer us so much more, and we need to bear this in mind as we look at how Bush explains and accounts for a variety of significant actions throughout his presidency.

God Made Me Do It?

In his book *The Faith of George W. Bush* (2004), Stephen Mansfield highlights the important influence of religion on Bush's beliefs, values, and politics. As Bush himself put it, "My style, my focus, and many of the issues that I talk about . . . are reinforced by my religion" (Bush, 2010 see also Bergen and Rae, 2006). Bush's critics used such claims as evidence for the right-wing Christianization of politics during the Bush presidency. Yet there are those who said Bush was not Christian enough, not Christian at all, and some who accused him of being against Christian fundamentalists. For example, when asked by a reporter from Texas about losing Christian votes if he supported trade with China, Bush said, "You only think that because you live around those whackos" (Damian Thompson, *Daily Telegraph* blog June 8, 2012). But wherever on the scale of Christianity Bush sits, Mansfield's most intriguing claim is that Bush told his friend and evangelist James Robinson that he had been called by God to run for president. According to a *Guardian* newspaper report on Mansfield's book:

> Bush said to James Robinson: "I feel like God wants me to run for President. I can't explain it, but I sense my country is going to need me. Something is going to happen . . . I know it won't be easy on me or my family, but God wants me to do it."

This is certainly a type of explanation. Bush became president because God wanted him to become president.

This is not said to be controversial, rather the aim is to show the problems we face in trying to determine when, if ever, one has a complete response to a "why" question, such as, why did George Bush become president? It is true that George W. Bush was happy to confirm, and proud to profess, his Christianity, and it is also true that Bush believes in "divine power": it is God who determines the world, its future, and all that is in it. Asked, for example, if Muslim terrorists go to heaven, Bush responded that it is not something he gets to decide; ". . . only the almighty God decides that." Given a belief in divine power, it would be hard to imagine anyone who is a Christian, and who is running for president, who would believe anything other than that God wanted them to do it.

While there is some skepticism about what Bush may or may not have said to James Robinson, we can also look at Bush's own words. In his book *Decision Points*, Bush tells us how he was struggling with the decision about whether he should or should not run for president. He explores his options with friends, family, and other supporters, but he is unsure of what to do. He then bemoans this fact to his mother and she says, "George get over it. Make up your mind and move on" (2010: 61). Bush continues in the book.

> Then Mark Graig struck. In his sermon he spoke about the book of Exodus, when God called Moses to action. Moses' first response was disbelief: "Who am I, that I should go to Pharaoh and bring the Israelites out of Egypt?" He had every excuse in the book. He hadn't led a perfect life; he wasn't sure if people would follow him: he couldn't even speak that clearly. That sounded a little familiar.
>
> Mark described God's reassurance that Moses would have the power to perform the task he had been called to do. Then Mark summoned the congregation to action. He declared that the country was starving for moral and ethical leadership. Like Moses, he concluded, "We have the opportunity, each and everyone of us, to do the right thing, and for the right reason."
>
> I wondered if this was the answer to my question. There was no mysterious voice whispering in my ears, just Mark Craig's high-pitched Texas twang coming from the pulpit. Then Mother leaned forward from her seat at the other end of the pew. She caught my eye and mouthed, "He is talking to you."
>
> After the service, I felt different. The pressure evaporated. I felt a sense of calm.

This narrative has a classic story shape, as defined for example by Labov and Waletzky (1967) (see also Chapter 4 in this volume). In their seminal work on narrative, Labov and Waletzky suggested that narratives have a general structural pattern containing the following elements:

A. An abstract which identifies the point or summarizes the action of the story;
B. An orientation which provides general background information and describes the particular circumstances of the action;

C. The complicating action reported in sequential order;

D. The result or resolution of the action;

E. A final coda to close the story, often relating it to the current context;

F. Evaluation at various points to guide the audience to the intended point of the narrative.

The formal structure, or shape of the story, is only one part of the process we need to consider in analyzing narratives (see Wilson and Stapleton, 2010), and Labov and Waltezky agree that the social and cognitive orientation of stories and how they function within interactional contexts is also significant.

When we look at Bush's story about Mark Craig, one of the first things to note is the opening sentence, "Then Mark Craig struck." The use of "then" suggests the possible elision of a "conjunction" (and): as in "and then Mark Craig struck." This use of "and" suggests a temporal process, as found in a standard pragmatic view of "conjunction." Consider for example:

He turned the key and opened the door.
She tripped and hit her head on the floor.

These are classic examples of the "and then" view of conjunction, which indicates a causal ordering of events; after all, while one can say "John got on his horse and rode into town," it is less acceptable to say "John rode into town and got on his horse." So how is this linked to Bush's comments about his mother telling him to "move on?" We can assume, as in any narrative, that Bush is ordering the events in time as they actually happened.

I wasn't sure whether to run for president.
Supporters encouraged me, but I still worried about it.
I told my mother about my worries and my indecision.
She told me to make my mind up and move on.
I still wasn't sure, and then Mark Craig struck.

But this is more than simply a list of events ordered in time; they are connected to the overall narrative that leads up to the story about "Mark Craig," since it is in this story that the general narrative is given its "point." Hence, "then Mark Craig struck" tells us we are at the endpoint of the sequence of elements that were relevant in the progress Bush made toward his final decision. In the story that is to follow, we can expect to find at least one answer to the question "Why did Bush run for president?

So what is that answer, what is it we are to take from the story of Bush's encounter with "Mark Craig?" Is it, for example, as we discussed above, that God told Bush to do it? It certainly looks like a form of revelatory narrative, since it is through Bush's indirect encounter with the story of Moses and Moses' doubts about whether he could fulfill God's task that Bush comes to see an answer to his own question: Should he run for president?

As noted above, narratives may be invoked as forms of "explanation." Narratives do this by being more than descriptions. In their organization, sequencing, characterization, plotting, and so on, they make events intelligible for the audience by providing scenarios and scripts (see Schank and Ableson, 1977), which the audience may use to infer specific forms of understanding. But this raises a core issue: Why use narratives at all? As Vellman (2003) argues, they must surely add something that a descriptive explanation does not. One option Vellman suggests is a form of "emotional resolution." Stories establish "an emotional cadence," and through a sequence of events some emotional endpoint is reached. The villain is captured, the family is reunited, or the hero is saved. Citing the work of Schank (1995) and his colleagues, Vellman (2003) notes that Schank claims we understand events in terms of the familiar, and the familiar is often stored in memory in terms of our experiences as stories. According to Vellman (2003: 8), we

> . . . put these experiences into words, by telling ourselves about them, and then remember them 'as told to' ourselves, a form that is richly indexed with keywords and inference readily accessible for purposes of understanding future experiences. When other people tell us a story, we understand it by assimilating it to stories of our own, retrieved from memory. . . . That is why people can explain something to us by telling us a story about it: their story helps us to assimilate the thing to what's familiar, by assimilating it to our own stories.

This process is part of how we "comprehend" such a text. The starting point of a narrative is essentially a pragmatic event, since our reaction to any such text is, why am I being told this? Why now, why here? Why these people? Why this context? Or in the general terms of Grice (1989) and Sperber and Wilson (1986), what is the "relevance" of this story? So what is Bush's intention in telling this story?

This is not a straightforward issue, since the story can be read literally, analogically, metaphorically, and so on. Let us begin by considering the story as that: a story. What is it about? In general terms, it's about a minister's sermon and the impact of that sermon on Bush. The fact that it is a sermon is something we might like to consider. One assessment of a sermon follows:

> To move from biblical text to biblical sermon, focus first on the power of Scripture to move beyond telling us *about* God to actually prompt an encounter *with* God. The words of Scripture mediate an encounter with the God we know in Jesus and through this encounter we are changed. (Working Preacher.org: posting 2008)

The important point here is that a sermon uses scripture to facilitate an encounter with God. Mark Craig provides a sermon for the congregation as a whole, but each individual may understand it in terms of how it facilitates an opportunity to encounter God or understand God's will. Bush sees the story of Moses' prevarication as an analogy for his own dilemma. Moses had to trust God, and understood that God expects all of us to do our duty when we are called upon to carry the burden of such a duty. Bush also tells us that his mother said to him, "He's talking to you." While the obvious interpretation of the pronoun "he" is that it refers to the minister, it is also possible, through the speech event of the sermon, to read "he" as the minister representing God, or even as God talking through the minister—where "he" could be ambiguous between God and the minister. The suggestion is that given the minister is a conduit and facilitator of God's message, there is a secondary level at which "he" could be seen as God speaking through the minister. Given this possibility, the point of the story would be that God called upon Bush to do his duty, which Bush interprets as running for president. Bush does not say this explicitly; it is presented indirectly through the story, the aim and structure of sermons, and the characters in the story, Mark Craig, Moses, and Bush's mother. Nevertheless, in assessing the resolution of the story, it is not unreasonable to suggest that Bush believed he had been called upon by God to run for president. And this is important for Bush in terms of the decisions he has to make, after all, and to paraphrase Bob Dylan, it is hard to be wrong when you have God on your side.

No More Heroes: Pragmatic Interpretation and Versions of Reality in the Iraq War

When Bush was first informed of the September 11, 2001 (9/11), attack on the World Trade Center in New York, he was reading a story to young children on a visit to a school. Bush was severely criticized for continuing to read to the children after he had been told that a second plane had crashed into the World Trade Center. Indeed, Osama bin Laden claimed in a video statement after the attack that Bush's lack of immediate action gave the hijackers all the time they needed to complete their task. Alternatively, Bush tells us that its was Karl Rove, his Deputy Chief of Staff, who told him about a plane crashing into the World Trade Center as they were walking into the school, and it was only when Bush spoke to Condoleezza Rice, Secretary of State, that he discovered it was a commercial airliner. Bush went ahead with the school visit, and as he was reading to the children, White House Chief of Staff Andrew Card whispered in his ear that a second plane had hit the second World Trade Center tower. Bush tells us:

> I saw reporters at the back of the room, learning the news on their cell phones and pagers. Instinct kicked in. I knew my reaction would be recorded and beamed throughout the world. The nation would be in shock; the president could not be. If I stormed out hastily, it would scare the children and send ripples of panic throughout the country. . . . I had settled on a plan of action. When the lesson ended I would leave the classroom calmly, gather the facts, and speak to the nation. (Bush, 2010: 127)

This is Bush's version of events. As we noted in Chapter 1, propositional attitude statements about beliefs, thoughts, desires, and so on, are difficult to accommodate within a formal truth conditional version of meaning, that is, we can't simply say they are true or false. We can't really say that Bush did not think the thoughts that he claims above, since they are his thoughts. We could, of course, check such things as who gave Bush what information and when. So we could speak to Karl Rove, or Condoleezza Rice, or Andrew Card, and confirm the truth of what Bush says they said, but even here this might not be as simple as one might think.

Former Vice President Dick Cheney discusses 9/11 in his book *In My Time* (2011). In the book he recalls during the 9/11 attack how he had to make the decision to tell the US Air Force to shoot down potential rogue planes even if they had ordinary passengers on board. As Bush recalls this, however, he says: "I told Dick that our pilots . . . had my authority to shoot them down. . . . I had just made my first decision as war time Commander in Chief" (Bush, 2010: 129). So who is right? As we can see, the same events may be remembered differently.

The media made much of the discrepancy between Bush's and Cheney's accounts of events. In a television interview it was suggested to Cheney that his version raised issues about who was in charge that day. Cheney's response was that ". . . there is no doubt that the President was in charge on that day, his version is in his book, my version is in my book." This is classic pragmatics; of course the president was in charge, this was the legal and constitutional position, so it is "necessarily" true. The real question was why did Cheney and Bush recall the same facts so differently? In everyday life it is frequently the case that similar events may be perceived in different ways. This is seen regularly in cases of eyewitness testimony. Studies have shown that witnesses can be manipulated into false beliefs through the introduction of false statements during witness questioning. For example, if the witness had seen a "yield sign" but was asked questions that referred to a "stop sign," the witness would come to believe what he saw was a stop sign, not a yield sign (see Loftus, 1996).

Equally, people's motivations and desires can also impact what they see or believe. The decision to give permission to shoot down potential rogue planes, which could have innocent passengers on board, as well as terrorists, was a difficult and courageous decision, and it could indicate leadership and strength of character. It may not be surprising, then, that both Bush and Cheney recall this differently. But Cheney has not explicitly said that Bush is mistaken or wrong in his version of events, he has merely said it is a different version from his own. But is there any more we can interpret from this? Does Cheney mean more than what he has said? We know Cheney is saying that different versions exist in different books, but one assumption we can draw upon is that Cheney must believe his own version of events; otherwise, what is it doing in his book? If we accept this, then we can infer that Cheney believes he is right; therefore does it follow that he believes Bush is wrong? Cheney does not state this, but it is a legitimate inference from what he has said. Yet both versions of events cannot be correct; this would be a contradiction. So if Cheney is not saying that Bush is wrong, only that his version is how he recalls events, what does that mean? There are a number of ways we might put this from Cheney's point of view.

a. Bush is lying.
b. Bush is wrong.
c. Bush is mistaken.
d. Bush remembers events differently.
e. There are two versions of events and that is that.

Some members of this list are stronger in their accusation and negativity than others, but all could be used to explain why two people describe the same set of events differently, including the last, which suggests that the speaker doesn't want to resolve the issue at all. This is a major issue for pragmatics. Since we are dealing with what is implied, and therefore that which can be canceled or denied, it is difficult on occasion to pin down what people actually believe, as opposed to what they imply. However, pragmatics can provide various avenues to explore in assessing whether language is being used to mislead or misdirect. In the rest of this chapter we want to consider the ways in which pragmatics helps us unpack Bush's language, and consider how this can add to and develop the way in which he has presented certain aspects of the Iraq War and its consequences.

Bush left office in 2008, and since then a wealth of information has emerged about the content and basis of those decisions made during his two terms as president. Many people now believe that Bush misled the public on a variety of matters, none more central than the Iraq War. Indeed, on June 10, 2008, Congressman Dennis Kucinich and co-sponsor Robert Wexler proposed 35 articles of impeachment for Bush's actions before and during the Iraq War. This was symbolic, however; since Bush was no longer president, nothing much was likely to happen. But was Bush's prosecution of the Iraq war a crime? Or is this, once again, just a matter of interpretation?

On September 18, 2002, CIA director George Tenet claimed he briefed President Bush on top-secret intelligence that Saddam Hussein did not have weapons of mass destruction (WMD). This seems particularly damming, but Bush dismissed this information as worthless as it was from the Iraqi foreign minister, a member of Saddam's inner circle. This may have seemed a reasonable argument back then; we now know, however, that the evidence turned out to be accurate in every detail. Critics argue, therefore, that Bush didn't want to hear the truth and he lied to the American people to get the war he wanted. This may or may not be true, but we can't decide it on the basis of Bush dismissing evidence from a potentially tainted source. Nevertheless, in both pre- and postwar contexts, as noted below, there is a sense in which any assessment of evidence and the validity of its source does seem to shift and change with time and political objectives.

When Bush was trying to get political support for a possible attack on Iraq, he says he wanted to declassify some of the intelligence to which he had access so that Congress and others could see what the real issues were. He says of a meeting in December 2002 (Bush, 2010: 242) that he ". . . asked George Tenet and his capable deputy John McLaughlin to brief me on what intelligence we could declassify to explain Iraq's WMD programs." When this arrived Bush noted "it was not very convincing," so he said to Tenet, "Surely you can do [a] better job of explaining the evidence against Saddam." George Tenet agreed, and in a now famous phrase, he said, "It's a slam dunk." This is the same George Tenet who, according to the information discussed above, said he had given Bush evidence that Saddam Hussein did not have WMD.

Tenet seems to be required by Bush to provide evidence that suits Bush's needs. Importantly here, since the evidence is coming from Tenet and the CIA, even though Bush asked for this evidence, it is still "third-party endorsed" evidence. In this case, should things not turn out as planned, Bush could always say he acted on the evidence he was given, which turned out to be wrong, and, as we'll see in a moment, this is what he did. Further, in justification of his position on this evidence at the time of going to war, Bush defends his decision as "reasonable" by arguing that everyone else believed the evidence Tenet presented. Bush says (2010: 242):

> I believed him (Tenet). I had been receiving intelligence briefings on Iraq for nearly two years. The conclusion that Saddam had WMD was nearly a universal consensus. My predecessor believed it. Republicans and Democrats on Capital Hill believed it. Intelligence agencies in Germany, France, Great Britain, Russia, China, and Egypt believed it. As German ambassador to the United States, not a supporter of the war, later put it "I think all of our governments believe that Iraq had produced weapons of mass destruction and we have to assume that they still have and that we have to assume that they still have . . . weapons of mass destruction. If anything, we worried that the CIA was underestimating Saddam, as it had before the Gulf War.

Bush also quotes a number of Democratic Congressional representatives who also believed Saddam Hussein had WMD:

> "One way or the other, we are determined to deny Iraq the capacity to develop **weapons of mass destruction** and the missiles to deliver them. That is our bottom line."
> **President Clinton**, February 4, 1998
> "If Saddam rejects peace and we have to use force, our purpose is clear. We want to seriously diminish the threat posed by Iraq's **weapons of mass destruction** program."
> **President Clinton**, February 17, 1998
> "Iraq is a long way from [here], but what happens there matters a great deal here. For the risks that the leaders of a rogue state will use **nuclear,**

chemical or biological weapons against us or our allies is the greatest security threat we face."

Madeline Albright, February 18, 1998

"He will use those **weapons of mass destruction** again, as he has ten times since 1983."

Sandy Berger, Clinton National Security Adviser, February 18, 1998

"[W]e urge you, after consulting with Congress, and consistent with the U.S. Constitution and laws, to take necessary actions (including, if appropriate, air and missile strikes on suspect Iraqi sites) to respond effectively to the threat posed by Iraq's refusal to end its **weapons of mass destruction** programs."

Letter to President Clinton, signed by **Sens. Carl Levin, Tom Daschle, John Kerry**, and others, October 9, 1998

"Saddam Hussein has been engaged in the development of **weapons of mass destruction** technology which is a threat to countries in the region and he has made a mockery of the weapons inspection process."

Rep. **Nancy Pelosi** (D, CA), December 16, 1998

(http://wiki.answers.com/Q/Did_George_Bush_lie_about_the_WMDs_in_Iraq#ixzz1yzIR25EQ)

If we question why Bush believed Iraq had WMD, the answer is because the available intelligence said so, the same/similar intelligence that convinced many others. This is, of course, a "justification," but it doesn't mean Bush was right. Indeed, looking back at the evidence on which he made his original judgment Bush now says, ". . . the intelligence was wrong."

Much has been made about the lack of real evidence for WMD, but less attention has been paid to the way Bush made use of what we might call "alternative world" evidence, that is, evidence presented from some possible world in which WMD exist, and where consideration is given to the consequences for Americans and others in such a world. In the pre-Iraq War assessment, Bush constructs what is known as a counterfactual argument, something like: "If Saddam Hussein did not have something to hide, he would not be willing to go to war." Counterfactuals are often associated with an analysis of "causal" relations such that where one gets "e" (the antecedent) one gets "c" (the consequent); if Saddam Hussein had nothing to hide (he has WMD) he wouldn't be willing to go to war. Bush had already convinced himself, based on Saddam's unwillingness to fully cooperate with UN weapons inspectors, that he was hiding something, and this was strengthened by that fact that Saddam was willing to go to war to protect or keep hidden the information that he has WMD. Given this type of argument, there is a sense in which the war on Iraq was justified by potential outcomes as much as actual outcomes. Consider the following interview from 2006:

> BUSH: . . . imagine a world in which you had a Saddam Hussein who had the capacity to make a weapon of mass destruction, who was paying suiciders to kill innocent life, who would—who had relations with

Zarqawi. Imagine what the world would be like with him in power. The idea is to try to help change the Middle East.

Now, look, I—part of the reason we went into Iraq: was—the main reason we went into Iraq: at the time was we thought he had weapons of mass destruction. It turns out he didn't, but he had the capacity to make weapons of mass destruction.

But I also talked about the human suffering in Iraq, and I also talked about the need to advance a freedom agenda. And so my question—my answer to your question is, is that imagine a world in which Saddam Hussein was there, stirring up even more trouble in a part of a world that had so much resentment and so much hatred that people came and killed 3,000 of our citizens.

You know, I've heard this theory about, you know, everything was just fine until we arrived and, you know, kind of—the "stir up the hornet's nest" theory. It just doesn't hold water as far as I'm concerned. The terrorists attacked us and killed 3,000 of our citizens before we started the freedom agenda in the Middle East. They were—

QUESTION: What did Iraq have to do with that?

BUSH: What did Iraq have to do with what?

QUESTION: The attack on the World Trade Center.

BUSH: Nothing, except for its part of—and nobody's ever suggested in this administration that Saddam Hussein ordered the attack. Iraq was a—Iraq—the lesson of September the 11th is take threats before they fully materialize, Ken.

Nobody's ever suggested that the attacks of September the 11th were ordered by Iraq. I have suggested, however, that resentment and the lack of hope create the breeding grounds for terrorists who are willing to use suiciders to kill to achieve an objective. I have made that case. And one way to defeat that—you know, defeat resentment, is with hope. And the best way to do hope is through a form of government.

Now, I said going into Iraq: we got to take these threats seriously before they fully materialized. I saw a threat. I fully believe it was the right decision to remove Saddam Hussein, and I fully believe the world was better off without him. Now, the question is, how do we succeed in Iraq? And you don't succeed by leaving before the mission is complete, like some in this political process are suggesting.

It looks very much like it didn't matter whether Saddam had WMD or not, as long as in some "possible world" he had the potential to produce WMD. In that world everyone is worse off, terrorists have a greater potential to spread death and destruction, Saddam's own people will suffer, the Middle East will suffer, and the world will be a more dangerous place. This is the "threat" as Bush saw it, and this is the "threat" Bush decided to remove. Hence, from what Bush says here, the debates about whether Saddam had or did not have WMD are second-ary to the "potential" threat Saddam had in a "possible world" constructed by Bush. But why should we believe all this, since Bush is talking about a "possible world," not the real world; in the real world the United States invaded Iraq, Saddam is dead, but there were no WMD.

Bush's text is essentially a set of stated or implied "counterfactual claims." Counterfactual statements consider what might have been the case, and they are a central part of our thinking and reasoning about our experiences of everyday life. Imagine that you are travelling to the train station, you decide to stop for a meal believing you will be in plenty of time to catch your train. However, while you are having your meal there is an accident on the road to the train station and this causes a traffic jam, and because of this there is a significant delay and you miss your train. You might say:

> If I hadn't stopped for that meal I would be on the train.
>
> *or*
>
> If there had not been an accident on the road I would have caught my train.

But why do we construct counterfactuals? For centuries philosophers puzzled over the meaning or relevance of counterfactuals since they referred to imaginary and nonexistent events; they are about what might have been, not about what was actually the case (Evans and Over, 2004; Byrne, 2002; Byrne and Johnson-Laird, 2009; Stalnaker, 1968; Lewis, 1973). The best-known theory in this area is that of David Lewis (1973, 2000).

Lewis made use of what is known as a "possible world semantics" to explain counterfactuals. In this semantics, truth conditions for the counterfactual are assessed in terms of relationships between possible worlds, a principle of "comparative similarity." As Menzies (2014) describes it: "the truth condition for the counterfactual 'If A were (or had been) the case, C would be (or have been) the case' is stated as follows:

> "If A were the case, C would be the case" is *true* in the actual world if and only if (i) there are no possible A-worlds; or (ii) some A-world where C holds and is closer to the actual world than is any A-world where C does not hold.

Such a definition generates a causal link between events.

> Where c and e are two distinct possible events, e *causally depends* on c if and only if, if c were to occur e would occur; and if c were not to occur e would not occur. (Menzies, 2014)

In our example above, c is stopping for a meal and e is missing the train. Hence, when c occurs e occurs, and when c does not occur e does not occur. Such assessments are central to our way of thinking about specific events, particularly when the outcome of those events may be bad. For example, historians have often speculated on what would have happened had Hitler won World War II. We would not have democracy as we know it, we would all have been controlled by Germany, the massacre of Jews would have continued, and so on. In this "possible world" the outcomes are particularly negative, and when we compare them to the actual world, the one in which Hitler did not win the war, our positive emotions and feelings toward the positive outcomes of winning the war become heightened, and our support for the objectives of World War II are strengthened (see Byrne, 2002).

Given this, when we look at how Bush explains both the Iraq War and the consequences of that war, against a background where we now know that many of the claims originally made for going to war were incorrect, he is forced to construct a "possible world" in which the consequences of not going to war become much worse than the consequences of going to war. He claims that:

> . . . imagine a world in which you had a Saddam Hussein who had the capacity to make a weapon of mass destruction, who was paying suiciders to kill innocent life, who would—who had relations with Zarqawi. Imagine what the world would be like with him in power.

Here he invites a counterfactual construction such as:

> If we had left Saddam in power (c) he would have had the capacity to make a weapon of mass destruction, he would have paid suiciders to kill innocent life, who would—who had relations with Zarqawi (e).

In the causal account given above where (e) is causally dependent on (c), (e) will only happen if (c) happens. All the bad and negative elements associated with Saddam only arise if we leave him in power. Equally, if (c) does not occur (e) does not occur. So we are all better off because Saddam has been removed from power.

Bush also introduces some other interesting post hoc arguments, for example:

> . . . the main reason we went into Iraq: at the time was we thought he had weapons of mass destruction. It turns out he didn't, but he had the capacity to make weapons of mass destruction.

Now whether the second claim here is actually true is a matter of contention, since it rested on the same discredited intelligence that claimed Saddam had weapons of mass destruction. But again Bush seems to be inviting us to infer, in some sense, we had to stop Saddam before he made nuclear weapons. Bush seems to want to us to believe:

> If Saddam had the capacity to make nuclear weapons (c) he would have made them (e).

This is again counterfactual, and given that it is almost certain that Saddam did not have the capacity to make nuclear weapons, here (e) is false and (c) is false, so in what possible world was there a case for war?

The Excuse for Torture and Tortured Excuses

One of the most controversial policies of the Bush administration involved the treatment of "terrorist" detainees, or prisoners, particularly those defined as "high value," those believed to have information essential in the "war on terror." Bush authorized the use of what were called "enhanced interrogation" techniques for such prisoners. These techniques included a variety of methods such a sleep deprivation, shouting and threatening detainees, stripping them naked, making then stand for long periods of time, and most controversial of all, "waterboarding," where detainees would have a wet towel, or other material, placed over their mouths and then water would be continuously poured into their mouths. The aim was to create a sense of drowning.

In several media interviews the main representatives of the Bush administration, particularly Cheney and Bush, denied that the United States carried out torture. They argued that torture was illegal and that the United States carried out interrogation using techniques that were within the law as confirmed by the Attorney General for the United States. They also argued that these techniques were necessary as part of the job of protecting the American people, and they had been used successfully in this regard. On Fox News (YouTube: "Bush on Torture") Bush makes all this clear in the following statement:

> I want to say something else, there's been a lot of talk in the newspapers and on TV about . . . a program that I put in motion to detain and question terrorists and extremists. I have put this program in place for a reason . . . and that is to better protect the American people and if we find somebody that may have information regarding a potential attack on America you bet we're gonna detain them and you bet we're gonna question them . . . because the American people expect us to find out information factual intelligence so we can help them . . . help protect them that's our job[,] secondly this government does not torture people you know we stick to US law and our international obligations[,] thirdly there are highly trained professionals questioning these extremists and terrorists now if we got professionals trained in this kind a work to a get information that'll protect the American people. The American people expect their government to take action to protect them from further attack and that is exactly what this government is doing and that's exactly what we'll continue to do.

Bush is responding to criticism in the media of his government's treatment of detainees, and in this sense the above statement is an "account." The account provides all the core elements that would appear again and again in response to this issue: the government is acting according to the law, the United States is meeting its international commitments, members of Congress are aware of what is taking place, the interrogation techniques are necessary to protect the American people, and the techniques have been shown to be successful. These claims provide a mixture of "justifications" and "excuses." Actions are justified under the law and are within international limits of acceptability, while others are excused because members of Congress know about them, or they are simply necessary to protect the American people.

All of these claims were questioned in different ways. The legal assessment was challenged by a variety of lawyers, while international condemnation of the interrogation techniques argued that they did not meet acceptable standards (many Americans also felt the use of some techniques was morally unacceptable), and there was disagreement within the intelligence community on the value of the information gained using "enhanced techniques."

In 2009 the Obama administration released a series of memos on "torture" during Bush's administration. These memos were issued by the Office of Legal Counsel between 2002 and 2005 and describe the interrogation techniques used on terrorist suspects (Huff Post: Politics, July 3, 2012). Referring to these memos, Patrick Leahy, Senate Judiciary Chairman, commented:

> These legal memoranda demonstrate in alarming detail exactly what the Bush administration authorized for "high value detainees" in US custody. The techniques are chilling. . . . We cannot continue to look the other way; we need to understand how these policies were formed if we are to ensure that this can never happen again.

There were those who disagreed with the release of the memos, and some former members of the Bush administration argued that giving terrorists the details of the techniques weakened the United States, because they cannot be used again, since suspects will know what to expect and prepare themselves accordingly. This was a point made previously by Bush and Cheney when they refused to comment on interrogation techniques because this would be telling the terrorists what their techniques were. Here we have the core difference in argument between those like Leahy and others, who focused on nuances of law and morality, and those who operate with a more basic argument, that if it works and helps America then that is justification enough.

Of course, if you can get these two arguments to coalesce, then that is much better. A review of the memos, and other linked material, shows that this was the basic policy. It all begins after 9/11 when on September 14, 2001, George W. Bush declares a "National Emergency by Reason of Terrorism." This is in essence the formal declaration of "war on terror," which is swiftly followed by the "Military Commission Order," November 13, 2001, whose subject was the "Detention, Treatment and Trial of Certain Non-Citizens in the War on Terrorism." This order declares the use of military force in the war on terrorism, and if this is to be successful it will be necessary for individuals "to be detained, and, when tried, to be tried for violations of the laws of war and other applicable laws by military tribunals. "The order provides for the unilateral authority of the President and Commander in Chief to detain prisoners indefinitely." Next, on January 25, 2002,

Alberto Gonzales, the White House General Counsel, rendered a decision on the ". . . Application of the Geneva Convention on Prisoners of War to the Conflict with Al Qaeda and the Taliban." In this he states:

> On January 18th, I advised you that the Department of Justice had issued a formal legal opinion concluding that the Geneva Convention 111 on the Treatment of Prisoners of War (GPW) does not apply to the conflict with al Qaeda. I also advised you that DOJ's opinion concludes that there are reasonable grounds for you to conclude that GPW does not apply with respect to the conflict with the Taliban. I understand that you decided that GPW does not apply, and accordingly, that al Qaeda and Taliban detainees are not prisoners of war under GPW. (lawofwar.org/**torture_memos_**analysis.htm)

On February 1, 2002, Attorney General John Ashcroft concurred with this and suggested that for protection against any subsequent legal actions ". . . a determination that the Geneva Convention does not apply will provide the United States with the highest level of legal certainty available under American law."

On February 7, 2002, George W. Bush confirmed that the Geneva Convention does not apply to al Qaeda and Taliban detainees. He argued that Geneva was designed for a conflict between "High Contracting Parties," or states, with standing armies. In the case of the war on terrorism there is a:

> . . . new paradigm in which groups with broad international reach commit horrific acts against innocent civilians, sometimes with the direct support of states. Our nation recognizes that this paradigm . . . ushered in not by us, but by terrorists—requires new thinking in the law of war, but thinking that nevertheless should be consistent with the principles of Geneva.

If Geneva does not apply, what will be the standards that will apply? Gonzales later commented on the outdated nature of the Geneva Convention and how he meant his memo to be interpreted: "The old ways may not work here. That's what the memo was intended to convey to the President. I never meant to convey to the President that the basic values in the Geneva Convention were outdated." Is this what Bush meant by "consistent with the principles of Geneva"? If so, how did this work? We know now that a range of interrogation techniques was employed, including dietary manipulation, slapping, sleep deprivation, water dousing, and waterboarding. In a memo of 2005, Alberto Gonzales reviews these methods and considers them in terms of legal assessments of what constitutes "torture." Gonzales comments that:

> [i]n defining the Federal Crime of Torture, Congress required that a defendant "*specifically intend*[]" to inflict *severe* physical or mental pain or suffering" and Congress narrowly defined "severe mental pain or suffering" to mean "the *prolonged mental harm* caused by" enumerated predicate acts, including "threat of *imminent* death" and procedures calculated to profoundly disrupt the sense of personality.

Much of the rest of the memo comes down to the definition of the terms "pain," "severe," and "extreme," and to contextual issues such as the medical assessment of detainees before, after, and during enhanced forms of interrogation.

As can be seen here, and in the decision on the Geneva Convention, and indeed in the very definition of war, much of the debate comes down to forms of "pragmatic interpretation." Consider, for example, the issue of "war." The argument used by the Bush administration was that the "war on terrorism" was not a "normally" defined war between nations. Terrorists do not represent specific states, they are not in any normal sense standing armies, and they do not abide by the international laws of war since they indiscriminately target innocent civilians. Of course, we might immediately counter here that this does not explain US actions in Afghanistan, which is a recognized state. The answer, again from Gonzales, is that under the Taliban it was a "failed" or "rogue" state and hence, again, standard rules did not apply! The fight with the Taliban may be understood in the same way as the war on terrorism in general.

There is nothing inherently wrong or problematic in setting up a definition X for "war" and then assessing the actions of those fighting against you in terms of that definition. Of course, it does not follow that if a combatant group does not abide by the laws of war when they attack you that you are required to abandon those rules yourself. Indeed, it could be argued that when you do abandon some or all of the rules of war because your aggressors have done so, then it follows if they are not fighting a standard war because they abandon the rules of war, then neither are you. By this I mean that if the aggressor's actions do not fit the definition X for war, and you then abandon or change some or all of the definition X for war, then neither side is fighting a "war" as standardly understood.

In essence "the war on terrorism" abandons at least some of the standard definitions of war. But then why refer to it as a "war" at all? The initial declaration of the Bush administration following 9/11 was one of "National Emergency." Clearly other terms are also available; could we have had a "fight" against terrorism, a "struggle" against terrorism, or even a "protection" against terrorism? But, of course, there is a good reason to use the term "war," even when you are not going to abide by standard rules yourself, and the reason is that it generates an ambiguity between "standard" war, and what we might call "non-standard" war. Here, the ambiguity can be manipulated for your ends, depending on your needs at any specific point in time. For example, in a time of "war," as standardly understood, the president as commander in chief is given much latitude in his actions. As Kenneth Roth (2004) put it

> The Bush administration has used war rhetoric precisely to give itself the extraordinary powers enjoyed by a wartime government to detain or even kill suspects without trial. In the process, the administration may have made it easier for itself to detain or eliminate suspects. But it has also threatened the most basic due process rights.

As Roth suggests, terms like "war on drugs" or "war on poverty" are harmless in their own way because the language is metaphorical. But the "war" on terrorism drives in two directions at once. First, as a "standard" war, emergency measures and powers are assured; second, as a "non-standard" war, it allows not only for actions outside the remit of the accepted laws of war, it provides a rational justification and excuse for such actions. Even if at a later date it is decided that the "non-standard" interpretation of war that underpinned such things as "enhanced interrogation" was wrong, personnel can argue that they acted under the best interpretation they had at the time.

As we have seen above, language is also central to the assessment of what is and what is not "torture," and here one of the main issues was, how does one define "pain" or "mental distress"? Both require a baseline, so we might apply such scalar adjectives as "severe" and "extreme" on a scale for "pain," and we could include a list with such things as mild-moderate-strong-severe-extreme-agonizing. This is a linguistic scale, of course, but pain is also a real physiological mechanism. Merskey (1991: *European Psychiatry*, 6, 4, 153–159) notes the definition adapted by the International Association for the Study of Pain in 1979 as:

> an unpleasant sensory and emotional experience associated with actual or potential tissue damage, or described in terms of such damage. It implies a monistic view of the experience of pain, and it is inappropriate to encumber it with concepts of pain behavior. Physicians recognize the individual's report because pain is subjective, and it varies both with the physical state of the individual and his/her state of mind.

What is interesting here is there is some allowance for a subjective element in interpretation and assessment, that is, what may be moderate pain for you may be extreme pain for me.

The Geneva Convention (1949) is clear on this:

> No physical or mental torture, nor any form of coercion, may be inflicted on prisoners of war to secure from them information of any kind whatever. Prisoners of war who refuse to answer may not be threatened, insulted, or exposed to any unpleasant or disadvantageous treatment of any kind.

This is not applied to terrorist detainees as defined by the Bush administration, however, because the war on terrorism is a non-standard "war," that is, it is one where terrorist detainees are not "prisoners of war." Nevertheless, Bush said he wanted to operate within the "principles of Geneva" and that the United States wanted to treat detainees in a "humane" way—yet this seems to have included assessing degrees of physical pain or mental distress to "enhance" interrogation. However, as well as the distinction between "standard" and "non-standard" definitions of war, the Bush administration also set up different definitions of detainees. Within the "non-standard" definition of "war," where detainees are not defined as "prisoners of war," there are some who are sub-categorized as "high value detainees," and it is these detainees who are selected for "enhanced interrogation." "High value detainees" are defined in Alberto Gonzales's memo of May 10, 2005 (page 3), as:

> a detainee who until time of capture, we have reason to believe: (1) is a senior member of al-Qia'da or an al-Qia'da associated terrorist group (Jemaah Islamiyyah, Eygptian Islamic Jihad, al-Zarqawi Group, etc.); (2) has knowledge of imminent terrorist threats against the USA its military forces, its citizens and organizations, or its allies; or that has/had direct involvement in planning and preparing terrorist actions against the USA or its allies, or assisting the al-Qai'da leadership in planning and preparing such terrorist actions; and (3) if released constitutes a clear and continuing threat to the USA and its allies.

Number (2) on the list of definitions is interesting. How do the US authorities know what "knowledge" the detainee has, and if they already know the detainee knows about X or Y, why would they need "enhanced interrogation?" Of course, the authorities may know that a detainee P has been involved in planning a bombing, but not know where the bombing is to take place, who else is involved, and at what date and time the bombing is to take place. This is exactly the point Bush (2010: 168) makes in the case of Abu Zubaydah, who under initial questioning by the FBI:

> . . . revealed bits and pieces of what he thought we already knew. Frighteningly, we didn't know much. For example, we received definitive information about a new alias for Khalid Sheikh Mohammed, who Zubaydah also confirmed had masterminded the 9/11 attacks. Then Zubaydah stopped answering questions.

The first thing to note is that the information Bush refers to was given under what one assumes to have been "normal" interrogation—and it seems the information was quite important, despite Bush's attempt to second-guess the detainee. However, because Zubaydah has now stopped answering questions, George Tenet of the FBI tells Bush he believes that Zubaydah has more information to give. The CIA suggests to the president the use of other "enhanced interrogation techniques," which, if applied, would be used only by professionally trained personnel and under medical supervision. One of these was "waterboarding," of which Bush notes, "No doubt the procedure was tough but medical experts assured the CIA that it did no lasting harm." This is a generalization, of course, and Gonzales's assessment of the use and impact of waterboarding is surrounded by many legal and medical caveats.

In the end Bush says that the techniques proved effective and that Zubaydah ". . . revealed large amounts of information. . . ." But the definition of "high value detainees" assumes the detainee has knowledge of "imminent attacks," and so on. In the case of Zubaydah, it was simply that Tenet believed Zubaydah had more to give—and indeed he did, but what if he didn't? If we interrogate an individual on the assumption that they know something, that is not a guarantee they do: but one might say that is exactly the point of interrogation, that is, to make the decision one way or the other. In this sense, since all senior Al Qaeda members could be assumed to have some knowledge of operations, they are all "high value," and for them the description in (2) seems redundant—unless, that is, it helps justify enhanced techniques and makes it sound like they were not generally used, and only used when it was assumed the detainees had some relevant knowledge of attacks or whatever. It is difficult to judge this generally, other than on a case-by-case basis, and perhaps this should have been part of (2) and part of what not only helped define "high value detainees" but also controlled the use and limits of "enhanced interrogation techniques."

Finally, one of the most remarkable comments and justifications for the use of "enhanced interrogation" is given by Bush (2010: 169) as:

> Zubaydah later explained to interrogators why he started answering questions again. His understanding of Islam was that he had to resist interrogation only up to a certain point. Waterboarding was the technique that allowed him to reach that threshold, fulfill his religious duty, and then cooperate. "You must do this for all the brothers," he said.

The suggestion here is that "enhanced interrogation" not only works, but that it assists certain detainees fulfill their religious duty.

Much of the justification Bush and members of his administration gave was either after the fact, or as part of an ongoing action, in both cases the main argument being that the ends justifying the means. When George W. Bush was asked in an interview why he believed "waterboarding" was legal, he replied, "Because the lawyers said it was legal." But there were critics who argued that it was Bush and his administration who asked the legal team to find a way to legally justify their actions. Thomas Kean, the joint Chair of the 9/11 Commission, said that ". . . the administration got the legal opinions they wanted."

Making use of the claim "because the lawyers said it was legal" sounds very much like an "excuse." Scott and Lyman (1968) defined excuses as those statements where the speakers know something is wrong but they deny full responsibility. In this case, if the Bush's actions could be shown to be "wrong," then he is not fully responsible because he acted on legal advice, given by people he said he "trusted." This is also an extension of the concept of "hedging," but in this case moving beyond single words or phrases to whole discourses. Instead of saying things like "as far as I remember" or "as I recall," one refers to legal definitions and documentation, not as agreed law but as an interpretive guide, and if this should prove wrong, it was still the professional advice one was given.

To be fair to Bush, he gave an answer to a direct question about why he believed "waterboarding" was legal, not whether it was wrong. But all of the forms of reasoning for "enhanced interrogation" suggest that it was a last resort, carried out only in cases where it was believed lives would be saved, only used under medical advice, and only where it was deemed to be legal. Why all these forms of explanation/justification? The answer is because many others did not believe that "waterboarding" was acceptable; they said it was wrong, dangerous, and illegal. Hence, the justifications and excuses arise because it is recognized that there is or could be something wrong, or at least that there are those who argued that the administration was wrong or behaving illegally.

George W. Bush's comments on Iraq, WMDs, and the treatment of detainees, including "enhanced interrogation" techniques, provide us with a series of "accounts" containing varying forms of justifications and excuses, and there is a familiar feel about all of these in that they often point to actions that were justified by evidence at the time. Recall how time-based constraints are frequently used by politicians: "when we said we would not raise taxes we did not know at that time that X was going to happen." These time-based arguments provide protection for politicians who can say things have changed since an original statement S, or we didn't know X at time Y. And this was very much the position adopted by the Bush administration as the consequences and full impact of the Iraq conflict began to emerge.

But the logic here is often confusing. If the United States is involved in a nonstandard war, where standard concepts defined within the Geneva Convention do not apply, this must work both ways—that is, terrorists are not expected to abide by the Geneva rules either. This is generally true, and terrorist groups have committed many horrific acts. However, such groups cannot claim that their actions were necessitated by a non-standard war, since Bush would argue that "they started it." Nevertheless, there are many in both the Western and Arab worlds, and elsewhere, who would dispute this, or at least see it as too simplistic. Some, such as Noam Chomsky and Christopher Hitchens, have asked the West and the United States in particular, to consider that the emergence of terrorist groups willing to attack America and the West could have been the outcome of American and other actions in areas such as the Middle East and elsewhere. And, they would further argue, that "enhanced interrogation," and indeed its convoluted justification, contribute to the continuation of the terrorism problem, and not its solution.

7

There and Back Again with Barack H. Obama

I am wary of politics. I think he's too much of a good guy
for the kind of brutality, the skepticism.

Michelle Obama on Barack Obama
(Remnick, 2010: 116)

Introduction

In his biography of Barack Hussein Obama, David Remnick asks his readers if
they can name their state senator? Remnick then suggests that if the reader can
name the person, or at least "Google" the name, they might like to consider the
possibility that such a person, within a very few years, could become the president of the United States. Remnick notes that while this feat requires a leap of
imagination, how much further are we stretching incredulity when we add that
the person is an African American—". . . every previous resident of the White
House, for more than two centuries has been a white male Protestant, except
for the thousand day interregnum when the President was a white male Roman
Catholic" (Remnick, 2010: 267).

When Barack Obama was elected president of the United States in 2008, it
was not only a historic moment, the election of an African American as president,
but it was, in Obama's own campaign terms, a triumph for "hope" and "change."
Throughout his campaign, the quality of Obama's rhetorical skills were noted
(Fallows, 2008; Heffernan, 2009). On a general level, Sam Leith (2012) discusses
a range of Obama's rhetorical techniques, from anaphora, through building a
rhythm using "syntheton" (using two words instead of one: "effort and determination," or "passion and dedication"; Inaugural Speech, 2013), to "trichodon"
(making use of groups of three phrases; see below). Leith also tells us that Obama's famous "Yes we can" chant was successful because it was three stressed syllables in a row, which he claims is rare in speeches. As we noted earlier, however, **199**

this type of rhetorical analysis refers to the mechanics of Obama's speech; it doesn't really tell us how it works. Why, for example, should three stressed syllables be important, why not four, why not five, which are presumably as rare in speeches, if not more so?

Whatever way we explain it, there is little doubt that Obama's rhetorical style assisted in sweeping him to power, not once but twice. After his first election, when the euphoria died down, Obama faced the cynical reality of politics. With a majority of Democrats in the Senate, but a majority of Republicans in the House, Obama had a difficult balancing act to achieve. By the time of his re-election campaign in 2012, there were varying views as to whether Obama had managed to balance the pro- and anti- forces within the political landscape of his first term, and there were signs that the once great rhetoric associated with Obama's original presidential campaign was beginning to temper toward the ordinary, if not the pedantic.

On October 15, 2012, NPR news's Alan Greenblatt ran a piece called, "The Not so Great Communicator," driven in the main by Obama's lackluster performance in the first of the presidential debates held on October 3, 2012. Greenblatt comments: "it's hard to think of a single speech he's (Obama) delivered as President that was as powerful as several he gave when originally running for the office." This is, of course, only one view, and in general the public still rank Obama as one of the best orators in the history of the presidency. Across the rest of the world, Obama's re-election as president in November 2012 was seen as a positive event. In a poll of 21 countries outside the United States, 50% of the people favored Obama over his Republican opponent Mitt Romney (YouGov/ Sunday Times: cited in *The Week*, November 10, 2012).

In this chapter we want to explore Obama's use of language in a number of political contexts, specifically, his anti-war speech on Iraq in 2002; his keynote address to the Democratic National Convention in 2004; and his "race" speech of 2008. As well as this, we want to look at the presidential debates of 2012, looking at the first debate in particular, when Obama was accused of putting in such a dismal performance that it helped reinvigorate his opponent's campaign. But we want to begin with a topic that would seem central to all great political and other speeches: the role of emotive language.

Emotion, Politics, and Pragmatics

According to Remnick (2010: 110) Barack Obama's first foray into public speaking on political issues took place at an anti-apartheid rally staged at his school in Hawaii.

Obama was to open the rally. "There's a struggle going on," he began. He could sense that only a few people had heard him. He raised his voice. "I say there is a struggle going on."

When Obama is not heard, he does what analysts refer to as "recycling his turn" (Schegloff, 1987; Mazeland and Huiskes, 2001), and he marks this turn with a meta performative comment, "I say," produced with a raised tone. This is a pragmatic act, and one not unusual in political speeches:

I say to you tonight
  I stand here before you
  We are gathered here
  Let me begin by saying

These are classic examples of historical sermon like forms that comment directly on one's actions. They reflect, in part, the nature of speeches as monologues and the need for forms of opening and closing. Classic research on ordinary conversation displays how participants make use of an opening section where such things as paired greetings may take place, hello/hello or hi/hi (see Chapter 1). This may then be followed by an introductory phase: What's new? How are things? This introductory phase is then developed through structured moves that introduce topics or narratives or other pairs such as question and answer (Schegloff, 1968; Hutchby and Wooffitt, 2008; Sidnell, 2010). In a speech there are also standard openings, as when the speaker is introduced, and this may include a brief biography of the speaker and an indication of the topic of the speech. But this introduction is mainly about the speaker; once the speaker is announced, she too has to go through an opening format. This often has a politeness phase, when the speaker thanks the hosts and the guests and then marks out what they will talk about. In this context, because the speaker holds the floor, she may make use of such things as "I will tell you tonight," "I am going to talk about," "I will discuss"; these moves perfomatively introduce the topic(s) that follow. Such meta-markers assist in a monologue context by creating a quasi-interactional moment where the speaker is both talking to and responding to themselves. Following this, they then state the core theme of the speech. This may be done in many ways, from a simple "I want to talk today about X," to a more complex emotional or emotive general statement, "Four years ago, I stood before you and told you my story" (Obama, 2008).

Once a speech is opened, there are many more possibilities for topics, themes, styles, organization, and so on. Consider the following from Obama's anti-war speech delivered in Chicago, October 2, 2002:

What I am opposed to is a dumb war. What I am opposed to is a rash war. What I am opposed to is the cynical attempt by Richard Perle and Paul Wolfowitz and other armchair, weekend warriors in this administration to shove their own ideological agendas down our throats, irrespective of the costs in lives lost and in hardships borne.

  or

I stand here today, grateful for the diversity of my heritage, aware that my parents' dreams live on in my precious daughters. I stand here knowing that my story is part of the larger American story, that I owe a debt to all of those who came before me, and that, in no other country on earth, is my story even possible. Tonight, we gather to affirm the greatness of our nation, not because of the height of our skyscrapers, or the power of our military, or the size of our economy. Our pride is based on a very simple premise, summed up in a declaration made over two hundred years ago, "We hold these truths to he self-evident, that all men are created equal. That they are endowed by their Creator with certain inalienable rights. That among these are life, liberty and the pursuit of happiness. (Keynote address to the Democratic National Convention, 2004)

We could look at both of these examples in structural terms and comment on pragmatic marking, use of pronouns, colloquial versus formal styles, and so on, but even a brief reading of these examples also makes clear that whatever structural forms are being used, there is also, in both examples, an appeal to our emotions. Terms such as "dumb" and "rash," or others such as "pride" and "precious," not only describe cognitive states and feelings, but also generate what are sometimes called "connotations," emotional associations of various types. But what are these, and can pragmatics say anything about them, given, in particular, that much of modern pragmatics is grounded within a rationalist view of meaning, where inferences and truth are calculated as logical formulas based on propositional representations, not on the description, delimitation, or measurement of emotions?

The reality is, however, that political speeches and debates, and much of everyday interaction, contain a variety of linguistic constructions that have emotive content or associations. It is a staple of great speakers and leaders that they arouse emotions. Social psychologists refer to "emotion" as "affect," and they contrast this with reason or rationality. The relationship between reason and affect, or emotion, as we will refer to it from now on, is a complex one. Neuroscientists argue that the brain has evolved to allow emotions and reasoning to work together; one without the other leads to problems of survival in the modern world. The classic example here is that of Phineas Gage, a young railroad construction worker who in 1848 suffered a bizarre accident when an explosion lodged a steel rod 2.5 centimeters thick and more than a meter in length in his head. The rod entered through his cheek and went through the frontal part of his brain. Gage was taken to the local doctor, John Harlow, and though Gage had lost a lot of blood and had had convulsions, he miraculously survived, being able to both walk and talk.

Some months after the accident, Gage underwent severe changes in both personality and mood. Perhaps most startling, particularly for those who knew him well, was his anti-social behavior, his display of bad manners, and his foul-mouthed language. Not surprisingly, Gage found it difficult to keep a job, or retain friends and family, and he died penniless in 1861. His doctor wrote of

Cage, "The equilibrium between his intellectual faculties and animal propensities seems to have been destroyed."

In his book *Descartes' Error*, neuroscientist Antonio Damasio (1996) drew on the example of Cage (among many others) to argue that Descartes' "dualist" view of the separation of body and mind was wrong. Not only do emotion and reason work and depend on each other, but they are also built out of an interaction with bodily experience to produce not a bifurcated body and mind but an integrated relationship of embodied cognition. In embodied cognition, mind, body, and world are integrated forces assisting our navigation through everyday life (Barsalou, 1999; Clark 1997; Lakoff and Johnson, 1999).

The Philosopher Andy Clark (1998) has written extensively on the concept of embodied cognition, and he shows how we see it in a host of areas from animal behavior to modern robotics. Clark tell us, for example, how the humble sponge utilizes water currents to position itself to access food, how tuna manipulate swirls and eddies to increase speed and maneuverability, and how simple robot forms called "mobots" utilize corners, angles, and spaces to move around a special environment. In the case of human beings, Clark points to wide range of examples of body-mind-world interaction, from the basic way we use pen and paper to assist mathematical calculations or as an aid memoir, to our complex use of language as an interactional resource for gaining information, manipulating others, or maintaining relationships.

As we have seen previously, the linguist and cognitive scientist George Lakoff has drawn on the general principle of embodied cognition to develop an explanation of metaphors as cognitive phenomena built out of our early experiences within the world. Lakoff has used this general picture to argue that political worlds can be manipulated and changed through shifts in the way language constructs different cognitive frames. Drew Westen (2007), in his book *The Political Brain*, makes a similar point, but in this case he emphasizes the important role that emotions play in voting behaviors, pointing out that for voters facts, figures, and logical reasoning to the best conclusions may fail when set against narratives and images that create passions such as fear, excitement, and anger (see Chapter 4).

But where does all this fit with language, and with pragmatics in particular? Andy Clark says, of all the tools we may use to advance our cognitive and social capacities, language is the "ultimate tool," and pragmatics, with its emphasis on meaning in context, is particularly relevant in explaining the interaction of emotion and reason in politics. On the other hand, many pragmatic tools emphasize the formal and the logical, the rational and the reasoned, rather than the emotional. In early work on semantics there was a distinction made between the denotative, referential, and descriptive use of language, and the connotative or the expressive and emotional use of language (see Lyons, 1977; Besnier, 1990). The connotative nature of language, while clearly displayed in a variety of ways within of the world's languages (see Besnier, 1990), has been given less attention;

it has been considered too variable and subjective. Yet at the same time, we all understand the emotional difference and relationship between words such as "killed" "dead," "slaughter," "massacre," "execution," and "murder." Can these differences be explained only by reason? If not, then where does emotion enter the construction of meaning within interaction, and political interaction in particular?

The situation is complicated further when we look at the seminal work of the social psychologist R. B. Zajonc. Zajonc (1980) published a paper in the *American Psychologist* entitled "Feeling and Thinking: Preferences Need No Inferences." In this paper Zajonc argues that not only are many feelings not based on cognitive processes, but some feelings, or emotions, may precede cognition. Zajonc says that emotions are more primitive than reason, are often nonverbal, and are less stable than cognitive outputs. Emotions may arise from different forms of what Zajonc calls "preferenda," interactions between stimuli and internal states of the individual. Researchers have known for some time that the decisions we make may be predicated on responses such as "I liked/didn't like X" without any rational justification for the choice, although if we ask someone why he said he "liked/didn't like X" he is capable of providing reasons and thoughtful arguments for his preferences. But this cognizing is coming after the emotional response; it is not necessarily what creates it.

One of the potential consequences of Zajonc's theory for pragmatics is that if meaning is rational and based on cognitive means-ends judgments, or judgments of appropriate social behavior, pragmatics can say little about how selected words or sentences lead voters to behave in specific ways, since those behaviors may be based on emotion and not reason. But there are two points to make. First, even if Zajonc is correct, the object/internal state relationship in the case of language will be words, sentences, and the utterance of these in context; these will be the objects that evoke emotion with or without reason. Second, given how we actually reason (see below), not all cognition may reflect the logical or procedural step-by-step approach assumed in formal pragmatic theories.

In his book *Thinking Fast and Slow*, Nobel laureate Daniel Kahneman (2011) distinguishes two of systems for thinking, system 1 and system 2. System 2 looks very much like our standard formal pragmatics model, where reasoning is rational, procedural, and logical, and also, Kanneman notes, "slow." In system 1, thinking looks much more intuitive and speculative and draws on such things as stereotypes and prototypes. Kahneman (2011: 7) gives us the following example:

> An individual has been described by a neighbor as follows: "Steve is very shy and withdrawn, invariably helpful but with little interest in people or in the world of reality. A meek and tidy soul, he has a need for order and structure and a passion for detail." Is Steve more likely to be a librarian or a farmer?

Most people presented with this problem opt for "librarian" As Kahneman states, "The resemblance of Steve's personality to that of a stereotypical librarian strikes everyone immediately." However, Kahneman then explains that what does not occur to us is that there are 20 farmers for every librarian in the United States. Statistically speaking, it follows that we are more likely to find people like Steve among the farming community than among librarians. We discussed previously how meanings can be inexact and that we often work on the basis of the typical example, or prototype, which has a set of stereotypical features, and because we do this (because we use the fast automatic system 1 style of thinking), we may get things wrong, or draw incorrect inferences. In many cases, however, this may not matter, as our swift processing of "best fit" has generally worked pretty well for us in the past.

Nevertheless, although many people selected "librarian" as the answer, this does not make the choice unreasonable, or unreasoned, since stereotypes or prototypes are often based on solid facts about our own experiences. Further, our propensity to use system 1 thinking in this way is something politicians make use of all the time in the hope of getting us to generalize beyond single cases or examples of X to all cases of X. In his 1976 campaign, Ronald Reagan used the following example of a woman from the South side of Chicago who was arrested for welfare fraud.

> She has eighty names, thirty addresses, and twelve Social Security cards and is collecting veteran's benefits on four non-existing deceased husbands. And she is collecting Social Security on her cards. She's got Medicaid, getting food stamps, and she is collecting welfare under each of her names. Her tax-free cash income is over $150,000.

The particular woman was never identified, and Reagan was accused of grossly exaggerating a single case, but because of Reagan's example the term "welfare queen" entered the American lexicon. This kind of exaggerated over-generalization is common in politics, and is frequently found in right-wing views of state welfare and immigration. Take the case of British Home Secretary Teresa May, who in a speech at a Conservative Party Conference in 2011 gave an example of the absurdity of immigration regulations. She claimed that an immigrant who was known to be in the country illegally could not be deported since he had bought a cat while in the United Kingdom, and the cat would be distressed if the immigrant were forced to leave the country. It later turned out the case was completely erroneous, but for those who believe immigration laws are wrong or absurd, the story had already served its purpose, engendering specific emotions or emotional reactions about immigration in general, going well beyond a single case example.

Consider the following taken from the beginning of Obama's speech, noted above:

> I stand here today, grateful for the diversity of my heritage, aware that my parents' dreams live on in my precious daughters.

What does that actually mean? It is metaphorical in that "dreams" are being considered as embodied within the lived individuals who are Obama's daughters. It is also possibly an analogy with genetic inheritance transferred to a more abstract plane of dreams. But it is also a classic stereotype, an example that we all want more for our children, we want them to be successful, to be safe, to prosper, and to have children of their own. In this example the statement is an emotional realization of our wishes for our children and future generations. But is all this cognitively processed by the audience? It is certainly available for "system 2" processing, but this is not the same as saying that everyone activates system 2. It is possible that some listeners may focus on selected words or phrases like "precious" or "daughter" or "parents" and react emotionally to these. Of course, reasoning and emotion can and do work together, but is it possible for us to respond to language without thought, or at least reflective thought, and if so, what would be the consequences for pragmatics and, indeed, for politics?

Language Emotions and Thought

Interestingly, if one Googles the phrase "language without thought," most articles that appear deal with the ability to think without the ability to use language, or fully formed human language (see Davidson, 1975; Leslie, 1988). Yet this is the reverse of the input phrase, which was "language without thought" not "thought without language." There are good reasons that this should be the case; after all, to have a language assumes that we use that language to represent things and as such to think (see Davidson, 1975). So while there is evidence from evolutionary biology that animals may have proto or other forms of cognition without language (see Hurford, 2007), one is less likely to find an argument that the use of language does not produce thought. Underlying much modern language philosophy, linguistics, and cognitive science is the belief that language in some way represents thought, the claim that communication is essentially a form of "telemention" (te Molder and Potter, 2005), wherein speakers produce their thoughts in sentences and these are then decoded, interpreted, and understood as thoughts by listeners.

Wittgenstein (1953) argued, however, that within ordinary language some forms of rule following are automatic; although they may give a sense of reflection, they are followed "blindly" (see Malcolm, 1971; cited in Coulter, 2005). To some extent this is in line with the embodied cognition position that thinking is not only in the head but an outcome of mind, body, world experience. Being in pain and seeing someone else in pain invokes in us a natural pre-linguistic (and shared) understanding that is "achieved" rather than "interpreted" (Coulter, 2005). We have seen how cognitive metaphor is assumed to use an experiential base as a source domain for representing target domains, which makes the source domain, in many cases, non-linguistic. While we can see this primitive, automatic and pre-linguistic understanding in reactions to pain, surprise, laughter, and so on; once sentences or phrases are involved these become mediating and therefore interpreted as representations of our feelings and thoughts. Coulter (2005) asks why should we assume this. Often such sentences as "he is going to hit me" are grafted onto non-linguistic experiences when someone may have been hit before, and their production is based on that experience, not an external and symbolic representation of that experience. In this way, many aspects of language become instinctive rather than forms of rational interpretation.

This is an odd argument for most of us because our background and training reflect the rational and modern computational view of the world, where language and thought are symbol manipulating and interpretation processes. But are we really as rational as we think?

Returning to the work of Daniel Kahneman (2011: 45), he gives us the following syllogism and asks us to "determine as quickly as we can" whether or not the conclusion follows from the premises:

> All roses are flowers.
> Some flowers fade quickly.
> Therefore some roses fade quickly.

Kahneman notes that when this syllogism was presented to college students a majority of them endorsed the conclusion; you may also have done this, but if so you are wrong. It is plausible that of the flowers that fade quickly none of them are roses.

But why are so many of us prone to get such assessments wrong? The answer resides in the two systems of thought, system 1 and system 2. Kahneman (2011: 20) describes these as follows:

> System 1 operates automatically and quickly with little or no effort and no sense of voluntary control.
> System 2 allocates attention to the effortful mental activities that demand it, including complex computations. The operation of system 2 is often associated with the subjective experience of agency, choice and concentration.

System 1 looks a bit like the emotional, non-inferring forms of thought noted by Zajonc, or the "blind" rule following of Wittgenstein, whereas system 2 reflects the classic representational, rational, and computational view of thought in modern cognitive science. However, as Kahneman argues, both systems 1 and 2 can be seen as interacting together. Imagine that after listening to a speech we are asked what we thought of the candidate; we might respond by saying that "we like him and we enjoyed the speech" (system 1). If we are asked to explain why we like him and why we enjoyed the speech we could, with some effort, explain aspects of the candidate and the speech as evidence for the position we have adopted (system 2).

The defining feature of system 2 is that its operations are effortful and one of its main characteristics is laziness a reluctance to invest more effort than is strictly necessary.

It is partly as a result of this "lazy" aspect of system 2 that we often rely on system 1, but, as a consequence, while our decisions will be swift they may also be inconsistent with the decisions we might have made had we taken more time and effort. Recall the example of the librarian and farmer; system 1 gave us access to a plausible response based on a general stereotype we have of librarians. This required little time and limited effort and it allowed us to solve the problem as it was put to us. Of course, such a response is not in itself irrational; we do have a process of reasoning we can draw on, that is, the inference from a stereotype of a librarian, to Steve's personality (see also Stanovich, 1999).

But what is the relevance of this for politics or pragmatics? For politicians, it means that focusing on logic and reason may not always be the best choice, and in some cases a more emotional, simplistic, or experiential-based argumentation may be more successful.

The importance of system 1 underlined our discussions of Ronald Reagan as a storyteller, and it helps explain how George W. Bush treated all "intelligence" on Iraq as "fact," because of the credibility of the source, the "intelligence community," and also, of course, because this, combined with his own objectives, allowed him to rationalize his actions of going to war with Iraq. But it does not always follow that system 1 is the best choice, and much of Clinton's rationalization of his behavior during his depositions was based on a detailed analysis of words, their definitions, and the motivations of his enemies. Clinton refused to make swift automatic responses to questions put to him, and instead manipulated the rational and underlying logic of language to present alternative interpretations that suited his needs (system 2).

Consider another example from Kahneman (2011: 50):

Banana   Vomit

These words are presented to the reader, and then Kahneman says:

> A lot happened to you during the last second or two. You experienced some unpleasant images and memories. Your face twisted slightly in an expression of disgust. . . . Your heart rate has increased, the hair on your arms rose a little and your sweat glands were activated. In short you responded to the disgusting word with an attenuated version of how you would react to the actual event, all of this was completely automatic, beyond your control.

If this is correct, how does this sit with a computational view, which would have located these words within a mental lexicon, where information on syntax, semantics, and pragmatics might interface, and where a type of Gricean logic would look for the relevance of this information in cooperative interaction.

On this, Kahneman suggests (2011: 50):

> There was no particular reason to do so, but your mind automatically assumed a temporal sequence and causal connection between the words banana and vomit, forming a sketchy scenario in which bananas caused the

sickness. . . . The state of your memory has changed in other ways; you are unusually ready to recognize and respond to objects and concepts associated with "vomit" such as sick, stink, nausea, and words associated with "bananas" such as yellow and fruit and perhaps apples and berries.

This is referred to as "associative activation"; it is automatic and effortless and, most significant, "You did not will it and you could not stop it" (Kanneman, 2011: 50). This last point needs careful consideration. The activation of ideas or concepts, or the construction of scenarios, is something semanticists and pramaticists refer to all the time; the only difference here is that it is always assumed to have some form of effortful or higher-level cognition involved, for example, constructing a script about the consequences of eating too many bananas, or eating a poisonous banana, or drinking too many banana daiquiris (Schank and Abelson, 1977). Kahneman's point is that his example reflects system 1 in action, not that there is no cognitive effort, or indeed representation; rather, it is the automatic nature of cognizing that is central, and this is built out of ideas and memories associated with words. Yet while all this may be automatic, the question is, why react at all? Kahneman (op. cit.: 51) suggests, "There was no particular reason to do so, but your mind automatically assumed a temporal sequence and causal connection between the words banana and vomit." In pragmatic terms, we have been presented with two words on a page, which drives us to try to make sense of what is before us, to look for "relevance." Remember that Sperber and Wilson argued a similar automaticity for utterance interpretation in that all utterances carry a presumption of their own "optimal relevance." In the case of the words on a page, we draw upon our understanding of the words in front of us and assume they appear for a reason. This leads to a cascade of not only related words and their connections, but also memories of scripts and scenarios relevant to how we make sense of words. System 1 and pragmatics relate in that system 1 offers a way of understanding and responding to the world around us, which has been built out of our associations and experiences with the world. Within interaction it seems that what we say may automatically trigger a range of associations (not all linguistic) before any reflective assessment about why the speaker said such and such at this time, or at this point in the interaction. So before we get to system 2, if in some cases we get to it at all, it is possible, through the use of language, to initiate a range of associations, or emotions, or as the linguists call them, "connotations."

Consider, for example, Barack Obama's middle name, "Hussein." During his first presidential campaign, and even after he was elected, some people tried to draw a connection between the name "Hussein" and the Middle East, even suggesting that Obama was a closet Muslim, that he had pro-Arab views, and negative attitudes toward Israel.

Obama is a lifelong Christian and not a Muslim; nevertheless, Obama himself, speaking in 2010 to the Israeli media, said, "it may just be the fact that my middle name is Hussein, and that creates suspicion" (cited in *The National Journal*, September 27, 2012). Wasimel-Manor and Stroud (2012) reported an experiment where Arab Israelis and Jewish Israelis both watched videos of President Obama talking to Israeli Prime Minister Benjamin Netanyahu. In one video the caption read "Barack Obama" and on the other "Barack *Hussein* Obama." When the middle name was introduced, Arab Israelis thought Obama would be fairer to Arabs, while Jewish Israelis thought he would be "less pro Israel."

In politics, as elsewhere, associations with particular terms, as we have said, may arise from everyday experiences, and the more one has certain experiences, or the more one is exposed to certain words in certain contexts, the tighter or more embedded those associations become. Consider, for example, the way in which the Bush administration's mention of "Saddam Hussein" would frequently occur in conjunction with the phrase "weapons of mass destruction (WMD)," and also either "al Qaeda" or "terrorism," or both (Kull, Ramsay, and Lewis, 2003). This may have reflected an effort to have the public create an associative link between Saddam Hussein and WMD, a link with terrorists, and al Qaeda in particular, and hence may have also created a further link to 9/11. This is not mere speculation, as the co-chairs of the 9/11 Commission put it:

> The Bush administration had repeatedly tied the Iraq war to September 11—insinuating in some people's minds a link between Iraq and the attacks themselves. . . . (A)t different junctures a majority of Americans believed that Saddam Hussein was involved in 9/11. (cited in Russomanno, 2011: 141)

Evidence of actual links between Saddam Hussein, WMD, al Qaeda, and 9/11 was considered questionable at the time of preparations for war with Iraq, and they were later confirmed as basically untrue (see Chapter 6 of this volume). However, through repeated references to links between Saddam Hussein, WMD, and al Qaeda, the American public came to believe that there was evidence for such links. Such was the impact of the use of repeated claims that even when evidence emerged that the links were unconfirmed, a large proportion of the public still continued (and continue) to believe that there were such links, including, despite evidence to the contrary, that Saddam Hussein had weapons of mass destruction. Reviewing selected public polls, Entman (2012: 168) comments that:

> In a Gallup Poll taken during January (2006), 53 percent of respondents said they thought the "Bush administration deliberately misled" Americans about Iraq's WMD. Yet 57 percent in a March 2006 Gallup Poll said they were either certain that Iraq had WMD or thought it likely. And 50 percent in a July Harris Poll said they believed WMD had been found. (Hanley, 2006)

It seems that once particular associations are established, they are hard to shift.

It is clear, then, that associative thinking at an automatic system 1 level could prove significant in generating public beliefs, and perhaps voter actions; consequently, it would seem remiss of any pragmatic analysis of political language to completely ignore such thinking, no matter how difficult it might prove to formally account for any specific emotional effects.

Embodied Pragmatics

In explaining the "associative" response to the words "banana" and "vomit," Kahneman also discusses a related phenomenon called "priming." As the name suggests, it refers to how interpretations and actions may be affected by the presentation of prior, or simultaneous, stimulus materials. For example, if you have been given the priming word "EAT" you are more likely to complete "SO-P" as "SOUP" as opposed to "SOAP" (Kahneman, 2011). There are also various studies that look at how linguistic priming may have bodily effects. In a number of famous studies Bargh et al. (2005; cited in Kahneman, 2011: 53) showed how students solving sentence construction problems were affected by associations related to the words they were working with. Students who were constructing sentences with words like "Florida," "old," "bald," and "forgetful" were found to move more slowly when sent to another location following the experiment. Paula Niedenthal (2007: 1002) asks us to imagine the following scenarios:

> A man walks into a bar to tell a joke. Two people are already in the bar, one is smiling and one is frowning. Who is more likely to "get" the punch line and appreciate the joke? . . . Two women are walking over a bridge. One is afraid of heights, so her heart pounds and her hands tremble. The other is not afraid at all. On the other side of the bridge, they encounter a man. Which of the two women is more likely to believe she has just met the man of her dreams?

What is going on here? Niedenthal tells us is that there is a link between the "bodily expression of emotion and the way in which emotional information is attended to and interpreted." This is what we might expect from an embodied view of the world where mind, body, and world interact. Significantly, the language-processing view of the world as only computational symbol manipulation ignores the way in which the interpretation of language may also reflect ". . . partial reactivations of states in sensory, motor, and affective systems . . ." (Niedenthal, 2007: 1003). Language use in general may initiate original cognitive states linked to the acquisition of language, and knowledge in general. Accepting this claim, along with the general process of priming, suggests that emotion in language will be linked to the associative experiential histories of words and phrases as shared by speakers and hearers, and central here is the general concept of empathy.

Research on the perception of emotion has shown that when we perceive emotion in others, there is often an equivalent or mirrored reaction in ourselves. We see someone recoil in pain and we may tense up and have an intake of breath as if we are suffering ourselves. The claim is not, however, that all language is processed emotionally. Experiments have shown that words such as "vomit" or "sick" can create a physical reaction, such as a grimace and change in facial muscles, when participants are asked whether the words are linked to emotions. On the other hand, if participants are simply asked whether the words have capital or lowercase letters, physiological or emotional reactions may not arise.

Returning now to political language in general, and Obama's political language in particular, we can see that if we want to understand both his successful and unsuccessful speeches, attending only to formal pragmatic symbol manipulation and processing may not always be enough; we also need to see how such language initiates system 1 reactions, associative thinking, an emotional mirroring triggered by selected words or phrases, and the connections to either generic or personal scenarios of emotional experience.

The Return of the President

We noted above that in the study of language, and particularly pragmatics, the denotative, representational, and formal view of meanings tends to hold sway. This is a generalization, of course, and there have been a variety of scholars who have given a place for the connotative or emotional aspects of language; Jacobson (1960), for example, or Bolinger (1980; see also Potts, 2007, Potts and Schwarz (2010). McConnell-Ginet (2008) argues that an "innate" view that all language is built from the same cognitive materials unaffected by society, and culture leads directly away from the social construction of meaning, where words carry "conceptual baggage," aspects of a word's meaning that it picks up on its way through the world (op. cit.: 512):

> I include under this rubric what traditional lexicographers and others have called connotations, but also encyclopedic knowledge, stereotypes or prototypes, and background assumptions, as well as knowledge about social practices in the course of which the word gets used.

McConnell-Ginet notes that much of the meaning generated in interaction does not come from what the speaker says, and may not even come from what the speaker means; rather, it is automatically generated through the broader cultural and conceptual history of words themselves. Here we come back, via linguistic analysis, to associative meaning and the operation of systems 1 and system 2.

Keeping this in mind, in this section I want to look more closely at a number of Obama's speeches. The aim will be to move beyond the descriptive aspects of the speeches (see Arwater, 2007) and pragmatically explain the operation of some of the connotative dimensions. We begin by looking at one of Obama's best known speeches, his 2004 address to the Democratic National Convention.

> Tonight is a particular honor for me because, let's face it, my presence on this stage is pretty unlikely. My father was a foreign student, born and raised in a

small village in Kenya. He grew up herding goats, went to school in a tin-roof shack. His father, my grandfather, was a cook, a domestic servant.

But my grandfather had larger dreams for his son. Through hard work and perseverance my father got a scholarship to study in a magical place: America, which stood as a beacon of freedom and opportunity to so many who had come before. While studying here, my father met my mother. She was born in a town on the other side of the world, in Kansas. Her father worked on oilrigs and farms through most of the Depression. The day after Pearl Harbor he signed up for duty, joined Patton's army and marched across Europe. Back home, my grandmother raised their baby and went to work on a bomber assembly line. After the war, they studied on the GI Bill, bought a house through FHA, and moved west in search of opportunity.

Consider the following words/phrases:

(1) Foreign student, Kenya, herding goats, tin roof, shack
(2) cook, domestic servant

We can see that our associative thinking could combine the words in (1) to indicate Africa, poverty, and limited farming. But also more than this, herding goats may produce thoughts about goat's milk, or feeding the family, perhaps a large family. In terms of "poverty" this might be sub-classified as not just poverty but African "poverty," which is worse or greater than American, British, or European "poverty." In terms of (2) the term "cook" seems neutral, that is, someone who cooks, although we might contrast it with the higher ranked category "chef." But when we set "cook" alongside "servant," things change. Here associations, or connotations, can run well beyond individual meanings. Although "cooks" can be found in all kinds of restaurants, a "cook" as "servant" evokes period style memories of the servants in a large house of a rich family. It is a "class" based view of "cook," and given that Africa has also been evoked this could link to colonialism; hence we may have dimensions of "status" and "power" in society, and in turn concepts of inequality, oppression, and freedom. Finally, having created such assumptions, we must ask where do we fit "foreign student?" We are told that Obama's father was a "foreign student" right at the outset. This may be fairly straightforward, meaning that his father came to American to study, and as a result met Obama's mother. But if we look at what follows, the description of Obama's father as a "foreign student"—as well as the associations we have highlighted—we can see how these might combine to generate links to one of the "grand narratives" (Lytoard, 1984) of American culture and history. The positive opportunities provided to those who come to the United States, a land of freedom and opportunity, where no matter what your lowly beginnings you are welcomed and given rewards for your hard work and enterprise. This is further strengthened if we see "foreign student" as a "primer"; this would make interpretations of earlier poverty and individual education and personal development all the more salient, in that to get from Africa and poverty to foreign student suggests strength, hard work, courage, and ambition.

But are these the kinds of associations Obama wants to generate? One can see the benefit of locating Obama through his family to the essential beliefs and philosophy underlying the American dream. Obama shows that his father benefited from American opportunities and freedoms, and that he (Obama) is one outcome of these opportunities, he is making the speech because he is, in a very specific sense, the product of American opportunity. One might criticize this analysis as speculative, and that not every member of the audience would have the same set of experiences with which to generate the same set of meanings. This is partly true, but it also points to an advantage and a problem. Some critics argue (see Schegloff, 1997) that when analysts comment on speech materials in this way they are dealing with a transcription and moving back and forth through a static presentation of the actual speech, while in the real world the audience who heard this speech would not have had such a reflective opportunity. This is a fair point, but in the embodied nature of associative thinking in real time, we can automatically process "script" based associations of the type we are highlighting. It doesn't matter whether all members of the audience get the same or all of the associations or connotations that might be derived from specific words in Obama's speech; it can be argued that many of them cannot help themselves from activating many of these associations because, as McConnell-Ginet suggests, these words carry "conceptual baggage."

Of course, one could argue that some of these associations may be accounted for in a standard pragmatic way, through Gricean principles and drawing on general knowledge or contextual assumptions, or a combination of both. But this is system 2 again, and in our analysis we are claiming that the associations were automatic and processed whether hearers willed them or not. Within pragmatics, several theories assume that the speaker is intending certain information to be constructed or inferred from the message, and that under the guiding rules/procedures of pragmatics the hearer can work out what information was conveyed. Many analysts working in pragmatics accept that this process is not always exact, but they see their job as explaining the rational and reasoned processes—cognitive, social, or otherwise—that underpin the activity of communication, and not any potentially random, unorganized, and emotional overlay of meaning. As we have seen previously (Chapter 1), such a case is cited by linguists as a reason to avoid the inclusion of emotional or connotative dimensions within either a semantic or a pragmatic theory. But perhaps many such associative meanings are not as random as we might think, and while they are not easily accommodated within present semantic or pragmatic theories, there is clearly something in them that deserves attention.

This is something McConnell-Ginet indicated in her definition of "conceptual baggage," but she goes further and suggests that a word's "conceptual baggage" (2008: 513):

> . . . can have profound communicative effects, triggering various kinds of (virtually automatic) inferences by interpreters, inferences not always explicitly

recognized by interpreters as such and often not intended by speaker. . . . Conceptual baggage, though not part of meaning as such, is often interactionally very significant even though not just implicit but (sometimes) difficult even to access.

Note how McConnell-Ginet comments on the (virtually automatic) nature of "conceptual baggage," and also that she would include under that heading "connotations." To endorse her final comment, she gives us the following example, taken from Kitzinger (2005; cited McConnell-Ginet, 2008: 513), which arose in a physician's office:

(3) My husband has a terrible headache and is running a high fever.

It is pointed out that Kitzinger's careful examination of (3) suggests a variety of assumptions—or in Kahenman's terms associations—become available based primarily the use of the phrase "my husband." McConnell-Ginet (2008:18) lists some of these as follows:

(4)

   a. The patient is an adult male married to the caller.
   b. The patient and the caller live together.
   c. The caller knows the patient's medical history.
   d. The caller will assume responsibility for the patient's care beyond
      making this call on his behalf—for example, driving him to see the
      doctor or picking up a prescription for him.
   e. The patient and the caller share their primary-care physician.

The point is that these assumptions would not follow in the same way "if the caller had referred to the patient as my friend." McConnell-Ginet sees these assumptions as forms of "conceptual baggage" because only (a) is semantic in the sense of being an entailment whose truth is guaranteed by (3). She goes on (ibid.: 513):

But no one would argue, I think, that if a person does not live with a man, is unfamiliar with his medical history, or is unwilling or unable to assume responsibility for his care when he is ill, then that man cannot be the person's husband.

McConnell-Ginet is aware that some analysts could argue that such assumptions are generated via Gricean implicatures, or perhaps "explicatures," but in line with Kahenman and our arguments above, McConnell-Ginet responds to such a possibility by noting (ibid.: 513–514):

But this move will not do the trick in general, because conceptual baggage can trigger inferences even if the speaker does not intend those inferences to be drawn, perhaps has not even considered them explicitly, and might even reject them on such consideration.

Let us turn now to an example from another well-known Obama speech, his anti-war speech on Iraq, delivered on October 2, 2002, at Federal Plaza, in Chicago. Specifically, in the first parts of the speech Obama makes clear he is not against war per se, his own family fought bravely in World War II, where essential freedoms were at stake and the war was necessary to maintain these freedoms and to defeat a "larger evil."

> Good afternoon. Let me begin by saying that although this has been billed as an anti-war rally, I stand before you as someone who is not opposed to war in all circumstances. The Civil War was one of the bloodiest in history, and yet it was only through the crucible of the sword, the sacrifice of multitudes, that we could begin to perfect this union, and drive the scourge of slavery from our soil. I don't oppose all wars.
>
> My grandfather signed up for a war the day after Pearl Harbor was bombed, fought in Patton's army. He saw the dead and dying across the fields of Europe; he heard the stories of fellow troops who first entered Auschwitz and Treblinka. He fought in the name of a larger freedom, part of that arsenal of democracy that triumphed over evil, and he did not fight in vain. I don't oppose all wars.
>
> After September 11th, after witnessing the carnage and destruction, the dust and the tears, I supported this administration's pledge to hunt down and root out those who would slaughter innocents in the name of intolerance, and I would willingly take up arms myself to prevent such tragedy from happening again. I don't oppose all wars. And I know that in this crowd today, there is no shortage of patriots, or of patriotism.
>
> What I am opposed to is **a dumb war**. What I am opposed to is **a rash war**. What I am opposed to is the cynical attempt by Richard Perle and Paul Wolfowitz and other armchair, weekend warriors in this administration **to shove their** own ideological agendas down our throats, irrespective of the costs in lives lost and in hardships borne.
>
> What I am opposed to is the attempt by political hacks like Karl Rove to distract us from a rise in the uninsured, a rise in the poverty rate, a drop in the median income—to distract us from corporate scandals and a stock market that has just gone through the worst month since the Great Depression. That's what I'm opposed to. **A dumb war. A rash war. A war based not on reason but on passion**, not on principle but on politics. Now let me be clear—I suffer no illusions about Saddam Hussein. He is a brutal man. A ruthless man. A man who butchers his own people to secure his own power. He has repeatedly defied UN resolutions, thwarted UN inspection teams, developed chemical and biological weapons, and coveted nuclear capacity. He's a bad guy. The world, and the Iraqi people, would be better off without him.
>
> But I also know that Saddam poses no imminent and direct threat to the United States or to his neighbors, that the Iraqi economy is in shambles,

that the Iraqi military a fraction of its former strength, and that in concert with the international community he can be contained until, in the way of all petty dictators, he falls away into the dustbin of history. I know that even a successful war against Iraq will require a U.S. occupation of undetermined length, at undetermined cost, with undetermined consequences. I know that an invasion of Iraq without a clear rationale and without strong international support will only fan the flames of the Middle East, and encourage the worst, rather than best, impulses of the Arab world, and strengthen the recruitment arm of al-Qaida. I am not opposed to all wars. I'm opposed to dumb wars.

We want to concentrate on the highlighted phrases in the above example. In looking at the video of the speech, the production of these phrases shows they were stressed, louder, and lengthened compared to surrounding talk. But why? These are passionate phrases, used mainly to express emotion. In this sense we would argue that they are similar to what Potts calls "expressives" (2007 1). Potts is one of the few analysts who has attempted to include connotations within semantics and pragmatics, and he refers to Kaplan (1999; cited in Potts, 2007: 1), who says:

> it seems to me quite possible to extend semantic methods [. . .] to a range of expressions that have been regarded as falling outside semantics, and perhaps even as being insusceptible to formalization.

As we noted in Chapter 1, it is not always clear what some formalizations actually buy us in terms of understanding the construction of meaning in social interaction. Potts does analyze "expressives" into semantic types, but more important for us is his definition of ". . . expressives as operators that actively change the context in specific ways." Potts suggests that "expressives" have the following characteristics, which he sees as following from a "single source" (2007: 2):

1. Independence: Expressive content contributes a dimension of meaning that is separate from the regular descriptive content.
2. Nondisplaceability: Expressives predicate something of the utterance situation.
3. Perspective dependence: Expressive content is evaluated from a particular perspective. In general, the perspective is the speaker's, but there can be deviations if conditions are right.
4. Descriptive ineffability: Speakers are never fully satisfied when they paraphrase expressive content using descriptive, i.e., nonexpressive, terms.
5. Immediacy: Like performatives, expressives achieve their intended act simply by being uttered; they do not offer content so much as inflict it.
6. Repeatability: If a speaker repeatedly uses an expressive item, the effect is generally one of strengthening the emotive content, rather than one of redundancy.

Potts is attempting to outline tests for "expressives," and as with many such tests in pragmatics, they always leave borderline cases. Potts says of the above set of features, for example:

> It defines some things as clearly expressive. It also defines some things as clearly nonexpressive. These exclusions can be surprising. To take just two quick examples: it has sometimes been suggested that the predicate 'lurk' has an expressive component (Harnish, 1975 provides data and references). But it fails all of the tests for expressivity identified here. Similarly, Keenan and Stavi (1986: 258) suggest that the determiner few might express an inherently subjective value-judgment by the speaker. This anticipates the language I use for expressives, but, like 'lurk,' this item simply fails to count as expressive. (This is not to say that the analyses of lurk and few are mistaken. I point out only that they don't count as expressive on the present view.) (Potts, 2007 26)

I think the last phrase is instructive, Potts says of "lurk" and "few" that they may be subjective or have an "expressive" component but they aren't defined as "expressives" by his tests. This is a bit like saying a three-legged dog may well be a dog but it is not dog under conditions which define a dog as a four-legged animal. In this weaker sense, then, we can see Potts's definition of "expressives" as a guide, a starting point from which to assess various forms; it is not an agreed and proven template which allows us to separate all and only "expressives" from other forms with only descriptive content.

If we consider "dumb" and "rash," for example, they would seem to fulfill many of the dimensions Potts highlights for "expressives." Under (1) dumb/rash do not affect the truth of the phrase they mark; for example, if its true that "there is a war in Iraq," it remains true even when modified as "there is a dumb/rash war in Iraq."

Potts defines (2) as:

> Expressives cannot (outside of direct quotation) be used to report on past events, attitudes, or emotions, nor can they express mere possibilities, conjectures, or suppositions. They always tell us something about the utterance situation itself. This is the nondisplaceability property.

One example given by Potts is as follows:

> That bastard Kresge was late for work yesterday. (# But he's no bastard today, because today he was on time.)

It seems possible to construct a similar argument with dumb/rash: "200 men died yesterday because of this dumb/rash war (but its not dumb/rash today because no men have lost their lives)."

We can interpret (3) in its generic sense as the use of a specific expressive where the speaker is adopting a particular emotional attitude to the host clause, and referring to the Iraq War as dumb/rash would seem to be in line with this.

Element (4) just means that it is hard to define the exact meaning as used by the speaker. Of course, one can say that "dumb" may be used to mean stupid or silly, but these are just word substitutions. Obama could have said this is a "stupid" war, but without the same impact. Or he could have said this is a "silly" war, but this is even worse, and seems to have connotations of jocularity or immaturity. Under (5) Potts is treating "expressives" as speech acts, that is, they are performative. So by calling the war in Iraq "dumb/rash" Obama is expressing his hostility toward the war. Finally, under (6) we have a generally recognizable aspect of the relationship between repeatability and increasing the emotional impact of one's use of expressive forms, for example, "This is a dumb, dumb war, as dumb a war as it is possible for a dumb war to be." Compare this to a simple descriptive use: "this is a war, a war as war, a war that is as much a war as it can be a war."

Our attempt to match "dumb" and "rash" in terms of Potts's model seems to support our initial intuitions that they are "expressive" and function to indicate an individual emotive attitude.

Let us now look at these again in the context of the speech and explore the emotional or other aspects of their expressive nature. One of the first things to note is that "dumb" and "rash" are used in two linked sentences.

What I am opposed to is **a dumb war**. What I am opposed to is **a rash war**.

They could have been conjoined, as in "What I am opposed to is a 'dumb' and 'rash' war," but this would lose the opportunity for repetition and parallelism. By using independent sentences, one can use repetition of the host clause "What I am opposed to is . . ." and which is further repeated a third time in "What I am opposed to is the cynical attempt. . . . " As we have seen, "the rule of three" can be used for a number of purposes in rhetoric (Leith, 2012; Atkinson, 1984) and one of these is to build tension as one reaches the end of a list. The Latin phrase *omne trium perfectum* suggests the completeness and perfection of things that come in threes. In terms of the rule of three, it is the phrase "What I am opposed to . . ." that is repeated to create the triad. But the rule appears in different formats; sometimes it is a repetition of the same word or phrase, as above, or in Lincoln's statement "Government of the people, by the people, for the people . . ." But it can also be related to conceptualizations, as in another Obama example: "Our security emanates from the justness of our cause; the force of our example; the tempering of qualities of humility and restraint." Such sets of three can show great variation and contribute to a range of emotions. But the content of the triad is also important and should be considered as much as the structural rule itself.

Consider "dumb," for example; while it can be ambiguous between reference to muteness or to stupidity it is quite clear in which sense Obama is using it. But if "dumb" is defined as "stupid" or "stupidity," can we substitute "stupid" for dumb without a change in semantic effect?

What I am opposed to is a dumb war.
What I am opposed to is a stupid war.

When I asked a group of students if these sentences had the same meaning, their first reaction was that the sentences were basically equivalent, then a few argued that "dumb" was stronger than stupid. Pushed on this, the closest they could explain the difference was in terms of comparative strength, that is, that "dumb" was in some sense even more stupid than simply stupid.

Webster offers a definition of "dumb" as "lacking intelligence; stupid," which treats dumb and stupid as synonymous. On the other hand, some commentators have argued that "dumb" is more of an American English usage. But consider the sentence: "That was a dumb and stupid thing to do." This seems a perfectly possible English sentence, yet in one sense it should be redundant if "dumb" and "stupid" mean the same thing as in the following two sentences:

That was a dumb and dumb thing to do.
That was a stupid and stupid thing to do.

These two sentences seem less plausible; by conjoining the same words, the conjunction becomes redundant and tautological. If "X was a dumb and stupid thing to do" is plausible, but the above two sentences are not, then in an intuitive way we seem to recognize that "dumb" and "stupid," while conveying a similar meaning, may be used in different contexts with perhaps a different emphasis.

Let's look at another related issue as displayed by these examples:

(a) You are either dumb or you are stupid but not both.
(b) You are either dumb or you are stupid or both.

Both of these sentences seem acceptable, but if so this is odd. The logical assessment of "or" suggests it can be exclusive or inclusive. For example, "John scored the goal or Bill scored the goal (but not both)," as opposed to "Bill is married or very rich" (or both). The problem is that (a) and (b) seem capable of being inclusive or exclusive, and this may be because the semantics of "dumb" and "stupid" are basically the same, but this can't be the full story since if (a) is acceptable then it suggests they are not the same. Maybe the answer is one of relatedness, perhaps on a scalar list, for example:

dumb, stupid, dim, dull, silly

Here "dumb" as an upper bounded member would entail "stupid," "dim," and so on. Equally, stupid would implicate "not dumb," and this would have to be cancelable: "You are stupid but not dumb." This seems possible, and the following sentence seems equally plausible: "You are dumb but not stupid." But under the entailment relation, where "dumb" entails "stupid," this sentence should be a contradiction of the type highlighted in "All of the boys came to the party but some of them did not," and this is clearly not the case.

What we can conclude from this is that not only is it difficult to discern the exact difference between "dumb" and "stupid" in terms of their semantics, we also don't fair much better in pragmatics, and this illustrates why "emotive" or affective marking in language is difficult to access.

While "dumb" and "stupid" share a similar semantic base, "dumb" may be a stronger variant in terms of its emotional expression. The fact that this intuitive reaction is not easily tracked in either semantics or pragmatics may be, as we suggested above, because both areas call for "formal" solutions—either A or B (exclusive), while emotive expressions may be weighted differently in different contexts. But this would suggest that whether one is emotively stronger than the other becomes relative to context. On the other hand, emotive or connotative aspects of words, phrases, or sentences cannot just vary in any old way, even if determined by context (Humpty Dumpty is not in control).

Another way of approaching this problem might be to consider something like the "Affective Norms for English Words Scale" (Bradley and Lang, 1999); here words are given an emotional weighting by giving them scores on a scale determined by informant reactions based on three main affective measures; pleasure, arousal, and dominance. In the case of the word "stupid," the mean scores were 2.31 for pleasure, 4.72 for arousal, and 2.98 for dominance. Unfortunately, there was no equivalent score for "dumb," since the word has not yet been assessed. The closest word to "dumb" is "dummy," which could of course be interpreted in different ways. "Dummy," however, scored 3.38, 4.38 and 3.67, which does suggest a higher average overall emotional reaction, but as we said, while "dummy" can mean one who is stupid, it can also mean an inanimate doll.

It seems the best that we can say is that words with similar semantic definitions such as "dumb" and "stupid" can occur in the same utterance without either contradiction or tautology and that as such the use of one as opposed to the other may carry different connotations in certain contexts, or that one as opposed to the other may have different weightings in terms of affective reactions. But this is important in that this emotive overlay can be a background for assessing the content of any argument that is to follow. As we suggested above, cognitive systems 1 and 2 are not necessarily mutually exclusive, and affective language can be used to generate feelings and emotions, which are then active as system 2 begins to work through claims or arguments that require more cognitive attention, a form of rhetorical priming (see above).

Within politics this suggests that affective language use, operating along with reasoned and detailed arguments, could influence political decision-making (see Utych 2012: 3; also Forgas and Locke, 2005).

When individuals are asked to arrive at an opinion about a political object, they will draw on the various considerations about that object they have in their minds (Zaller, 1992). When individuals receive political information intertwined with affective language, this language should create a particular mood in them, giving them another consideration that seems relevant.

Consequently, Obama's emotional framing of his argument against any war in Iraq places the pro-war lobby's case within a context of irrationality, and lack of intelligence. Hence, Obama's repetition of what we might call his slogan against the war, that this war is "dumb" and this war is "rash":

> A dumb war. A rash war. A war based not on reason but on passion.

Obama's complaint is that the reasoning behind the war is "emotional," not rationally considered; it is rushed, based on the wrong reasons, and hence just "dumb." Given that political speeches are carefully crafted, and given that the contrast is between "reason" and "rationality" versus "ignorance" and "lack" of intelligence or thoughtfulness, why not just say the war is irrational and it hasn't been thought through, or even that it's just stupid. One reason is that "irrational" may not evoke the same emotive state represented by either "stupid" or "dumb," and we have argued that "dumb" is even stronger than "stupid," so it is "dumb" that is chosen because it does a better job in this context.

Let us consider some other aspects of Obama's speech, in particular his use of two metaphors; first, "armchair warriors," leveled against a range of individuals, but naming directly Richard Perle and Paul Wolfowitz; and second, ". . . shove their own ideological agendas down our throats. . . ." We have noted in a number of places the significance of the work of George Lakoff and colleagues on cognitive metaphors and the centrality of the experiential foundation of such metaphors. And we can see how Obama wants to distinguish between those who sit around and talk about war (ideology) and those who suffer directly because of that talk, where the content and beliefs underlying such talk are forced on us. This "force" is linked by analogy to an experiential base of "force feeding," as in either benign examples, such as parents getting a baby to eat its food, or in the more sinister sense of forcibly making someone eat what he doesn't want. To highlight this more clearly, we want to draw on the work of Giles Fauconnier and his concept of mental or conceptual spaces, which is also grounded in embodied cognition. We want to make use of Fauconnier's work because of its broader conceptual base, which moves beyond metaphors to language and cognition in general, and because it draws on original work by Koestler (1964) on what he called "bisociation":

> I have coined the term 'bisociation' in order to make a distinction between the routine skills of thinking on a single 'plane,' as it were, and the creative act, which, as I shall try to show, always operates on more than one plane.

Bisociation is interesting for us in that it links quite closely to the general notion of system 1 as an "associative engine." Koestler used bisociation to try to explain "creativity" in such areas as the arts, humor, and the sciences. His main point is that creativity is manifest when two seemingly disparate or diverse bodies of thought are brought together in the production of something new or original. The process ". . . uncovers, selects, re-shuffles, combines, and synthesizes already existing facts, ideas, faculties, (and) skills" (Koestler, 1964: 120). For example, consider the classic joke:

Q: Why did chicken cross the road?
A: To get to the other side.

This joke works, in part, by setting up a bisociation between the intentional actions of a human being and the actions of chickens. Through the anthropomorphism, or personification, of the chicken as human, we seek a resolution to the question through intentions and rationality, but the core of the joke is the clash between such assessments and the simple outcome of moving from one side of the road to the other. Or consider the famous example of Archimedes. It is claimed that he came up with the scientific concept of "displacement" by noting how the water level in his bath varied relative to his weight. Assuming that Archimedes had had several baths in his life prior to his "Eureka" moment, the rise in the bath water did not previously trigger any interest. It was only when he was considering a specific problem that the displacement of water—which was previously unconnected to any problem he was trying to solve—became relevant. Thus two seemingly unconnected areas were combined to provide the creative outcome of scientific discovery.

Building on the general idea of bisociation, Fauconnier and Turner (1996: 1; see also Fauconnier and Turner, 2002) develop what is referred to as "conceptual blending theory."

> Conceptual blending is a basic mental operation that leads to new meaning, global insight, and conceptual compressions useful for memory and manipulation of otherwise diffuse ranges of meaning. It plays a fundamental role in the construction of meaning in everyday life, in the arts and sciences, and especially in the social and behavioral sciences. The essence of the operation is to construct a partial match between two inputs, to project selectively from those inputs into a novel "blended" mental space, which then dynamically develops emergent structure. It has been suggested that the capacity for complex conceptual blending ("double-scope" integration) is the crucial capacity needed for thought and language.

Fauconnier and Turner (2002: 63–65) give an example of how this works by asking us to consider an article called "The Boat Race." Here a modern boat in 1993 sails a course originally taken by a clipper in 1853.

The Boat Race
A sailing magazine reports:
As we went to press, Rich Wilson and Bill Biewenga were barely maintaining a 4.5 day lead over the ghost of the clipper *Northern Light*, whose record run from San Francisco to Boston they're trying to beat. In 1853, the clipper made the passage in 76 days, 8 hours. ("Great America II," *Latitude 38*, volume 190, April 1993, p. 100)

While in reality there are two clearly distinct runs over the same course; in the magazine they have become merged, or as Fauconnier and Turner (2002) argue, the two distinct events have become "blended" into a single event (see figure 5).

The two distinct events correspond to two input mental spaces, which reflect salient aspects of each event: the voyage, the departure and arrival points, the period and time of travel, the boat, its positions at various times. The two events share a more schematic frame of sailing from San Francisco to Boston; this is a "generic" space, which connects them. Blending consists in partially matching the two inputs and projecting selectively from these two input spaces into a fourth mental space, the blended space:

In the blended space, we have two boats on the same course, both having left San Francisco, on the same day. A process of 'pattern completion' allows us to construe this situation as a race (by importing the familiar background frame of racing and the emotions that go with it). This construal is emergent in the blend. The motion of the boats is structurally constrained by the mappings. Language signals the blend explicitly in this case by using the expression "ghost-ship." By "running the blend" imaginatively and dynamically—by unfolding the race through time—we have the relative positions of the boats and their dynamics.

As another example, and one more relevant to the aims of this book, consider the following comment on Clinton's presidency after he had been in office a few months:

By this point, Roosevelt was far ahead of Clinton.

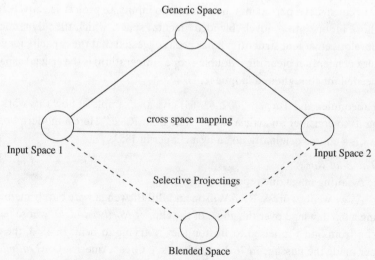

FIGURE 5 The four-space model: (Fauconnier and Turner, 2003:59)

Here Roosevelt's and Clinton's presidencies become the two inputs that become mapped onto each other. This would be seen in terms of time points, political achievements, problems they faced, and so on. Each is being compared on a set of political variables at a specific point in time to achieve some "political" understanding or explanation of either or both presidencies, and this understanding is emergent not from one or other set of achievements but through their blending.

Now if we take this approach to the anti-war speech of Obama, the opening statement is about war in general and the fact that Obama is not against war per se; indeed, he suggests the Civil War and World War II as examples of wars that proved necessary in the removal of slavery and the destruction of a particular evil represented by reference to "Auschwitz and Treblinka." Obama further tells us that he has family history associated with involvement in war, but a war that was necessary to maintain a "greater freedom," specifically the maintenance of "democracy." Compared to such wars, with their noble and necessary objectives, the Iraq war is "dumb" and "rash," waged by people who will not be going to war ("armchair warriors"), but who yet expect the ultimate sacrifice of others.

In Obama's speech, two main mental input spaces are being presented from the outset, which we might call "war 1," as exemplified by the Civil War and World War II, and "war 2," as in the case of Iraq, with a "generic space" for "war in general".

Here the input spaces represent alternative views of war, and as such they clash when placed in blended space. This forces the listener to contrast these alternatives, to set each one against the other for comparison. It is unlikely that many people would want war for its own sake; most of us understand that

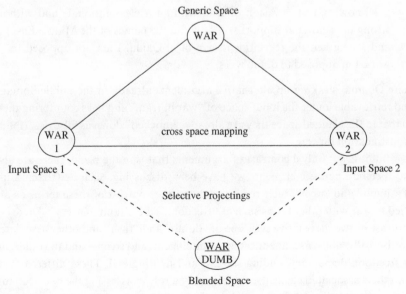

FIGURE 6

politicians lead us to war while they and their advisors remain safe at home. Most of us also recognize that war is sometimes necessary, for the protection of our country, our way of life, our family, and our children. Given the blended space, the questions for the listener are, what is the purpose of the Iraq War? Why is it necessary? Is there evidence that its causes and objectives could be computed in comparison with such things as the Civil War or World War II? Can the objectives be achieved without war?

The outcome of any assessment between the "war 1" and "war 2" input spaces is not guaranteed one way or the other. Remember that the Bush administration's arguments for war are also in the public domain. Arguments about terror and support of terror from Iraq, arguments about the actions of a dictator who was compared with Hitler (see Chapter 5; also Wilson et al., 2012), and who had murdered many of his own people. What is central is that the "blended space" allows listeners not just to consider arguments about war, but to see how Obama's speech has set up a contrast between "war 1," which is just and necessary, with positive and worthwhile outcomes, and "war 2," which is unnecessary, unmotivated, with no clear rationale or objectives.

Obama is well aware of the alternative Bush administration arguments; hence he adds such comments as:

> But I also know that Saddam poses no imminent and direct threat to the United States or to his neighbors, that the Iraqi economy is in shambles, that the Iraqi military a fraction of its former strength . . .
>
> I know that even a successful war against Iraq will require a U.S. occupation of undetermined length, at undetermined cost, with undetermined consequences.
>
> I know that an invasion of Iraq without a clear rationale and without strong international support will only fan the flames of the Middle East . . . and strengthen the recruitment arm of al-Qaida. I am not opposed to all wars. I'm opposed to dumb wars.

Here Obama is taking up alternative arguments already in the public domain, and retrievable under the input space of "war in Iraq," and he is countering them so that in the blended space they are already "knocked" down as false descriptors of justification for war.

But it is not only a contrast of arguments that is in the blend; there are also the specific linguistic elements we have been discussing, such as Obama's use of "dumb" and "rash," their repetitions, and the contrast of these terms as applied to war with other terms such as "freedom," "evil," and "slavery." There is a contrast of two associative sets, one of "dumb" and "rash" and other associated words—silly, nonsense, uneducated, unintelligent, and so on—and the other one of freedom, democracy, ending slavery, and fighting evil. These different sets, with their associated elements, can also play a role in assessing the two accounts of "war 1" and "war 2." These can assist in providing an emotional overlay for the assessments of "war 1" and "war 2" and produce as output an Orwellian mantra: "war 1" good, "war 2" bad. Further, there is another level of processing, which may assist Obama in making his case, and this is the input space in the model described as "generic space."

In the generic space for "war," one would find a range of associations, such as the cost of war in economic and human terms, the impact on vulnerable groups such as children and the old, the horror of war through such images as the dead, the mutilated, lost limbs, and so on. These negative associations connected with "war" may also tip the balance in Obama's favor in an audience assessment of the blended space, such that they come to understand and agree with Obama that the war in Iraq is unnecessary.

We see here how Obama's speech may be described in relation to pragmatic processing and understanding. It is not only the logic of system 2 arguments, set up as types of war as in "war 1" (Civil War, World War II) and "war 2" (Iraq War), but also system 1 associations connected with the account of such war types. The mix of conceptual input from these areas, along with "generic" associations linked to war in general, drive home Obama's argument and help make it memorable and successful in terms of its own rhetoric, and in terms of the developing reputation of Obama as an important and powerful public speaker.

A Different Kind of "Race"

In considering Obama's language, there is also a more general sense in which we can draw on conceptual blending to explain Obama's style. As the first black US president, he was always going to have to walk the line between the idealization of American democracy and the reality of the continuing inequalities in American society, including the issue of race. In his 2004 address to the Democratic National Party Convention, Obama repeats the claims of the Constitution:

> Our pride is based on a very simple premise, summed up in a declaration made over two hundred years ago, "We hold these truths to he self-evident, that all men are created equal. That they are endowed by their Creator with certain inalienable rights. That among these are life, liberty and the pursuit of happiness." (Keynote address, 2004)

But on March 18, 2008, in a famous speech called "A More Perfect Union," Obama tackles the issue of race more directly:

> The document they produced was eventually signed but ultimately unfinished. It was stained by this nation's original sin of slavery, a question that divided the colonies and brought the convention to a stalemate until the founders chose to allow the slave trade to continue for at least twenty more years, and to leave any final resolution to future generations.

During this speech, as Obama had done before, and would do again, he refers to his own personal family story, which we can view as a conceptual "motif" for the clash of the "idealization of American democracy" (as in the Constitution) and the reality of American society, where race issues are still a matter of concern. Obama's solution to this was to continually tell his own story, to talk of his white mother and his black father. He refers to the dreams he sees instantiated in his children, as his own father had dreams in coming to the United States. Race is blended within Obama himself, as is the American dream. He says (A More Perfect Union, 2008):

> I am married to a black American who carries within her the blood of slaves and slave-owners—an inheritance we pass on to our two precious daughters. I have brothers, sisters, nieces, nephews, uncles and cousins, of every race and every hue, scattered across three continents, and for as long as I live, I will never forget that in no other country on Earth is my story even possible.

The fact that he is president is the outcome of ". . . [his] own American story." This story is referred to frequently both directly and indirectly. In understanding the story as one of progression of American ideals Obama has set up two conflicting conceptual spaces which when blended create a clash, and that clash is resolved by the generic space which Obama and his story inhabits.

Here American ideals clash with American reality in a number of ways, but centrally if we see the generic space as Obama himself and Obama's story we see how Obama provides us with a resolution, by treating everyone the same and providing the same opportunities for all; anyone who works hard enough can achieve his or her goals in a modern America, even an African American.

Presidential Debates

On October 7, 2012, President Barack Obama appeared at the Nokia Theatre in Los Angeles. He was joined by high-profile supporters from the world of film and music, including George Clooney, Stevie Wonder, Katy Perry, and Earth Wind and Fire. Obama thanked all those who were supporting him and he told the audience of some 6,000 that the celebrities who had already performed or spoken had done so "flawlessly." He then said, "I can always say the same," which drew laughter and cheers from the crowd. What the crowd was responding to was Obama's self-deprecation, as only four days earlier, on October 3, he had taken part in the first presidential debate of the 2012 campaign in Denver, Colorado, which many viewed as one of his worst public and political performances.

On October 4 the *National Journal* cited some high-profile tweets on Obama's debate performance:

> Commentator and blogger Andrew Sullivan . . . tweeted, "Look, you know how much I love the guy, and how much of a high-info viewer I am, but this was a disaster for Obama."

Comedian Bill Maher . . . tweeted, "I can't believe I'm saying this, but Obama looks like he DOES need a teleprompter."

Jim Manley, a former longtime aide to Senate Majority Leader Harry Reid and the late Sen. Edward Kennedy, tweeted, "What can I say? Romney lives to fight another day."

And these are all Obama supporters! The Hill Blog, October 7 (2012), commented:

Senior Obama campaign adviser Robert Gibbs on Sunday acknowledged that the president was unhappy with his performance in last week's first debate.

"It's not rocket science to believe that the president's disappointed," Gibbs said, in an interview on NBC's *Meet the Press*.

Explaining his lackluster performance to radio host Tom Joyner, Obama suggested that "I was just too polite," and he promised to be more aggressive in future debates. While recognizing the concerns of his supporters, Obama suggested: "By next week a lot of the hand wringing will be complete."

Why was there such concern over Obama's performance? One immediate reason seemed obvious at the time. In the weeks prior to the debate, polls showed a small but important lead for Obama. Following the first presidential debate, the gap in the polls was not only closed, with Mitt Romney drawing alongside Obama, there were some polls that began to suggest Romney was pulling ahead.

Within the media, presidential debates are given an almost mythical position in the pantheon of events that take place during a presidential election. Given the viewing figures for such debates, this is not surprising. The 1960 presidential debates were one of the most watched events in US television history, with 66 million viewers. In 2012 there were around 67 million viewers who watched the first presidential debate.

Such figures make good reading for the media, but do they make any difference to the outcome of presidential elections? Writing in "The National Interest" on October 4, Robert W. Merry comments that:

This is important to keep in mind because the political media attribute almost total impact to not just the debates as a whole but to specific moments of drama or zing or to matters of appearance. But did Richard Nixon's sweaty upper lip in his first 1960 debate with John Kennedy seal his fate as a loser that year? No. Did Michael Dukakis lose to George H. W. Bush in 1988 because he didn't show outrage at Bernard Shaw's outrageous hypothetical question involving the rape of Dukakis's wife? No. Did Ronald Reagan win in 1980 because he uttered his two famous debate lines—"There you go again"; and, "Ask yourself: Are you better off than you were four years ago?" No.

Most academic research seems to endorse Merry's assessment, although in an article in *American Politics Research*, John G. Greer (1988) argued that while debates reinforced the public's preference for specific candidates, there was more impact among the undecided than previously assumed. Tom Holbrook in the journal *Political Behavior* (1999: 67) suggests that presidential debates have a positive impact on voters' "information acquisition," and, most important, this acquisition is more significant in the initial debates: ". . . early debates generate more learning than do subsequent debate[s]."

The debates themselves have been highly controlled since the formation of a Commission on Presidential Debates (CPD) in the 1980s. The CPD, which is supported and endorsed by both the Democrats and the Republicans, is the only organization allowed to host presidential debates. It arranges four debates, including at least one vice presidential debate. The CPD's control has been criticized for producing banal and highly formalized debates, with little real "bite" or argument. Senator John Kerry, the presidential candidate in 2004, said of the debates:

> You could have picked ten people off the street who didn't know Jerusalem from Georgia and they would have had better questions.

Debating Troubles

The first presidential debate in the 2012 campaign was held on October 3, 2012, and as soon as it had ended, media pundits were immediately assessing who had "won." Almost everyone agreed that Romney had won, and everyone also agreed, including Obama himself, that the president had not performed well in the debate—the question was why? Some people thought he seemed personally disengaged or uninterested. Others thought he did not use any of his "big guns" against Romney, for example, the leaked recording of Romney telling a business dinner that he could more or less "write off" 47 percent of Americans who wanted the government to look after them and who were never going to get the basics of the Republican philosophy (see Chapter 1).

Interestingly, those who thought Romney did well in the debate were no clearer in explaining his success than others were in explaining why Obama had performed badly. There were those who suggested that Romney won by default, simply because Obama never turned up. Others suggested that Romney came across as someone in command of the facts, more statesman-like, a man with experience of leadership. As Robert Merry put it, "He won on demeanor. He won on the crispness of his arguments. He simply won, hands down."

By the time of the second presidential debate on October 16, things had changed; in this debate, most saw Obama as the victor. So what changed, and can we use the second debate to help us understand what went wrong in the first debate? In an analysis of the second presidential debate, a University of Southern Illinois debate coach, Todd Graham, claims that Obama won this time because he used the two most important techniques of debate (CNN online October 17, 2012):

> The first is the primacy effect, and the second is using your opponent's language against him. If you want to win a debate, you've got to master these techniques.

The "primacy effect" is simply that the first things a speaker says are more important than what follows. Given Graham's comments, we can look backward in time to the first debate and consider whether Obama was making use of these techniques. A cursory glance at the transcript of the first debate does show Obama using the "primacy effect," and on many occasions he uses Romney's own language against him. Here are two examples from the early section of the debate, where both Obama and Romney adopt a very similar style in reporting each others' views.

> OBAMA: Governor Romney has a perspective that says if we cut taxes, skewed towards the wealthy, and roll back regulations, that we'll be better off. I've got a different view.
>
> ROMNEY: The president has a view very similar to the view he had when he ran four years ago, that a bigger government, spending more, taxing more, regulating more—if you will, trickle-down government—would work.

As regards using your opponent's language against him, both Obama and Romney continually refer to what the other has said, either directly or indirectly, as in the following:

> OBAMA: And this is where there's a difference, because Governor Romney's central economic plan calls for a $5 trillion tax cut—on top of the extension of the Bush tax cuts—that's another trillion dollars—and $2 trillion in additional military spending that the military hasn't asked for. That's $8 trillion.
>
> ROMNEY: First of all, I don't have a $5 trillion tax cut. I don't have a tax cut of a scale that you're talking about. My view is that we ought to provide tax relief to people in the middle class. But I'm not going to reduce the share of taxes paid by high-income people. High-income people are doing just fine in this economy. They'll do fine whether you're president or I am.

This kind of exchange is repeated throughout the debate, so it cannot be simply that Obama does not use a "primacy effect," or that he does not use his opponent's language or claims against him. So what was Obama's problem?

If one looks at the history of presidential debates, in particular media coverage of the debates, the media does not normally focus on the overall quality of the debate; rather, the media concentrates on those memorable "sound bites" that could be said to have changed or decided not only the debate but the future direction of the election. The comments of Merry above referred to some famous examples, and there are others, such as those selected by Clayman (1995: 118) in his discussion of "Defining Moments . . . " in presidential debates:

> In 1976 it was Gerald Ford's unexpected assertion that Poland was not subject to Soviet domination. In 1980 it was the way Ronald Reagan deflected Jimmy Carter's attacks with "there you go again." In 1984 it was Walter Mondale's colorful "where's the beef" put-down of Gary Hart. And in 1988 it was Lloyd Bentsen's withering assessment of Dan Quayle: "Senator, you're no Jack Kennedy."

Focusing on this last example, Clayman argues that what makes "Defining Moments" quotable events is their conspicuousness, their narrativity, their direct and indirect criticism, and audience reaction. In most of the "defining moments" quoted by both Merry and Clayman, one can see or audibly hear a reaction to the quotable statements. In the first presidential debate of 2012, despite Romney's win and Obama's slack performance, there are no clear quotable moments given by either candidate. So one cannot point to what Romney did that destroyed Obama the way Bentsen did Quayle, and there is no clear moment in Obama's debating language that stands out and says, "I have just shot myself in the foot," or "I walked into that one." Hence, much of the media reaction to the first debate concentrated not on the fact that Romney won the debate but that Obama lost the debate. It is the failure of expectations that is the defining moment. Obama was the favorite, he was expected to win "hands down," he was the better speaker, the incumbent, and so on. The shock is not that Romney did so well, it is that Obama did so badly. As a result, most analysts were left scratching their heads as to what went wrong.

You Can't Argue When There Is Nothing to Argue About

Since 1992 presidential debates have moved away from a "panelist" format to a range of other format types, including a town hall format, a single moderator format, and a mixed version of panel and moderator. The 2012 series of debates focused on a moderator and town hall format. The variation in format and the tight control over questions and answers, along with a strict monitoring of time given for responses, have suggested to some that such variation and control affect the opportunities for serious political debate. Research has shown, however, that there are a complex set of factors that impact the quality and nature of the debate, and no single factor stands out from the rest (see Benoit and Wells, 1996; Carlin, Morris, and Smith, 2001; Bilmes, 1999). For example, Carlin, Morris, and Smith (2001) looked at the impact of "format" on what they called "clash" and "non-clash" argument strategies, and they found no significant difference by "format." Equally, Bilmes (1999) applied a pragmatic approach, using "Conversation Analysis," in considering vice presidential debates. Bilmes noted that there were concerns over the nature, structure, organization, and position of questions and answers as appropriate turn configurations, as well as concerns with timing, content, and topic. However, these types of issues are found in many forms of interaction, not just vice presidential or presidential debates.

In the first debate between Barack Obama and Mitt Romney, the format was a single moderator, Jim Lehrer, the host of PBS's *NewsHour* (see transcript at http://www.npr.org/). The debate was to focus on domestic policy and was divided into six time segments of approximately 15 minutes each, on topics that were selected by the moderator and announced several weeks before the debate. Each segment would be opened with a question from the moderator, and each candidate was given two minutes to respond. The time in each segment would be assessed by the moderator and used to develop further discussion. During the opening of the first debate, Jim Lehrer explained the structure to the audience, and added:

> The audience here in the hall has promised to remain silent—no cheers, applause, boos, hisses, among other noisy distracting things, so we may all concentrate on what the candidates have to say. There is a noise exception right now, though, as we welcome President Obama and Governor Romney.

This constraint means that political tactics such as inviting applause, laughter, or support from the audience becomes more difficult. The debate lasted 90 minutes, and the most central element of the debate, which had a role to play in almost all segments, was the economy, and this is where we will focus our attention.

It is quite clear that each camp will have fully prepared for the debate by looking at the differences between them on specific issues. The aim for each candidate would be to highlight their own strengths while attacking their opponent's weaknesses. For the challenger in such debates there is the clear and available record of the incumbent on the economy. The sitting president will have been in office for at least three years and his actions and policies, successes and failures, will be on record. On the other hand, the incumbent has to target what are often plans or aspirations as presented by the challenger, and these can sometimes prove more tricky to critique, since the evidence about whether such plans will work is something that is yet to be proven; although it is also true that such plans will be evidenced in various other ways, as for example through the use of independent expert assessment, or through evidence that a similar plan has worked/not worked before.

We will look at the economic arguments in general terms first, and then consider what a deeper pragmatic analysis might tell us about these, and whether this can contribute to our understanding of Obama's failings and weaknesses in the first debate.

Jim Lehrer's opening question was given first to Obama.

> Gentlemen, welcome to you both. Let's start with the economy, segment one, and let's begin with jobs. What are the major differences between the two of you about how you would go about creating new jobs?

Note that Lehrer does not ask Obama how he will create jobs or tackle unemployment; he explicitly asks Obama to "debate with himself." Obama is expected to express his view on jobs and unemployment and also to consider how his views differ from those of Romney. This is important, because it forces each candidate to explain their understanding of their opponent's policy. This is not unusual, and would probably have happened under a general question such as "What's your view on the economy?" However, by formalizing the process, it makes it more difficult to simply describe your opponent's policy in "sound bites," or only in negative terms, since this could suggest a limited understanding, or a limited debate strategy of negative attack.

Obama opens by saying:

> OBAMA: Well, thank you very much, Jim, for this opportunity. I want to thank Governor Romney and the University of Denver for your hospitality.
>
> There are a lot of points I want to make tonight, but the most important one is that 20 years ago I became the luckiest man on Earth because Michelle Obama agreed to marry me.
>
> And so I just want to wish, Sweetie, you happy anniversary and let you know that a year from now we will not be celebrating it in front of 40 million people.

[laughter]

This opening includes a good example of the disruptive influence of "parentheticals" (see Chapter 2) as Obama inserts "Sweetie" into the flow of his sentence. It occurs almost as an afterthought, and could be considered to be almost dysfluent. But we can see immediately, despite Lehrer's attempt to silence the audience, that Obama has generated "laughter" by starting the debate, and the public defense of his presidency, by wishing his wife a "happy anniversary" in front of millions of people.

When Romney takes his turn, he responds to Obama's opening remark by offering his own congratulations to the Obamas on their anniversary; hence Obama's remarks have generated a return token from Romney, which matches Obama's "break" in the flow of debate, and in turn Romney's own comments generate laughter.

> And congratulations to you, Mr. President, on your anniversary. I'm sure this was the most romantic place you could imagine, here—here with me. So I . . .
> [laughter]
> Congratulations.

As classic work on the interactional construction of laughter shows (see Jefferson, 1979), there are a number of structural techniques that may be employed to invite recipients' laughter. One is to end an utterance by producing laughter tokens and hence invite others to join in, or one can hint at the invitation to laugh within an utterance prior to completion, or, interestingly, one can hedge on the invitation by making sounds at the end of a turn, a cough, or breath type, which may be suggestive of an invitation to laugh. This last option is important since one cannot guarantee that invitations to laugh will be taken up, so it allows the speaker to withdraw the invitation to laugh, or rather negate it as an invitation altogether. As Jefferson (1979: 90) puts it:

> Should others decline to laugh, the equivocal sound may be terminated, and remain just a breath, throat clearing etc., or may be followed by more sound which retroactively formulates the prior as definitely not laughter.

In Obama's opening turn, he offers only the hint of a smile as he approaches the end of his comment, and even when laughter arises he does not himself offer any clear reciprocal laughter. Indeed, at one point in his turn around just after ". . . marry me" a lone audience member offers some laughter but quickly closes this off because Obama's interactional clues remain ambiguous.

In the case of Romney, things are much simpler, given that laughter has already occurred in response to Obama's turn. Romney matches not so much Obama's slightly ambiguous invitation to laugh, but rather he matches a pragmatic clash of the type we discussed above in blended "conceptual" spaces. For Obama, it was saying happy anniversary—a personal event—in front of millions of people; for Romney, it was the clash between those romantic places one might express such personal emotions, and being in a presidential debate.

In very formal or serious events, laughter can sometimes play a role in relaxing both speakers and audience, and while we cannot unequivocally prove that this was Obama's aim, we can at least say it was what he, and in turn Romney, achieved.

Turning to the substance of Obama's response, he starts by outlining the historic difficulties faced by the nation, and how the nation and the American people have responded. He notes achievements that have been made but accepts there is more to be done:

> You know, four years ago we went through the worst financial crisis since the Great Depression. Millions of jobs were lost, the auto industry was on the brink of collapse. The financial system had frozen up.
>
> And because of the resilience and the determination of the American people, we've begun to fight our way back. Over the last 30 months, we've seen 5 million jobs in the private sector created. The auto industry has come roaring back. And housing has begun to rise.
>
> But we all know that we've still got a lot of work to do. And so the question here tonight is not where we've been, but where we're going.

The metaphor of "travel" and being "on a road" or "path" to a destination is invoked here, and we should note this will become relevant when we look at

Romney's response. But before we do this, let us consider the rest of Obama's comments:

> Governor Romney has a perspective that says if we cut taxes, skewed to-wards the wealthy, and roll back regulations, that we'll be better off. I've got a different view.
>
> I think we've got to invest in education and training. I think it's important for us to develop new sources of energy here in America, that we change our tax code to make sure that we're helping small businesses and companies that are investing here in the United States, that we take some of the money that we're saving as we wind down two wars to rebuild America and that we reduce our deficit in a balanced way that allows us to make these critical investments.
>
> Now, it ultimately is going to be up to the voters—to you—which path we should take. Are we going to double on top-down economic policies that helped to get us into this mess or do we embrace a new economic patriotism that says America does best when the middle class does best? And I'm look-ing forward to having that debate.

In the rest of the response, Obama takes up the invitation to debate his oppo-nent's alternative views. Obama's assessment is short, suggesting that all that is on offer from Romney is a tax cut for the wealthy with, in addition, some minor changes in regulation. At the end of his response, Obama returns to a "path-goal" metaphor (see Lakoff and Johnson, 1999) and explicitly sets up a choice between two paths—his own and that of Governor Romney—and he contrasts the failure of the past with a "new economic patriotism." This is a contrast that not only negates Romney's position but also positions a sub-contrast between the "new" and the "old," and since the "new" has been co-positioned with being "patriotic," there is an invited inference (Geis and Zwicky; 1971: Chapter 3, this vol) that the "old," as in opposition to the "new," is unpatriotic.

Turning now to Romney, he begins by taking up Obama's "path-goal" meta-phor and suggests that's Obama's path is the issue (concern), because taking this path has been a failure and Obama's solution to this failure is to continue on the same path, that is the wrong path:

> ROMNEY: Now, I'm concerned that the path that we're on has just been un-successful. The president has a view very similar to the view he had when he ran four years [ago], that a bigger government, spending more, taxing more, regulating more—if you will, trickle-down government—would work.
>
> That's not the right answer for America. I'll restore the vitality that gets America working again. Thank you.

This is a short response, but it highlights the struggle between both camps over the "path-goal" metaphor. This metaphor is an exemplar of "cognitive meta-phor" and invokes a schema in human cognition (Johnson, 1987; Lakoff, 1993) manifested literally in movement: a human being crawls, walks, runs, leaps, rides, and uses other forms of movement from point A to point B. The movement is intentional and purposeful, with the goal of achieving an objective.

As we have seen, Obama uses the "path-goal" metaphor to indicate a positive move to a brighter future, and his whole campaign was predicated on a single word linked to this "path-goal" metaphor: "forward." Clearly, Romney is appropriating the metaphor to his own ends, where keeping on the "path" (Obama's path) is to keep heading in the wrong direction. This struggle over the use of the "path-goal" metaphor looks like it was a strategic move by Romney because we see it occurring in different places prior to the first debate. In an interview with ABC television almost a month before the first presidential debate, the Republican nominee for vice president, Paul Ryan, said the following about Obama's Presidency:

> Ryan: I think President Obama has placed us **on the path to decline**.
>
> Ryan: . . . for every person who got a job last month four stopped looking for work, **that's not a good direction** that's **the wrong direction**. I mean George we have to create 150,000 jobs every month just to keep up with population growth and we didn't even do that. It's **on the wrong path** . . .
>
> Ryan: We have been growing under 2% George we **are not on that kind of a path we need to get on that kind of path, we need to get on a faster growth path** . . .

This highlights the point we discussed above about the difference between an incumbent president and a challenger. Obama's record on the economy is on public record, and while there are many positive aspects that can be mentioned at the time of the election, the fact was that the US budget deficit was still the highest in its history. Hence, the challenge to Obama's "path-goal" metaphor may be a good move to attract voters who believe that nothing has changed in the economy, or who may believe it has gotten worse.

Following Romney's response, Jim Lehrer asks Obama to respond to what Governor Romney has just said, and here Obama takes the opportunity to go into greater detail on both his own policy and on Romney's economic policy. Obama expands slightly on how he wants to improve education, he comments on issues concerning the tax code and reduction in deficit, and then he comes to what was for him, and the Democratic Party, the core philosophy of Romney's position, and, presumably, the weak point the Democrats wanted to attack:

> OBAMA: And this is where there's a difference, because Governor Romney's central economic plan calls for a $5 trillion tax cut—on top of the extension of the Bush tax cuts—that's another trillion dollars—and $2 trillion in additional military spending that the military hasn't asked for. That's $8 trillion. How we pay for that, reduce the deficit, and make the investments that we need to make, without dumping those costs onto middle-class Americans, **I think is one of the central questions of this campaign.**

We have highlighted the last sentence to indicate the importance of what Obama calls the "central question." It had also been at the center of debates in the weeks prior to the first presidential debate. In a number of interviews and newspaper articles, Romney and his team had been challenged on the figures that underpinned their plan to reduce the budget deficit through tax cuts. The figures Obama quotes are calculations made by the Democrats based on the Republicans' fiscal plans. Obama and his team continually challenged the Republicans to explain the financial details of their plan. In one speech Obama said:

> No matter how many times they try to tell you they are talking specifics really soon, they don't do it and the reason is cause the math doesn't work.

In an interview just a week before the first presidential debate, Republican vice presidential nominee Paul Ryan was asked in an interview about the Republicans' tax plans and how they would work (Fox News, September 30, 2012).

> INTERVIEWER: Let's go through the plan, the Obama camp say
>   independent groups say if you cut those tax rates for everybody by 20%
>   it costs 5 trillion dollars over ten years—true?
> RYAN: Not in the least bit true . . . .
> INTERVIEWER: How much would it cost?
> RYAN: It's revenue neutral it doesn't . . .
> INTERVIEWER: [No I'm just talking about the (?) deductions we'll get to the
>   the deductions I'm talking about the deductions
> RYAN: The cut in tax rates is lower () all American tax rates by 20%
> INTERVIEWER: [Right How much does it cost
> RYAN: It's revenue neutral

The interviewer carries on in this vein, with Ryan continuing to deny the figure of $5 trillion, and refusing, as he said, to get into a "baseline argument." In the end, the interviewer uses Obama's phrase:

> INTERVIEWER: You haven't given me the math
> RYAN: Well . . . no I don't have the time . . . Ehen it would take me **too long**
>   to go through the math.

Ryan was severely criticized by the media for this response. It suggested to many analysts either that the Republicans didn't know or understand the math, or that they were so arrogant that they didn't think the ordinary voter would understand the math. Either way, this seemed a perfect target for Obama in the first debate and he went for it.

In response Romney says:

> First of all, I don't have a $5 trillion tax cut. I don't have a tax cut of a scale that you're talking about. My view is that we ought to provide tax relief to people in the middle class. But I'm not going to reduce the share of taxes

paid by high-income people. High-income people are doing just fine in this economy. They'll do fine whether you're president or I am.

This response was in line with Republicans' defense of their plans for tax reductions. The figure of $5 trillion had been used on several occasions by the Democrats and followed up by the media. We saw this above in the interview with Paul Ryan when he said it wasn't true that there was a tax cut of $5 trillion. So we have a stalemate on the figures, the Democrats saying $5 trillion is what the Republicans' plans will cost, the Republicans denying this. The problem was the Republicans had not given any exact figures as to what the reduction would be, and once again Romney denies the figure of $5 trillion, but he doesn't give an alternative figure. We can see this should provide an opening for Obama to further attack Romney, as there is still no clarity, still no "math." However, within his response Romney also included the concluding comments:

> And finally, with regards to that tax cut, look, I'm not looking to cut massive taxes and to reduce the—the revenues going to the government. My—my number-one principal is, **there will be no tax cut that adds to the deficit. I want to underline that: no tax cut that adds to the deficit.**
>
> But I do want to reduce the burden being paid by middle-income Americans. And I—and to do that, that also means I cannot reduce the burden paid by high-income Americans. So any—any language to the contrary is simply not accurate

The highlighted statement is important because it introduces an implicit "block" not only on any talk about $5 trillion tax cuts, but on any figure that could be produced which could be shown to increase the deficit. We will have more to say on this in a moment. But for now we also want to briefly highlight Romney's last claim above. It has two important parts: first, "I do want to reduce the burden being paid by middle-income Americans"; and second, "I cannot reduce the burden paid by high-income Americans." In the first claim, Romney positions himself with the middle class, whom both Obama and Romney recognized as central to the outcome of the election, and he does so, rather clumsily, by suggesting that any benefits or gains for the middle class rely on upper income Americans continuing to pay their share of taxes. He is explaining that by removing tax breaks within the system it will be higher earners who will carry the burden. The problem in this example is the phrase "cannot reduce" in relation to high earners. In debates on tax during this campaign, the term "reduction" has become associated with "tax reduction," and for those critical of the Republicans there was an association between "tax reduction" and higher income Americans. Hence, given system 1 automatic first reaction thinking (discussed above), there is a danger that the phrase "cannot reduce" used in relation to higher income earners could have been interpreted as leaving them alone, that is, that they would not have to contribute more, but this was not what Romney wanted to say.

Returning to the debate, Jim Lerher invites Obama to comment on what Governor Romney has just said, and once again Obama repeats the claim of $5 trillion tax cut, and emphasizes that Romney has had numerous opportunities to refute or explain this figure but has failed to do so.

Now, Governor Romney's proposal, which he has been promoting for 18 months, calls for a $5 trillion tax cut, on top of $2 trillion of additional spending for our military. And he is saying that he is going to pay for it by closing loopholes and deductions. The problem is that he's been asked over 100 times how you would close those deductions and loopholes, and he hasn't been able to identify them.

Obama also drives home this point by using a standard technique of claiming that it is not Barack Obama making these claims, with all his individual and political bias, it is an independent assessment.

OBAMA: But I'm going to make an important point here, Jim.

OBAMA: When you add up all the loopholes and deductions that upper-income individuals can—are currently taking advantage of, you take those all away, you don't come close to paying for $5 trillion in tax cuts and $2 trillion in additional military spending.

OBAMA: And that's why independent studies looking at this said the only way to meet Governor Romney's pledge of not reducing the deficit or—or—or not adding to the deficit is by burdening middle-class families. The average middle-class family with children would pay about $2,000 more.

Now, that's not my analysis. That's the analysis of economists who have looked at this. And—and that kind of top—top-down economics, where folks at the top are doing well, so the average person making $3 million is getting a $250,000 tax break, while middle-class families are burdened further, that's not what I believe is a recipe for economic growth.

In Romney's response he utilizes, again, the generic claim that his plans will not raise the deficit, hence neutralizing any figure mentioned by Obama.

ROMNEY: So if the tax plan he described were a tax plan I was asked to support, I'd say absolutely not. I'm not looking for a $5 trillion tax cut. What I've said is I won't put in place a tax cut that adds to the deficit. That's part one. So there's no economist that can say Mitt Romney's tax plan adds $5 trillion if I say I will not add to the deficit with my tax plan.

The centrality of this clash between the $5 trillion figure, and the lack of response from the Republicans on the "math," and so on, carries on through the first part of the debate. Here are two further examples:

OBAMA: Jim, I—you may want to move onto another topic, but I—I would just say this to the American people. If you believe that we can cut taxes by $5 trillion and add $2 trillion in additional spending that the military is not asking for, $7 trillion—just to give you a sense, over 10 years, that's more than our entire defense budget—and you think that by closing loopholes and deductions for the well-to-do, somehow you will not end up picking up the tab, then Governor Romney's plan may work for you.

ROMNEY: I think first of all, let me—let me repeat—let me repeat what I said. I'm not in favor of a $5 trillion tax cut. That's not my plan. My plan is not to put in place any tax cut that will add to the deficit. That's point one.

So you may keep referring to it as a $5 trillion tax cut, but that's not my plan.

In terms of the argument it looks like we have a simple clash:

A. You said X.
B. I didn't say X.

But it is slightly more sophisticated than this. Obama's attack is based on a set of figures which he claims have been independently assessed. Romney rejects these figures, and rejects the basis of their assessment. But Romney is doing more than this, he is not simply rejecting a figure and its assessment, he is rejecting any figure that, if accepted, would increase the deficit. Clearly, Obama's use of the figure of $5 trillion has been chosen because it would not match Romney's aims and it certainly wouldn't assist in reducing the budget deficit. But why is Romney's strategy important here? It is important because Obama has based his attack on example figures, the outcome of the math, if you will, but what Romney has done is not only rejected a single figure but all figures that do not meet the metric of not increasing the budget deficit. Hence, each of Obama's attacks based on his figures is an attack on a position that does not exist in any universe of figures that Romney uses, because Obama's figures will increase the budge deficit. As a result all figures that would increase the deficit are "blocked," but these are the very figures that Obama needed for his criticism of Romney; this is the very objective of the attack set by Obama and his team.

Pragmatic Blocking or "Talk to the Hand"

In simple terms, in any argument one can deny claims made against your position.

You said X.
No I didn't.

Indeed, this is how arguments emerge, because there is a conflict between the claims of one opponent and the claims of another. But this is also a constructionist claim, that is, that arguments arise out of the failure of A to accept the claims of B and vice versa. It is an argument because both sides cannot be correct at the same time.

But all disagreements need not be arguments in this sense, and here we want to consider one form of disagreement which I have called elsewhere "pragmatic blocking." In a paper written in 2007, with my colleague Dr. Karyn Stapleton, we explored how the nationalist community in Northern Ireland reacted to major changes within the structure, organization, and practice of the Police force. Nationalists and Republicans in Northern Ireland had for many years been suspicious of what was called the "Royal Ulster Constabulary." This force was seen as "anti-Catholic" and an arm of the British state as embodied within a mainly Protestant and Unionist Northern Ireland Government. Following a major report known as the "Patton Report," major changes were to take place. The police force would be renamed as the "Police Service of Northern Ireland," there would be efforts made to ensure that membership of the force was equally distributed between Catholics and Protestants, and the Police service itself would be overseen by a Police Commission representative of the full political, religious, and social diversity of Northern Ireland.

Several years into the change, we ran a number of focus groups within Nationalist areas of Belfast and one of the questions we asked was about "Police change." What surprised us was that informants said there had been no change, but then they went on to discuss aspects of the changes that had taken place. Consider the following:

R: . . . I was just wondering about your views on the current (.) state of policing, or (.) the policing situation at the moment?
F3: There virtually isn't one. (.) There's nobody in here, um (.) The police is not accepted. And I don't think they'll ever be accepted here. Because they have never proved themselves, uh, along the way. (.) The people don't trust them.
F: Yeah
F3: You know? (.) And even with the joy-riding issue here, we see them going about, and chasing (.) they chase the joy-riders, and they stop the joy-riders and the next thing, they let them go. I mean what's that all about? (.) You know, they don't even arrest them, they just (.) "get out of the car and away you go."

We at first thought that the informants were caught in a contradiction:

There is a policing situation and there is not a policing situation.

There are many similar exchanges throughout our data, where in one sense the concept of "policing change" is rejected, while at the same time informants continue to refer to examples of "policing change."

Looking at this seemingly contradictory stance, we argued that what we have here is an instance of "metalinguistic negation" (see Chapter 2), the negation of something said previously. One important aspect of metalinguistic negation is referred to as the "representation distinction" The distinction takes two possible forms.

Carston (2002: 27) sets these out in the following examples:

a.i. We didn't see two hippopotamuses. But we did see the rhinoceroses.
b. We didn't see two hippopotamuses. But we did see two hippopotami.
a.ii. She is not pleased with the outcome. She is angry it didn't go her way.
b. She is not pleased with the outcome: She is thrilled to bits.

In the (a) sentences some descriptive representation is negated and the following statement is consistent with this reading (Not P; Q). In the (b) sentences a similar assessment creates a contradiction; that is, P is negated and then P is affirmed (Not P; P). In this case an objection is being made about a "non-descriptive" aspect of the prior utterance; in (a.i) the inappropriate plural, and in (a.ii) that a weaker adjective has been used.

Now in the case of "there is no police situation," this is a response to the interviewer's comments and acts to negate their claim. In this sense, the issue seems to be one of representation.

INTERVIEWER: There is a police situation.
F3: There is no police situation.

But this is (P; Not P) as opposed to (Not P; Q). As such, therefore, it is simply a negation of the affirmative claim made by the interviewer. So both turns together give us a contradiction:

There is a police situation and there is no police situation.

But what is being objected to? And what is being corrected? At best, we can speculate on what "police situation" means for both the interviewer and F3. While we might consider that "police situation" has different meanings for the interviewer and for F3, there would still be something odd here. F3 says there is not a "police situation" because the police are not accepted. However, a normative interpretation of either a context where a community has problems with the police or a context where the police have problems with the community would seem quite logically to be a "situation."

To explain this, we argue that the informants' use of "There is no police situation" is formulated to "pragmatically block" any inferences that flow from the interviewer's understanding of what a "police situation" is. A similar concept is also found in Conversation Analysis under what Pomerantz (1986) has called an "extreme case formulation." These are turns that attempt to stop others from undermining the speaker's claims. Sacks (1992: 23) gives an example of a telephone call from a suicide prevention center where it becomes clear that there is a gun in the house. The prevention desk attempts to get an account of why there is a gun in the house, but the caller simply says "everyone has one don't they." Sacks suggests this cuts off the basis for an account, or in our terms, "blocks" certain aspects of any account.

Returning to the Romney/Obama debate, we suggest that Romney has "pragmatically blocked" any discussion of his tax plans as they are interpreted by Obama. There is no need to do "the math" and no need to explain any potential impact on the deficit, because Romney does not have any plan as explained by Obama, particularly if he uses any figure that increases the budget deficit.

This "blocking" approach is more than a form of disagreement. Disagreement follows from argument, debate, and counterargument. Romney has "blocked" off these avenues and left Obama nowhere else to go; hence Obama ends up repeating several times the same point, allowing Romney the opportunity on each occasion to explain to the audience that Obama's claims are not relevant to any concept within Romney's agenda or policy, and to suggest not so much that Obama is mistaken, but that he is referring to an alternative world of his own making, and not one recognized by Romney and his team.

This tactic not only throws Obama off his argument, but it allows Romney to avoid an awkward debate around his fiscal policy, and at the same time makes him sound thoughtful and reasonable. For example, he says if his policy was anything like Obama describes then he, Romney, would vote against such a policy. Further, by "blocking" debate on the issues as Obama sees them, this allows Romney to agree with Obama that the group in most need of help is the "middle class."

When one views the video of the debate, as Romney "blocks" aspects of the deficit argument while referring to helping the "middle income" group, Obama can be seen to be nodding in agreement. While this may only be agreement to the statements about the "middle income" group or the middle classes, it occurs in the same statement where Romney rejects and "blocks" Obama's claims about Romney's fiscal plans. Hence, for some audience members Obama may be seen as agreeing that he doesn't understand Romney's plans.

The claim is not that this blocking tactic is what made Obama's performance so limited within the debate, merely that it can be seen as one major contributing factor, and one that has not been given consideration within either mainstream media or academic considerations of the debate, possibly because the problem has not been given any pragmatic attention.

So once again we have seen in this chapter, and at a number of different levels, how pragmatic considerations offer insights in to presidential language and its operation in speeches and debates. With only a limited amount of data we have been able to capture several different pragmatic phenomenon in action, and to show how their social and cognitive links ground presidential language and context.

Afterword

In Chapter 1, I stated that the aim of this text was to consider what a pragmatic analysis could tell us about examples of the language used by several different presidents of the United States. The inferential nature of pragmatics was highlighted, and it was noted that there were almost no book length studies of the pragmatics of presidential language, let alone those which focused on several different presidents. The objective, therefore, was to select only a small number of examples of language use from each president to exemplify pragmatic analysis, and not to carry out any comparative assessment or attempt the construction of any unified pragmatic theory of presidential language. As we have seen, pragmatic issues abound within presidential language, and given our emphasis on sociopragmatics, this is what we would predict. It is not that in each case those aspects of language we have considered have not been noticed or indeed discussed before; rather, we have highlighted the way in which pragmatic analysis may bring further detail, insight, or even controversy to the debates about presidential style and rhetoric.

For example, the detailed analysis given to Kennedy's famous phrase "I am not the Catholic candidate for president. I am the Democratic Party's candidate for president who happens to be a Catholic," highlights the intersection of language, logic, and representation in the use of referential forms. Kennedy's phrase and speech have both been touted in historical, theoretical, and rhetorical analysis as a clear separation of church and state, but a pragmatic analysis helps us understand the way in which personal, social, and professional roles may be delimited linguistically for political and other purposes. Or consider Nixon. Everyone now tends to accept that he lied, yet at the same time most of us also accept that lying seems to have various degrees of interpretation (white lies, justified lies, and so on), but who is to be the arbiter of such degrees of lying, and where in this area does the use of inference or implication to direct misleading beliefs sit? Or consider Clinton, who pushed at the very edges of linguistic interpretation for his own ends; was this wrong or simply so exaggerated that at times it became absurd? Either way, pragmatics helped us see what Clinton was doing and why, and also helped us understand that we all manipulate language, but it is the degree, the extent, and the person that sometimes make this manipulation socially or politically problematic, and nowhere is this clearer than when we see a president obfuscate, mislead, redirect—and yes, even "downright" lie.

The application of pragmatics also helped us see how certain linguistic tools and formats might be particularly suited to political ends, as in Reagan's use of "storytelling" to connect with his audiences and enliven often dull and dusty facts and figures. Or consider the interconnected ways in which Obama made use of his own personal family story to capture the underlying core of the American dream or the enduring American ideology in which every person, through hard work and effort, may achieve his or her dreams, and hence be perceived as being equal in terms of opportunity. But equally, as with all tools, if we understand their use and how they operate, we might find ways to subvert them or block them, as we saw in the first Obama/Romney presidential debate.

One of the first scholars to draw our attention to the use of political language was George Orwell, who suggested that political language was often used to defend the indefensible. This could be argued for Nixon and Clinton, and certainly we saw this in the case of Bush and his administration, that language was used not necessarily to describe the world as it was, but rather as it might be in counterfactual frames; further, language was also used to create specific views of the world, bounded by facts or not, which may have progressed policy first and reality second.

The claim of this book, then, is that the tools provided within the broad scope of sociopragmatics should be considered in efforts to explain specific and general presidential language, and that this will add to already existing work on intuitive, structural, rhetorical, or other forms of communicative analysis of such language. The analysis provided throughout this text is in line with the linguistic study of language in that its aim was to be descriptive. Hence, while I have noted the manipulative and deceptive use of language by some presidents, or the positive emotive and rational use of language by others, I have attempted to describe and understand the objectives involved, as opposed to making specifically moral judgments. This does not exclude the use of pragmatics for "critical" reflection or assessment; I merely wanted to descriptively highlight the way in which linguistic forms become utilized in context and for what purpose, without, as far as possible, imposing any prescriptive values on linguistic choices in specific political contexts.

We have clearly seen that there is much detail that pragmatics can bring to the analysis of presidential language, and from a range of differing perspectives and theories. It is also clear that many differing theories share core underlying components that may contribute to various higher levels of cognitive or social debate. The aim was not to become embroiled in such debates or to decide between them, since at a practical level it is the impact of specific inferences that is as important as how they are explained socially, cognitively, or culturally. Hence, we have used a variety of differing approaches, which do not always coalesce theoretically but which when combined in this study deliver productive insights.

In this sense I believe this text adds to the literature on presidential language, mapping out further the breadth and depth available through pragmatic analysis, and I hope also that this has indicated the exciting landscape of research awaiting those who wish to carry this project further, at both the level of individual case studies and at the level of comparative analysis across a range of presidents.

REFERENCES

Aikhenvald, Alexandra Y. (2004) *Evidentiality* (Oxford: Oxford University Press).

Alterman, Eric. (2004) *When Presidents Lie: A History of Official Deception and Its Consequences* (New York: Viking).

Antaki, Charles. (ed.), (1988) *Analysing Everyday Explanation: A Casebook of Methods* (London: Sage).

Antaki, Charles. (1994) *Explaining and Arguing: The Social Organisation of Accounts* (London: Sage).

Archer, Dawn. (2005) *Historical Sociopragmatics: Questions and Answers in the English Courtroom (1640–1760). Pragmatics and Beyond New Series* (Amsterdam/Philadelphia: John Benjamins).

Atkinson, Max. (1984) *Our Masters' Voices: The Language and Body Language of Politics* (London: Methuen).

Atkinson, Maxwell J., and Drew, Paul. (1979) *Order in the Court: The Organization of Verbal Interactions in Judicial Settings* (London: Macmillan).

Atwater, Deborah F. (2007) "Senator Barack Obama; The Rhetoric of Hope and the American Dream," *Journal of Black Studies*, 38(2), 121–129.

Augoustinos, Martha, LeCouteur, Amanda, and Fogarty, Kathryn. (2007) "Apologizing-in-Action: On Saying 'Sorry' to Indigenous Australians," in Alexa Hepburn and Sally Wiggins (eds.), *Discursive Research in Practice* (Cambridge: Cambridge University Press), 88–103.

Austin, John L. (1962) *How to Do Things with Words* (Cambridge, MA: Harvard University Press).

Bach, Kent. (1994) "Semantic Slack: What Is Said and More," in Savas L. Tsohatzidis (ed.), *Foundations of Speech Act Theory* (London: Routledge), 267–291.

Bach, Kent. (1997) "The Semantics/Pragmatics Distinction: What It Is and Why It Matters," *Linguistische Berichte*, 8, 33–50.

Bach, Kent. (2006) "The Top 10 Misconceptions about Implicature," in Betty J. Birner and Gregory Ward (eds.), *Drawing the Boundaries of Meaning: Neo-Gricean Studies in Pragmatics and Semantics in Honor of Laurence R. Horn* (Philadelphia: John Benjamins), 21–30.

Bachelor, Alexandra. (1988) "How Clients Perceive Therapist Empathy: A Content Analysis of 'Received' Empathy," *Psychotherapy: Theory, Research, Practice, Training*, 25(2), 227–240.

Baddeley, Alan D. (1990) *Human Memory: Theory and Practice* (Hove: Lawerence Erlbaum Associates).

Baker, Peter. (2000) *The Breach: Inside the Impeachment and Trial of William Jefferson Clinton* (New York: Scribner).

Bakhtin, Mikhail M. (1981) *The Dialogic Imagination: Four Essays*, Michael Holquist (ed.), trans. Caryl Emerson and Michael Holquist (Austin and London: University of Texas Press).

Bakhtin, Mikhail M. (1986) *Speech Genres and Other Late Essays*, trans. Vern W. McGee (Austin: University of Texas Press).

Bal, Mieke (1977). *Narratology*. Introduction to the Theory of Narrative (Toronto: University of Toronto Press).

Ballim, Afzal, and Wilks, Yorick. (1991) *Artificial Believers: The Ascription of Belief* (Hillsdale, NJ: Lawrence Erlbaum Associates).

Balitzer, Alfred A., Bonetto, Gerald M., A (eds) (1983) *Time For Choosing: The Speeches Of Ronald Reagan, 1961–1982*. Chicago : Regnery Gateway In Cooperation With Americans For The Reagan Agenda.

Bargh, John, Chen, Mark, and Burrows, Lena. (1996) "Automaticity of Social Behaviour: Direct Effects of Trait Construction and Stereotype Activation on Action," *Journal of Personality and Social Psychology*, 71, 17–21.

Barsalou, Lawrence W. (1999) "Perceptual Symbol Systems," *Behavioral and Brain Sciences*, 22, 577–660.

Bates, Elizabeth, and MacWhinney, Brian. (1982) "Functionalist Approaches to Grammar," in Eric Wanner and Lila Gleitman (eds.), *Language Acquisition: The State of the Art* (New York: Cambridge University Press).

Bateson, Gregory. (2000) *Steps to an Ecology of Mind* (Chicago: University of Chicago Press).

Bell, Allan. (1984) "Language Style as Audience Design," *Language in Society*, 13, 145–204.

Bell, Madison S. (2000) *Narrative Design:Working with Imagination, Craft and Form* (London:Norton and Company).

Benoit, William L. (1995) *Accounts, Excuses, and Apologies: A Theory of Image Restoration Strategies* (Albany: State University of New York Press).

Benoit, William L., and Wells, William T. (1996) *Candidates in Conflict: Persuasive Attack and Defense in the 1992 Presidential Debates* (Tuscaloosa: University of Alabama Press).

Benson, Thomas W. (2004) *Writing JFK: Presidential Rhetoric and the Press in the Bay of Pigs Crisis* (College Station: Texas A&M University Press).

Bergen, D. Jason, and Rae, Nicol C. (2006) "Jimmy Carter and George W. Bush: Faith, Foreign Policy, and an Evangelical Presidential Style," *Presidential Studies Quarterly*, 36(4), 606–632.

Berry, Joseph P. (1987) *John F. Kennedy and the Media: The First Television President* (Lanham, MD: University Press of America).

Besnier, Niko. (1990) "Language and Affect," *Annual Review of Anthropology*, 19, 419–451.

Bharuthram, Sharita. (2003) "Politeness Phenomena in the Hindu Sector of the South African Indian English Speaking Community," *Journal of Pragmatics*, 35, 1523–1544.

Bilmes, Jack. (1999) "Questions, Answers, and the Organization of Talk in the 1992 Vice Presidential Debate: Fundamental Considerations," *Research on Language and Social Interaction*, 32, 213–242.

Bishop, Dorothy, and Leonard, Lawrence. (2000) *Speech and Language Impairments in Children: Causes, Characteristics, Intervention and Outcome* (East Sussex: Psychology Press).

Blakemore, D. (2002). *Relevance and Linguistic Meaning: The Semantics and Pragmatics of Discourse Markers* (Cambridge: Cambridge University Press).

Blakemore, Diane. (2006) "The Division of Labour Between Syntax and Pragmatics: Parentheticals," in Robyn Carston, Diane Blakemore, and Hans van de Koot (eds.), *Language, Mind and Communication: Essays in Honour of Neil Smith,* Special Issue of *Lingua* 116, 1670–1687 (Amsterdam: Elsevier).

Blakemore, Diane. (2009) "Parentheticals and Point of View in Free Indirect Style," *Language and Literature,* 18(2), 129–153.

Bochner, Arthur, Ellis, Carolyn, and Tillmann-Healy, Lisa. (1997) "Relationships as Stories," in Steve Duck (ed.), *Handbook of Personal Relationships: Theory, Research, and Interventions,* 2nd ed. (Chichester, UK: Wiley), 107–124.

Bolinger, Dwight. (1980) *Language, the Loaded Weapon: The Use and Abuse of Language Today* (London: Longman).

Bradley, Margaret M., and Lang, Peter J. (1999) *Affective Norms for English Words (ANEW): Stimuli, Instruction Manual, and Affective Ratings.* Tech. Report C-1. (Gainesville: University of Florida, Center for Research in Psychophysiology).

Brice-Heath, Shirley. (1983) *Ways with Words: Language, Life, and Work in Communities and Classrooms* (New York: Cambridge University Press).

Brinkly, Alan. (2012) *John F. Kennedy* (New York: Henry Holt).

Brown, Penelope, and Levinson, Stephen. (1978) "Universals in Language Usage: Politeness Phenomena," in Esther Goody (ed.), *Questions and Politeness: Strategies in Social Interaction* (Cambridge: Cambridge University Press), 56–311.

Buchanan, Patrick J. (2005) *Where the Right Went Wrong: How Neoconservatives Subverted the Reagan Revolution and Hijacked the Bush Presidency* (New York: Thomas Dunne Books).

Bruner, Jerome. (1986) *Actual Minds Possible Worlds* (Cambridge MA: Harvard University Press).

Bruner, Jerome. (1990) *Acts of Meaning* (Cambridge MA:Harvard University Press)

Buring, Daniel, and Christine Gunlogson. (2000) "Aren't Positive and Negative Polar Questions the Same?," manuscript, UCSC. www.academia.edu/1580527/Polarity_Alternatives_and_Scales (accessed September 2012).

Bush, George W. (1999) *A Charge to Keep: My Journey to the White House* (New York: Morrow).

Bush, George W. (2010) *Decision Points* (London: Virgin).

Butler, Clayton D. (2001) *The Role of Context in the Apology Speech Act: A Socio-Constructivist Analysis of the Interpretations of Native English-Speaking College Students.* Unpublished doctoral dissertation (Austin: The University of Texas).

Byrne, Ruth, M. J. (2002) "Mental Models and Counterfactual Thoughts about What Might Have Been," *Trends in Cognitive Sciences,* 6(10), 426–431.

Byrne, Ruth M., and Johnson-Laird, Philip N. (2009) "'If' and the Problems of Conditional Reasoning," *Trends in Cognitive Sciences,* 13(7), 282–287.

Cambridge Advanced Learner's Dictionary (2008). Cambridge: Cambridge University Press.

Campbell, John. (2002) *Reference and Consciousness* (Oxford: Oxford University Press).

Capps, Lisa & Ochs, Elinor. (1995) *Constructing panic: The discourse of agoraphobia.* Cambridge, MA: Harvard University Press.

Cappelen, Herman, and Lepore, Ernie. (2007) "Relevance Theory and Shared Content," in Noel Burton-Roberts (ed.), *Pragmatics* (Basingstoke: Palgrave), 115–135.

Carlin, Dana B., Morris, Eric, and Smith, Shawna. (2001) "The Influence of Format and Questions on Candidates' Strategic Argument Choices in the 2000 Presidential Debates," *The American Behavioral Scientist*, 44(12), 2196–2218.

Carston, Robyn (2002) *Thoughts and Utterances* (Oxford: Blackwell).

Chafe, Wallace, and Nichols, Johanna (eds.). (1986) *Evidentiality: The Linguistic Encoding of Epistemology* (Norwood, NJ: Ablex).

Chase, Susan. E. (1995) *Empowerment: The Work Narratives of Women School Superintendents* (Amherst:University of Massachusetts Press).

Charteris-Black, Johnathan. (2014) *Analysing Political Speeches* (Houndmills: Palgrave MacmIllan).

Cheney, Richard B. (2011) *In My Time: A Personal and Political Memoir* (London: Threshold Editions).

Chilsom, Malcolm. (2012) *Blog*, March. http://definitionsinsemantics.blogspot.co.uk/2012/03/humpty-dumpty-principle-in-definitions.html (accessed December 2012).

Chomsky, Noam. (2006) *Language and Mind* (Cambridge: Cambridge University Press).

Clark, Herbert H. (1996) *Using Language* (Cambridge: Cambridge University Press).

Clark, Andy. (1998) *Being There: Putting Brain Body and World Together Again* (Cambridge, MA: MIT Press).

Clark, Herbert H. and Gerrig, Richard J.(1984) On the Pretense Theory of Irony. *Journal of Experimental Psychology:General*, 113, 121–126.

Clark, Herbert H. (1999) "Passing Time in Conversation," *Proceedings of the Workshop on the Structure of Spoken and Written Texts*, January 29–31 (University of Texas, Austin).

Clayman, Steven. (1995) "Defining Moments, Presidential Debates, and the Dynamics of Quotability," *Journal of Communication*, 45(3), 118–147.

Clayman, Steven. (2002) "Tribune of the People: Maintaining the Legitimacy of Aggressive Journalism," *Media, Culture, and Society*, 24, 191–210.

Clayman, Steven, and Heritage, John. (2002) *The News Interview: Journalists and Public Figures on the Air* (Cambridge: Cambridge University Press).

Cohen, Andrew D., and Shively, Rachel L. (2007) "Acquisition of Requests and Apologies in Spanish and French: Impact of Study Abroad and Strategy-Building Intervention," *Modern Language Journal*, 91(2), 189–212.

Colston, Herbert. L. (1997). Salting a wound or sugaring a pill: The pragmatic functions of ironic criticisms. *Discourse Processes*, *23*, 24–45.

Cotterill, Janet. (2004) "Collocation, Connotation, and Courtroom Semantics: Lawyers' Control of Witness Testimony Through Lexical Negation," *Applied Linguistics*, 25(4), 513–537.

Coulter, Jeffrey P. (2005) "Language Without Mind," in Hedwig te Molder and Jonathan Potter (eds.), *Conversation and Cognition* (Cambridge: Cambridge University Press).

Coupland, Nik. (2007) *Style*. Cambridge: Cambridge University Press.

Craig, Holly. K. (1995). Pragmatic impairments. In P. Fletcher & B. MacWhinney (Eds.), *The Handbook of Child Language* (pp. 623–640). Oxford: Blackwell.

Culpeper, Jonathan. (2009) "Historical Sociopragmatics: An Introduction," *Journal of Historical Pragmatics*, 10(2), 179–186.

Cunningham, Michael. (1999) "Saying Sorry: The Politics of Apology," *The Political Quarterly*, 70(3), 285–293.

Dallek, Robert. (2003) *An Unfinished Life: John F. Kennedy, 1917–1963* (Boston: Little, Brown).

Dallek, Robert, and Golway, Terry. (2007) *Let Every Nation Know: John F. Kennedy in His Own Words* (Naperville, IL: Soursebooks).

Damasio, Antonio. (1996) *Descartes' Error: Emotion, Reason, and the Human Brain* (London: Papermac).

Danet, Brenda (ed.). (1984) "Studies of Legal Discourse," *Special Issue of TEXT: An Interdisciplinary Journal for the Study of Discourse*, 4, 1–3.

Darby, Bruce W., and Schlenker, Barry R. (1982) "Children's Reactions to Apologies," *Journal of Personality and Social Psychology*, 43, 743–753.

Davidson, Donald. (1975) "Thought and Talk," in Samuel Guttenplan (ed.), *Mind and Language* (Oxford: Oxford University Press), 7–23.

Davidson, Donald. (1986) "A Nice Derangement of Epitaphs," in Ernest LePore (ed.), *Truth and Interpretation: Perspectives on the Philosophy of Donald Davidson* (Oxford and New York: Blackwell), 433–446.

Dean, John. (1976) *Blind Ambition: The White House Years* (New York: Simon & Schuster).

De Fina, Anna. and Alexandra. Georgakopoulou (2008) Analysing narratives as practices. *Qualitative Research*, 8(3): 379–387.

Deutschmann, Mats. (2003) *Apologising in British English* (Umeå: Umeå Universitet).

Devitt, M. and Sterenly, Kim (1999) Language and Reality: An Introduction to the Philosophy of Language.Massachusetts: MIT Press.

Devitt, Michael. (2004) "The Case for Referential Descriptions," in Marga Reimer and Anne Bezuidenhout (eds.), *Descriptions and Beyond* (Oxford: Oxford University Press), 280–305.

Dews, Shelly., & Winner, Ellen. (1995). Muting the meaning: A social function of irony. *Metaphor and Symbolic Activity*, 10, 3–19.

Donnellan, Keith. (1966) "Reference and Definite Descriptions," *The Philosophical Review*, 75, 281–304.

Doyle, Charles. (2010) Perjury Under Federal Law. *Congressional Research Service*. http://fas.org/sgp/crs/misc/98-808.pdf (accessed December 2012).

Draper, Stephen. (1988) "What's Going on in Everyday Explanation?" in Charles Antaki (ed.), *Analysing Everyday Explanation: A Casebook of Methods* (London: Sage), 15–31.

Draper, Robert. (2007) *Dead Certain: The Presidency of George W. Bush* (London: Free Press).

Druckman, James N. (2003) "The Power of Television Images: The First Kennedy-Nixon Debate Revisited," *Journal of Politics*, 65(2), 559–571.

Du Bois, John W. (2004) "Searching for Intersubjectivity: Too and Either in Stance Alignment," Paper given at the *25th Conference of the International Computer Archive of Modern and Medieval English* (Verona, May 19–23).

Du Bois, John W. (2007) "The Stance Triangle," in Robert Englebretson (ed.), *Stancetaking in Discourse: Subjectivity, Evaluation, Interaction* (Amsterdam: Benjamins), 139–182.

Edelman, Murray (1988) Constructing the Political Spectacle (Chicago:Chicago University Press).

Emmott, Catherine. (1997) *Narrative Comprehension: A Discourse Perspective* (Oxford: Oxford University Press).

Emonds, Joseph. (1979) "Appositive Relatives Have No Properties," *Linguistic Inquiry*, 10, 211–243.

Entman, Robert M. (2012) *Scandal and Silence: Media Responses to Presidential Misconduct* (Cambridge: Polity).

Erikson, Paul D. (1985) *Reagan Speaks: The Making of an American Myth* (New York: New York University Press.

Espinal, M. Teresa. (1991) "The Representation of Disjunct Constituents," *Language*, 67, 726–762.

Evans, Jonathan, St. B. T and Over, David E. (2004) *On Hypothetical Thinking: Lessons from Logic and from the Lab. IF* (Oxford: Oxford University Press).

Fairclough, Norman. (1984) *Discourse and Social Change* (Cambridge: Polity).

Fallows, James. (2008) "Rhetorical Questions," *The Atlantic Magazine*, September. www.theatlantic.com/magazine/archive/2008/09/rhetorical . . . /306943/. (accessed December 1, 2012).

Facuonnier, Gilles, and Turner, Mark. (1996) Blending as a Central Process of Grammar. In Adele Goldberg (ed.) Conceptual Structure Discourse and Language. (Standford: Centre for The Study of Language and Information.)

Fauconnier, Gilles, and Turner, Mark. (2002) *The Way We Think* (New York: Basic Books).

Fauconnier, Gilles, and Turner, Mark. (2003) *Recherches n Communication, n 19. 58–86.* (http://tecfa.unige.ch/tecfa/maltt/cofor-1/textes/Fauconnier-Turner03.pdf.

Fetzer, Anita. (2013) *The Pragmatics of Political Discourse: Explorations across Cultures* (Amsterdam: Benjamins).

Fisher, Simon E., et al. (1998) "Localisation of a Gene Implicated in a Severe Speech and Language Disorder," *Nature Genetics*, 18, 168–170.

Fisher, Walter R. (1987) Technical Logic, Rhetorical Logic, and Narrative Rationality. *Argumentation*, 1, 3–21.

Flank, Lenny. (2010) *JFK: Selected Speeches of President John F. Kennedy* (St. Petersburg, FL: Red and Black Publishers).

Fodor, Janet D., and Ferreira, Fernanda (eds.). (1998) *Reanalysis in Sentence Processing* (Dordrecht: Kluwer Academic Publishers).

Forgas, J. P., & Locke, J. (2005). Affective influences on causal inferences: The effects of mood on attributions for positive and negative interpersonal episodes. Cognition and Emotion, 19, 1071–1081.

Fraser, Bruce. (1999) What are Discourse Markers. *Journal of Pragmatics*, 31, 931–952

Frege, Gottlob. (1892/1980) "'Über Sinn und Bedeutung,' Zeitschrift für Philosophie undphilosophische Kritik 100," in Peter Geach and Max Black (eds.), *Translations from thePhilosophical Writings of Gottlob Frege* (Oxford: Oxford University Press).

Fries, Charles C. 1940. *American English grammar.* (New York: Appleton Century Crofts).

Fromkin, Victoria A. (1973) *Speech Errors as Linguistic Evidence* (Paris: Mouton).

Frost, David. (2007) *Frost/Nixon* (London: Macmillan).

Funk-Unrau, Neil. (2004) "Potentials and Problems of Public Apologies to Canadian Aboriginal Peoples," *Interaction*, 17(1–2), 20–21.

Gamson, William A. (1996) Media Discourse as a Framing Resource in Ann N. Crigler (ed), *The Psychology of Political Communication* (Ann Arbor: University of Michigan Press, pp. 111–132).

Garfinkel, Harold. (1956) "Conditions of Successful Degradation Ceremonies," *American Journal of Sociology*, 61, 420–424.

Garfinkel, Harold. (1967) *Studies in Ethnomethodology* (Englewood Cliffs, NJ: Prentice-Hall).

Cassirer, Ernst. (1954). *Language and Myth*, trans. S.K. Langer (New York: Dover).

Gazdar, Gerald. (1979) *Pragmatics: Implicature, Presupposition, and Logical Form* (New York: Academic Press).

Gee, Paul. (1991) A Linguistic Approach To Narrative, Journald of Narrative and Life History, 1, 1, 15–39.

Geach, Peter., and Black, Max. (1980) Tranlations from the Philosophical Writings of Gottlieb Frege, 3rd edition (Oxford:Blackwell).

Geeraerts, Dirk. (2008) "Prototypes, Stereotypes and Semantic Norms," in Gitte Kristiansen and Rene Dirvin (eds.), *Cognitive Sociolinguistics* (Berlin: Mouton), 21–44.

Geis, Michael (1987) *The Language of Politics* (New York: Springer).

Geis, Michael, and Zwicky, Arnold. (1971) "On Invited Inferences," *Linguistic Inquiry*, 2(4), 561–566.

Gibbs Jr Raymond. (2002) "A New Look at Literal Meaning in Understanding What Is Said and Implicated," *Journal of Pragmatics*, 34, 457–486.

Gibbs Jr Raymond (ed.). (2008) *Cambridge Handbook of Metaphor and Thought* (New York: Cambridge University Press).

Gibbs Jr, Raymond W., and Colston, Herbert L. (eds.). (2007) *Irony in Language and Thought* (New York: Lawrence Erlbaum Associates).

Gibbs Jr, Raymond W., and Colston, Herbert L. (2012) Interpreting Figuartive Language (Cambridge: Cambridge University Press).

Giglio, James N. (2006) *The Presidency of John F. Kennedy*. 2nd ed., rev. (Lawrence: University Press of Kansas).

Goffman, Erving. (1955) "On Face Work," *Psychiatry*, 18, 213–231.

Goffman, Erving. (1959) *The Presenation of Self in Everyday Life* (New York: Doubleday Anchor Books; reprinted by Penguin, 1990).

Goffman, Erving. (1974) *Frame Analysis: An Essay on the Organization of Experience* (London: Harper and Row).

Goffman, Erving. (1981) *Forms of Talk* (Philadelphia: University of Pennsylvania Press).

Golway, Terry, and Grantz, Les. (2010) *JFK: Day by Day* (Philadelphia: Running Press).

Gopnik, Myrna. (1990) "Feature-Blind Grammar and Dysphasia," *Nature*, 344, 715.

Gopnik, Myrna, and Crago, Martha. (1991) "Familial Aggregation of a Developmental Language Disorder," *Cognition* 39(1), 1–50.

Green, Georgia M. (1989) *Pragmatics and Natural Language Understanding* (Hillsdale, NJ: Lawrence Erlbaum Associates).

Greenhalgh, Trisha, and Hurwitz, Brian (eds.). (1998) *Narrative Based Medicine: Dialogue and Discourse in Clinical Practice* (London: BMJ Books).

Greenwald, Anthony, and Banaji, Mahzarin. (1995) "Implicit Social Gognition, Social Attitude and Stereotype," *Psychological Review*, 102(1), 4–27.

Greer, John G. (1988) "The Effects of Presidential Debates on the Electorates Preferences for Candidates," *American Politics Research*, 16, 486–501.

Grice, Paul H. (1967) *Logic and Conversation: The William James Lectures* (Cambridge, MA: Harvard University Press).

Grice, Paul H. (1989) *Studies in the Way of Words* (Cambridge, MA: Harvard University Press).

Guan, Xiaowen, Park, Hee Sun, and Lee, Hye Eun. (2009) "Cross-cultural Differences in Apology," *International Journal of Intercultural Relations*, 33(1), 32–45.

Haig, Robin. (1988) *The Anatomy of Humor* (Springfield, IL: Charles Thomas).

Halberstam, David. (1972) *The Best and the Brightest* (London: Barrie and Jenkins).

Hamn, Bernd. (2005) *Devastating Society: the Neo-Conservative Assault on Democracy and Justice* (London: Pluto Press).

Han, Chung-Hye, and Romero, Maribel. (2002) "Ellipsis and Movement in the Syntax of Whether/Q . . . or Questions," *Proceedings of the 32nd Annual Meeting of the North East Linguistics Society* (NELS 32) (Amherst, MA), 197–216.

Hanley, Charles. (2006) "Half of US Still Believes Iraq Had WMD," *Washington Post*, August 7.

Hargie, Owen, Stapleton, Karyn, and Tourish, Dennis. (2010) "Interpretations of CEO Public Apologies for the Banking Crisis: Attributions of Credit, Blame and Responsibility," *Organization*, 17(6), 721–742.

Harnish, Robert M. (1975) "The Argument from Lurk," *Linguistic Inquiry*, 6, 145–154.

Harris, Sandra, Grainger, Karen, and Mullany, Louise. (2006) "The Pragmatics of Political Apologies," *Discourse and Society* 17(6), 715–737.

Hart, Roderick P. (1987) *The Sound of Leadership* (Chicago: University of Chicago Press).

Harvey, John, Weber, Ann, and Orbuch, Terri. (1990) *Interpersonal Accounts: A Social Psychological Perspective* (Oxford: Basil Blackwell).

Heffernan, Virginia. (2009) "The YouTube Presidency—Why the Obama Administration Uploads So Much Video," *New York Times*, April 12. <http://www.nytimes.com/2009/04/12/magazine/12wwln-medium-t.html?> (accessed November 2012).

Hempel, Carl (1962), Explanation in Science and in History, in *Frontiers of Science and Philosophy*, R. G. Colodney (ed.), Pittsburgh, PA: University of Pittsburgh Press, pp. 9–33.

Hiller, Ulrich. (1983) "Contracted Forms im gesprochenen: Ihre und Distribution als Funktion des Sprachregisters," *Die Neueren Sprachen*, 82, 15–27.

Hinchman, Lewis P., and Hinchman, Sandra K (eds.). (1997) *Memory, Identity, Community: The Idea of Narrative in the Human Sciences* (Albany: State University of New York Press).

Hitchens, Christopher. (1999) *No One Left to Lie To: The Triangulations of William Jefferson Clinton* (London: Verso).

Holbrook, Thomas M. (1999) "Political Learning during Presidential Debates," *Political Behavior*, 21, 67–89.

Holmes, Janet. (1990) "Apologies in New Zealand English," *Language in Society*, 19, 155–199.

Horn, Larry A. (2001) *Natural History of Negation*. 2nd ed. (Chicago: University of Chicago Press).

Huang, Yan. (2007) *Pragmatics* (Oxford: Oxford University Press).

Hurford, James R. (2007) *The Origins of Meaning: Language in the Light of Evolution* (Oxford: Oxford University Press).

Hurford, James R., and Heasley, Brendan. (1983) *Semantics: A Coursebook* (Cambridge: Cambridge University Press).

Husserl, Edmund (1936)Die Krisis der europäischen Wissenschaften und die transzendentale Phänomenologie. Eine Einleitung in die phänomenologische Philosophie.

[The crisis of European sciences and transcendental philosophy. An introduction to phenomenology.] *Philosophia*. Belgrad. 1: 77–176.

Hutchby, Ian, and Wooffitt, Robin. (2008) *Conversation Analysis*. 2nd ed. (Cambridge: Polity).

Jakobson, Roman. (1960) "Linguistics and Poetics," in Thomas Sebeok (ed.), *Style in Language* (Cambridge, MA: MIT Press) 350–377.

Jebahi, Khaled. (2011) "Tunisian University Students' Choice of Apology Strategies in a Discourse Completion Task," *Journal of Pragmatics*, 43(2), 648–662.

Jefferson, Gail. (1979) "A Technique for Inviting Laughter and Its Subsequent Acceptance/Declination," in George Psathas (ed.), *Everyday Language: Studies in Ethnomethodology* (New York: Irvington Publishers), 79–96.

Jefferson, Thomas, (1802) Letter to the Danbury Baptisits: http://www.loc.gov/loc/lcib/9806/danpre.html.

Joffe, Helene. (1997) "The Relationship Between Representational and Materialist Perspectives: AIDS and 'the Other,'" in Lucy Yardly (ed.), *Material Discourses of Health and Illness* (London: Routledge), 132–149.

Johnson, Mark. (1987) *The Body in the Mind: The Bodily Basis of Meaning, Imagination and Reason* (Chicago: University of Chicago Press).

Johnson-Laird, Philip N. (1983) *Mental Models: Towards a Cognitive Science of Language, Inference, and Consciousness* (Cambridge: Cambridge University Press).

Kahneman, Daniel. (1973) *Attention and Effort*. Prentice-Hall Series in Experimental Psychology (Englewood Cliffs, NJ: Prentice-Hall).

Kahneman, Daniel. (2011) *Thinking Fast and Slow* (New York: Farrar, Strauss, Giroux).

Kahneman, Daniel, and Tversky, Amos. (1973) "On the Psychology of Prediction," *Psychological Review*, 80, 237–251.

Kaplan, David. (1999) *What Is Meaning? Explorations in the Theory of Meaning as Use*. Brief version, draft 1, manuscript, UCLA.

Keenan, Edward L., and Stavi, Jonathan. (1986) "A Semantic Characterization of Natural Language Determiners," *Linguistics and Philosophy*, 9(3), 253–326.

Kissine, Mikhail. (2013) *From Utterances to Speech Acts* (Cambridge: Cambridge University Press).

Kitzinger, Celia. (2005) "Speaking as a Heterosexual: (How) Does Sexuality Matter for Talk-in-Interaction?" *Research on Language and Social Interaction*, 38(3), 221–265.

Kjeilmer, Goran. (1998) "On Contraction in Modern English," *Studia Neophilologica*, 69, 155–186.

Kleinman, Arthur. (1988) *The Illness Narratives: Suffering, Healing and the Human Condition* (New York: Basic Books).

Koesten, Joy, and Rowland, Robert C. (2004) "The Rhetoric of Atonement," *Communication Studies*, 55(1), 68–87.

Koestler, Arthur. (1964) *The Act of Creation* (London: Hutchinson).

Kornprobst, Markus. (2007) Comparing Apples and Oranges: Leading and Misleading Uses of Historical Analogies, *Millennium* 36/1.

Kövescses, Zoltan. (2010) *Metaphor: A Practical Introduction* (New York: Oxford University Press).

Kraus, Sidney. (2000) *Televised Presidential Debates and Public Policy*. 2nd ed. (Hillsdale, NJ: Erlbaum).

Kripke, Saul. (1977) "Speaker's Reference and Semantic Reference," in Peter A. French, Theodore E. Uehling, Jr., and Howard K. Wettstein (eds.), *Contemporary Perspectives in the Philosophy of Language* (Minneapolis: University of Minnesota Press), 6–27.

Kristeva, Julia. (1986) "Word, Dialogue, and Novel," in Toril Moi (ed.), *The Kristeva Reader* (Oxford: Basil Blackwell), 34–61.

Kristeva, Julia. (2002) "Nous deux or a (Hi)story of Intertextuality," *Romanic Review*, 93(1–2), 7–13.

Kull, Steven, Ramsay, Clay, and Lewis, Evan. (2003) "Misperceptions, the Media, and the Iraq War," *Political Science Quarterly*, 118(4), 569–598.

Kumon-Nakamura, Sachi, Gulksman, Sam, and Brown, Mary. (1995) "How about Another Piece of Pie: The Allusional Pretense Theory of Discourse Irony," *Journal of Experimental Psychology*, General 124, 3–12.

Kunda, Ziva. (1999) *Social Cognition* (Cambridge, MA: MIT Press).

Kurtzman, Daniel. *Funny Ronald Reagan Quotes* Politicalhumor.about.com.

Kutler, Stanley I. (1998) *Abuse of Power: The New Nixon Tapes* (London: Simon and Schuster).

Labov, William (1972), *Language in the Inner City: Studies in Black English Vernacular* (Philadelphia: University of Philadelphia Press), 354–396.

Labov, William. (1997). "Some Further Steps in Narrative Analysis," *Journal of Narrative and Life History*, 7, 395–415.

Labov, William, and Waletzky, Joshua. (1967) "Narrative Analysis: Oral Versions of Personal Experience," in June Helm (ed.), *Essays on the Verbal and Visual Arts* (San Francisco: American Ethnological Society).

Ladd, Robert D. (1981) "A First Look at the Semantics and Pragmatics of Negative Questions and Tag Questions," in *Papers from the Seventeenth Regional Meeting of the Chicago Linguistic Society* (Chicago Linguistics Society), 164–171.

Lai, Cecilia S., et al. (2001) "A Novel Forkhead-Domain Gene Is Mutated in a Severe Speech and Language Disorder," *Nature*, 413, 519–523.

Lakoff, George. 1971. Presuppositions and relative well-formedness. In D.D. Steinberg and L. A. Jakobovits (eds), *Semantics: An Interdiscliplinary Reader.* Cambridge: CUP.

Lakoff, George. (1972) "Hedges: A Study in Meaning Criteria and the Logic of Fuzzy Con-cepts," in Paul Peranteau, Judith Levi, and Gloria Phares (eds.), *Papers from the Eighth Regional Meeting* (Chicago Linguistics Society), 183–228.

Lakoff, George. (1987) *Women, Fire, and Dangerous Things: What Categories Reveal about the Mind* (Chicago: University of Chicago Press).

Lakoff, George. (1993) "The Contemporary Theory of Metaphor," in Andrew Ortony (ed.), *Metaphor and Thought*. 2nd ed. (Cambridge: Cambridge University Press), 202–251.

Lakoff, George. (2002) *Moral Politics: How Liberals and Conservatives Think* (Chicago: University of Chicago Press).

Lakoff, George. (2004) *Don't Think of an Elephant: Know Your Values and Frame the Debate* (London: Chelsea Green Publishing).

Lakoff, George. (2008) "The Neural Theory of Metaphor," in Raymond W. Gibbs (ed.), *The Cambridge Handbook of Metaphor and Thought* (Cambridge: Cambridge University Press) 17–38.

Lakoff, Geoge, and Johnson, Mark. (1980) *Metaphors We Live By* (Chicago: University of Chicago Press).

Lakoff, George, and Johnson, Mark. (1999) *Philosophy in the Flesh: The Embodied Mind and Its Challenge to Western Thought* (New York: Basic Books).

Lawrence Windy Y., & Carpenter, Ronald H. (2007) On the Conversational Style of Ronald Reagan: A – E = <Gc" Revisited and Reassessed. *Speaker and Gavel*, 44, 1–12.

Leech, Geoffrey N. (1983) *Principles of Pragmatics* (London: Longman).

Leith, Sam. (2012) *Words Like Loaded Pistols: Rhetoric from Aristotle to Obama* (New York: Basic Books).

Lenk, Uta. (1997) "Discourse Markers," in Jef Verschueren et al. (eds.), *Handbook of Pragmatics* (Amsterdam: John Benjamins), 1–17.

Leonard, Lawrence B. (2000) *Children with Specific Language Impairment* (Cambridge, MA: MIT Press).

Leslie, Alan M. (1988) "The Necessity of Illusion: Perception and Thought in Infancy," in Lawrence Weiskrantz (ed.), *Thought Without Language* (Oxford: Clarendon Press/Oxford University Press), 185–210.

Levinson, Stephen C. (1989) "A Review of Relevance" (book review of Dan Sperber and Deirdre Wilson, *Relevance: Communication and Cognition*), *Journal of Linguistics*, 25, 455–472.

Levinson, Stephen C. (2000) *Presumptive Meanings* (Cambridge, MA: MIT Press).

Levinson, Stephen C. (2003) *Pragmatics* (Cambridge: Cambridge University Press).

Lewis, David. (1973) *Counterfactuals* (Oxford: Blackwell).

Lewis, William F. (1987) "Telling America's Story: Narrative Form and the Reagan Presidency," *Quarterly Journal of Speech*, 73, 280–302.

Lewis, David. (2000) "Causation as Influence," abridged version, *Journal of Philosophy*, 97, 182–197.

Liddy, G. Gordon. (1980) *Will: The Autobiography of G. Gordon Liddy* (New York: St. Martin's Press).

Linde, Charlotte E. (1993) *Life Stories: The Creation of Coherence* (New York: Oxford University Press).

Loftus, Elizabeth F. (1996) *Eyewitness Testimony* (Cambridge, MA: Harvard University Press).

Luchjenbroers, June. (1997) "'In Your Own Words . . .': Questions and Answers in a Supreme Court Trial," *Journal of Pragmatics*, 27, 477–503.

Lycan, William. (1991) "Even and Even If," *Linguistics and Philosophy*, 14, 115–150.

Lycan, William. (1995) "Philosophy of Language," in Robert Audi (ed.), *The Cambridge Dictionary of Philosophy* (Cambridge: Cambridge University Press), 586–589.

Lyons, John. (1977) *Semantics*, Vol. 1 (Cambridge: Cambridge University Press).

Lyotard, Jean-Francois. (1984) *The Postmodern Condition: A Report on Knowledge* (Manchester: Manchester University Press).

Maines, David R. (1993) "Narrative's Moment and Sociology's Phenomena: Toward a Narrative Sociology," *The Sociological Quarterly*, 34, 17–38.

Malcolm, Norman. (1971) *Problems of Mind: Descartes to Wittgenstein* (London: Harper). andler I

Mandler, Jean and Johnson, Nancy S. (1977) Remembrance of things parsed: story structure and recall *Cognitive Psychology* 9, 111–51.

Mansfield, Stephen. (2004) *The Faith of George W. Bush* (Lake Mary, FL: Charisma House).

Markkanen, Raija, and Schröder, Hartmut (eds.). (1997) *Hedging and Discourse: Approaches to the Analysis of a Pragmatic Phenomenon in Academic Texts* (Berlin and New York: Walter de Gruyter).

Martin, Robert M. (1987) *The Meaning of Language* (Cambridge, MA: MIT Press).

Mates, Benson. (1986) *The Philosophy of Leibniz: Metaphysics and Language* (Oxford: Oxford University Press).

Mazeland, Harrie, and Huiskes, Mike. (2001) "Dutch '*but*' as a Sequential Conjunction: Its Use as a Resumption Marker," in Margret Selting and Elisabeth Couper-Kuhlen (eds.), *Studies in Interactional Linguistics* (Amsterdam: Philadelphia: Benjamins), 141–169.

Medhurst, Martin. J. (2008) Before the Rhetorical Presidency. Texas: Texas A&M University Press.

MacAndrew, A. "FOXP2 and the Evolution of Language," http://www.pnas.org/cgi/reprint/0503739102v1.pdf (accessed November 12, 2012).

McConnell-Ginet, Sally. (2008) "Words in the World: How and Why Meanings Can Matter," *Language* 84(3), 497–527.

McTear, Michael, and Conti-Ramsden, Gina. (1992) *Pragmatic Disability in Children* (London: Whurr).

Meier, Ardith J. (1998) "Apologies: What Do We Know?" *International Journal of Applied Linguistics*, 8, 215–231.

Menzies, Peter. (2014) "Counterfactual Theories of Causation," *Stanford Encyclopedia of Philosophy* (Stanford, CA: Stanford University Press). http://plato.stanford.edu/entries/causation-counterfactual/.

Merskey, Harold. (1991) "The Definition of Pain," *European Psychiatry*, 6, 153–159.

Mey, Jacob L. (1994) "How to Do Good Things with Words: A Social Pragmatics for Survival," (adapted version of a plenary lecture delivered during the 4th International Pragmatics Conference, Kobe, Japan, on July 30, 1993), *Pragmatic*, 4(2), 239–263.

Mey, Jacob L. (ed.). (2001) *Pragmatics: An Introduction*. 2nd ed. (London: Wiley-Blackwell).

Minsky, Marvin. (1975) "A Framework for Representing Knowledge," in Patrick H. Winston (ed.), *The Psychology of Computer Vision* (New York: McGraw-Hill), 211–281.

Mishler, Elliot. (1999) *Storylines: Craftartists' Narratives of Identity* (Cambridge, MA: Harvard University Press).

Morgan, Pamela S. (2001) "The Semantics of an Impeachment: Meanings and Models in a Political Conflict," in René Dirven, Roslyn Frank, and Cornelia Ilie (eds.), *Language and Ideology*. Vol II: *Descriptive Cognitive Approaches* (Amsterdam and Philadelphia: John Benjamins), 77–105.

Müller, Vincent C. (ed.). (2013) *Theory and Philosophy of Artificial Intelligence SAPERE, 5* (Berlin: Springer).

Murata, Kumiko. (1998) "Has He Apologized or Not?: A Cross-Cultural Misunderstanding Between the UK and Japan on the Occasion of the 50th Anniversary of VJ Day in Britain," *Pragmatics*, 8, 501–513.

Nash, Walter (1980) *Designs in Prose* (London: Longman).

Niedenthal, Paula M. (2007) "Embodying Emotion," *Science*, 316, 1002–1005.

Nordquist, Robert. *Garden Path Sentences.* Grammar.about.com.

Norrick, Neal R. (2001) "Discourse Markers in Oral Narrative," *Journal of Pragmatics,* 33, 849–878.

Obama, Barack. (2004) Keynote Address, Democratic National Convention: Boston, July 27th

Obama, Barack. (2008) *The Audacity of Hope: Thoughts on Reclaiming the American Dream* (New York: Random House).

O' Barr, William M. (1982) *Linguistic Evidence: Language, Power, and Strategy in the Courtroom* (London: Academic Press).

Oborne, Peter. (2005) *The Rise of Political Lying* (London: Free Press).

Ochs, Elinor, and Lisa Capps. (2001) *Living Narrative* (Cambridge, MA: Harvard University Press).

Olsson, John. (2004) *Forensic Linguistics: An Introduction to Language, Crime, and the Law* (London: Continuum).

O'Neill, Barry. (1999) *Honor, Symbols and War* (Ann Arbor: University of Michigan Press).

Orbuch, Terri L., et al. (1994) "Account-making and Confiding as Acts of Meaning in Response to Sexual Assault," *Journal of Family Violence,* 9(3), 249–264.

Orbuch, Terri L., Veroff, Joseph, and Holmberg, Diane. (1993) "Becoming a Married Couple: The Emergence of Meaning in the First Years of Marriage," *Journal of Marriage and the Family,* 55, 815–826.

Owen, Marion. (1983) *Apologies and Remedial Interchanges: A Study of Language Use in Social Interaction* (The Hague: Mouton).

Palin, Sarah. (2008) *RCN Nomination Acceptance Speech*: http://www.uatrav.com/article_c28f289c-8bdb-5401-816a-44b9f31996c9.html.

Palin, Sarah. (2010) *America by Heart: Reflections on Family, Faith, and Flag* (New York: Harper Collins).

Panagiotidou, Maria-Eirini. (2010) "The Language of Landscapes Mapping Intertextuality: Towards a Cognitive Model," *PALA* (Genoa).

Peale, Norman V. (1953) *The Power of Positive Thinking* (London: Cedar).

Penn, Claire. (1999) "Pragmatic Assessment and Therapy for Persons with Brain Damage: What Have Clinicians Gleaned in Two Decades?," *Brain and Language,* 68, 535–552.

Pfiffner, James O. (1999) The Contemporary Presidency: Presidential Lies. *Presidential Quaterly.* 4, 903–917.

Pfiffner, James P. (2006) "Do Presidents Lie?," in George Edwards (ed.), *Readings in Presidential Politics* (Belmont, CA: Thompson Wadsworth), 159–181.

Pfiffner, James P. (2007) *The Modern Presidency.* 5th ed. (Belmont, CA: Wadsworth). mason.gmu.edu/~pubp502/DoPresidentsLie1sp.pdf.

Philips, Susan U. (1987) "The Social Organization of Knowledge and Its Effects on Discourse in Bureaucratic Contexts," in Monica Heller and Sarah Freeman (eds.), *Discourse as Organizational Process, special issue of Discourse Processes,* 10(4), 429–433.

Phoenix, Cassandra, and Sparkes, Andrew C. (2009) "Big Stories, Small Stories and the Accomplishment of a Positive Ageing Identity," *Qualitative Research,* 9, 219–236.

Pietarinen, Ahti, V. (2005) "Relevance Theory Through Pragmatic Theories of Meaning," in Bruno G. Bara, Lawrence Barsalou, and Monica. Bucciarelli (eds.), *Proceedings of the XXVII Annual Conference of the Cognitive Science Society (July).*

Pinker, Steven. (1995) *The Language Instinct: The New Science of Language and Mind* (London: Penguin).

Polkinghorne, Donald. (1988) *Narrative Knowing and the Human Sciences* (New York: State University of New York Press).

Polyani, Livia. (1985) *Telling the American Story* (Norwood, NJ: Ablex).

Pomerantz, Anita. (1986) "Extreme Case Formulations: A Way of Legitimizing Claims," *Human Studies*, 9, 219–230.

Posner, Richard A. (2000) *An Affair of State: The Investigation, Impeachment, and Trial of President Clinton* (Cambridge, MA: Harvard University Press).

Potter, Jonathan, Wetherell, Margaret, and Chitty, Andrew. (1991) "Quantification Rhetoric- Cancer on Television," *Discourse and Society*, 2, 333–365.

Potts, Christopher. (2002) "The Lexical Semantics of Parenthetical-As and Appositive-Which," *Syntax*, 5(1), 55–88.

Potts, Christopher. (2005) *The Logic of Conventional Implicatures* (Oxford: Oxford University Press).

Potts, Christopher. (2007) "The Expressive Dimension," *Theoretical Linguistics*, 33(2), 165–197.

Potts, Christopher. (2008) "Conventional Implicature and Expressive Content," to appear in Claudia Maienborn, Klaus von Heusinger, and Paul Portner, (eds.), *Semantics: An International Handbook of Natural Language Meaning* (Berlin: Mouton de Gruyter). http://people.umass.edu/potts/papers.shtml (accessed January 4, 2013).

Potts, Christopher, and Schwarz, Florian. (2010) "Affective 'this,'" *Linguistic Issues in Language Technology*, 3(5), 1–30.

Prince, Gerald. (1983) "Narrative Pragmatics: Message and Point," *Poetics*, 12, 527–536.

Putnam, Hilary. (1975) *Mind, Language and Reality: Philosophical Papers*. Vol 2 (Cambridge: Cambridge University Press).

Quine, Willard V. (1960) *Word and Object* (Cambridge, MA: MIT Press).

Recanati, François. (1998) "Pragmatics," in Edward Craig (ed.), *Routledge Encyclopaedia of Philosophy*, Vol. 7 (London and New York: Routledge), 620–633.

Recanati, Francois. (2010) *Truth-Conditional Pragmatics* (Oxford: Oxford University Press).

Reid-Gold, Eileen R. (1988) "Ronald Reagan and the Oral Tradition," *Central States Speech Journal*, 39(3–4), 159–175.

Remnick, David. (2010) *The Bridge: The Life and Rise of Barack Obama* (London: Picador).

Reston, James, Jr. (2007) *The Conviction of Richard Nixon: The Untold Story of the Frost/Nixon Interviews* (New York: Harmony).

Ricketts, Tom, and Potter, Michael (eds.). (2010) *Cambridge Companion to Frege* (Cambridge: Cambridge University Press).

Riessman, Catherine K. (2004) "Narrative Analysis," in Michael Lewis-Beck, Alan Bryman, and Tim Futing Liao (eds.), *Encyclopedia of Social Science Research Methods* (Thousand Oaks, CA: Sage), 705–709.

Riessman, Catherine K. (2008) *Narrative Methods for the Human Sciences* (London: Sage).

Risen, Jane L., and, Gilovich, Thomas,. (2007) "Target and Observer Differences in the Acceptance of Questionable Apologies," *Journal of Personality and Social Psychology*, 92, 418–433.

Robinson, Jeffrey D. (2004) "The Sequential Organization of 'Explicit' Apologies in Naturally Occurring English," *Research on Language and Social Interaction*, 37, 291–330.

Rogan, Randall, and Hammer, Mitchell (1994). "Crisis Negotiations: A Preliminary Investigation of Facework in Naturalistic Conflict Discourse," *Journal of Applied Communication Research*, 22, 216–231.

Rosenwald, George C., and Ochberg, Richard L. (eds.). (1992) *Storied Lives: The Cultural Politics of Self-Understanding* (New Haven, CT: Yale University Press).

Roth, Kenneth. (2004) "The Law of War," *Foreign Affairs*, Jan/Feb. http://www.foreignaffairs.com/articles/59524/kenneth-roth/the-law-of-war-in-the-war-on-terror (accessed December 4, 2012).

Rumelhart, David. (1975) "Notes on a Schema for Stories," in Daniel Bobrow and Allan Collins (eds.), *Representation and Understanding* (New York: Academic Press), 211–236.

Russell, Bertrand. (1905) "On Denoting," *Mind*, 14, 479–493.

Russell, Bertrand. (1920) *Introduction to Mathematical Philosophy* (London: George Allen and Unwin).

Russell, Bertrand. (1956) *Logic and Knowledge: Essays 1901–1950*, Robert C. Marsh (ed.), (London: George Allen and Unwin).

Russomanno, Joseph. (2011) *Tortured Logic: A Verbatim Critique of the George W. Bush Presidency* (Washington, DC: Potomac).

Ryan, Marie-Laure. (2003) *On Defining Narrative Media: Image and Narrative*. http://www.imageandnarrative.be/mediumtheory/marielaureryan.htm (accessed December 14, 2013).

Sacks, Harvey. (1992) *Lectures on Conversation*. 2 vols. (Oxford: Blackwell).

Sanders, Stephanie A., and Reinisch, June M. (1999) "Would You Say You 'Had Sex' if . . . ?" *Journal of the American Medical Association*, 281(3), 275–277.

Sarbin, Theodore R. (ed.). (1986) *Narrative Psychology: The Storied Nature of Human Conduct* (New York: Praeger).

Sartre. Jean-Paul (1965) *Nausea*. London: Penguin.

Schank, Roger C. (1975) *Conceptual Information Processing* (New York: Elsevier).

Schank, Roger. (1995) *Tell Me a Story: Narrative and Intelligence* (Evanston, IL: Northwestern University Press).

Schank, Roger C., and Abelson, Robert P. (1977) *Scripts, Plans, Goals and Understanding: An Inquiry into Human Knowledge Structures* (Hillsdale, NJ: Erlbaum).

Schank, Roger C. (1990) *Tell Me A Story: A New Look at Real and Artifiical Memory*. New York: Scribers.

Schegloff, Emmanuel. (1968) "Sequencing in Conversational Openings," *American Anthropologist*, 70(6), 1075–1095.

Schegloff, Emmanuel. (1987) "Analyzing Single Episodes in Interaction: An Exercise in Conversation Analysis," *Social Psychology Quarterly*, 50, 101–114.

Schegloff, Emanuel A. (1997) "Whose Text? Whose Context?" *Discourse and Society*, 8, 165–187.

Schiffrin, Deborah. (1987) *Discourse Markers* (Cambridge: Cambridge University Press).

Schiffrin, Deborah. (2001) "Discourse Markers: Language, Meaning and Context," in Deborah Schiffrin, Deborah Tannen, and Heidi Hamilton (eds.), *The Handbook of Discourse Analysis* (Oxford: Blackwell), 54–75.

Schiffrin, Deborah. (2003) "We Knew That's It: Retelling the Turning Point of a Narrative," *Discourse Studies*, 5, 535–562.

Schlesinger, Arthur M., Jr. (2002) *A Thousand Days: John F. Kennedy in the White House* (Boston: Houghton Mifflin).

Schourup, Lawrence. (1999) "Discourse Markers," *Lingua*, 107, 227–265.

Schroedel, Jean, Bligh, Michelle, Merolla, Jennifer, and Gonzalez, Randall. (2013) "Charismatic Rhetoric in the 2008 Presidential Campaign: Commonalities and Differences." *Presidential Studies Quarterly*, 41(1), 101–128.

Scott, Marvin, and Lyman, Stanford. (1968) "Accounts," *American Sociological Review*, 31, 46–62.

Searle, John R. (1969) *Speech Acts: An Essay in the Philosophy of Language* (Cambridge: Cambridge University Press).

Searle, John R. (1987) "Indeterminacy, Empiricism, and the First Person," *Journal of Philosophy*, 84(3), 123–146.

Semino, Elena. (2008) *Metaphor and Discourse* (Chicago: University of Chicago Press).

Sheey, Gail. (2000) "The Accidental Candidate: George W. Bush," *Vanity Fair*, October.

Shaw, Russell (2011) The Separation of God from public life. *The Catholic World Report*. http://www.catholicworldreport.com/Item/536/the_separation_of_god_from_public_life.aspx (accessed November 2012).

Shuy, Roger W. (1996) *Language Crimes: The Use and Abuse of Language Evidence in the Courtroom* (Oxford: Blackwell).

Shuy, Roger W. (1998) *The Language of Confession, Interrogation and Deception* (Thousand Oaks, CA: Sage Publications).

Sidnell, Jack. (2010) *Conversation Analysis: An Introduction* (Malden, MA: Wiley-Blackwell).

Simons, Herbert W. (2000) "A Dilemma-Centered Analysis of Clinton's August 17th Apologia: Implications for Rhetorical Theory and Method," *Quarterly Journal of Speech*, 86(4), 438–453.

Sintonen, Matti. (1993) "In Search of Explanations: From Why-Questions to Shakespearean questions," *Philosophica*, 51, 55–81.

Solan, Lawrence M. (2002) "The Clinton Scandal: Some Legal Lessons from Linguistics," in Janet Cotterill (ed.). *Language in the Judicial Process* (Houndmills, UK: Palgrave Macmillan).

Solan, Lawerence M. (2003) "Presidents and Scandals: Bush and Uranium, Clinton and Sex, Reagan and Iran-contra: What Do They Have in Common?" *MSNBC News*.

Sperber, Dan. (1996) *Explaining Culture: A Naturalistic Approach* (Oxford: Blackwell).

Sperber, Dan. (2009) "Culturally Transmitted Misbeliefs (Commentary on Ryan T. McKay and Daniel C. Dennett, 'The evolution of misbelief')," *Behavioral and Brain Sciences*, 32, 534–535.

Sperber, Dan, and Wilson, Deirdre. (1985/1986) "Loose Talk," *Proceedings of the Aristotelian Society*, LXXXVI, 153–171.

Sperber, Dan, and Wilson, Deirdre. (1986). "On Defining Relevance," in Richard Grandy and Richard Warner (eds.), *Philosophical Grounds of Rationality: Intentions, Categories, Ends* (Oxford: Oxford University Press), 143–158.

Sperber, Dan, and Wilson, Deirdre. (1995) *Relevance: Communication and Cognition* (Oxford: Blackwell).

Sperber, Dan, and Wilson, Deirdre. (2005) "Pragmatics," in Frank Jackson and Michael Smith (eds.), *Oxford Handbook of Contemporary Philosophy* (Oxford: Oxford University Press), 468–501.

Stalnaker, Robert. (1968) "A Theory of Conditionals," in Nicholas Rescher (ed.), *Studies in Logical Theory* (Oxford: Oxford University Press), 98–112.

Stalnaker, Robert. (1970) "Pragmatics," *Synthese*, 22, 272–289.

Stalnaker, Robert (with R. H. Thomason). (1973) "A Semantic Theory of Adverbs," *Linguistic Inquiry*, 4, 195–220.

Stalnaker, Robert. (1974) "Pragmatic Presuppositions," in Milton Munitz and Peter Unger (eds.), *Semantics and Philosophy* (New York: New York University Press, 1974), 197–213.

Stalnaker, Robert. (1998) "On the Representation of Context," *Journal of Logic, Language and Information*, 7, 3–19.

Stalnaker, Robert. (2002) "Common Ground," *Linguistics and Philosophy*, 25, 701–721.

Stanovich, Keith E. (1999) *Who Is Rational? Studies of Individual Differences in Reasoning* (Mahwah, NJ: Lawrence Erlbaum Associates).

Stanton, Frank. (2000) "The First Debate over Presidential Debates." *Newsweek*, September 25, 3.

Stapleton, Karyn, and Wilson, John. (2010) "Community Discourse about Politics in Northern Ireland," *Text & Talk*, 30, 311–331.

Summers, Anthony. (2000) *The Arrogance of Power: The Secret World of Richard Nixon* (London: Gollancz).

Tannen, Deborah. (1993) "Introduction," in Deborah Tannen (ed.), *Framing in Discourse* (New York: Oxford University Press), 3–13.

Tannen, Deborah. (2006) "Intertextuality in Interaction: Reframing Family Arguments in Public and Private," *Text & Talk* 26(4), 597–617.

Tavuchis, Nicholas. (1991) *Mea Culpa: A Sociology of Apology and Reconciliation* (Stanford, CA: Stanford University Press).

te Molder, Hedwig, and Potter, Jonathan (eds.). (2005) *Conversation and Cognition* (Cambridge: Cambridge University Press).

Ten Have, Paul. (2007) *Doing Conversation Analysis: A Practical Guide.* 2nd ed. (London: Sage).

The Hill Blog, Oct 7, 2012, ehill.com/ . . . /260667-gibbs-obama-disappointed-by-performance-in (accessed January 5, 2013).

Thomas, Jenny. (1995) *Meaning in Interaction: An Introduction to Pragmatics* (London: Longman).

Thompson, Damian. (2012) *Daily Telegraph Blog* June 8th.

Thompson, John B. (1990) *Ideology and Modern Culture* (Cambridge: Polity Press).

Thompson, Sandra A., and Mulac, Anthony. (1991) "A Quantitative Perspective on the Grammaticization of Epistemic Parentheticals in English," in Elizabeth C. Traugott and Bernd Heine (eds.), *Approaches to Grammaticalization.* Vol. 2: *Types of Grammatical Markers* (Typological Studies in Language 19.2) (Amsterdam/Philadelphia: John Benjamins), 313–327.

Tiersma, Peter. (1990) "The Language of Perjury: 'Literal Truth,' Ambiguity, and the False State ment Requirement. *Southern California Law Review.* 373–433.

Tiersma, Peter. (2004) Did Clinton Lie? Defining 'Sexual Relations'," 79 *Chicago Kent Law Review* 927 (2004). *Southern California Law Review*, 63, 373–431.

Thornborrow, Joanna and Coates, Jennifer. (2005) *The Sociolinguistics of Narrative* (Amsterdam: Benjamins).

Utych, Stephen M. (2012) "Negative Affective Language in Politics," *35th Annual Meeting of the International Society of Political Psychology*, Chicago July 6–9, www.vanderbilt.edu/political . . . /utych-affective-language-ispp.pdf (accessed December 2012).

Vandelanotte, Lieven. (2007) "Mister So-called X: Discourse Functions and Subjectification of So-called," in Christopher S. Butler, Raquel Hidalgo Downing, and Julia Lavid (eds.), *Functional Perspectives on Grammar and Discourse: In Honour of Angela Downing* (Studies in Language Companion Series 85) (Amsterdam: Benjamins), 359–394.

van Dijk, Teun. (1998) *Ideology: A Multidisciplinary Approach* (Thousand Oaks, CA: Sage).

Vellman, J. David. (2003) "Narrative Explanation," *Philosophical Review*, 112(1), 1–25.

Verschueren, Jef. (1998) *Understanding Pragmatics* (London and New York: Arnold).

Verschueren, Jef, Östman, Jan-Ola, and Blommaert, Jan (eds.). (1995) *Handbook of Pragmatics* (Amsterdam: Benjamins).

Vipond, Douglas, and Hunt, Russell A. (1984) "Point-Driven Understanding: Pragmatic and Cognitive Dimensions of Literary Reading," *Poetics*, 13, 261–277.

Waismel-Manor, Israel, and Stroud, Natalie J. (2012) *The Influence of President Obama's Middle Name on Middle Eastern and U.S. Perceptions*, http://link.springer.com/content/pdf/10.1007%Fs11109-012-9210-4 (accessed October 2012).

Walker, Anne Graffam. (1987) "Linguistic Manipulation, Power, and the Legal Setting," in Leah Kedar (ed.), *Power Through Discourse* (Norwood, NJ: Ablex Publishing), 57–80.

Weisberg, Jacob. (2001) *George W. Bushisms—Deluxe Election Edition* (New York: Simon and Schuster).

Westen, Drew. (2007) *The Political Brain: The Role of Emotion in Deciding the Fate of the Nation* (New York: Public Affairs).

White, Michael, and Epson, David. (1990) *Narrative Means to Therapeutic Ends* (New York: Norton).

Wichmann, Anne. (2001) "Spoken Parentheticals," in Karin Aijmer (ed.), *A Wealth of English* (Gothenburg: Gothenburg University Press), 171–193.

Wilks, Yorick. (1986) "Default Reasoning and Self-Knowledge," in M. King and Michael Rosner (eds.), *Special Issue of IEEE Transactions on Knowledge Representation. Proceedings of IEEE*, 74, 1399–1405.

Wilks, Yorick, and Bien, Janusz. (1983) "Beliefs, Points of View and Multiple Environments," *Cognitive Science*, 8, 120–146.

Wilson, Deidre. (2003) "Relevance Theory and Lexical Pragmatics," *Italian Journal of Linguistics/Rivista di Linguistica*, 15, 273–291.

Wilson, Deirdre. (2004) "Relevance and Word Meaning: The Past, Present and Future of Lexical Pragmatics," *Modern Foreign Languages*, 27, 1–13.

Wilson, Deirdre. (2010) "Parallels and Differences in the Treatment of Metaphor in Relevance Theory and Cognitive Linguistics," *UCL Working Papers in Linguistics*, 22, 41–55.

Wilson, Deirdre, and Carston, Robyn. (2006) "Metaphor Relevance and the Emergent Property Issue," *Mind and Language*, 21(3), 404–433.

Wilson, Deirdre, and Sperber, Dan. (1991) "Pragmatics and Modularity," in Steven Davis (ed.), *Pragmatics: A Reader* (Oxford: Oxford University Press), 583–595.

Wilson, Deirdre, and Sperber, Dan. (1992) "On Verbal Irony," *Lingua*, 87, 53–76.

Wilson, Deirdre, and Sperber, Dan. (2002) "Truthfulness and Relevance," *Mind*, 111, 583–632.

Wilson, Deirdre, and Sperber, Dan. (2004) "Relevance Theory," in Laurence Horn and Gregory Ward (eds.), *The Handbook of Pragmatics* (Oxford: Blackwell), 607–632.

Wilson, Deirdre, and Sperber, Dan. (2012) *Meaning and Relevance* (Cambridge: Cambridge University Press).

Wilson, John. (1980) "Why Answers to Questions Are Not Enough in Social Discourse," *Belfast Working Papers in Linguistics*, 3, 20–41.

Wilson, John. (1990) *Politically Speaking* (Oxford: Blackwell).

Wilson, John, and Henry, Alison. (1998) "Parameter Setting in a Socially Realistic Linguistics," *Language and Society*, 27(1), 1–21.

Wilson, John, Sahlane, Ahmed and Somerville, Ian. (2012) Argumentation and Fallacy in newspaper op/ed coverage of the prelude to the invasion of Iraq. *Journal of Language and Politics*, 11 (1), 1–31.

Wilson, John, and Stapleton, Karyn. (2007) "The Discourse of Resistance: Social Change and Policing in Northern Ireland," *Language in Society*, 36(3), 393–425.

Wilson, John, and Stapleton, Karyn. (2010) "The Big Story about Small Stories: Narratives of Crime and Terrorism," *Journal of Sociolinguistics*, 14(3), 287–312.

Wittgenstein, Ludwig. (1953) *Philosophical Investigations*, trans. G. E. M. Anscombe (London: Blackwell).

Wittington, Keith E. (2000) "Bill Clinton Was No Andrew Johnson: Comparing Two Impeachments," *University of Pennsylvania Journal of Constitutional Law*, 2, 422–465.

Wodak, Ruth. (2011) The Discourse of Politics in Action.Politics as Usual. London:Palgrave MacMillan.

Woodbury, Hanni. (1984) "The Strategic Use of Questions in Court," *Semiotica*, 48(3–4), 197–228.

Wynn, Rolf, and Wynn, Michael. (2006) "Empathy as an Interactionally Achieved Phenomenon in Psychotherapy: Characteristics of some Conversational Resources," *Journal of Pragmatics*, 38(9), 1385–1397.

YouGov/Sunday Times: cited in *The Week*, November 10, 2012.

Zaller, John (1992) The Nature and Origins of Mass Opinions (Cambridge:Cambridge University Press).

Zajonc, Robert B. (1980) "Feeling and Thinking: Preferences Need No Inferences," *American Psychologist*, 35(2), 151–175.

Zwicky, Arnold M. (1970) "Auxiliary Reduction in English," *Linguistic Inquiry*, 1(3), 323–336.

INDEX